VOICES OF RESURGENT ISLAM

CONTRIBUTORS

CHARLES J. ADAMS is Professor of Islamic Studies, McGill University.

KHURSHID AHMAD, a leader in the Jamaat-i-Islami, is currently Director: Institute of Policy Studies, Islamabad.

LISA ANDERSON is Assistant Professor of Government and Social Studies, Harvard University.

JOHN J. DONOHUE is Director: Center for the Study of the Modern Middle East, Beirut.

JOHN L. ESPOSITO is Professor of Religious Studies, College of the Holy Cross.

KEMAL A. FARUKI is a barrister and scholar of Islamic law.

ISMAIL R. AL-FARUQI is Professor of Islamic Studies, Temple University.

MICHAEL M.J. FISCHER is Associate Professor of Anthropology, Rice University.

YVONNE Y. HADDAD is Associate Professor of Islamic Studies, Hartford Seminary Foundation.

JAVID IQBAL is a Justice of Pakistan's High Court.

KHALID M. ISHAQUE is a barrister and former member of Pakistan's Islamic Ideology Council.

AL-SADIQ AL-MAHDI is the former Prime Minister of the Sudan where he remains an Islamic political leader.

ABDULAZIZ SACHEDINA is Associate Professor of Religious Studies, University of Virginia.

HASSAN AL-TURABI was a founder of Sudan's Muslim Brotherhood and is currently Attorney General of the Sudan.

JOHN O. VOLL is Professor of History, University of New Hampshire.

FRED R. VON DER MEHDEN is Albert Thomas Professor of Political Science, Rice University.

VOICES
OF
RESURGENT ISLAM

Edited by
John L. Esposito

New York   Oxford
OXFORD UNIVERSITY PRESS
1983

Library of Congress Cataloging in Publication Data

Esposito, John L.
Voices of resurgent Islam.

1. Islam—20th century—Addresses, essays, lectures.
I. Title.
BP60.E86 1983   297′.09′04   82-24544
ISBN 0-19-503339-6
ISBN 0-19-503340-X (pbk.)

Printing (last digit): 9 8 7 6 5 4

Printed in the United States of America

For
Mom, Dad, Lou & Rick
Mary & Paul Pagliaro

Preface

During the past few years, the re-emergence of Islam in Muslim politics has attracted a great deal of attention in the media, the press, conferences, and innumerable publications. Our purpose is to provide in a single volume, through biographical studies and Muslim statements, perspectives on the "Islamic resurgence": its formative influences, the religio-political world views of its ideologues and the perceptions of contemporary Muslim actors.

The reader will find common themes but a diversity of interpretations. While there is a unity in Islamic belief, there is also a variety of understandings both as to its implications and its implementation. The studies of Muslim ideologues in section II and the statements of contemporary Muslim activists in section III bear witness to the divergence (ikhtilaf) of thought and action which has existed and continues to exist in the Muslim world.

A major emphasis in this volume is on state and society, the political and social goals of Islamic activists. Their approach is reflected in the biographical studies of men like Ayatullah Khomeini, Muammar Qaddafi, Sayyid Qutb. It is especially evident in the selections of contemporary activists like Al Sadiq al-Mahdi, Khurshid Ahmad, and others who address questions regarding the political, social, and economic goals of Islamic societies. The concern here is less with individual personalities than with Islamic issues.

Where possible, translation has been standardized. For proper names, the more common spellings have been utilized. Similarly, because this volume is meant for non-specialists as well as specialists, diacritical marks have been omitted to simplify reading.

There are many colleagues and friends who have contributed to this volume in an informal rather than a formal manner. Some did so through their participation in a conference "Islamic Resurgence: Prospects and Implications," sponsored by the College of the Holy Cross, in October 1980 through a U.S.I.A. grant. Others have been helpful in their advice and encouragement. Among those acknowledged are: Hamid Enayat, James P. Piscatori, Anwar Ibrahim,

Wilfred Cantwell Smith, L. Carl Brown, Nikki R. Keddie, Richard P. Mitchell, Hasan Hanafi, Peter Gran, Anis Ahmad, Sheila McDonough, Lois al-Faruqi, and Abdul Hamid Abu Sulayman. While none are responsible for the viewpoints expressed here, their interest has been greatly appreciated.

I would also like to thank the Islamic Council of Europe, London, for excerpts from chapter X of Ismail R. al-Faruqi's *Islam and the Problem of Israel.*

A special note of thanks to Mary Cerasuolo, a superb and patient typist; Jennifer Carey, a careful and tireless proofreader; my wife, Jean, who is always a constructive and supportive critic.

Worcester, Massachusetts   J. L. E.
June 1983

Contents

VOICES OF RESURGENT ISLAM

INTRODUCTION

Islam and Muslim Politics

The Muslim world extends from North Africa to Southeast Asia. In addition to some forty-three Muslim (majority) countries, Muslims constitute a significant minority in another twenty countries. The more than 800 million Muslims comprise almost a fifth of the world's population. The size and geographic expanse of the Muslim world and its emergence as a world economic power whose political stability is of increasing importance to the Western world have made an understanding of events in the Muslim world a critical concern.

The purpose of this volume is to provide some insight into a phenomenon that has swept the Muslim world. It has been described by various titles: Islamic Resurgence, Islamic Revival, Militant Islam, Rise of Islamic Fundamentalism. This volume will explore the origins, development, prospects, and implications of the Islamic resurgence through both analytical studies (on the history and major influences of the resurgence) as well as the statements of Muslim scholar/activists engaged in the political, social, and economic aspects of the Islamic resurgence today.

THE ISLAMIC WORLD-VIEW: RELIGION AND THE STATE

In order to understand the sources and inspiration of the contemporary resurgence, some appreciation of the relationship of religion to politics and society in Islam is essential. As we shall see, both in Muslim belief and in Muslim history, Islam has occupied an important place in the ideology of the state and in the conduct of Muslim politics from its seventh-century beginnings to the twentieth century. Thus, the current resurgence of Islam in Muslim politics should not be all that unexpected. For Muslims, Allah (God) is the central fact of reality; he is the same God who revealed himself to all the Prophets (Adam, Moses, Jesus) and finally, and most completely, to the Prophet Muhammad. This revelation to Muhammad, the last of the Prophets, is contained in the Quran, the actual, literal living word of God. A Muslim's duty is obedience and submission *(islam)* to the will of God. However, the submission incumbent upon the Muslim is not that of mere passivity or acceptance of a set of dogmas or rituals; rather it is submission to the divine command, to strive *(jihad)* to actively realize God's will in space-time, in history. Thus, the Quran declares that man is God's vicegerent or representative *(khilafah)* on earth (S. 5:55; 6:166); God has given creation to man as a divine trust *(amanah)* (S. 33:72; 31:20–29); and it is on the basis of how man carries out his vicegerency that he is to be either rewarded or punished (S. 17:14–14).

The Muslim's obligation to realize God's will in history is communal as well as individual (S. 3:104, 110). In the Islamic community *(ummah),* religious solidarity replaced tribal ties; the *ummah* serves as the dynamic vehicle for realization of the divine mandate in society, as an example to other people of the world (S. 2:143). Thus, Islam, like Christianity, is a world religion with a universal mission. However, it is distinguished from Christianity by the unity and totality of the Islamic view of reality. As God is one *(tawhid),* so all of his creation has an underlying unity and is subject to His rule. God is sovereign ruler, and man, as His vicegerent, must implement His rule on earth. Therefore, religion is not separate but rather integral to every aspect of life: prayer, fasting, politics, law, and society. This belief is reflected not only in the doctrine of *tawhid* but also, quite concretely, in the development of the Islamic state and Islamic law (the *shariah*).

The Islamic state is a community of believers. Allah is the ultimate sovereign of the state and, indeed, of all creation. Political and religious leadership was vested in Muhammad, God's messenger on earth, who served as both Prophet and political leader of the Islamic community/state. Upon Muhammad's death, his political successors (caliph, "successor," or imam, "leader") were to ensure the faithful following of God's will as embodied in Islamic law. Law was rooted in divine revelation, the Quran and Sunna (example or model behavior of the Prophet Muhammad). It provided the blueprint for Muslim society—a comprehensive code of life which includes laws that regulate prayer and alms-giving as well as family, criminal, commercial, and international law. Religious scholars (ulama, "the learned") served as the guardians of the tradition and, therefore, they were often advisers to governments (caliphate). They ran the schools and universities *(madrasas);* developed, applied, and interpreted the law; and administered the social welfare system (traditional system of social services).

This belief in the divinely ordained nature and mission of the Muslim community was validated and reinforced by their success and power throughout Islamic history. Within one hundred years of the Prophet Muhammad's death, the original Islamic community, through expansion and conquest, became an empire more extensive than any the world had known. In time the Islamic world extended from Arabia, west to North Africa and Spain, and east to Indonesia. In addition to developing political, social, and legal institutions, Islam gave birth to a great civilization. Muslims contributed to philosophy, mathematics, geometry, optics, the physical sciences. and the arts. While Western Christendom passed through its Dark Ages, Islamic civilization flourished; the Muslim world was the locus for major centers of learning and culture.

The fall of Baghdad to the Mongols in 1258 (a traumatic period in Islamic history) marked the end of the Islamic Caliphate. Yet, within several centuries, three Muslim empires (the Ottoman in the Middle East, the Safavid in Persia, and the Mogul in the Indian subcontinent) again rose up to extend the continuum of Muslim rule and culture. Throughout the period from 1258 to the eighteenth century, Muslims continued to live under Muslim rulers in states governed by Islamic law. Although often characterized as medieval, despite a certain degree of stagnancy culture did continue to develop and, at times, to flourish.[1] Therefore, Muslims were able to look back upon their history as one in which, despite internal and external battles and disruptions, a general continuity of Muslim rule and life had been maintained. Indeed, throughout their history, Islamic law had remained the ideal blueprint for Muslim society. The basic criterion for the legitimacy of Muslim governments was the ruler's commitment to *shariah* rule. Thus, to be a Muslim was to live in an Islamic state, governed by Islamic law, pursuing a divinely mandated mission. Success and power were signs of both divine guidance and the community's fidelity. For Muslims, history was indeed inherently meaningful. The traditional Islamic worldview provided a holistic approach toward life, a life in which religion was intimately and organically related to politics, law, and society.

RELIGION AND POLITICS IN MODERN ISLAMIC HISTORY

A major crisis in Islamic history and in Muslim identity was precipitated by the advent of colonialism. During the nineteenth century the Islamic world succumbed to Western Christendom—militarily, economically, and finally, politically. As a result, the very meaning of Muslim history was challenged. What had gone wrong in Islam? Why had Muslim fortunes been so dramatically reversed? The disintegration of the traditional Islamic political order and the struggle against European colonialist intervention and rule provided both an identity crisis and a political purpose for Muslims in the twentieth century. Under Western influence and colonial rule, modernization had begun. Generally speaking, Muslim countries followed a path of Westernization and secularization as they increasingly adopted Western models in politics, law, and education. In many areas of the Muslim world, clear trends toward a separation of religion from the state could be identified. The caliph and sultans were gone; much of Islamic law was replaced by Western legal codes; and modern secular, political, economic, and educational systems were established under colonial tutelage.

During the twentieth century, religion re-emerged in the politics of the Muslim world, inspiring anti-colonial, nationalist movements and their struggle for independence. The ground had been prepared by the late nineteenth-century Muslim reformer Jamal al-Din al-Afghani, the father of modern Muslim nationalism. Traveling from India to Egypt, he called upon Muslims to resist imperialism, seek political liberation and undertake an intellectual reawakening rooted in a return to Islam. Independence and Islamic reform were the necessary conditions to restore Islam's lost power and glory. Under Afghani's disciples, the Egyptian Muhammad Abduh (1849–1905) and the Syrian Rashid Rida (1865–1935), the Salafiyyah movement through its reformist journal *al-Manar* sought to restate classical doctrines in order to bring about Islamic political, legal, and intellectual reform.[2] Its impact was felt throughout the Muslim world and informed independence movements and Muslim nationalism from North Africa to Southeast Asia.

In North Africa, faced with the ethnic division of Arab and Berber, Islam became the basis for anti-colonial solidarity. Islamic slogans, symbols, and religious leaders played important roles in the nationalist movements of Tunisia's Abd al-Aziz al-Thaalibi and Morocco's Allal al-Fasi established political parties such as the Destour (Constitution) and the Istiqlal (Independence) parties which placed the nationalist struggles with France within an Islamic context. Similar attempts occurred in Algeria under the leadership of the Algerian People's party (Parti du Peuple Algerien) and the Association of Algerian Ulama.[3]

In the Indian subcontinent, what had originally been a common Hindu-Muslim independence movement sparked by anti-British sentiment, redirected its focus as Muslims increasingly worried about their own communal status in an independent state dominated by a large Hindu majority. This communal concern eventually led to the call for a separate Muslim homeland. In 1930, Muhammad Iqbal (1875–1938), the great Islamic reformer and poet of South Asia, had called for a Muslim homeland.[4] Muhammad Ali Jinnah (1876–1948), the "Founder of Pakistan" and his Muslim League Party, increasingly recognized the value of Islam in mass mobilization and from 1940 championed the cause of Muslim nationalism. Appeals to Islam and the demand for a separate Muslim state proved to be effective rallying cries in a mass movement which, by 1947, led to the partitioning of British India and the birth of Pakistan as a separate Muslim nation—in the words of its first constitution: "The Islamic Republic of Pakistan."

In the Arab East countries such as Syria, Lebanon, and Egypt, Islam's role was more limited since a significant, well-educated, and articulate Christian minority had been a major force in the formation and development of an Arab nationalism that emphasized Arab ethnic/linguistic bonds. Despite this, Islam played an important role in the formulation of nationalist ideology. The legacy of Afghani and Abduh's Salafiyya movement would develop in many directions. However, during this period, whether in the writings of Rashid Rida, Shakib Arslan, Lutfi al-Sayyid, or Abd al-Rahman al-Bazzaz, Islam remained an important factor in defining national identity and ideology.[5] Emphasis was not placed on Islamic unity or pan-Islam. Rather, religion was seen as a foundational source for Arab nationalism, given the central place of Islam in Arab history and, conversely, given the Arab character of Islam: its Central Arabian origins, its language (the Quran), its Prophet Muhammad, early leadership and victories.

Finally, in Indonesia, which lacked a single language, history, and ethnic background, Islam had provided the basis and leadership for Indonesia's first mass nationalist movement (through the leadership of the Sarakat Islam party). During the post World War II period, Muslim organizations joined with other nationalist forces in achieving independence from Dutch role in 1949.[6]

During the post-independence period, Islam again receded from the political arena as newly-established Muslim states sought to modernize and to develop as separate nations. In general, they continued to look to Western models in their development efforts. Under the leadership of secular elites, Western political theories and institutions were carried over as part of the colonial legacy and thus, as the models to be emulated: nationalism, popular sovereignty, parliamentary government, legal codes, and educational systems. Two points should be noted about this process. First, Western models of development had been abruptly transplanted; they were adopted, not adapted, to their new environments. Institutions and codes that were the product of the West's historical/cultural experience, spanning several centuries of development, were often uncritically and suddenly applied to people with a different historical tradition, experience, and values. Second, with the exception of Turkey which opted for a completely secular state and Saudi Arabia which advocated a more traditionally inspired Wahhabi Islamic state, most Muslim countries reveal a more complex, eclectic process. Despite the inclusion of a few Islamic provisions requiring that: the state religion be Islam, the head of state be a Muslim, and the *shariah* be a source of law, the constitutions and laws of Muslim countries were largely based upon Western models. National ideology, state institutions, and political elites and parties were secularly oriented. Religion was restricted to the area of personal belief and morality. For many, this path of secularization was inherent in the process of political development.

However, in the late 1950s and 60s, Islam again can be clearly identified as a factor in Muslim politics as North African states gained their independence and radical governments came to power in Egypt, Syria, and Iraq. In North Africa, it was only logical, in light of the role that Islam had played in national independence movements, that the leadership in Morocco and Algeria should continue to appeal to Islam. In Morocco, the sultanate of Muhammad V had become a nationalist symbol during the independence movement. He continued to use Islam to buttress the monarchy. Thus, the monarchy became both the key political and religious institution of the state.[7]

In 1965, three years after independence, Houari Boumedienne gained power in Algeria in a *coup d'état*. Educated in Cairo at al-Azhar University, center of Islamic learning, Boumedienne placed greater emphasis on Islam and Arabization. Algeria's National Charter of 1976 articulated this commitment, linking Islam to its social revolution.[8]

In Syria, Iraq, and Egypt, old regimes were overthrown and replaced by more radical groups (socialist in orientation) and committed to Arab unity. The old liberal nationalism gave way to Arab nationalism/socialism—Nasserism in Egypt (1952), and the Baath party in Syria (1958) and Iraq (1963, 1968). These radical governments distinguished themselves from their predecessors by rooting their ideology in an Arab/Islamic heritage. They insisted that unlike previous regimes, theirs was not a borrowed or foreign ideology. Neither Western capitalism nor communism, their Arab socialism was true to their own glorious history and values and was able to address the major failure of government—the lack of radical socioeconomic reform. Both Gamal Abdel Nasser and leaders of the Baath party recognized that the appeal to religion was an important factor in winning mass support for their rule and policies. Islam, or more specifically, Islamic slogans, vocabulary, and symbols re-emerged as a source of and a force in this undertaking. The earlier tendency to modernize through secularization was somewhat altered. Religion was no longer relegated to private life alone, as Muslim governments employed Islamic symbols, values, and institutions to legitimate and justify reforms. However, this was *not* a return to classical ideology for an Islamic polity. Islam was not *the* central principle, but rather it emerged as "a" component in the state's national ideology. There was a growing tendency to assert national independence by shunning the posture of wholesale reliance on the West and to appeal more to cultural pride and identity. Acknowledgment of indebtedness to the West for governmental structures and institutions as well as science and technology was distinguished from acceptance of Western values. Government leaders were coming to grips with the political and social reality of their countries in which the vast majority of citizens (in urban as well as rural areas) were spiritually and psychologically indebted to and influenced by the beliefs, practices, and values of their common

Islamic heritage. Thus, governments sought to legitimate their policies through a controlled use of religion.

We can see this process quite clearly in the formulations of Arab nationalism and Arab (Islamic) socialism preached by Gamal Abdel Nasser within Egypt and throughout the Arab world. From the nineteenth century, Egypt had pursued a path of increasing secularization beginning with the rule of Muhammad Ali (1805–49) and continuing through the Free Officers' revolution of July 1952. In the first years after the revolution, Egyptian nationalism continued along a secular path; yet after 1955, as Nasser sought to propound an ideology that would both unify the Egyptian people behind him and strengthen his position as the spokesman for the Arab world, he increasingly broadened Egyptian nationalism into an Arab nationalism, rooted in a common Arab/Islamic past. Nasser's nationalism provided a sense of common history, identity, and solidarity that served as a basis for Arab unity.[9] The lure of this brand of Arab nationalism was demonstrated by the popularity Nasser enjoyed among many Muslim Arabs outside Egypt as well as attempted unions between Egypt and other Arab states (Syria, Libya, Jordan, and Sudan) under the umbrella of United Arab Republic.

Radical Arab governments also made major use of Islam to justify socio-economic reforms. Turning to a rich Islamic heritage, they interpreted Quranic texts and Prophetic traditions in order to legitimate and gain popular support for their Islamized brand of socialism. Traditional Islamic beliefs and values, such as the unity of the Muslim community (*ummah*), equality of its members, and social justice epitomized by Islamic practices like *zakat* (a tithe or wealth tax imposed for the general welfare of the poor), were reinterpreted. This emphasis on the Arab/Islamic character of government socialism may be seen in Nasser's Arab socialism, Algerian socialism, and the early writings of the Baath party of Syria and Iraq.[10] In addition, Islam and Islamic institutions were used to support government programs and policies. Egypt founded the Islamic Congress in conjunction with Saudi Arabia and Pakistan and created the Supreme Council of Islamic Affairs which, among other activities, published *Minbar al-Islam* (The Pulpit of Islam), a leading journal that espoused religious reform in the Muslim world and served as a primary source for articles supporting Nasser's Arab (Islamic) socialism. Similar developments occurred in other Muslim countries as governments obtained *fatwas* (formal legal opinions issued by specialists (muftis) in religious law) supporting government reform programs in birth control, land reform, nationalization, etc.

The role of Islam in Muslim politics was not restricted to government activity alone. Islamic organizations or movements continued to be active as well. Among the more significant and influential movements was the Muslim Brotherhood (al-Ikhwan al-Muslimun).[11] The Muslim Brotherhood was founded in 1928 by Hasan al-Banna (1906–1949), an Egyptian teacher who had received both a traditionally religious and a modern education. The Brotherhood grew out of al-Banna's deep concern about the effects of a Western secular form of modernization upon Islamic life and values and the failure of the government to address adequately the widespread socio-economic disparities in Egyptian society. In common with previous Islamic revivalist (*tajdid*) movements, al-Banna attributed the ills of society to its departure from the Islamic ideal as found in early Islam—during the time of the Prophet Muhammad and his companions. Therefore, he too advocated a return to Islamic sources—the Quran and the Example or practice of the Prophet. It is important to note that al-Banna did not reject modernization and technology but rather the Westernization and secularization of Muslim society. He reaffirmed the political nature of Islam and the need for political action to realize or re-establish a proper state based upon Islam in order to assure an Islamic society, governed by Islamic law and belief. He not only preached his message of social reform but also tried to implement it by establishing hospitals and cottage industries. Internationally, the Brotherhood emphasized the unity of the Muslim community (*ummah*) and denounced the continued foreign domination of Egypt and of other Muslim countries as well as the birth of neocolonialism in Palestine caused by the establishment of Israel in 1948.

After World War II, the Brotherhood emerged as an increasingly militant, activist, political organization. In 1949 the Brotherhood was implicated in the assassination of Egypt's prime minister and, shortly thereafter, Hasan al-Banna was assassinated (on February 12, 1949). The Brotherhood was a major supporter of the Free Officers' revolution of July 1952 with whom it shared common concerns: foreign domination, the failure of liberal nationalism, and the need for radical socio-economic reform. Despite its ties with the Free Officers, through Anwar Sadat, the Brotherhood's initial co-operation with the government gave way to disaffection and opposition due to Nasser's authoritarian rule and his refusal to establish an Islamic state. In 1954 and again in 1966 the Brotherhood was accused of plotting to assassinate Nasser. As a result, some of its leaders were executed, many of its members imprisoned, and the organization was finally suppressed. The Muslim Brotherhood inspired similar movements throughout the Arab world and re-emerged publicly in Egypt during Anwar Sadat's rule (1970–81).[12]

Despite these examples, the re-emergence of Islam during the 1960s was a rather limited phenomenon both geographically and politically. It was a partial retreat by political leaders in a number of countries from a secular, political path as they selectively appealed to Islam for legitimation and support. However, during the latter half of the 1970s, Islam dramatically re-emerged in Muslim politics across the Islamic world; in General Zia ul-Haq's *coup d'état* in Pakistan in 1977 and his call for establishment of an Islamic system of government

(*Nizam-i-Islam*); in the Iranian "Islamic revolution," in the seizure of the Grand Mosque in Mecca, in the assassination of Anwar Sadat in Egypt, and in the bloody suppression of the Muslim Brotherhood in Hama by the Syrian government. Islam has played a more active and widespread role in Muslim politics from North Africa to Southeast Asia. However, this political phenomenon has been rooted in a deeper, widespread, and more profound religious revival which has encompassed both the personal and the political sphere. The personal aspect of the Islamic revival is reflected in increased emphasis upon religious observances (mosque attendance, Ramadan fast, outlawing of alcohol, and gambling), religious programming in the media, the proliferation of religious literature, the rebirth of the Muslim Brotherhood, the rise of new Islamic associations, the success of Muslim student associations in university elections, and the vibrant *dawah* (missionary) movements which seek not simply to convert non-Muslims but to "Islamize" the Muslim population, i.e., to deepen their knowledge of and commitment to Islam.[13]

The current resurgence of Islam has attracted attention both because of its geographic expanse and its geopolitical significance. Religion is used both by incumbent governments and opposition movements in contemporary Muslim politics.[14] Political coalitions, operating under the banner of Islam, have toppled the Shah of Iran and Zulfikar Ali Bhutto in Pakistan, while Muslim resistance movements continue to operate in Afghanistan, Egypt, Syria, etc. Saudi Arabia,[15] Morocco,[16] Khomeini's Iran,[17] and Zia ul-Haq's Pakistan[18] legitimate their rule and policies in the name of Islam. Throughout the Muslim world, Islamic symbols, slogans, ideology, and actors have become prominent fixtures in Muslim politics.

The causes of the resurgence are many and need to be appreciated within the specific contexts of individual countries and regions. However, several phenomena may be identified as common to the contemporary Muslim experience: 1) an identity crisis precipitated by a sense of utter impotence, disillusionment, and loss of self-esteem; 2) disillusionment with the West and the failure of many governments to respond adequately to the political and socio-economic needs of their societies; and, 3) the new-found sense of pride and power which resulted from military (Arab-Israeli war) and economic (oil embargo) success in 1973.

If Islam's past strength, success, and power were signs of God's guidance and pleasure with the Islamic community's realization of His Will, modern Muslim history has instead been a record of the *ummah's* failure. Colonial rule, continued dependence on the West, and the disastrous Arab-Israeli war of 1967 were clear signs of an errant, debilitated community. Since Islamic belief and history taught that success and power were signs of a faithful community, Muslims might well ask "What had gone wrong in the Islamic world?" and "Why had

God seemingly abandoned his community?" Religious leaders and traditionists in general countered that God had not abandoned the Muslims; rather the Muslims in pursuing a Western secular path of development had departed from and must now "return" to the straight path of Islam.

Modern elites were particularly disillusioned. They had cast their lot as members of developing nations with a Western-oriented future. Yet, they continued to find themselves victims of Western neo-colonialism—politically, economically, and militarily dependent upon the superpowers—often seeming to be pawns in the struggle between the West and the Soviet Union. Nothing symbolized the reality of Western neocolonialism more than the creation and expansion of the state of Israel—a Western state established in the midst of the Arab world—protected and sustained by massive American aid. Finally, the quick and total defeat of Egypt, Syria, and Jordan by Israel in the '67 war and Israeli annexation of Sinai, Gaza, and the West Bank, with its capital Jerusalem—a sacred symbol and Islam's third holiest city—constituted the clearest testimony of the depths of the Muslim world's impotence.

If the West had failed Muslims as an ally, what of the Western models of development so eagerly adopted by Muslim governments? The record of elite policies in nation building was judged to be dismal indeed. Neither liberal nationalism nor the radical Arab nationalism/socialism of Gamal Abdel Nasser or the Baath party had succeeded. Problems of authoritarianism, legitimacy, and political participation continued to plague most Muslim countries. Although parliamentary forms of government, democratic elections, and political party systems were adopted in many countries, the reality of Muslim politics was often one of dictatorship and authoritarian rule. In addition, corruption and the concentration of wealth persisted as twin pillars of Muslim society while poverty, illiteracy, and overpopulation galloped along unchecked. Government promises for a more prosperous future, coupled with government development programs, created rising but, too often, unrealized expectations. The positive benefits of modernization seemed to benefit the few, while the lot of the masses remained relatively unchanged.

The negative fallout from the effects of modernization were of equal concern: migration from the villages and rapid urbanization of overcrowded cities with insufficient social support systems; the breakdown of traditional family, religious, and social values; the adoption of a "Western lifestyle," enthusiastically pursued as a symbol of modernity but now increasingly criticized as a source of moral decline and spiritual malaise. The climate of despair and disillusionment throughout the Muslim world during the late 1960s is amply documented in secular as well as religious literature issuing from North Africa, the Middle East, and South Asia.

Writers representing a spectrum of religious and ideological orientations questioned the Westernization of their societies and advocated a reaffirmation of their own cultural heritage. Islamic history, civilization, and values were re-examined in an attempt to build a present and future which were not simply the product of a Western transplant but rooted more indigenously in Islamic history and values. Of course, the meaning, interpretation, and approaches varied from religious to cultural and from fundamentalist to reformist. Renewal (*tajdid*), reform (*islah*), authenticity (*asala*), and renaissance (*nahda*) were common themes throughout the Muslim world.[19]

Events in 1973 provided a new source of pride and served as a positive motivation for Islamic revivalism. The ignominious Arab defeat of 1967 was reversed by the October War. While the Israelis were ultimately victorious, the Arab world felt vindicated by Egyptian successes in the war which many believed had been saved for the Israelis by the United States. Most importantly, Anwar Sadat's use of Islamic symbols and rhetoric to mobilize and motivate Egyptian forces gave a decidedly religious character to its battles and made this war an Islamic victory.[20] This was the Ramadan war (the sacred month of fasting during which the war occurred); its code name was Badr, a famous early Islamic victory led by Muhammad; its battle cry Allahu Akbar (God is Most Great), the traditional Islamic call to the defense of Islam; those who died in this holy war (jihad) were not simply patriots but martyrs (*shahid*).

The Arab oil embargo of 1973 was a second major catalyst for the resurgence. For the first time since the dawn of colonialism, the West was dependent upon the Muslim world. The Arabs were no longer simply client states but a world economic power to be reckoned with. Their economic and, hence, geopolitical importance was a source of enormous pride and a sign to many of a return of Allah's blessings. Such wealth and success were reminiscent of a glorious past—a new renaissance was at hand. The fact that Saudi Arabia is the birthplace of Islam, encompassing its two holiest cities, Mecca and Medina, reinforced such sentiments. Moreover, major oil powers like Saudi Arabia and Libya used their petrodollars to foster Islamic revivalism in other Muslim countries, supporting Islamic movements, assisting governments that introduced Islamic reforms, and underwriting the publication and distribution of Islamic literature.[21]

The extent and significance of the Islamic resurgence have raised many questions, among them: 1) Why have both analysts (academic as well as government) and the general public so misunderstood this significant phenomenon? 2) What voices have contributed to the beliefs and attitudes reflected in the Islamic revival? 3) What do contemporary Muslims say about a resurgent Islam and its political, economic, and social implications for the future? These are the questions which this volume addresses.

Muslim revivalists insist that the current religious revival is not simply a reaction to the West, but rather is part of an ongoing process of revival (*tajdid*) and reform (*islah*) which reflects a continuing tradition in Islamic history. John O. Voll, in "Renewal and Reform in Islamic History," maintains that central to the process of renewal in Islam is the revivalist call for a return to the fundamentals of Islam. However, the meaning and method of renewal varies with changing historical circumstances. What emerges is the picture of a tradition which, although fixed and stable, is neither stagnant nor monolithic. When the existing conditions and institutions of Islam seemed to warrant it, Muslim reformers have felt free to challenge the blind following of tradition (*taqlid*) and the Islamic establishment. They claimed their right to engage in independent analysis or interpretation (*ijtihad*) in order to re-form their societies.

In contemporary Islam, there has been a renewed call for the reform of Muslim societies through a return to Islamic sources. In "Islam and the Quest for Identity in the Arab World," John J. Donohue maintains that while the Arab defeat in the '67 war and oil wealth/power are important factors, the modern reaffirmation of Islamic identity is a response to a deeply rooted, century-old clash of cultures which has remained unresolved. Through a content analysis of Arab literature, Donohue reveals the increasing prominence of Islam as an element in Arab identity. Growing disenchantment with the West and a reactive quest for a more indigenously rooted identity is well illustrated in a broad spectrum of literature: popular, intellectual, and religious.

Notes

1. Marshall S. G. Hodgson, *The Venture of Islam*, vol. 2 (Chicago: University of Chicago Press, 1974).

2. Albert Hourani, *Arabic Thought in the Liberal Age* (London: Oxford University Press, 1970), chs. 5–9; and Malcolm Kerr, *Islamic Reform* (Berkeley: University of California Press, 1966).

3. For a brief overview of this development, see John O. Voll, *Islam: Continuity and Change in the Modern World* (Boulder, Colo.: Westview Press, 1982), pp. 207–14.

4. Muhammad Iqbal, selection from his Presidential Address before the Muslim League, "A Separate Muslim State in the Subcontinent," in *Islam in Transition: Muslim Perspectives*, ed. by John J. Donohue and John L. Esposito (New York: Oxford University Press, 1982), pp. 91–93.

5. *Islam in Transition*, pp. 55–90. Sylvia G. Haim, ed., *Arab Nationalism* (Berkeley: University of California Press, 1976).

6. Fred R. von der Mehden, *Religion and Nationalism in Southeast Asia* (Madison: University of Wisconsin Press, 1968), p. 212.

7. Clifford Geertz, *Islam Observed* (New Haven: Yale University Press, 1968), p. 75ff.

8. *Charte Nationale* (1976); see *Islam in Transition,* pp. 129–30.

9. Daniel Crecelius, "The Course of Secularization in Modern Egypt," in *Islam and Development: Religion and Sociopolitical Change,* ed. by John L. Esposito (Syracuse, N.Y.: Syracuse University Press, 1980), ch. 3; Guenther Lewy, "Nasserism and Islam: A Revolution in Search of Ideology," in *Religion and Political Modernization,* ed. by Donald Eugene Smith (New Haven: Yale University Press, 1974), ch. 14.

10. See, for example, Shaykh Mahmud Shaltut's justification for the acceptability of Nasser's Arab socialism in *Islam in Transition,* pp. 99–102, as well as excerpts from the writings of Michel Aflaq, a founder of the Baath party, and the Algerian *Charte Nationale,* ibid., pp. 107–12, 129–30.

11. The best study to date is R. P. Mitchell's *The Society of the Muslim Brothers* (London: Oxford University Press, 1969). Cf. C. P. Harris, *Nationalism and Revolution in Egypt* (The Hague: Mouton, 1964) and I. M. Husaini's *The Moslem Brethren* (Beirut, 1969).

12. Abd al-Moneim Said Aby and Manfred W. Wenner, "Modern Islamic Reform Movements: The Muslim Brotherhood in Contemporary Egypt," *The Middle East Journal,* 36:3 (Summer 1982), 336–61.

13. Fred R. von der Mehden, "Islamic Resurgence in Malaysia," in *Islam and Development,* chap. 9.

14. There are now many articles and volumes appearing at a rather steady rate. For a review of six such volumes see John L. Esposito, "Islam and Politics," in *The Middle East Journal,* 36:3 (Summer 1982), 415–20. Among the better overviews of the role(s) of Islam in contemporary politics are: Michael C. Hudson, "Islam and Political Development," in *Islam and Development,* ch. 1; Ali E. Dessouki, "The Islamic Resurgence: Sources, Dynamics, and Implications," in *Islamic Resurgence in the Arab World,* ed. by Ali E. Dessouki (New York: Praeger, 1982), ch. 1; H. R. Dekmejian, "The Anatomy of Islamic Revival," *The Middle East Journal,* 34:1 (Winter 1980).

15. James P. Piscatori, "The Roles of Islam in Saudi Arabia's Political Development," in *Islam and Development,* ch. 7; and Ronald R. MacIntyre, "Saudi Arabia," in *The Politics of Islamic Reassertion,* ed. by Mahammed Ayoub (New York: St. Martin's Press, 1982), ch. 2.

16. K. R. Singh "North Africa," in *The Politics of Islamic Reassertion,* ch. 4.

17. Mangol Bayat, "Islam in Pahlavi and Post-Pahlavi Iran: A Cultural Revolution?" in *Islam and Development,* ch. 5; and Kambiz Afracteh, "Iran," in *The Politics of Islamic Reassertion,* ch. 6.

18. John L. Esposito, "Pakistan: Quest for Islamic Identity," in *Islam and Development,* ch. 8; and William L. Richter, "Pakistan," in *The Politics of Islamic Reassertion,* ch. 8.

19. See, for example. John J. Donohue, "Islam and the Quest for Identity in the Arab World," in this volume; Ali Merad, "The Ideologisation of Islam in the Contemporary Muslim World," in *Islam and Power,* ed. A. S. Cudsi and Ali E. Dessouki (Baltimore: Johns Hopkins University Press, 1981), ch. 3; and Waheed-uz-Zamaan, ed., *The Quest for Identity* (Islamabad: Islamabad University Press, 1974).

20. Yvonne Y. Haddad, *Contemporary Islam and the Challenge of History* (Albany: State University of New York Press, 1982), chs. 2–3.

21. Daniel Pipes, "Oil Wealth and Islamic Resurgence," in *Islamic Resurgence,* ch. 2. While this chapter provides a store of information, the author's reductionist position regarding oil power and the resurgence is questionable.

I

UNDERSTANDING ISLAMIC IDENTITY

The Iranian revolution brought a startling revelation—the vast majority of Americans knew little about Islam and the Muslim world despite the fact that Islam is the second largest of the world's religions and the predominant religion of an increasingly important area of the world. Even professionally trained analysts in academia and government seemed totally oblivious to the religious revival taking place in many parts of the Muslim world and to its political implications. This oversight among professionals was due to the tendency of development theory to presuppose that the secularization of society was integral to the process of modernization.[1] Religious traditions were viewed as, at best, important in a medieval past. However, they were a part of the passing of traditional societies and, if anything, potential obstacles to change.[2]

Secondly, most analysts, whether consciously or not, operate on an assumption that religion and politics are or ought to be separate spheres of life. The tendency of Christianity to distinguish between Church and State ("Render to Caesar the things that are Caesar's and to God ...") coupled with a modern secular understanding of the nature of the state blinded many to the different perspectives of Islam.[3] But why in a society which prides itself on a high rate of literacy was the public so totally ignorant of Islam and the Muslim world? Moreover, where information did exist, why was it often simply a collection of stereotypes: camels and tents, menacing or cunning wealthy oil sheiks, harems, and veiled women. In the first chapter of this volume, Fred R. von der Mehden analyzes the causes for the ignorance, confusion, and misinformation which have characterized American public's perceptions of Islam.

1. Donald E. Smith, *Religion and Political Development* (Boston: Little, Brown, 1970).
2. See. for example, Daniel Lerner's *The Passing of Traditional Society: Modernizing the Middle East* (Glencoe, Ill.: The Free Press, 1958).
3. Michael C. Hudson, "Islam and Political Development," in *Islam and Development: Religion and Sociopolitical Change,* ed. by John L. Esposito (Syracuse, N.Y.: Syracuse University Press, 1980), ch. 3.

ONE

American Perceptions of Islam

FRED R. VON DER MEHDEN

There can be little doubt that the public's perceptions of Islam have tended to be characterized by ignorance, confusion, and misinformation. Until the national trauma of the Embassy hostage situation in Iran, our knowledge of this religion of over 700 million adherents was weak on Islam's basic tenets, recent history, internal schisms, and regions of dominance. Although informed about the Crusades in school, the average citizen knows little of the Five Pillars, the expansion of Islam to Southeast Asia and Black Africa, differences among sects, and the basic fact that the majority of Muslims live outside the Arab world. Beyond this, Islam and its causes have generally not received a sympathetic hearing and have been the subject of considerable criticism related to such issues as the Iranian crisis, the Black Muslims in the United States, or the Arab-Israeli conflict. My basic thesis in this study is that views of Americans toward Islam are framed by attitudes toward issues that involve Muslims. These issues are generally not fundamentally religious in content but help to establish stereotypes that are transferred to Islam itself.

Several of the most salient reasons for this picture: 1) the historical environment; 2) educational patterns; 3) the Arab-Israeli issue; 4) the oil crisis; 5) the Iranian Revolution; and 6) stereotyped perceptions. These are obviously interrelated factors which reinforce one another.

HISTORICAL ENVIRONMENT

The fundamental ignorance and, at times, antipathy of Americans regarding Islam needs to be judged in the light of our history. It can be argued that past cultural and racial biases against Third World societies in general has clouded our views of Islam as well as other "foreign" belief systems. Thus, Muslims were just another target of a type of international "Jim Crowism." Some observers, such as Professor E. W. Said, have asserted that Islam has been singled out for abuse, in part due to the historical confrontation between Islam and Christianity.[1] Without rejecting the accuracy of this latter view in terms of historical attitudes of Americans, it would appear that current perceptions of Islam rise out of a combination of ignorance of the religion and negative reactions against the rhetoric and activities of a minority of its adherents.

The rather huge lacunae in our knowledge are the result of several somewhat obvious factors. As a nation, we have historically been parochial in our understanding of the rest of the world, tending to display relatively little interest in other languages and cultures. As to Islam in particular, the United States never colonized a large Muslim population, the only significant group being the Moros of the southern Philippines after 1898. The people who arrived on our shores from the Middle East were generally not Muslims and, in fact, many felt persecuted by them. These included Christian Armenians, Syrians, and Lebanese, as well as the Jews who claimed historic ancestry in the area. Muslims remained a small minority and even in 1981 were less than .2 percent of the U.S. population. In part because of this lack of national and personal interraction, even our academic leadership in Islamic studies tended to be composed of foreigners, a pattern that has only begun to change significantly in the past decade. As one might expect, this overall ignorance was transferred into our general educational system.

EDUCATIONAL PATTERNS

Public education in the United States normally devotes to the non-Christian world a relatively small part of World Civilization courses. What data we have on teaching about Islam show that recent texts used at the high school level can be characterized by brevity and incidents of confusion and bias. One example of such short shrift is A. Mazour and J. Peoples's *Men and Nations: A World History*.[2] In this 878-page text for high school students, fewer than 700 words are given to an explanation of Islam as a religion. and less than five pages are devoted to the religion, its spread, culture, and law. There is no reference to the fact that the Muslim religion is the faith of Islam's largest nation, Indonesia. In a study of twenty such texts, Gerald Perry found that, while they provided basically accurate definitions of the Five Pillars, many were weak on other aspects of the religion, such as the caliphate, *shariah,* and the Sunni-Shia schism.[3] Even regarding the most essential Pillar, there was some confusion expressed about the characterization of Allah. Americans have generally lacked an understanding of the Muslim view of the Supreme Deity or the role of Muhammad and the Judeo-Christian heritage of Islam. In the texts a statement such as "Allah is the Arabic word meaning God" was exceptional, while comments such as

"Muslims worship a God called Allah" reinforced misconceptions that there were fundamental differences in interpretation of the Deity between Christians and Muslims. Regarding the caliphate, one particularly erroneous text, which kept referring to the caliphate in the present tense, asserted that:

> Moslems are also united under the Caliph and other religious leaders. One group of Moslems, who are trained in Islamic law and religion, make up the "Supreme Spiritual Committee of Islam." This group of high officials meets in Cairo.[4]

As well, these books tended to picture Islam as an intolerant religion, lacking in gentleness.

Finally, these texts were mixed as to their interpretations of the Arab-Israeli conflict, a factor in American attitudes toward Islam, which we will comment upon below. While some books were even-handed and others simply did not present reasons for Arab views and actions, a third set was biased in favor of Israel, and all were laudatory toward the image of Israel.

In a study of eight texts distributed in Canada and the United States, a committee of the Middle East Studies Association reported similar conclusions.[5] It found that some texts still referred to the "Mohammedan Religion" and occasionally showed Islam as distinct from the Judeo-Christian tradition or left out one of the Five Pillars. No hostility toward Islam was displayed, but there was a tendency to point to the strangeness and to the violent nature of Islam. Scores of minor errors were also noted in the texts, from calling all Arabs Muslim to inaccurate characterizations of the caliphate.

Ethnic stereotypes were also present: Arabs were viewed as farmers or nomads, the Turks as cruel, and all dressed strangely, etc. Yet, as one Committee member commented, "The overall impression one gets from these textbooks is not willful bias and prejudice, but rather the lack of thorough knowledge and understanding of the Middle East, its multifaceted civilization, and the forces at work there today."[6]

A more recent survey of texts written since 1975 shows some improvement[7]—none of the authors refers to "Mohammedanism." The texts do tend to understate the number of Muslims (about 500 million), emphasize the war and violence in Islam, give an inaccurate account of the role of women, and include a number of incorrect or misleading statements.

To this data we can add Michael Suleiman's studies of high school teacher and student reactions in several states.[8] He also finds a paucity of information provided American youth regarding Muslims. While not concentrating on Islam as such, he found that approximately two-fifths of those teaching world history and social studies devoted two weeks or less to the Middle East. As well,

37 percent of one sample of teachers found them skipping the Middle Eastern sections of their courses: always (3%), most of the time (8%), and frequently (28%). In contrast, 67 percent spent six weeks or more on Europe.

Suleiman further noted that in a sample of 520 high school teachers, their students saw Islam as "strange," leading to fear and hostility. "Thus, to some students Muslims are followers of a 'strange religion, peculiar religion, weird,' 'people with a funny religion,' 'stupid religion,' 'infidels.' Furthermore, Muslims 'dress strangely and practice polygamy.'"[9] He does not provide any percentages of such hostile opinions. Nor does he quantify the "frequent" remarks among teachers praising Islam for its contribution to science, the arts, and architecture. Teachers tended to be more favorably disposed than students toward Muslims. A very important finding, which will be discussed later, was that students and teachers generally tended to see Muslims in terms of their religion.

We thus find that Americans start with a weak foundation in their knowledge of Islam. World history forms only one year in the normal education of an American high school student and, while in recent years the non-Western world has been given greater stress, it is still a minor part of most such courses. Within discussions of the Third World, the Middle East is given no greater consideration than other areas. It is against this paucity of formal background that we can see the impact of other factors.

In this analysis it is argued that issues not central to an understanding of Islam as a religion have helped to determine overall attitudes. It is hypothesized that Islam itself has not been the issue, but such factors as the Arab-Israeli conflict, the oil crisis, and Iran's Islamic Revolution have influenced our view of Islam. It is further argued that the media have reinforced these views.

ARAB-ISRAELI CONFLICT

The Arab-Israeli conflict has made objective assessments of Islam and its adherents difficult, in part because, as James Reston once explained, "You may put it down as a matter of fact that any criticism of Israel will be met with the cry of anti-Semiticism."[10] From the beginning of the formation of Israel, American opinion has displayed greater sympathy for its cause than for that of its Arab opponents, with only a small percentage showing pro-Arab attitudes. Public opinion polls through the years have provided evidence for this stability of popular support. This can be compared with Canada in 1973 where 5 percent sympathized with the Arabs, 22 percent with the Israelis, and 73 percent with neither or no opinion. It can also be compared with the earliest Gallup Poll in 1949

Table I. Gallup Polls on the Arab-Israeli Conflict[11] (statistics shown in percentages).

Question: In the Middle Eastern situation, are your sympathies more with Israel or more with Arab nations?

Date	Israel	Arab Nations	Neither
August 1981	44	11	34
January 1979	40	14	31
May 1978	44	10	33
March 1978	38	11	33
June 1977	44	8	28
January 1975	44	8	22
December 1973	50	7	25
March 1970	44	3	32
January 1969	50	5	28
June 1967	66	4	25

that gave Israel 24 percent, the Arabs 12 percent, and neither 38 percent. The percentages not noted were primarily "don't knows."

Recent actions of the Begin government in the West Bank and Lebanon have led to considerable criticism. American opinion polls showed strong negative reactions to the attack on the Iraqi reactor, and Anwar Sadat's conciliatory moves were generally commended, but these views have not been translated into pro Arab-cum-pro Muslim attitudes. A number of journalists have noted major changes in American opinion since the October War and Sadat's trip to Israel.[12] By late 1978—asked if Israel was doing all it could to bring about peace in the Middle East—Gallup found 27 percent responding positively, 49 percent negatively, and 24 percent with no opinion.[13] At the same time, Sadat began to be seen more as a man of peace than the Israeli Prime Minister, with more than twice as many Americans having a highly favorable view of Sadat than of Begin in 1978. However, Sadat's popularity did not affect perceptions of Arabs or Muslims as a whole. Yet the Palestinian case, while viewed more sympathetically by the American public, was clouded by charges of "terrorism" and, when polled, Americans held a 4-to-1 ratio of sympathy for Israel over the PLO as late as 1981. Ironically, given the generally secular nature of the PLO, its activities helped to reinforce the view of Muslims as intransigent and fanatical.

When asked to rate Egypt and Israel on a 10-point favorable-unfavorable scale, American responses were as shown in Table II.

However, these positive changes must be viewed against years of sympathetic reactions to "tiny," "democratic," and "embattled" Israel.[14] In turn, then, these

Table II.   Gallup Poll Index – March 1980.

	+5	+4	+3	+2	+1	Don't Know	−1	−2	−3	−4	−5
Egypt	5	7	22	28	19	6	9	5	4	1	4
Israel	10	10	21	16	17	5	7	4	4	1	5

attitudes have influenced public views of Israel's enemies. While the argument can be made that the media have biased our perceptions (this will be discussed later), the activities of some Arab states have frequently not helped matters. Against the Israeli sensitivity to the media has more often been a seeming Arab unwillingness to open satisfactory communications with the West. Only Sadat was equally as capable of manipulating public opinion in the United States as the Israelis. In the past, the tendency toward hyperbole in the Arabic and Farsi languages often lent credence to those pointing up the dangers of Muslim success.[15] More limited than the Israelis in their ability to use domestic interest groups in the United States in the past, some Arab groups turned to strong language, anomic disturbances, and threats. Again, these reinforced views of what Muslims are like.

ENERGY CRISIS

Unfortunately for Muslims, the changed image of Israel that was catalyzed by the 1973 October War was correlated with the AOPEC (Arab Organization of Petroleum Exporting Countries) boycott and followed by the Iranian Revolution. Again we must note that a key element in the American stereotype of the Muslim relates to Middle Eastern events. To all too many, Arab equals Muslim, and vice versa, and OPEC (Organization of Petroleum Exporting Countries) equals Arabs and vice versa. The public does not perceive the difference between AOPEC and OPEC, and the existence of often hardline non-Arab members of the latter, such as Nigeria or Venezuela, goes by with little notice. The use of rich oil sheiks in political cartoons to exemplify OPEC readily gives credence to the general stereotype. Threats by Muslim states to use the boycott in the Arab-Israeli conflict, and the paramount role of the often traditionally dressed Wahhabi Saudis in oil negotiations, all lend further evidence to support these perceptions. And, as we shall see, that particular stereotype has not been attractive. At the same time, it would be incorrect to give too much emphasis to the energy issue. It is true that regular price increases by OPEC focus attention on the Middle East, and "Arab oil money" is a regular topic of conversation. Again, however, polls tend to show that Americans have often blamed the large petroleum companies and their own government for their situation. For example, a poll immediately after the 1973 oil crisis found 25 percent blaming the oil companies, 23 percent the U.S. government, 19 percent the Nixon administration, 16 percent the public, and only 7 percent the Arab nations—few blamed the Israelis.[16]

IRAN'S ISLAMIC REVOLUTION

Finally, the Islamic Revolution in Iran has been a two-edged sword in the battle to increase American understanding of Islam. There is no question that the number of newspaper and magazine articles, editorials, and television spots covering Muslim-oriented subjects has increased tremendously since its inception. Even academics have been called upon by government, business, social organizations, television, and newspapers to clarify the situation. A perusal of the *Readers' Guide* to popular periodicals displayed an astounding growth in articles related to Islam and its adherents. During the year from March 1976 to February 1977, there were only half a dozen pieces on various Islamic subjects, while in the first six months after the taking of the American hostages, there were more than fifty. There were similar increases in articles on Islam in newspapers, and general media coverage grew dramatically. Without the hostage issue and what preceded it, Americans would probably have remained even more ignorant of differences between Shiites and Sunnis, as well as the rising Islamic "fundamentalist" revival. However, along with explanations of the meaning of Islam there came other articles less illuminating, such as those entitled "Khomeini's Contagion," "Portrait of an Ascetic Despot," and "A Regime of Fanatics."

This reaction to the perceived excesses of the Iranian Revolution is the negative side to the problem. Americans became extremely antagonistic toward the Iranians due to the hostage issue. A survey in March 1980 showed that on a +5 to −5 scale, 90 percent of the sample rated Iran from a −1 to −5, and 69 percent −4 and −5. No other country reached that low. Polls in the months immediately after the capture of the hostages found a large majority of the public supporting punishment of the Iranians in one form or another.[17] Chanting in the streets by demonstrators declaring, "Kill the American dogs," and attacks on the U.S. Embassy in Pakistan and on American facilities elsewhere after the fighting in Mecca tended to color the public's view of Islam as a whole. Nor did the statements of Ayatullah Khomeini aid friendly relations. The comments by historian Kemal Karpat that "Khomeini has done more to harm the Islamic image in one month than all the propaganda of the past 15 years"[18] may be too strong, but to many Americans Khomeini came to symbolize fanaticism and atavism in Islam. As the title of *Time*'s article read when he was named "Man of the Year," he was viewed as "The Mystic Who Lit the Fires of Hatred." Certainly, quotes of the Ayatullah have not helped, such as "The nation voted for an Islamic Republic and everyone should obey. If you do not obey, you will be annihilated."[19] Cartoons of the Ayatullah have Muslim symbols around them; his views are often characterized as the rising tide of a new Islam in the world; jokes, commercial dart boards with his picture, Country-Western songs, etc., became part of the stereotypes being formulated in the American mind.

While newspaper editorials following the hostage-taking and later attacks on U.S. posts were generally careful not to blame Islam as a whole, many of them added to the confusion about the role of the religion. The picture of Islam as intolerant, extremist, and reactionary was fostered in some editorials. Thus, the *Miami Herald* referred to "a maddened clique of Islamic clergy that draws its power from the frenzy of murderous slogans"; threats to try the Shah and Embassy hostages brought out statements of "so-called Islamic justice"; and the attacks on other American facilities often condemned "Moslem mobs" rather than the nationalism of the offenders.[20] In sum, the Iranian Revolution and particularly the hostage issue, when combined with the rhetoric of Iranian Muslim leaders, imprinted upon the American mind a picture of excess, intolerance, and fanaticism which may be difficult to erase. This was particularly unfortunate, as we now turn to the historic role of the media as reinforcers of Muslim stereotypes.

THE ROLE OF THE MEDIA

Assessing the role of the media on any issue that encompasses the Middle East immediately raises the dangers of paranoia. Let it be stated at the outset that I do not see a major Zionist conspiracy which controls our media, although I recognize full well the efforts of pro-Israeli interests to influence what Americans see and read.[21] This does not mean, however, that there has not been an historic bias in favor of Israel and an unattractive stereotypic view of the Arab Muslim. What does affect our media and how they influence us are the following:

1. Stereotypes of Muslims in the Middle East predate the Arab-Israeli crisis and can be found in literary references to Turks and Arabs as well as in World War I anti-Turkish propaganda.[22]

2. America's reactions to the Holocaust, early support of Israel as the perceived underdog, and the dangers of appearing anti-Semitic, all are reflected in the media.

3. Although it is no longer acceptable to use most U.S. ethnic groups as villains, the inaction, until recently, of Arab Americans in putting pressure on the

media, has made the Arab a good target. (It should also be noted that the majority of Americans of Arab descent are not Muslim.) The perceived actions of OPEC and Iran have made the role of villain easy for the public to accept.

4. Americans tend to consider Islam as primarily identified with the Arab world. If most Arabs find it difficult to disengage religion and ethnicity, so do Americans. Thus, the ferment that appears omnipresent in the Middle East tends to be viewed as an integral aspect of Islamic life.

Against this background we find considerable evidence that the American media have not been entirely even-handed and have not expanded the public's knowledge greatly past the aforementioned school textbooks. Perhaps more recently newspapers are not as biased as some would believe, as seen in Robert Trice's analysis of editorials in our elite press (New York Times, Washington Post, Chicago Tribune, Los Angeles Times, Denver Post, Atlanta Constitution, Christian Science Monitor, St. Louis Post-Dispatch, Wall Street Journal, Louisville Courier-Journal, Dallas Morning News).[23] In viewing editorials from 1966 to 1974, he found that both support and criticism of Israel and the Arab states were weaker than expected, and that Israel was constantly criticized over retaliatory raids and the annexation of Jerusalem. However, the Arab cause was never able to get much sympathy from the American press; only the Christian Science Monitor showed an overall positive view of the Arabs, and only the Monitor and Post-Dispatch had an overall negative assessment of Israel. During this period news-reporting itself tended to be unbiased, although words such as "terrorist" were used one-sidedly to describe Palestinian activities. Part of this was the aforementioned problem of Arab states which were not as aware as the Israelis of the usefulness of public relations and made access to their countries difficult.

However, it should be noted that this more even-handed pattern has emerged after years of more biased reporting. For example, a study of six news magazines and the New York Times's "News of the Week" during the second half of 1956 (the Suez Crisis period) found the Arab typically pictured as a desert nomad; the Israelis were viewed as the "good guys" while the Arabs were the "bad guys."[24] Again, there were differences in the coverage and neutrality of these magazines, with the New Republic the best on both counts, followed by Time and the New York Times. A later analysis by Suleiman showed the difference in coverage of the 1973 October War.[25]

As has been noted previously, however, another part of the editorial page—the political cartoon—has not aided American-Islamic understanding. While the Ayatullah may have been Time's "Man of the Year," he has become the cartoonist's breadwinner. In pinpointing the oil issue, the symbol of the despised OPEC is invariably the caricature of a greedy, sinister Arab, perhaps with a minaret in the background. PLO members are broadly characterized as knife- and gun-wielding fanatics in many of the cartoons. Two ameliorating factors should be noted: these negative pictures do not attack Islam as such; and all political cartoonists are not biased on this matter. Again, the *Christian Science Monitor* stands out for its long-term fairness, and there has been a general move toward greater understanding, except in the case of the Iranian issue.[26] In sum, while press stories have become more even-handed (particularly with the opening of Arab states to American reporters), and editorials less pro-Israeli, stereotypes are maintained through cartoonists and some of the perceived excesses of extremists.

Insofar as the rest of the media is concerned, the April/May 1980 copy of *The Link* provides an interesting, if committed, analysis of the stereotypic view of the Arab on American television.[27] After strong comments by liberal journalist Nicholas Von Hoffman ("no religious, national, or cultural group . . . has been so massively and consistently vilified") and by Jonathan Raban ("Arab is a word that people learn to hate when they hear it on television"), author Jack Shaheen provides examples of stereotyping. He notes the tendency to picture the Arab at different times as extremely wealthy, cruel, stupid, oriented toward the use of terror, and generally unattractive. The stereotypic pattern which categorizes whole peoples has thus put the Arab and his religion in the role of villain. Regrettably, Erik Barnouw is probably correct when he states:

> Viewers feel that they understand, from television alone, what is going on in the world. They unconsciously look to it for guidance as to what is important, good, and desirable, and what is not. It has tended to displace or overwhelm other influences such as newspapers, school, church, grandma, and grandpa. It has become the definer and transmitter of society's values.[28]

If this is true, we need to consider carefully Shaheen's argument in another piece that asserts, "A negative, unjustifiable, and erroneous image of the Arab and his life style is offered to American viewers on a continuing basis."[29]

American television news has been particularly vulnerable to accusations of unbalanced reporting on matters dealing with Arabs and Israelis. In part the situation has been due to easier access to news sources in Israel, where direct satellite coverage is available. However, there is also the problem of U.S. television news centers being in New York, where Israel is an important political and emotional issue.[30] As well, it is argued that general American attitudes taint coverage of the news, as ABC's Steve Bell commented, "I call it the audience factor—in this case a tremendous interest in and sympathy for Israel. It's a factor in how editorial judgements are made." NBC's Steve Mallory asserted that the U.S. viewer is less interested in news about people with darker skins and "Arabs are the people you see wearing kaffiyehs and riding camels, right? And those aren't your neighbors in California or Kansas."[31] To the extent that these charges are true, they buttress the points made earlier regarding perceptions of Islam influenced by the Israeli issue and attitudes toward the Third World in general.

This pattern of stereotyping has also been obvious in motion pictures, whether it be the romantic sheik of the 1920s, slapstick comedy Arabs of the postwar years, or adventure films located in a celluloid Baghdad. On the other hand, we have also seen pro-Israeli movies such as *Exodus, Cast a Giant Shadow,* and *Judith.*

Thus, the actions of Muslims have helped to establish images of Islam that emphasize intransigence, fanaticism, war-like behavior, "foreignness," and antagonism toward modern democratic precepts. This is not based upon an extensive knowledge of the religion itself but upon the perceptions of self-identified professors of the Islamic faith, filtered through the media. Misperceptions of Islam are generally not due to a natural antagonism, although former President Carter overstated the case when he said that, "We have the deepest respect and reverence for Islam and all those who share the Moslem faith." More properly, there are stereotypical images based upon limited knowledge of unfamiliar cultures.

Against this background of general ignorance and pre-formed ideas, it is not surprising that the American public finds it difficult to understand the current Islamic resurgence that has manifested itself throughout the Muslim world. Given this nation's intimate involvement with the Iranian Islamic Revolution and the hostage issue, we can see several elements come into the public perception of the resurgence:

1. To understand the American reaction to Islamic resurgence, it is necessary to recognize the images that have influenced its collective mind. Those who have appeared in the media professing one form or another of "Islamic resurgence" include many who are identified in unfavorable terms. Among them are Ayatullah Khomeini himself who has referred to Americans as "devils" and held their people hostage; Libya's Colonel Qaddafi, charged with assassination attempts on his opponents; those responsible for attacks on Mecca and U.S. facilities in Asia; those leading demonstrations against this country in Iran; and the alleged assassins of Anwar Sadat.

2. There is little knowledge of the resurgence outside of Iran and perhaps Pakistan, although there is a vague understanding that it is taking place elsewhere. Certainly, the movement in Indonesia and Malaysia is totally unknown outside the academic and corporate communities. The pre-empting of the move-

ment by Iran insofar as the media are concerned means that the Ayatullah Khomeini and militants tend to define the resurgence for the American people.

3. Comments by Khomeini and the rhetoric of his followers have led Americans to view the resurgence as fanatical or extremist, missing other elements in the movement.

4. There is a tendency to believe that the Islamic revival is reactionary in its entirety. Pictures of women in traditional dress, rhetoric attacking foreign investment and Western culture, and demands to cleanse elements of modern morality, all provide a picture that dominates the media. Americans are generally unaware of the complex mosaic of beliefs in the movement; particularly misunderstood is the desire of many "fundamentalists" to modernize within a religious context acceptable to the indigenous culture and not to launch a modern Islamicized Luddite movement.[32]

To conclude, this chapter has attempted to show that the average American's views of Islam arise out of a brief and at times inaccurate description of the religion and its adherents presented in the schools. Beyond this perhaps murky picture he is influenced not by definitions of what Islam as a religion preaches, but by what he sees acted out by groups and individuals identified as Muslim. Lacking sufficient keys from his history, education, and the media as to why these actions are taking place, the citizen reacts to events. Thus, he sees the cost of living rise due to what his government says are unreasonable OPEC (read Arab) price increases, the long Arab-Israeli conflict in which the Arabs are characterized as militarily incompetent and prone to terrorism, and, most recently, a self-declared Islamic Revolution which has imprisoned his diplomats, endangered his investments, and called his country criminal.

It would be improper to end with this bleak picture, for changes are apparent. The news media have shown a greater penchant for even-handedness in the Arab-Israeli dispute; Sadat's overtures created a favorable image of a devout, tolerant Muslim interested in peace; Arab Americans have launched a campaign to pressure the networks regarding Arab stereotypes; and, with it all, the Iranian Islamic Revolution made Americans more acutely aware, and to a degree more knowledgeable, of the role of Islam as a religion and as a political force. As well, a number of private and government organizations have stepped forward to attempt to educate the general public on the basics of Islam. These have included such diverse groups as the National Committee To Honor the Fourteenth Centennial of Islam with its large budget and prestigious boards, the Hartford Seminary, the International Communications Agency, and various U.S. corporations and universities. It would be comforting but inaccurate to state that the wall of past ignorance has been destroyed, but, without doubt, some major cracks have appeared.

Notes

1. E. W. Said, *Orientalism* (New York: Pantheon, 1978) and the "Review Symposium" of the book in the *Journal of Asian Studies,* 39 (May 1980):481–517.

2. A. Mazour and J. Peoples, *Men and Nations: A World History* (New York: Harcourt Brace Jovanovich, 1975).

3. G. Perry, "Treatment of the Middle East in American High Schools," *Journal of Palestine Studies,* 4 (Spring 1975):45–58.

4. Ibid., p. 49.

5. W. Griswold, *The Image of the Middle East in Secondary School Textbooks* (New York: Middle East Studies Association, 1975).

6. Ibid., p. 26.

7. Ayad Al-Qazzaz. "The Perception in Some U.S. World History Textbooks," paper presented at the Dimension of Islam Conference in North America, University of Alberta, May 1980.

8. Michael Suleiman, "The Middle East in American High School Curricula: A Kansas Case Study," *Mesa Bulletin,* 8 (May 1974):8–19: idem, "National Stereotypes as Weapons in the Arab-Israeli Conflict," *Journal of Palestine Studies,* 3 (Spring 1974): 109–21; and idem, *American Images of Middle East Peoples: Impact of the High Schools* (New York: Middle East Studies Association, 1977).

9. Suleiman, *American Images,* p. 45.

10. Quoted in "The American Media and the Palestinian Problem," *Journal of Palestine Studies,* 5 (Autumn 1975/Winter 1976): 176. Several other journalists interviewed agreed with this assertion.

11. *Gallup Public Opinion Index,* Report 161 (1978), p. 27, and Report 191 (1981). For an excellent review of U.S. public opinion, see M. Suleiman's "American Public Support of Middle Eastern Countries: 1939–1979," a paper for the Fourth Annual Symposium of the Georgetown University Center of Contemporary Arab Studies, 1979.

12. "The American Media."

13. *The Gallup Poll,* 1978 (Wilmington: Scholarly Resources, 1979).

14. See S. Lipset, "The Polls in the Middle East," *Middle East Review,* 11 (Fall 1978): 24–31. He notes that in 1978 Israel was favored 43 percent to 11 percent for Arab states.

15. See M. Suleiman, "The Arabs and the West: Communication Gap," *Il Politico.* 32 (1967):511–29.

16. *Gallup Public Opinion Index,* Report 104, 1974, p. 5.

17. *Newsweek,* Dec. 17, 1979.

18. *Time,* Dec. 17, 1979.

19. *Time,* Jan. 7, 1980.

20. *Editorials on File,* 10 (Nov. 1–15, 1979):1210–59. Obviously, this was a highly traumatic period that would expectedly bring forward emotional statements. Perhaps it is remarkable that comments were so muted.

21. For a book that does see a conspiracy, see A. Lilienthal, *The Zionist Connection* (New York: Dodd. Mead, 1979). An example of such views is the statement of I. F. Stone that "Finding an American publishing house willing to publish a book which departs from the standard Israeli line is about as easy as selling a thoughtful exposition of atheism to *L'Observatore Romano* in Vatican City."

22. A number of important English writers such as Arnold Toynbee wrote propaganda pieces pointing to alleged Turkish atrocities.

23. Robert Trice, "The American Elite Press and the Arab-Israeli Conflict," *Journal of Palestine Studies,* 3 (Spring 1974):116, 118.

24. M. Suleiman. "An Evaluation of Middle East News Coverage in Seven American Newsmagazines: July–December 1956," *Middle East Forum,* 41 (Autumn 1965):9–30.

25. See Tables III and IV in M. Suleiman, "National Stereotypes as Weapons in the Arab-Israeli Conflict," *Journal of Palestine Studies,* 3 (Spring 1974):116. 118.

26. See G. Damron, "A Survey of the Political Cartoons Dealing with the Middle East," in E. Ghareeb, ed., *Split Vision: Arab Portrayal in the American Media* (Washington, D.C.: Institute of Middle Eastern and North African Affairs, 1977), pp. 153–62. For example, see L. Michalak's "Exoticism and Cruelty: The American Stereotype of Arabs," unpublished paper, Department of Anthropology, University of California, Berkeley, 1975.

27. J. Shaheen, "The Arab Stereotype on Television," *The Link,* 13 (April/May 1980). Also see his "The Image of the Arab on American Television," in *Split Vision,* pp. 163–71.

28. Ibid., p. 3.

29. Shaheen, "The Image of the Arabs," p. 164. Perhaps proof of this can be seen in the "Abscam" incidents based upon alleged bribes of public officials by an Arab. Americans of Arab descent have asked what the reaction would have been if it had been called "Jewscam." See also F. R. von der Mehden, "Religion and Development in Southeast Asia: A Reassessment," paper prepared for the International Rural Sociology Congress, Mexico City, August 1980.

30. See J. Weisman, "Blind Spot in the Middle East," *TV Guide* (Oct. 24–30, 1981): 6–14. He reports on an extensive survey of television coverage of the Middle East and quotes correspondents on this issue.

31. Ibid., p. 12.

TWO

Renewal and Reform in Islamic History: *Tajdid* and *Islah*

JOHN O. VOLL

Contemporary resurgent Islam contains new elements, but it also has deep roots in the Muslim historical experience. Some Islamic organizations may be new, and contemporary movements may not have direct institutional connections with past groups. However, the contemporary activities of Islamic renewal reflect a longstanding and continuing dimension of Islamic history. It is, of course, important to understand the particular conditions of individual groups and their specific experiences. In addition, it is of great importance to be aware of the broader Islamic historical context within which these movements operate. The historical heritage provides at least some of the symbols and concepts available for Muslims in the contemporary resurgence. In this way, even in the absence of direct organizational continuity, contemporary Muslim actions are influenced by the past experience of the Islamic world.

Two of the great concepts in the Islamic vocabulary of resurgence are *tajdid* and *islah*.[1] *Tajdid* is usually translated as "renewal" and *islah* as "reform." Together they reflect a continuing tradition of revitalization of Islamic faith and practice within the historic communities of Muslims. It provides a basis for the conviction that movements of renewal are an authentic part of the working out of the Islamic revelation in history. Even when the terms *tajdid* and *islah* are not explicitly used, the attitude and mode of faith to which they refer can still be seen.

Over the centuries the specific meanings of *tajdid* and *islah* have changed, depending on the evolution of Islamic thought and the changing circumstances of the Islamic community. In general terms, however, there has been a continuity of mood that lies behind the changing specifics of meaning. At its core, this broad tradition of renewal-reform represents the individual and communal effort to define Islam clearly and explicitly in terms of God's revelation (as recorded in the Quran) and the customs or Sunna of the Prophet Muhammad (as recorded in the hadith literature which describes his reported sayings and actions.) In changing circumstances and with different implications, *islah* and

32

tajdid have always involved a call for a return to the basic fundamentals of Islam as presented in the Quran and Sunna of the Prophet.

The effort to bring communal and individual realities into line with the basic norms and values of the belief system is not unique to Islam. However, the specific ways in which this effort is manifested do have characteristically Islamic modes. The sources of the terms *islah* and *tajdid* as names for this effort can give some indication of the way the "renewalist" mode operates within Islam.

Although the term *islah* is frequently translated as "reform," the term and other related words have a strong sense of moral righteousness as well as a sense of reshaping for the sake of improving effectiveness. This mood is part of the usage of the term and related words in the Quran and helps to define the tone of "reform" within the Islamic tradition. *Islah* is directly related to the task of the long line of God's messengers whose works are described in the Quran. The Prophet Shuayb, for example, tells the people to whom he was sent: "I want only *islah* to the extent of my powers."[2] Those who work for *islah*, the *muslihun*, are frequently praised in the Quran, and they are described as being engaged in the work of God. Their reward is said to be sure (S. 7:170). In this way, although the era of the prophets and their *islah* efforts is over, the work of *islah*, righteous reform, continues as a part of the responsibility of believers. This reform is not simply working for increased efficiency or prosperity. It is the effort to increase the righteousness of the people.

Tajdid has similar connotations of faithfulness to God's revelation. The basis for most Muslim discussions of *tajdid* is a tradition from the Prophet Muhammad. He is reported to have said, "God will sent to this *ummah* (the Muslim community) at the head of each century those who will renew its faith for it." This activity of renewal is *tajdid* and the person who brings it about is called a *mujaddid*. This saying of the Prophet has had many different interpreters who have disagreed over details, but the basic tone is remarkably constant. The Muslim community over time is seen as departing from the path defined by the Quran and the Sunnah, and *mujaddids* are needed to bring about a regeneration of the authentic Islamic spirit. In this way, *tajdid*, like *islah*, has a basic moral dimension. Renewal, like reform, must serve the purpose of fulfilling God's will rather than human practicality alone.

This mode of revitalization has certain necessary characteristics. In particular, it is based in a special way upon a sense of knowledge of the will of the divinity. *Islah* and *tajdid* are modes of "reform" that start from a basic standard that is believed to be permanently available to the believers in an unchanging form. In Islam, this standard for judgment is the Quran and the Sunna of the Prophet.[3] Knowledge of this standard is gained by examination of these fundamental sources. This is different from subjective awareness based on personal intuition or illumination. In a profound sense, *islah* and *tajdid* as modes of reform are scriptural rather than illuminationist.

A corollary of this scriptural basis is that *islah* and *tajdid* are modes of reform that do not depend upon a concept of "progress" for their validity. The perfect model is already available in the revelation. The purpose of the *mujaddids* or the *muslihun* is not to perfect the model, it is to implement an already existing ideal. These renewer-reformers are thus not messiahs or apocalyptic figures coming at the end of time and human history. While there are messianic figures in the traditions of Islam, their anticipated role is to bring in the last days, while the actions of the renewer-reformer are clearly in the realm of historical human experience.

The sense of having a complete model and of the historicity of that model is strengthened by the recognition of the practice or Sunna of the Prophet as a basic source of guidance. The Prophet is believed to have established a community which is a model for how the revelation is to be applied in human society. In this context, one may strive to create a society using the Prophet's community as a model, but this *islah* is a process of restoration and renewal, not one of self-conscious innovation. The renewer and reformer is not compelled to re-create the exact conditions of the first Islamic century, but the process of *tajdid-islah* is inspired by the example of a past experience rather than impelled by a hope for a future utopia.

This special role of the experience of Muslims during the period of the Prophet's lifetime is well defined by a modern Muslim reformer in this tradition, Sayyid Qutb. He states,

> That was a remarkable period, a sublime summit, an exceptional generation of men, a bright beacon. It was, as we have said, decreed and willed by God, so that this unique image might be materialized in the situations of real life and recourse might later be had to it, in order to repeat it within the limitations of human capacity.[4]

This early era of righteous excellence sets the challenge to subsequent generations of humans and it is in this challenge that the spirit and task of *islah* and *tajdid* are defined. Sayyid Qutb said, "The fact is that this period was not the result of an unrepeatable miracle; rather it was the fruit of human exertion made by the first Muslim community. It can be achieved whenever that exertion is again made."[5] This special effort is the heart of the traditions of *islah* and *tajdid* in the Islamic community.

The main foundations of this renewalist tradition remain remarkably constant. The great effort is to continue the work of righteousness and submission to God's will. This was the mission of the *muslihun* described in the Quran and the goal of *islah* after the days of the Prophet Muhammad. It is an effort of socio-moral construction or reconstruction making use of a normative standard found in the Quran and the Sunna of the Prophet. This standard is independent from the changing historical conditions and specific contexts and it is available as a criterion to be used by renewers as a standard for judging the value of existing conditions and institutions. Although the guardians and interpreters of this special standard might become an elite, the fact that the Quran was recorded in permanent form and available to all meant that it could be used as a basis for a profound criticism of such an elite and its organizations as well as other social institutions.

The basic standard of judgment which inspires Islamic reform and renewal may not depend upon particular conditions of time or place. However, the specific forms that *tajdid* and *islah* take do reflect the nature of the society in which they are undertaken. Thus, while the effort to bring society into conformity with the norms defined by the Quran and Sunna is, in general terms, a constant element in the *tajdid-islah* tradition, the role of the *muslihun* and *mujaddids* in any given social context will vary. Over the centuries, as a result, the contextual significance of the effort of moral renewal has changed and evolved.

CONTINUING THEMES IN TAJDID-ISLAH

The renewalist tradition in Islam is a special style or mode of dealing with the faith, particularly as it involves the life of the believer within the Muslim community. The long term continuity of this mode of Islam can be seen by examining three themes which appear in the manifestations of *tajdid-islah* in the major eras of Islamic history, both pre-modern and modern. They are: 1) the call for a return to, or a strict application of, the Quran and the Sunna of the Prophet; 2) the assertion of the right of independent analysis *(ijtihad)* of the Quran and the Sunna in this application, rather than having to rely upon and imitate the opinions of the preceeding generations of the learned men of Islam (which is called *taqlid*); and, 3) the reaffirmation of the authenticity and uniqueness of the Quranic experience, in contrast to other Islamic modes of synthesis and openness.

Return to the Quran and the Sunna. The first decades of the Islamic era were a unique time. They were the years of the lifetime of the Prophet Muhammad and his immediate companions. In this period and the years following, not only was the record of revelations to Muhammad fully recorded, but there was also a beginning of the recording of the statements and actions of the Prophet in various situations. These reports, or hadiths, assumed increasing importance in the minds of Muslims as guides for faith and behavior. They were seen as defining the Sunna or practice of the Prophet. However, during the first century and a half, the process of hadith gathering and recording was still developing. It was not until well into the second century that formal and organized collections of hadith began to be compiled and the study of hadith began to be an organized discipline. In this, the works of Muhammad al-Shafii (150–204 A.H./767–820 A.D.) and Ahmad ibn Hanbal (164–241 A.H./780–855 A.D.) in analysis, and the great collections of hadith, the most famous of which was compiled by Muham-mad al-Bukhari (194–256 A.H./810–870 A.D.), meant that by the end of the third Islamic century, there was a formal, generally accepted body of traditions that could be used by Muslims for guidance.[6]

Before this time there were men and groups who insisted on no compromises in adherence to the faith. These rigorists did not have a fully developed corpus of rules and organized precedents to serve as a rallying point for their call. As a result, they moved in the direction of simple asceticism, like Hasan al-Basri,[7] or in the direction of developing their own body of organized thought and rules that began to diverge from the mainstream of Muslim thought and life, as hap-pened with the Kharijites.[8]

By the beginning of the third Islamic century, the perceptions of the life of the Prophet had become sufficiently codified for teachers like Ahmad ibn Han-bal to call for a strict adherence to the Quran and the Sunna of the Prophet.[9] He could reject the earlier alternatives of simple personal opinion and other methods and he criticized local traditions of practice and legal interpretations that had developed in the various parts of the Islamic world.

Strictly speaking, renewal and reform movements are not possible until a basic tradition is formulated.[10] With the presence of an established canon of the Quran and the Sunna, it became possible to use that canon as a standard by which to judge contemporary events and practices. It provided a basis for efforts to purify Islamic society and could be used as a basis for rejecting post-prophetic customs and formulations. The existence of this basic standard of judgment makes it possible to issue a call for re-forming society on the basis of the estab-lished scriptures. The early strict asceticism and sectarian rigorism were part of the process of the original formative efforts. However, once the Quran and the Sunna became fully defined as a basis for judgement within an established Mus-lim community, the spirit and mood that had originally led to sectarian rigorism and asceticism could provide the motivation for *islah* and *tajdid*.

Since the ninth century (A.D.), the call for a return to a strict application of the Quran and the Sunna has been heard in different areas and in varying forms. The acceptance of the Quran and Sunna is certainly the identifying feature of the Islamic community as a whole. However, from time to time, men and groups emerged who demanded a particular kind of adherence to the Quran and the Sunna. The "renewalists" insisted on a more literal interpretation and application than the general community did. Their rigorism was recognized as distinctive by their contemporaries in all ages.

This rigorism most frequently manifested itself in opposition to practices current in society. The call for *tajdid* took many forms in this context: opposition to the belief that it was a specially pious act to visit tombs of major men of the faith, prohibition of consumption of intoxicating beverages, imposition of Quranic punishments for certain crimes, and other specific regulations. In broader terms, *mujaddids* were recognized as being more literalist in their interpretations and less likely to utilize symbolic or esoteric interpretations of the Quran. Over the centuries, the emphasis has varied, depending upon the particular circumstances. Often, as in the case of Ibn Taimiya (661–728 A.H./1262–1327 A.D.) and the Wahhabis in the eighteenth century, there was strong opposition to practices which the general population accepted as Islamic, but for which the renewer-reformer found no justification in the Quran or Sunna.[11] Popular religion was thus a common target. At other times the target would be the whole structure of the Islamic establishment. Ahmad ibn Hanbal battled the learned men supported by the caliph. Uthman dan Fodio in nineteenth-century West Africa opposed what he saw as a politico-religious establishment that was lax to the point of infidelity.[12] A third basic target was innovation inspired by the practices and ideas of non-Islamic civilizations. While the Greek philosophical tradition came to play an important role in the Islamic experience, there were always some who mistrusted this tradition and opposed its implications.[13] Similarly, in modern times, while many leaders accept Western techniques and ideas, there are always those who believe that these mean, at times at least, a departure from the path of the Quran and the Sunna.[14]

Whether against popular Islam, "establishment" Islam, or an Islam of synthesis, the *tajdid-islah* response is similar: the Muslim, as individual and as part of a community, must adhere in a strict and relatively literal way to the Quran and the Sunna of the Prophet. Anything that works against or dilutes that adherence approaches ungrateful unbelief and needs to be eliminated by the processes of *tajdid* and *islah*.

The need for ijtihad. The call to direct adherence to the Quran and the Sunna has a basic corollary. If these two are the essential and perfect sources for judgment and guidance, other sources of advice may be helpful but they do not have to be followed. Authorities other than the Quran and the Sunna can, and if they are associated with practices that are being opposed, should be rejected or at least ignored. The renewer-reformer generally has claimed the right to make his own judgment based directly on an independent analysis of the Quran and the Sunna. The *mujaddid* has not felt bound by the interpretations and ideas of the teachers and schools that emerged after the times of the Prophet and his companions. This process of independent analysis is called *ijtihad* and is traditionally seen as the opposite of *taqlid*. the following of the views and rulings of earlier teachers.[15]

Although individuals throughout Islamic history have claimed to be *mujtahids* (rightful practitioners of *ijtihad*), for most of the Muslim world, *taqlid* came to be the generally accepted method for analysis. As a modern Muslim scholar explains, Muslim teachers wanted to give due care and attention to the faith. When "jurists became apprehensive lest inefficient people should practice *ijtihad*, they closed the door of legal deduction upon themselves and those who came after them."[16]

An example of the defense of *taqlid* can be seen in a legal opinion issued early in the twentieth century in Tunisia: "It is generally admitted that, ever since the codification of the doctrine of Islam by the four great orthodox imams, this door [of *ijtihad*] is closed and that Muslims must conform their opinions strictly to the opinions enumerated by these imams, without seeking to arrive by means of their own reasoning at a personal opinion about the tenets of Islam."[17] It should be noted that this is not true for Muslims in the Shiite tradition. In contrast to the majority or Sunni Muslims, the Shia Muslims believe that the community receives continued direct guidance through the *ijtihad* of special teachers in each age. Thus, within Shia Islam there has not been the same style of claim to *ijtihad* or the same form for the issue of *taqlid* as in the Sunni world.[18]

Within Sunni Islam, however, *ijtihad* was an important part of the ideas and methodology of *tajdid* and *islah*. Early renewers in the days of the formalization of Islamic thought, like Ahmad ibn Hanbal, were generally recognized as engaging legitimately in *ijtihad*. He was the last of the great founders in the era of "the four great orthodox imams." However, the claim to be a legitimate *mujtahid* soon became both a cause for dispute and a hallmark of major *mujaddids* (or those aspiring to that rank). For example, Ibn Taimiya was recognized by his students as a *mujtahid*.[19] A modern renewalist has said that Ibn Taimiya "was not simply bold in rejecting stagnant *taqlid*, but he was, even more, an example in the practice of *ijtihad*."[20] At the same time, an opponent said that Ibn Taimiha had isolated himself from the Islamic community by his "inventions" which ran counter to the basic consensus of the community.[21] Similarly, in the fifteenth century, Jalal al-Din al-Suyuti made his ability to exercise *ijtihad* a part of his self-description as a *mujaddid* for his century.[22]

For the person engaged in *tajdid*, *ijtihad* is not simply an intellectual exercise. It is the legitimizing basis for opposition to the existing conditions and institutions in a seemingly already Muslim society. Basing his views directly on the Quran and the Sunna, he feels free to challenge the communal consensus and institutional tradition. In the face of the demand to follow the decisions of the great medieval thinkers as they had been accepted for centuries, Muhammad al-Shawkani (1172–1250 A.H./1758–1834 A.D.), a supporter of *ijtihad* in Yemen, could say that there is "the pure path of the Quran and the pure Sunna of the Messenger of God," and "there is no third like them." [23] This is an often-stated position among the renewalist reformers.

The broader significance of claiming the right of *ijtihad* is clear in the cases of movements like the Sanusiyyah Tariqah and the Wahhabis. The Sanusiyyah was established in the middle of the nineteenth century by Muhammad ibn Ali al-Sanusi. This scholar from North Africa developed firm renewalist convictions. His claim to *ijtihad* brought him into sharp conflict with some of the most prominent Islamic "establishments" of his day. In Cairo, for example, he clashed with the scholars of al-Azhar, perhaps the best-known Islamic educational center of the time. He rejected their inflexible conservatism and rigid adherence to opinions of earlier scholars.[24]

The Wahhabi case shows that *ijtihad* is not just a challenge to existing conservative elites. *Ijtihad* was maintained in a framework of rigorous fundamentalist literalism by the founder, Muhammad ibn Abd al-Wahhab, a scholar in the eighteenth-century Arabian Peninsula. However, even in this narrowly circumscribed framework, the appeal to *ijtihad* could have major long term significance. The Wahhabi "insistence on the right of *ijtihad* (independent thinking) and their condemnation of *taqlid* acted as a great liberating force, and . . . has affected the temper of subsequent Islamic developments perhaps more than any other single factor."[25]

In the twentieth century the terminology has sometimes changed and the debates are not always framed in terms of *ijtihad* and *taqlid*. However, even these traditional terms remain frequently used. The vigor of the argument and the appeal to *ijtihad* can be seen in the statements of one of the major modern Islamic thinkers, Muhammad Abduh, who was both a renewer and a modernist. Abduh argued that "Islam encouraged men to move away from their clinging attachment to the world of their fathers and their legacies, indicting as stupid and foolish the attitude that always wants to know what the precedents say."[26] Although the specific context of Abduh's presentation is the modern situation in which Muslim thinkers were defending Islam against the charge of being stagnant, it should be clear that Abduh's attack on *taqlid* and advocacy of *ijtihad* reflect a longstanding element in efforts of *islah* and *tajdid*. He was not, in this, introducing a new element into renewalist-reform.

People undertaking *islah* and *tajdid* in the twentieth century claim the right to return directly to the fundamental sources of Islam, the Quran and the Sunna. Later interpretations are not considered binding and are often rejected. Few, for example, call for the full reconstruction of the medieval political system of the caliphate, although that was an issue in the 1920s. Few insist that the medieval legal rulings must be accepted in the later medieval forms. As in the past, this mode of Islam represents a challenge to many established social and intellectual traditions.

It should be clear, at least as a result of noting the emphasis on *ijtihad,* that *tajdid* and *islah* are not "traditionalist" or "conservative" modes of Islamic experience and attitude. The revivalist-reformer is more likely to criticize and attack existing institutions and customs than he is to support them. It should not be surprising that organized movements created by *mujaddids* have been system challenging, often with revolutionary consequences. The transformation of the socio-political scene in West Africa by the Fulani jihad of Uthman dan Fodio, or in the Arabian Peninsula by the movement of Muhammad ibn Abd al-Wahhab, or in Libya in the nineteenth century by the Sanusiyyah provides illuminating perspectives.[27]

This aspect of *tajdid* is often overlooked in twentieth-century analysis. Outside observers sometimes become confused or describe it as paradoxical when a group within the *tajdid* tradition appears to be revolutionary rather than conservative. This can be seen, for example, in discussions of the Muslim Brotherhood in the 1930s and 1940s which express surprise at the socially revolutionary program of the Brothers, or in analyses of the Libyan revolutionary regime after 1969 that see the regime as being "paradoxically" both "radical" and "reactionary." Others are surprised that a great Islamic university like al-Azhar in Cairo is not in the forefront of any fundamentalist movement in Egypt, although historically such "establishment" institutions have more often been the object of revivalist attack than they have been the center of support for renewalist-reformism.

The "paradox" is resolved by viewing such contemporary currents from the perspective of the broader context of *tajdid* and *islah* in Islam. This mode of Islam is willing to use the Quran and Sunna as a standard by which to judge traditional and current institutions and, when they are found wanting, to oppose them. This *ijtihad* does not necessarily mean an attempt to recreate the conditions of the seventh-century Arabian Peninsula. Even the most naïve renewer goes beyond that. What this *ijtihad* means is using individual effort to apply the Quran and the Sunna to existing conditions. Thus, President Qaddafi in Libya can support a strict application of the Quran, noting that any attempt to draft law for society outside of the sources of religion and tradition (and "religion embraces tradition"[28]) "is invalid and illogical,"[29] and yet have the actual political system proposed be quite different from existing models inside or outside the Islamic tradition.

The *tajdid-islah* tradition in Islam thus usually not only calls for a return to the Quran and the Sunna. It also claims the right of *ijtihad,* with the possible rejection of existing institutions and traditional interpretations. These two dimensions of *tajdid* provide the basis for a potentially revolutionary type of thought or movement that, at the same time, remains rooted within the Islamic perspective rather than attempting to "go beyond" the fundamental sources of Muslim inspiration.

Reaffirmation of Authenticity. The basic framework for the *tajdid-islah* tradition is the continuing reaffirmation of the uniqueness and authenticity of the Quranic message.[30] This involves maintaining a special mood and observing special limits beyond which the *mujaddid* will not go in thought or action. The Quran and the Sunna are maintained as the authentically complete and universally applicable guidance from God for man. In this context, *ijtihad* may be necessary in order to determine the proper application of the Quranic message in changing circumstances, but this, in the tradition of *tajdid-islah,* need not, and must not, involve borrowing from non-Islamic traditions as a way of adding to basic Islamic principles.

In this position the *tajdid-islah* mode can be distinguished from other great modes of Islamic expression by the degree of willingness to accept or engage in great cultural syntheses in a conscious way. In the great interactions of cultures and civilizations that have occurred within the history of Islam, *tajdid-islah* efforts have opposed syntheses that risked undermining the special Quranic foundation of Islamic society. This is in contrast, for example, to the more contemplative mystic mode of Islam in which there is a greater conscious willingness to recognize the universality of authentic religious experience. The mystic mode thus tends to create rather than oppose syntheses.[31]

Other contrasting modes might be the preservationist mode of a conservative religious establishment. In this mode one finds a high degree of toleration for a variety of non-Islamic practices in the life of rulers and the general population. Throughout much of Islamic history this "latitudinarian interpretation of the nature of an Islamic society" has been held by many of even the representatives of the learned tradition in Islam.[32] The tacit assumption seems normally to be that anarchy or challenge to existing institutions poses a greater danger than tolerance for divergences from a strict application of Islamic rules.

Another contrasting mode might be that of the rulers, where again the methods of accommodation and toleration are used. Consciously or unconsciously, even very religiously oriented rulers utilize techniques and approaches that are not Islamic in origin.[33] The result is often a fruitful and dynamic synthesis producing a new Islamic framework, but one which might be opposed by the renewalist-reformer who insists on the unique and universal authenticity of the Quranic message.

One way of noting this is to observe matched pairs of these modes as they interact in the context of Muslim history. One of the great and continuing dialogues within the Islamic historical experience has been between the authenticity-emphasizing renewalists and the more universalist representatives of Islamic mysticism. The position of these mystics was comprehensively defined in the works of Muhyi al-Din Ibn al-Arabi (560–638 A.H./1165–1240 A.D.). Ibn al-Arabi's mysticism sees the divinity as expressed in many forms and does not limit the expression of that divinity to one religious tradition. Thus, "the mystic's God can obviously be neither Muslim nor Christian, Buddhist, Jewish nor pagan."[34] This thinking provides the basis for a profoundly open, syncretistic mysticism that was frequently the object of renewalist concern.

In the early years of the dialogue between this type of mysticism and the renewalists, Ibn Taimiha clashed with the followers of Ibn al-Arabi. This clash can also be seen in the experience of later renewalists like Ahmad Sirhindi in Mughal India and the seventeenth-century Southeast Asian renewalist, Abd al-Rauf al-Sinkili.[35] A recent reflection of this longstanding debate on Ibn al-Arabi can be seen in the rejection of books by Ibn al-Arabi on the part of Islamic fundamentalist students in Egypt in 1978–79, and the resolution of the Egyptian People's Assembly in February 1979, which banned writings by Ibn al-Arabi from general circulation. An illustrative pair indicating the *tajdid-islah* and "mystic" modes is thus Ibn Taimiya vs. Ibn al-Arabi and the interaction between their intellectual heirs.

There are other pairs which show the contrasts between *tajdid-islah* and other Islamic modes. Among these are Ahmad Sirhindi in India against the syncretism of the Mogul ruler Akbar;[36] Muhammad ibn Abd al-Wahhab against the champions of popular religious customs in the eighteenth-century Najd;[37] Uthman dan Fodio against the venal ulama and the semi-pagan rulers of West Africa;[38] or Muhammad Ahmad, the Sudanese Mahdi, against a corrupting government and also popular religious customs.[39]

In more recent times the tradition of *tajdid-islah* can be seen in twentieth-century Egypt in the opposition of the Muslim Brotherhood to secular socialist and liberal Islamic modernist trends.[40] It is well illustrated in the early opposition of Abu al-Ala Mawdudi to the Pakistan movement and his later opposition to many of the governments in independent Pakistan.[41]

In these and many other social and historical contexts, people within the mode of *tajdid-islah* have worked to create a society based on a rigorous application of what they believe to be the essential heart of the Islamic message. This has involved a self-conscious alertness to the possible dangers of diluting the Islamic message as presented in the Quran and the Sunna. In this, visible syncretism and adoption of ideas and methods clearly originating from outside the historical Islamic experience have been rejected. In place of such actions, the *tajdid-islah* mode vigorously affirms that the Quran and the Sunna are complete as guides for humanity and they apply in all times and places. While it may be necessary, in the view of the renewalist, to exercise informed personal judgment in analyzing the Quran and the Sunna, this *ijtihad,* to be legitimate, is to be solely an interpretive effort rather than an effort to supplement an already complete guidance framework. This reaffirmation of the authentic completeness of the Quran and the Sunna is the third characteristic element of *tajdid-islah*.

CONCLUSION

In the contemporary period, at the beginning of the fifteenth Islamic century, the *tajdid-islah* tradition has a special meaning and relevance. In the great dynamism within the Islamic world, which has been called the "Islamic resurgence" in the 1970s, the themes of the renewalist tradition emerge as significant in country after country. The distinctive conditions of contemporary modern (really "post-modern" because of the new circumstances of global societies and interactions) society provide productive opportunities for reform in the *tajdid-islah* style.

The global context of the last quarter of the twentieth century is in many ways specially suited for the re-emergence of the renewalist Islamic tradition. The "resurgence of Islam" is, at least in some of its aspects, a utilization of tones and symbols that have deep roots within the Islamic tradition. This does not mean that Islamic movements are inherently "conservative" or "reactionary." On the contrary, it means that a long-standing revolutionary or revitalizing tradition within Islam is being more fully reactivated.

There are specific aspects of the post-modern social and global context which provide direct openings for *tajdid-islah* movements. The first of these is the growing attention on a global scale to the issues of morality in society. In many areas and cultures this requires the creation of a type of movement that runs counter to longstanding modes of operation. In the United States, for example, activist movements of social morality, at least at times, clash with the self-perceived tradition of the "separation of church and state."[42] In other areas, the activism of Buddhist monks has appeared to be a departure from long traditions of pacifism and political quietism.[43]

Within Islam, however, the calls for the creation of a moral economic order based on divine revelation or the rejection of the so-called "value free social sciences" are resonant with the longstanding moral dimension of the *tajdid-islah* tradition. Within Islamic communities, in other words, the symbols and conceptualizations of this increased awareness of the demands of morality are already in existence and can be utilized by contemporary activists.

The continuing themes of the *tajdid-islah* tradition themselves are of a character to appeal to the contemporary mood. In particular, there are two different sides to the post-modern mood that often clash or represent contradictory elements in various societies. These two sides are the desire to create institutions and modes of action that have authenticity and firm foundations in meaningful identities, and also the unwillingness to accept existing formulations or traditional ones without radical questioning. Usually the striving for authenticity involves a reacceptance of some traditional expression while the critical mood rejects such acceptance.

In this context, the critical mood becomes, in the extreme cases, the nihilistic anarchism of some of the terrorist organizations of Europe. At the same time, the search for authenticity becomes a form of rigid neo-conservatism that rejects, in its extreme form, any critical scientific thought, or it may become a punitive ritualism in support of the state and in opposition to modernist liberal elements, as it did in the case of the authenticity movement in Chad. The issues are real but the available cultural or ideological vocabulary in many societies is limited.

Within Islamic societies, the *tajdid-islah* tradition provides a long-standing mode of reaffirmation of authenticity. At the same time, this same mode represents a critical exercise of independent judgment in dealing with existing institutions. The combined themes in the Islamic tradition of *tajdid-islah* of the claiming of the right of *ijtihad* while reaffirming the authentic sources provides a set of conceptualizations that is very helpful in the contemporary context. It is, thus, not surprising to find this mode of Islamic expression becoming important in recent years.

It is important to remember that the *tajdid-islah* tradition has never been a static one. The significant expressions of this tradition that are most readily available to contemporary Muslims are those that are currently called "fundamentalist." However, these are not the only possible ways of expressing this tradition. The current "fundamentalism" has its roots in the eighteenth century. Lines of conceptual similarity can be drawn, for example, between the eighteenth-century Wahhabis and the twentieth-century Muslim Brotherhood even though there are no direct organizational connections between the two movements. It is this fundamentalist structuring of the *tajdid-islah* tradition that has provided conceptual aid to contemporary Muslim revivalists. However, there are signs that a new formulation of the *tajdid-islah* tradition may be emerging. If it does, it would be in keeping with the dynamic nature of the tradition itself.

In Iran, for example, there are many reasons for the struggle between the Ayatullah Khomeini and the Mujahidin-i Khalq. In the context of the history of renewalism in Islam, it is possible to say that one aspect of this struggle is that, while both represent some aspects of the *tajdid-islah* tradition, the Ayatullah Khomeini is in a more established mode of fundamentalism while the Mujahidin are part of the process of the definition of a new style of *tajdid-islah*.[44] Similarly, this same distinction might be made between the established, fundamentalist position of the thinkers of the Muslim Brotherhood in Egypt and the ideas of some one like Professor Hassan Hanafi of the University of Cairo, who is working to define an authentically Islamic "left."[45]

Regardless of what form it takes in the future, it is clear that the *tajdid-islah* tradition remains a vital part of Islamic life. Working within the opportunities provided by the challenges of post-modern society, the *tajdid-islah* tradition has proven its continuing vitality. It continues to represent one of the dynamic dimensions of the Islamic experience.

Notes

1. For discussions of the definitions of these concepts and their history, see Fazlur Rahman, "Revival and Reform in Islam," *The Cambridge History of Islam,* ed. P. M. Holt, Ann K. S. Lambton, and Bernard Lewis, 2 vols. (Cambridge: Cambridge University Press, 1970), vol. 2, pp. 632–42; Abu al-Ala Mawdudi, *A Short History of the Revivalist Movement in Islam,* trans. al-Ashari (Lahore: Islamic Publications, 1976); A. Merad, "Islah," *Encyclopaedia of Islam* (new edition), vol. 4, pp. 141–63.

2. Translations from the Quran are done by the author unless otherwise indicated.

3. For further discussion of the impact of the availability of this standard of judgment see John O. Voll, "Wahhabism and Mahdism: Alternative Styles of Islamic Renewals," *Arab Studies Quarterly,* 4 (1982):110–26.

4. Sayyid Qutb, *This Religion of Islam* (Gary, Ind.: International Islamic Federation of Student Organizations, n.d.), p. 65.

5. Ibid., p. 38.

6. For a current Muslim description of this process see Bakri Shaykh Amin, *Adab al-Hadith al-Nabawi* (Beirut: Dar al-Sharq, 1976/1396). pp. 29–48.

7. H. Ritter, "Hasan al-Basri," *Encyclopaedia of Islam* (new edition), vol. 3:247–8.

8. Henri Laoust, *Les Schismes dans l'Islam* (Paris: Payot, 1965), pp. 36–48.

9. Ira M. Lapidus, "The Separation of State and Religion in the Development of Early Islamic Society," *International Journal of Middle East Studies,* 6 (1975):382–83.

10. Rahman, "Revival and Reform," p. 632.

11. See, for example, Muhammad Umar Memon, *Ibn Taimiya's Struggle Against Popular Religion* (The Hague: Mouton, 1976).

12. For further discussions of these men and their movements, see Lapidus, "The Separation of State and Religion," and Mervyn Hiskett, *The Sword of Truth: The Life and Times of the Shehu Usuman dan Fodio* (New York: Oxford University Press, 1973).

13. See, for example, the discussion in Marshall G. S. Hodgson, *The Venture of Islam,* 3 vols. (Chicago: University of Chicago Press, 1974), vol. 1. For the analysis of the development of the school of Ahmad ibn Hanbal and later scholars in this tradition, the works of Henri Laoust and George Makdisi are of great importance. See, for example, Laoust's *Les Schismes dans l'Islam* and George Makdisi, "Hanbalite Islam," *Studies on Islam,* ed. and trans. by Merlin L. Swartz (New York: Oxford University Press, 1981), pp. 216–74.

14. See, for example, the following articles in Altaf Gauhar, ed.. *The Challenge of Islam* (London: Islamic Council of Europe, 1978): I. H. Qureshi, "Islam and the West:

Past, Present and Future" (pp. 236–47); Hamid Algar, "Islam and the Intellectual Challenge of Modern Civilization" (pp. 284–96); and Altaf Gauhar, "Islam and Secularism" (pp. 298–310).

15. For a brief introduction to the concepts, see the articles by J. Schacht and D. B. Macdonald under "Idjtihad" in *Encyclopaedia of Islam* (new edition), vol. 3, pp. 1026–27. Interesting modern discussions of *ijtihad* in the traditional Islamic scholarly format appear in the papers by Sheikh M. Nour El-Hassan and Sheikh al-Fadil Ben Ashour in *The First Conference of the Academy of Islamic Research* (Cairo. al-Azhar, 1964/1383).

16. Sheikh Abdul-Rahman al-Qalhud, "Al-Talfeek and Its Rule in Jurisprudence," *The First Conference*, p. 76.

17. This translation appears in Arnold H. Green, *The Tunisian Ulama, 1873–1915* (Leiden: Brill, 1978), pp. 188–89.

18. For the Shii context, there are many recent publications. Further discussions of issues raised here can be found in Nikki Keddie, "Religion, Society, and Revolution in Modern Iran" and Mangol Bayat-Phi!lip, "Tradition and Change in Iranian Socio-Religious Thought," both in Michael E. Bonine and Nikki R. Keddie (eds.) *Continuity and Change in Modern Iran* (Albany, N.Y.: State University of New York Press, 1981). Also, see Shahrough Akhavi. "Shii Social Thought and Praxis in Recent Iranian History," *Islam in the Contemporary World,* ed. by Cyriac K. Pullapilly (Notre Dame, Ind.: Cross Roads Books, 1980), pp. 171–98.

19. Abu Hafs Umar b. Ali al-Bazzar, *al-Alam al-aliyyah fi manaqib shaykh al-islam ibn taymiyyah,* ed. by Salah al-Din al-Munajjid (Beirut: Dar al-Kitab al-Jadid, 1976/1397), p. 18.

20. Abu al-Ala Mawdudi, *Mujaz tarikh tajdid al-din wa ihyaihi* (Beirut: al-Shirkah al-Muttahidah, 1975/1395), p. 77. In the English translation, *A Short History of the Revivalist Movement in Islam,* the discussion of Ibn Taymiyyah appears on pp. 67–70.

21. Abu al-Hasan Taqi al-Din Ali b. Abd al-Kafi al-Subki, *al-Durur al-madiyyah li al-radd ala ibn taymiyyah* (Damascus: al-Qudsi, 1347), p. 6.

22. See the discussion of this figure in J. O. Hunwick, ed., "Ignaz Goldziher on al-Suyuti," *The Muslim World,* 68 (1978):79–99.

23. Muhammad b. Ali al-Shawkani, *al-Qawl al-mufid fi adalah al-ijtihad wa al-taqlid* (n.p.: m.n., 1929/1347), p. 3.

24. See B. G. Martin, *Muslim Brotherhoods in 19th-Century Africa* (Cambridge: Cambridge University Press, 1976), pp. 102–3. For al-Sanusi's teachings on *ijtihad,* see Nicola A. Ziadeh, *Sanusiyah* (Leiden: E. J. Brill, 1968), pp. 81–82.

25. Fazlur Rahman, *Islam* (Garden City, N.Y.: Doubleday, 1966), p. 243.

26. Muhammad Abduh, *The Theology of Unity,* trans. by Ishaq Musaaad and Kenneth Cragg (London: George Allen and Unwin, 1966), p. 127.

27. For further discussion of this, see Hiskett, *The Sword of Truth,* and Ziadeh, *Sanusiyah.*

28. Muammar Qaddafi, *The Breen Book,* Part One, p. 76.

29. Ibid., p. 68.

30. For a further definition of this, see John Voll, "The Sudanese Mahdi: Frontier Fundamentalist," *International Journal of Middle East Studies,* 10 (1979):150–52.

31. This more universalistic, synthesis-creating mode is well described in Martin Lings, *What Is Sufism?* (Berkeley: University of California Press, 1975).

32. G. E. von Grunebaum, "The Problem: Unity in Diversity," *Unity and Variety in Muslim Civilization.* ed. by Gustave E. von Grunebaum (Chicago: University of Chicago Press, 1955), p. 20.

33. See, for example, the analysis in H. A. R. Gibb, "The Evolution of Government in Early Islam," *Studies on the Civilization of Islam,* ed. by Stanford J. Shaw and William R. Polk (Princeton: Princeton University Press, 1982), pp. 34–46.

34. Rom Landau, *The Philosophy of Ibn Arabi* (New York: Macmillan, 1959), p. 28.

35. John Obert Voll, *Islam: Continuity and Change in the Modern World* (Boulder, Colo.: Westview Press, 1982), pp. 20, 59, 69.

36. Aziz Ahmad, *Studies in Islamic Culture in the Indian Environment* (Oxford: Clarendon Press, 1964), Ch. 6 and 7 in Part Two.

37. Abdallah al-Salih al-Uthaymayn, *al-Shaykh Muhammad bin Abd al-Wahhab: Hayatuhu wa Fikruhu* (al-Riyad: Dar al-Ulum, n.d.).

38. A very helpful introduction to the ideas of Uthman dan Fodio, along with an excellent description of the history of his movement, appears in Uthman ibn Fudi, *Bayan wujub al-hijra ala l'ibad.* ed. and trans. by F. H. El Masri (Khartoum: Khartoum University Press; and London: Oxford University Press, 1978.)

39. Voll, "Sudanese Mahdi."

40. For a comprehensive discussion of the Muslim Brotherhood, see Richard P. Mitchell, *The Society of the Muslim Brothers* (London: Oxford University Press, 1969).

41. See, for example, the discussions in John L. Esposito, "Pakistan: Quest for Islamic Identity," in John L. Esposito (ed.), *Islam and Development.* (Syracuse, N.Y.: Syracuse University Press. 1980), pp. 139–62; and Freeland Abbott, *Islam and Pakistan* (Ithaca, N.Y.: Cornell University Press, 1968), pp. 171–82.

42. In the early 1980s, this issue was frequently raised with regard to the organization called the Moral Majority. Some of the lines of debate can be seen by comparing the following: Jerry Falwell, "Future-Word: An Agenda for the Eighties," in Jerry Falwell (ed.), *The Fundamentalist Phenomenon* (Garden City, N.Y.: Doubleday, 1981), pp. 186–223; and Robert McAfee Brown, "A Response to 'Listen, America!': Listen, Jerry Falwell," *Christianity and Crisis* 40:21 (Dec. 22 1980), 360–64.

43. Many of the major lines of development within Bujddhism are discussed in the essays in Heinrich Dumoulin, *Buddhism in the Modern World* (New York: Macmillan, 1976). A useful specific study of the development of the attitudes and roles of monks in a particular country is David Gosling, "New Directions in Thai Buddhism," *Modern Asian Studies* 14:3 (1980), 411–39.

44. Voll, *Islam: Continuity and Change,* pp. 300–304.

45. See, for example, Hanafi's articles in *al-Yasar al-Islami* 1 (1401/1981). and Hassan Hanafi, "The Relevance of the Islamic Alternative in Egypt," *Arab Studies Quarterly* 4:1/2 (1982), 54–74.

THREE

Islam and the Search for Identity in the Arab World

JOHN J. DONOHUE

Political events in the Middle East these past few years have pushed Islam to center stage and set the audience astir. The victorious return of Ayatullah Khomeini to Teheran in early 1979 seemed to mark an abrupt change in the logic and direction of events on the Middle Eastern scene. Observers and scholars who had forgotten that Islam was in the wings waiting its chance suddenly began revising their theories.

Khomeini represents the most dramatic entry on the scene; but he was, in fact, a latecomer. Islamic actors were already on stage and active, though their roles were much less spectacular. The troubles in Syria over the place of Islam in the new constitution in 1973,[1] the attack on the Military College in Cairo by the Party for Islamic Liberation in 1974,[2] and the debate in Egypt on the application of the *shariah*[3] were just some of the signs of a revitalization of Islam several years before Ayatullah Khomeini's name became a household word.

Some would date the new vitality of Islamic actors from the defeat of the Arabs in their war with Israel in 1967. Certainly there was a marked increase in religious observance among youth in Egypt following that war, and in the Arab Middle East, the Khartoum Summit of August 1967 marked a fall in the fortunes of the "Arab Progressives" in their contest with Saudi Arabia and its Islamic Pact supporters.

Undoubtedly, the rise in pitch of Islamic spokesmen in the area can be explained in part by internal politics and the astounding wealth generated by petroleum in the past decade. It would be an error to attribute all to these aspects, but it would be equally erroneous to neglect them. The predominant motives are more deeply rooted; they spring from the clash of cultures or, as some would have it, of civilizations—a clash which is over a century old but, as yet, unresolved.

Islam has always been a constant in Arab identity. The Western military occupation of Arab lands in the nineteenth and early twentieth century and the subsequent encroachment of industrial and technological civilization have provoked change, dislocation, and repeated efforts to shape a contemporary Arab identity. Rarely have these efforts neglected Islam. A brief look at some of the major attempts during the past century will make this clear. But even more interesting is the presence of the Islamic element in the period following World War II. A recent content analysis of Arab writings between 1945–70 clearly indicates not only the presence of Islam in the Arab search for identity but also the variety of configurations in which it is found. The nuances which this study offers give us a better perspective on present crises and future possibilities.

HISTORICAL OVERVIEW

The first contacts were relatively benign. Europe was an awesome but attractive model for Middle Eastern Muslims who voyaged abroad in the early nineteenth century. They were convinced that certain European values and institutions integrated into the fabric of Islamic society would produce the progress necessary to give strength and prosperity to their flagging fortunes. One has only to read Khayr al-Din[4] and Tahtawi[5] to see that their turning to the West was in no way a detachment from their Islamic convictions.

By the end of the nineteenth century, the clash had revealed its real proportions with the gradual dismemberment of the only remaining Islamic empire, the Ottoman, by Western military occupation of North Africa and Egypt and the loss of "Islamic" territory to Western-supported independence movements in the Balkans. In this context Jamal al-Din al-Afghani made his appeal for a reaffirmation of a true Islamic identity as the sole means to resist the Western invasion, and Muhammad Abduh began his rereading of Islam to show that Islam was completely in harmony with modern civilization.[6]

But Islamic identity while permanent is somewhat amorphous politically. Islamic identity in the form of loyalty to the sultan-caliph at Istanbul prevented sentiments for Arab autonomy from developing into a political force for several years. The early formulations of Arab identity were thoroughly Islamic. Abd al-Rahman al-Kawakabi[7] is the most frequently cited representative of this line of thoughts: only the Arabs because of their pristine ties with Islam could restore Islam to its original vigor; the Turks, in fact, had deformed Islam. Then in 1916 when Arab sentiment, aided by the political conjuncture, crystallized into the "Great Arab Revolt" under Sharif Husayn and his sons, the official statement of grievances justifying the revolt was thoroughly Islamic.[8]

The period of the mandates and the struggle for independence generated a variety of local and regional "nationalisms" in which cultural and historical elements took precedence over the religious in the attempt to formulate the rationale for modern political entities. For thinkers like Rashid Rida and Shakib

Arslan[9] sliding from local nationalism to a sort of pan-Islamism presented no problem. For others, Islam was one element among others in the constellation which formed Egyptian or Arab civilization; and in any case, for them, Islam could not furnish the basis for a contemporary state. Christian Arab thinkers, fully engaged in the Arab renaissance, neglected or played down religious identity as a divisive element.

When more reasoned formulations of Arab nationalism appeared in the 1940s, Islam was very much part of the theory, but was cast in a subordinate role. For Michel Aflaq (Baath party) and Abd al-Rahman al-Bazzaz, Islam is fundamentally the spirit of Arab nationalism.[10]

Thus, even a rapid survey of the thinkers whose writings have become standard references for the development of Arab nationalist thought indicates the persistence of Islam and the constant, though varied, role it maintains in Arab thought. But are these thinkers representative, or are they isolated examples without resonance in Arab society at large? It was with this question in mind that we set about sampling Arab periodical literature.

THE CONTENT ANALYSIS STUDY

In an attempt to discover how the problem of Arab culture and change was presented to the general Arab reading public, we established a corpus of 246 articles selected from Arab periodicals published between 1945 and 1970. This corpus represents a sample of the Arab world including North Africa, and it also incorporates three levels of readership: popular (e.g., *al-Hilal* and *al-Arabi*), religious (e.g., *Majallat al-Azhar* and *Majallat al-Hajj*), and intellectual (e.g., *al-Katib* and *al-Adab*). The twenty-five-year span was broken into three periods: 1945–50, 1955–60, and 1965–70. The articles studied represent a random selection from all the articles on the subject of Arab culture and change in the given periodicals during the three periods of time mentioned.

Themes on Arab and non-Arab culture were sifted out of these articles according to a grid established by a pilot study. Three elements established a theme: 1) an attitude toward Arab or non-Arab culture (pro, con, neutral with several nuances); 2) an aspect or element of culture (religion, tradition, politics, social structure, etc.); and 3) the motivation expressed to justify the attitude taken. In addition, the basic argumentation of each article was analyzed and classified. Five basic arguments were found: 1) Islam; 2) Arab-Islamic civilization; 3) Arab and human civilization; 4) national and cultural revival and reform; and 5) openness for basic changes. The first two make clear reference to the Arab past as a norm; the third situates Arab civilization in a broader context;

the fourth focuses more on reform which takes Arab realities into consideration, and the fifth focuses on radical change.

The attitudes expressed vary from a need for authenticity (national, Arab, or Islamic identity) to a need for openness to other cultures. In between lies a whole gamut of attitudes from selective authenticity (choosing only what is apt for today) to criticism of Western culture.

The elements of culture discussed include culture, in general, religion, traditions and values, economy, politics and ideology, intellectuals and education, and language.

The motivations are multiple but fall into groups: dynamic/static, objective/credulous, spiritual/material, social and cultural relations. For instance, authenticity concerning language and literature is advocated as a means for achieving *strength* and *independence* (cultural relations vis-à-vis the West), or Western culture is criticized for its lack of *spiritual* values.

INCREASE IN AUTHENTICITY

The extremes in the gamut of attitudes—authenticity and openness—came out clearly in the random sample used to establish the grid of attitudes; they were not imposed. Declarations that the sole hope for progress lay in adopting Western science and the scientific mentality, or in following European educational systems, or imitating European civic virtues represented the extreme of openness, whereas a return to true Islamic values or to Arab or national cultural values represented the pole of authenticity. In between are found praise of Islamic society in the Golden Age, criticism of aspects of Western culture, and also neutral attitudes, i.e.. positive and negative statements about society without reference to Arab or to non-Arab culture.

The study revealed an increasing concern for authenticity over the three time periods as illustrated in Table I where we see a significant increase especially in the Popular and Intellectual reviews. In 1945–50, one-half of the popular articles and 56 percent of the intellectual articles were expressing attitudes advocating the need for authenticity in Arab society or praising authenticity achieved; but in 1965–70, the percentage had risen to 80 percent (popular) and

Table I. Proportion of Articles Expressing Attitudes of Authenticity.

	Popular	Religious	Intellectual
Period I (1945–50)	9/18, 50%	22/33, 67%	10/13, 56%
Period II (1955–60)	18/24, 75%	25/30, 83%	24/30, 80%
Period III (1965–70)	24/30, 80%	27/33, 82%	27/30, 90%

90 percent (intellectual). The increase in religious periodicals is less dramatic, but also higher in the 1945–50 period.

As we will see later, this authenticity is not univocal; it embraces a variety of views all of which represent a reaffirmation of identity.

This increased concern for authenticity in Arab society is accompanied by a similar increase in criticism of Western culture (64 percent of all the articles in Period I contain criticism of Western culture, 85 percent of those in Period III) and in criticism of Arab society for its lack of authenticity (42 percent of all the articles in Period I have expressions of this attitude, 67 percent of those in Period III). The criticism of Western culture most frequently focuses on one or other aspects of imperialism or is phrased in general terms. When the criticism is specific, it is aimed at religion, education (including intellectuals and Orientalists), and politics. In these criticisms, the West is seen as domineering, subversive, hypocritical, egoistical, materialist, anti-Islamic, amoral, and unrealistic. Arabs who follow Western ways and those who adopt foreign ideologies are stigmatized as lacking authenticity and aiding foreign cultural subversion of Arab or Islamic society.

All three periods selected contain a major crisis. The 1945–50 period bridges the Arab war for Palestine which ended in the creation of Israel, the 1955–60 period contained the Suez war, and the 1965–70 period, the six-day Arab-Israeli war. The reactions to the first crisis expressed in cultural reaction to the West and restatement of identity were less prominent than the reactions in the late fifties and late sixties when the Egyptian revolution and the formulation of Nasserism took effect along with the ascent of the Baath party and independence movements in North Africa.

Concomitant with this increased concern for authenticity was an increase in the number of articles on religious subjects on the popular and intellectual levels.

The percentage of articles on religious subjects when all three levels are merged increases only slightly from Period I to Periods II and III (42 percent to 45 percent), but as Table II illustrates, the increase on the popular and intellectual levels is very marked. It should be noted that the increased interest in

Table II. Proportion of Articles on Religious Subjects.

	Popular	Religious	Intellectual
Period I (1945–50)	3/18, 17%	23/33, 70%	3/18, 17%
Period II (1955–60)	6/24, 25%	22/30, 73%	10/30, 33%
Period III (1965–70)	9/30, 30%	20/30, 61%	11/30, 37%

authenticity (Table I) and the increase in articles on religious subjects (Table II) over the three time periods is most dramatic in the articles from popular and intellectual periodicals. The articles from religious reviews have an initially higher and more constant concern with authenticity and are much more frequently centered on religious subjects. This is natural given the affiliation of the authors and the projected audience. What is unexpected is that the popular and intellectual articles, which in 1945–50 are quite separated from the religious concerning authenticity and religious topics, by 1965–70 draw much closer to the religious on both counts. In fact, the popular and intellectual surpass the religious articles in their concern for authenticity, but articles from religious periodicals still have almost twice as many articles on religion in the 1965–70 period. It should be noted that the articles chosen from religious periodicals were on Arab culture and change; articles on purely religious topics were not included.

It would appear that the articles from religious periodicals remained constant through the three periods and served as a magnet drawing the popular and intellectual articles toward a religious point of view both in concern for a restatement of authentic identity in the face of the West and in a concern for Islam. However, a close analysis of the type of authenticity expressed and of the basic argumentation of the articles reveals significant differences.

Types of Authenticity

These references can be grouped into four distinct types of authenticity which emerge in the literature: Islamic, Arab, Arabo-Muslim, and national. The differences are clear in the following illustrations.

Arab Authenticity

Excerpts from two articles from popular reviews illustrate an Arab authenticity. An article from *al-Hilal* (Egypt, June 1966, pp. 30–39) explains the Charter of 1962 as thoroughly Arab and contemporary. The sixties in Egypt marked the Arab socialist phase of Nasserism which was embodied in the Charter. This socialism is presented as fully authentic, not as a system imposed from outside. The Charter is "the Arab mind confronting its specific reality"; and it "marks a new phase of the political, social, and cultural awareness of the Arab mind." Religion is not ignored but Islam is not singled out; rather we are told that "Religions are the spiritual energy animating revolutionary actions through ideals, a progressive message, and faith linked to the will for a good life, virtue and progress."

The Charter is specifically Arab, thus authentic. But, in fact, the authenticity is not a return to the past or to religion; it is rather confronting Arab reality.

A second article, from the popular review *al-Arabi* (Kuwait, Nov. 1965, pp. 20–23) focuses more on the past and Arab specificity. The Arabs are "distinct" and form "a distinctive nation within the human community." The author complains of attempts to erase Arab authenticity, of "those who have adopted imported traits and have dropped their authentic characteristics." The solution is to "return to the characteristics which made our ancestors great."

Two examples from intellectual reviews add refinement to Arab authenticity; both are from the Beirut monthly *al-Adab*. The first (July–Aug. 1967, pp. 71–75) criticizes "those who have strayed from that scientific, objective and realistic path which is true Arabism." The culprits have "cooperated with Americans and spread the American mentality." Their plight is that they do not know "how to return to Arab culture and Arab customs."

The other article (April 1968, pp. 25–28) has the same point of view. It describes three positions possible when faced with cultural imperialism: 1) reaction and withdrawal; 2) heightened consciousness; and 3) dislocation. Consciousness forms the sage middle position between the two extremes of a reactionary turning in on oneself and a complete loss of identity through imitation of the West. The middle path is described thus:

> Our roots are in Arabism. . . . We must present an alternative which preserves the personality of the original, living (Arab) nation and guarantees its development: an Arab, national, socialist society. . . . This is not incompatible with our heritage. We must present our heritage and tradition with progressive, scientific explanations. . . . Hamurabi, Akhnaton and Muhammad were revolutionaries; Muhammad was the greatest. . . . We must uncover Arab reality.

All four articles define authenticity in an Arab frame, set off from the "other," the West. And the first, third, and fourth are clearly rereadings of the Arab heritage. If religion enters at all, it is in terms of its social, revolutionary values.

Islamic Authenticity

Authenticity can also be centered squarely on Islam as in the following three examples. An article in the religious review of Saudi Arabia, *Majallat al-Hajj* (24:2 (1969):109–12), makes a distinction between Islam and Muslims: the backwardness which exists in Islamic countries is not from Islam but from the deviation of Muslims who have forsaken the essential elements of Islam. A return to

Islam is imperative in order to progress ("there is no progress apart from religion") and to protect the Islamic cultural personality against the threat of cultural imperialism ("Islam is the best vehicle of protest and resistance"). According to the author, Islam confers a "primitive spirit" on the *ummah,* and it is not in man's power to confer a new spirit. Islam has also given a specific intellectual structure to Muslims. Consequently, those who adopt Western values on the pretext that Islam has the capacity to change and, therefore. incorporate these values are in error. So, also, do those err who try to explain the *shariah* in terms which justify the adoption of Western intellectual and social modes.

Another Saudi article from the intellectual review *al-Manhal* (29: (1968):38–41) presents Islam as the middle path between two extremes—but here the extremes are communism and the forces of imperialism. "Nothing can replace Islam in the Islamic and Arab world. It is a third force, a force for good, right, justice, mercy, charity, and humanism, values which are missing in other religions but are complete in Islam. . . . Tomorrow is for Islam no matter what the power of Communism or the force of Imperialism."

An article from the Lebanese Shiite review *al-Irfān* (April 1959, pp. 759–65) calls for a return to "our true values" based on Islam. The values Muslims rejected in order to import and impose Western values and principles were not "our true values." Islam deviated after the first four caliphs lay sleeping for thirteen centuries. And Western values have spawned lack of faith, disunity, insincerity, and lack of responsibility.

In all three examples, Islam, as such, and not as part of a cultural complex, is the basis of authenticity.

Arab-Muslim Authenticity

Expressions of this type of authenticity represent an attempt to integrate Islam into an Arab "progressive" perspective as the following citation from the Iraqi intellectual review *al-Aqlam* (March 1965, pp. 43–51) illustrates:

The human and cultural motives behind the application of socialism to Arab society are identical with the goals set by Islamic doctrine for Arab civilization: social justice incarnated in law and human rights. Islam fought against usury and did away with oppression and monopoly. . . . What is needed is the efficacious application of that socialism which has its roots in Arab existence and had its pilot experience under the religion of Islam.

Since Arab socialism is Muslim in its principles and national in its goals, it is necessary that contemporary Arab nationalist socialist thought be tied to Arab-Muslim thought. . . . The new Arab Islamic renaissance is represented by the resurrection of the Arab-Muslim cultural and human heritage as a point of departure for building a modern Arab culture.

National Authenticity

This type of authenticity appeared most frequently in articles from North African reviews. For instance, a program proposed in an article from the Tunisian intellectual review *al-Fikr* speaks of the need to "rediscover national authenticity and the characteristics of the Tunisian personality by extirpating the foreign tendencies the occupiers tried to plant in us." Progress will come only with "a revivification of national culture."

The popular Algerian review *al-Moujahid* (Mar. 6, 1966, p. 16) criticizes those who cooperate with imperialism and follow a route other than that which leads to the discovery of "our personality . . . our special gifts and genius." The aim is to "resurrect our history" so as to "link today with tomorrow and make the present a continuation of our personality of yesterday and a basis for our future."

As we noted previously, there is an increase in concern for authenticity in the period 1965–70 in the articles from popular and intellectual reviews which brings the latter more in line with the articles from religious reviews. Fundamental differences, however, remain. This is clear if we examine the types of authenticity which predominate in the three types of review.

Articles from religious reviews most frequently propose Islam as the basis of authenticity, whereas the popular and intellectual articles more frequently see authenticity as Arab, national, or Arabo-Muslim.

There is a basic difference in mentality involved here. An appeal to Arab or national authenticity places Arab or national identity in first place and though a denial of Islam is not involved *ipso facto,* it is at best reduced to a secondary role in the process of change. The same may be said for Arab-Muslim authenticity. This expresses a mentality which sees the Arab heritage as embracing various elements among which is Islam. Whereas an appeal to Islamic authenticity most often implies a mentality which considers that everything has been given by God, once for all.

Table III. Distribution of Articles in Period III According to Types of Authenticity and Review.

	Popular	Religious	Intellectual	Total
Arab Authenticity	7	4	11	22
Islamic	6	20	4	30
Arab-Muslim Authenticity	2	1	7	10
National Authenticity	4	1	5	10
Total	19	26	27	72

But even the appeal to Islamic identity requires further investigation and distinction.

The Basic Argumentation of the Articles

In coding the articles, the attitudes expressed, the element of culture discussed, and the motives singled out were extracted from each paragraph. Lest this fragmenting of articles into themes overlook the basic logic of the article, provision was made to extract the basic argument of each article. When we spoke earlier of types of authenticity, we singled out the various poles to which authenticity was tied. Here, it is the argument underpinning the article as a whole that was extracted. These arguments fall into the following categories:

1. *Islam:* We find statements to the effect that "Islam is matter and spirit" in contradistinction to Western materialism, or that "Islam embodies human values" which will save the world from its present plight. Or again, "Islam is up to date and it alone can solve today's problems." Some articles are based on the principle that "only fidelity to Islam can give us strength and force," while others agree that "Islam is a social revolution."

2. *Arabo-Islamic Civilization* is the basis of some of the articles which present the Arabs and Islam as the pinnacle of civilization and argue that because of its glorious past Arab civilization can floursh once again. Some other articles focus on the need to guard the specific Arab-Muslim personality.

3. *Arab and Human Civilization:* A few articles laud Arab civilization but place it squarely in the frame of human civilization, singling out the contribution the Arabs have made to human civilization and its openness to and interaction with other civilizations. Some authors argue that civlization is one with only superficial differences; a few place the Arabs in the context of Mediterranean culture. But more frequent are articles pointing out Arab or Egyptian contributions to civilization as a whole or to poetry, philosophy, and science.

4. *National and Cultural Revival and Reform* is also the basis for some articles which propose "national culture as the strength of a nation," or claim that "national culture and language will assure independence." Still others center on the need to guard Arab specificity, to reject cultural imperialism, and to form a new culture fitting Arab reality.

5. *Openness for Basic Change:* A few articles neglect authenticity even in the most minimal form and argue that only radical change can bring the Arabs into line with contemporary civilization. For instance, science is proposed as the sole means for progress, or a radical change in mentality is given priority among needs. In a few cases, openness to the West is seen as the only means to overcome cultural decline.

What we wish to single out here is the increasing use of Islam as the basic argument in the popular and intellectual articles in the 1955–60 and 1965–70 periods.

However, basic differences remain and can be seen when the argumentation is inspected more closely. Twenty of the twenty-four articles on the religious level in Period III use unnuanced arguments concerning Islam. For example, Islam is matter and spirit and a locus of human values or fidelity to Islam will give us force, or we need to guard our Muslim personality and morals, or Islam can solve today's problems. Whereas, in the popular and intellectual articles there are only five out of the sixteen articles in Period III with these arguments. Instead, we find seven of the sixteen which reread Islam to find therein a social revolution. This particular use of Islam is not found at all on the religious level.

The difference can be illustrated by comparison of a few articles from Egypt, Syria, and Saudi Arabia. An article from The Egyptian journal *al-Katib* (June 1966, pp. 122–29) states that the Quran offers basic *principles* to solve today's problems by promoting development, assuring justice to all, and regulating international disputes. In fact, Islam is in harmony with Arab socialism. Objections from fundamentalist quarters are precluded by arguing that the Prophet's words should not be applied literally. Another article from the same review (Mar. 1968, pp. 10–29) repeats the argument that "Islam is *principles*, not detailed prescriptions" and that Islam is open to science and, therefore, to socialism which is science. Both these instances are based on Islam—but Islam is seen as principles supporting Arab socialism.

A very different conception of Islam is presented by examples from religious articles such as that from the Saudi review *Majallat al-Hajj* (23:12 (1969):776–79) which argues that youth is mistaken in thinking that religion is an obstacle to science and social revolution. Islam, in fact, is confirmed by science and the institution of *zakat* which assures the distribution of wealth is proof of Islam's social concern. Islam, for the author, is the religion of human nature and intellect. Another religous article from the Syrian review *al-Tamaddun al-Islami* (36 (1969):185–92) declares that Islam is intended for all peoples and that only a "return to Islam—text and spirit—will give us victory." In these two examples Islam is presented, not as principles, but as texts and institutions.

Table IV. The Proportion of Articles Using Islam as the Basic Argument.

	Popular	Religious	Intellectual
Period I (1945–50)	1/18, 5%	18/33, 54%	0/18, 0%
Period II (1955–60)	2/24, 8%	23/30, 76%	5/30, 17%
Period III (1965–70)	10/30, 33%	24/33, 73%	6/30, 20%

The analysis of the corpus of 246 articles reveals many nuances and differences between regions, and they do reveal the growing concern for Islam as an element of identity in the late 1950s and even more in the 1960s in the periodical literature. Despite fairly strict control of publications in many of the countries during at least part of the periods studied, the variety of approaches to the subject of identity and change emerges clearly, and woven into that variety, Islam takes an increasingly prominent place. The increasing prominence given to Islam is even more accentuated during the 1970s as we indicated at the beginning of this article. Were we able to complete the sample with a fourth period, 1975–80, the references to Islam would be much more pronounced, but with a similar variety of outlook.

CONCLUSION

Islam is an element of the basic substratum of Arab-Muslim identity. Of this there is no doubt. What is not clear is the form that Islam will take finally in contemporary Arab-Muslim society. It is not easy to imagine a contemporary society in which Islamic institutions of another age continue to play a vital role as some proponents of an "Islamic society" seem to champion, nor is a new identity witout a prominent Islamic element very likely.

In a recent seminar on Arab nationalism and Islam, one of the participants opined that there is a sort of pendular motion governing the relationship between the two—now Arabism dominates, now Islam.[11] This may be apt to describe the fluctuations of a transitional period in which a new relationship is still being forged; it is certainly not a formula for stability and development.

Moreover, the fluctuation between nationalism and Islam can also be explained in function of the dominant personalities who served to crystalize the elements of identity, first in one form then in another, during the past quarter-century in the Middle East. First, Gamal Abdel Nasser, with his charismatic appeal to Arab identity, mobilized to assure independence, development, and a role on the international political scene. That charisma withered in the war of 1967. In the decade which followed the stage was set for the entry of another, but very different, charismatic character. Saudi Arabia stepped in to fill, partially, the void left by Nasser and to assure both that the Arabs' first real war against Israel in 1973 would carry an Islamic stamp and that Saudi aid would foster Islamic consciousness throughout the Islamic world.[12] Then the incredible revolution in Iran brought to prominence another charismatic leader, Ayatullah Khomeini. His vision of the world and society is poles apart from that of

Nasser, but his immediate impression on the area was equally dazzling. It brought into sharp focus that element of identity which has marked the difference between "East" and "West" for fourteen centuries—Islam. But once the initial euphoria had faded, it became clear that appeals to Islam are not without a divisive aspect which dampens its effect as an instrument of political mobilization. Now, as the Iraqi-Iranian war drags on into its second year, there are signs that Arab identity still has force in separating out and defining political and economic interests, in the Gulf area most especially.

Certain effects of the Islamic resurgence, however, give signs of continuing for sometime—namely, the refocusing of attention on the *shariah* as the touchstone of an Islamic society and the consequent re-emergence of the ulama as a political force after their having been shunted aside in the process of change for nearly a century.[13] This situation should provide the occasion for an honest confrontation of the various tendencies within society which will permit the formulation of an identity apt for contemporary Arab-Muslim society.[14]

Notes

1. John J. Donohue, "The New Syrian Constitution and the Religious Opposition: A Chronology of Events January-April 1973," in *CEMAM Reports* (Beirut: Dar El-Mashreq, 1976), vol. 1, no. 1, pp. 81–96.

2. Cf. Shereen Khairallah, "The Islamic Liberation Party, Search for a Lost Ideal," *CEMAM Reports* (1975), vol. 2, pp. 87–95.

3. Cf. Maurice Martin and Rose-Marie Masad's "Return to Islamic Legislation in Egypt," *CEMAM Reports* (1976), vol. 4, pp. 47–81.

4. Cf. Leon Carl Brown, *The Surest Path* (Cambridge: Harvard University Press. 1976), p. 74.

5. See the excerpt in John J. Donohue and John L. Esposito, eds., *Islam in Transition: Muslim Perspectives* (New York: Oxford University Press, 1982), p. 11.

6. Ibid., pp. 20, 24.

7. Muhammad Amarah, ed., *Complete Works of al-Kawakabi* (Beirut: al-Muassah al-Carabiyah, 1975), pp. 355–58.

8. See C. Ernest Dawn's *From Ottomanism to Arabism* (Champaign, Ill.: University of Illinois Press, 1973), ch. 3.

9. Donohue and Esposito, *Islam in Transition*, pp. 57, 60.

10. Ibid., pp. 84, 107.

11. *al-Qawmiyah al-Arabiyah wal-Islam* (Beirut: Markaz Dirasat al-Wahdah al-Carabiyah, 1981), p. 738.

12. On Saudi interpretations of the October War, see *CEMAM Reports* (1974) vol. 1, no. 2, p. 33, and on the Lahore Conference of February 1974 where some proposed proclaiming King Faysal as Caliph; see Ibid., vol. 2, p. 37.

13. The Kuwaiti daily *al-Siyasah* carried an interesting discussion on the *shariah* and the constitution which brings out the desire of the Ministry of Awqaf and Islamic Affairs to take a more prominent role. See *al-Siyasah,* (Mar. 26, 1980), p. 1.

14. Abdallah Laroui, *L'Idéologie arabe contemporaine* (Paris: Maspero, 1967), pp. 19–28, proposes three typical reactions to change, each of which leaves "dogma" untouched. The reflections of Gilbert Grandquillaume, "Islam et politique au Maqhreb," are apropos: Islamic identity is a notion which is deeply felt and states must pay attention to it; though it is widely felt, the understanding of it is feeble: it can accommodate very different contents extending from extreme religiosity to atheism (in O. Carré (ed.), *L'Islam et l'état* (Paris: POF, 1982), p. 53.

11

PIONEERS OF THE ISLAMIC RESURGENCE

As seen in Section I, the concerns of the Islamic resurgence were clearly reflected in periodical literature for several decades. Similarly, self-criticism, the quest for Islamic identity, and the formulation of Islamic responses or alternatives to the challenge of modernity existed throughout the twentieth century.[1] This section highlights six major Muslim activists from the Arab world, Iran, and South Asia who have had a formative influence on current developments and contemporary revivalists. These Muslims represent both fundamentalist and modernist orientations. All are critical of the West and advocate a return to Islam as an alternative to Western capitalism and communism. Moreover, despite distinctive differences in their blueprints for society, each reflects the belief that rectification of the plight of modern Islam requires the recognition and reappropriation of Islam as a total way of life. This will enable, indeed require, Muslims to be faithful both to Islam's private and public—political, legal, and social—dimensions. The following chapters focus on the contribution of these Muslim voices to a resurgent Islam's political and social thought. Who are they?

Perhaps the two most influential figures in contemporary Muslim revivalist thought are Sayyid Qutb (1906–1966) of al-Ikhwan al-Muslimun (the Muslim Brotherhood) and Mawlana Abu al-Ala Mawdudi (1903–1979) of the Jamaat-i-Islami (the Islamic Association). Both were prodigious writers whose books have been translated and circulated widely throughout the Islamic world. They identified and responded to many of the concerns which continue to trouble

---

1. John J. Donohue and John L. Esposito, eds., *Islam in Transition: Muslim Perspectives* (New York: Oxford University Press, 1982), and John O. Voll, *Islam: Continuity and Change in the Modern World* (Boulder, Colo.: Westview Press, 1982).

Islam today. Their interpretations of Islam inform much of contemporary Islamic revivalism: its worldview and agenda.

Yvonne Haddad in "Sayyid Qutb: Ideologue of Islamic Revival" demonstrates why Qutb is a model for a process common to many Muslim revivalists. Born in an Egyptian village, his early traditional upbringing was followed by exposure to and enchantment with the West. However, he progressively became disaffected with the West, believing that alien models were incapable of providing the sense of identity and moral purpose which the Islamic world required. He "returned" to Islam convinced that only an Islamic alternative could provide the ideology and values so sorely needed by Muslim society. Qutb joined the Muslim Brotherhood and spent the remainder of his life as an Islamic activist. Imprisoned for ten years and finally executed by Nasser in 1966, Sayyid Qutb has since that time been known as "the martyr" (shahid) of the Islamic revival. Like Sayyid Qutb, Mawlana Abu al-Ala Mawdudi may be viewed as an ideologue of a resurgent Islam. In 1941 he founded the Jamaat-i-Islami, a Muslim religio-political movement intimately involved in South Asia. A prolific writer, Mawdudi's major contribution and legacy was his systematic interpretation of Islam. Charles Adams in "Mawdudi and the Islamic State" shows how Mawdudi, responding both to this South Asian experience as well as the general condition of Muslims throughout the world, called upon Muslims to restore Islam's primacy in their personal as well as their political lives. Convinced that Islam is a comprehensive way of life, he wrote extensively on the nature and character of an Islamic state and through the Jamaat-i-Islami worked to implement politically the Islamic ideal. His writings have been translated from Urdu into Arabic, Farsi, and English and may be found in libraries and book stalls throughout the Muslim world.

From a Western perspective, the two names most commonly associated with Islamic politics are probably Libya's Muammar Qaddafi and Iran's Ayatullah Khomeini. Lisa Anderson in "Qaddafi's Islam" assesses the Islamic character of Qaddafi's Libya. Colonel Qaddafi's early appeals to Islam shortly after seizing power, the introduction of Islamic laws, his attempt to follow in the footsteps of Nasser as an Arab leader, and his use of petrodollars to extend Libya's influence in the Muslim world would seem to support assumptions that his is an Islamic government. However, while the West continues to view Libya as an Islamic state, to what extent is that really true today? What is Qaddafi's Islamic legacy?

While both Qaddafi and Khomeini are often viewed as heads of Islamic governments, their ideology and interpretation of Islam are as different as their professions—Colonel and Ayatullah. The symbol of Iran's revolution, the Ayatullah Khomeini emerged from this struggle as the key political and religious leader in the newly established Islamic Republic of Iran. Under his guidance,

Iran has become the first Shiite religious state and the only Muslim nation to be dominated politically by clerics. The increased control by fundamentalist clergy in the post-revolution period and their effective ouster of more moderate Muslim leaders such as Mehdi Bazargan, Khomeini's first prime minister, and the Sorbonne-educated Abul-Hasan Bani-Sadr, former protégé of Khomeini and Iran's president, as well as repressive government measures in the name of Islam, raise many questions about the nature of Iran's Islamic state. Michael Fischer's "Imam Khomeini: Four Levels of Understanding" analyzes a man who has proven far more complex than most expected. To get at his subject, Fischer studies Khomeini from four perspectives: his biography, projected persona, specific programs, as well as the religious and the political contexts in which Khomeini has functioned. The result is a penetrating study of the Ayatullah Khomeini: an insight into the man, his rise to power, his popular revolutionary appeal, his understanding of Islamic government, and thus a fuller appreciation of the spirit behind the sometimes austere, harsh character of Islamic rule in Iran today.

While all Muslim revivalists may share a desire to shed Western domination and to reroot their ideological foundation and modernization more authentically in their Islamic heritage, their approach and methods differ markedly. So, too, in contrast to the four previous Muslim voices, Muhammad Iqbal (1875–1938) and Ali Shariati (1933–1977) represent a more reformist Islam. Both shared with their more fundamentalist colleagues (whether traditional or radical) similar concerns and attitudes: excessive dependence upon the West, self-alienation, a call for a return to Islam, and the implementation of an Islamic alternative to effect a more Islamic state and society or order. However, reformer modernists differ in the nature and degree of change, reinterpretation (*ijtihad*) which they advocate. While all Muslims look with pride to their Islamic past, Islamic reformers pursue a path that is more one of renovation than restoration or replication. Thus, Islam's successes and glorious formative period are not looked to for the detailed blueprint for society. Rather, they supply the inspiration, example, principles, and values in light of which new forms must be developed. We see this clearly in "Muhammad Iqbal and the Islamic State." Iqbal, the leading Muslim modernist of South Asia, was a forerunner of contemporary Islamic reformism. His emphasis on the unity and totality of the Islamic worldview and his call for a reconstruction of Islamic thought and practice are keystones for contemporary Islamic reformers. For Iqbal, the remedy for a depressed community was a new synthesis of Western and Islamic sciences which would provide a bridge between tradition and modernity. It has remained the elusive desideratum and continues to constitute the principal challenge to contemporary reformers who seek "Islamic modernization."

Ali Shariati, like Iqbal, first received a traditional Islamic education before earning his doctorate in Europe. Strongly influenced by Iqbal's writings, he too sought a synthesis, a return to a revolutionary Islam which he distinguished from the previously clerical dominated, established Islam. Rejecting both secular elites with their uncritical apeing of the West (Westoxification) and the traditional religious leadership, Shariati's sociology of Islam proved an attractive alternative for an alienated, searching generation of growth. If the Ayatullah Khomeini was the symbol of opposition and resistance, Shariati was the revolutionary ideologue. Although he and Khomeini were the revolution's early heroes—their pictures often placed side by side on wall posters and in parades—as time and a close study of each reveals, their visions of the nature and character of Islam and Islamic government are poles apart.

FOUR

Sayyid Qutb:
Ideologue of Islamic Revival

YVONNE Y. HADDAD

The twentieth century has seen several spokesmen for Islam whose ideas have had a wide impact on their contemporaries as well as on the succeeding generations. Their writings have assumed a primary position in providing a comprehensive Islamic vision, a synthesis necessitated by the rapid change accompanying the impact of modernization and Westernization with their direct challenge to prevalent institutions. In the early part of the century, it was the work of Muhammad Abduh which provided the foundation for a liberal, rational, and humanistic Islam which became the intellectual justification of the "secular" national experiments in the Arab world.

Few Muslim thinkers have had as significant an impact on the reformulation of contemporary Islamic thought as has Sayyid Qutb. Since his execution in Cairo in 1966, his writings have inspired numerous revivalist movements throughout the Muslim world. They have captured the imagination and the commitment of young Muslims and transformed them into working for the cause of Islam in the world. His life experiences as well as his death became a perfect illustration of one of the processes through which a revolutionary passes from enchantment with the West to the helplessness and marginality that it may inspire in those who find its values and norms not only foreign but inadequate, and finally the return to the roots where reintegration, conversion, and a new vibrant identity cohere and the human being becomes part of the revolutionary movement aimed at changing the world and bringing in a new ethical moral order based on freedom, brotherhood, and justice for all.

Qutb's works carefully analyzed what he believed to be the disease of Muslims who struggle to fit alien models, attempting to replicate them in their own countries. He captured the hopes and dreams of those who sought to bring about change, to elevate the social order, and to provide equitable distribution of wealth and power in society. He moved from a stance of an observer and interpreter of society, reflecting on its currents of thoughts and goals, to a revolutionary who charted the vision of a new order to which he wanted to lead all people. Having been disillusioned by all other solutions he formulated his own, grounded in the Quranic vision yet relevant for the everyday life of Muslims in the Arab world.

Those influenced by his writings include the revolutionary Iranian students who helped topple the Shah's regime, also their most popular ideologue, Ali Shariati. A number of Qutb's books have been translated into foreign languages.[1] The office of the International Islamic Federation of Student Organizations in Kuwait has made several of his books available in English translation. They are highly recommended to members of the Muslim Student Association in the United States, who avidly read them to help raise consciousness for an Islamic order they hope to bring about when, upon their return to their respective countries, they will assume roles of leadership. His writings are also popular among members of the American Muslim Mission (popularly known as Black Muslims) who find his "evangelical" rhetoric and Quranic centeredness strongly supportive of their worldview as they seek to transform American society and convert others to the faith of Islam.

Sayyid Qutb's interpretation of the Quran has become very popular because of its clear literary style and its appealing didactic and homiletic approach. Thousands of copies of the thirty-volume interpretation have been purchased by people in all walks of life. It has become the standard by which the Quran's message is interpreted in many mosques and homes throughout the Muslim world. It has been extensively used by the author of *Tafsir al Muminin,* a popular exegesis of the Quran which has had wide distribution in Syria and is credited by a Syrian official as being the "secret weapon" of the Muslim Brotherhood revolution in that country.

Qutb's writings have also had a special impact on Islamic groups in Egypt, especially after 1971 when Sadat allowed them to resume their activities in an effort to combat his socialist opposition. His writings had special poignancy for those who shared the torture of Egyptian prisons under the Nasser regime. Sadat's assassins came from one of the many groups who quote Qutb for justification of their revolutionary fervor.

Sayyid Qutb was born in 1906 in the village of Qaha in Asyut Province to al-Hajj Qutb Bin Ibrahim, a well-respected and relatively affluent gentleman farmer who was a member of the nationalist party. He attended a local school for four years where he memorized the Quran by the age of ten. His intimate and comprehensive knowledge of the Quran in the context of his religious upbringing[2] seems to have had an abiding influence on his life. It was the anchor of his existence and functioned as the parameter of his intellectual endeavor as in the 1950s he turned to Islam to provide meaning and direction for his life.

At the age of thirteen Qutb was sent to an uncle in Cairo to continue his education. He graduated from Dar al-Ulum where he came under the influence of Abbas Mahmud al-Aqqad and his Westernizing tendencies. He became extremely interested in English literature and read avidly anything he could lay his hands on in translation. Upon graduation he was appointed as inspector of the ministry of education, a position he eventually gave up to devote himself exclusively to writing.

Qutb's written work was prolific. Besides the interpretation of the Quran, he is credited with twenty-four books.[3] He also contributed many articles to magazines, especially *al-Risalah*,[4] discussing the issues that were being debated in the intellectual circles of Egypt at the time. The first phase of his work was mostly literary, including poetry, stories and articles, and literary criticism. He was later to renounce all these works and regret ever having written them. In the late 1940s he wrote two books on Quranic topics, asserting in the introduction, "I have found the Quran."

Like other Egyptian intellectuals who had been enamoured of the West, such as Taha Husayn, Ahmad Amin and his mentor Abbas Mahmud al-Aqqad, Sayyid Qutb underwent a transformation in the late 1940s. This came as a result of British war policies during World War II and as an aftermath of the creation of the state of Israel. The latter he perceived as a rejection of the rights of the Arabs to self-determination and a rejection of their equality to Western man. In 1949 he came to the United States to study educational administration in Washington, D.C., and in California. Hence he witnessed the wide and unquestioning support of the American press for Israel. This along with what he felt to be the denigration of the Arabs left Qutb with a bitterness he was never able to shed.

Sayyid Qutb was small in build, very dark, and soft spoken. He was described by his contemporaries as extremely sensitive, humorless, very intense, and issue oriented. (He also appears to have suffered from a variety of ailments; at the end of his life he is reported to have carried medication with him where he went.)[5] The swarthiness of his complexion may have been a contributing factor in his sensitivity to what he experienced as strong racial prejudice in the United States. He now felt that this country, which like many other young Arabs he had idolized, rejected him, his being, and his identity. He saw the injustice of the uprooting of the Palestinians, fully supported by America, with its implicit rejection of all Arab peoples.

AN ISLAMIC ALTERNATIVE

Upon his return to Egypt, Sayyid Qutb joined the Muslim Brotherhood and began writing on Islamic topics. In his books he proposed an Islamic ideology as an alternative to those systems competing for Egyptian allegiance, dedicating the rest of his life to articulating the content, scope, and method of this ideology. Thus in his early books on Islamic subjects, the Islamic ideology is proposed as an alternative to those of communism, capitalism, nationalism, liberalism, and secularism. These writings, along with those of later periods of his life, continue to provide contemporary Muslims with the ideological and emotional content presently undergirding the Islamic revival. Qutb's work has had extensive dissemination throughout the Muslim world, and his ideas have become the accepted definition of Islam and its role in shaping the social, political, economic, intellectual, cultural, and ethical aspects of society. At the time, however, the content of the ideology was tentative in his mind. His writings were a kind of careful crafting of a variable synthesis of ideas which he felt might replace all others in the marketplace of ideologies. Writing almost in the spirit of dialogue, he wrote in 1959:

> If it becomes evident that Islam possesses or is capable of solving our basic problems, of granting us a comprehensive social justice, of restoring for us justice in government, in economics, in opportunities and in punishment ... then without doubt it will be more capable, than any other system we may seek to borrow or imitate, to work in our nation.[6]

During this period, Qutb was influenced by the writings of Muhammad Assad (Leopold Weiss) and Abu al-Ala Mawdudi, writings which became available in Egypt in 1951. His early Islamic writings are filled with references to their work. His later works continue where they left off, and in fact are the radical conclusion of ideas expressed by them.

Qutb believed that the Islamic ideology would present a potent argument against capitalism as well as help solve all the problems that make communism appealing to the masses, such as the uneven distribution of wealth, unemployment, low wages, unequal opportunity, corruption of the labor force, and poor productivity, as well as a myriad of social problems. Furthermore, the system would free the Muslims from subservience to either capitalism or communism, providing social justice, international respect and dignity as well as freedom from the evils of strife and war, "A system that provides us with the bread that communism provides, and frees us from economic and social disparity, realizing a balanced society while sustaining us spiritually."[7]

Thus not only would the Islamic ideology solve social and economic problems, it would provide Muslims with a sense of self-worth. "The individual without a comprehensive ideology that binds him to heaven and earth is a wretched dwarf and a neglected foundling. The ideology is necessary." The ideology "provides the individual with a goal greater than himself, the goal becomes the society in which he lives and humanity of which he is a member."[8]

In this tentative proposal, Qutb suggested that the Islamic system had room for a wide range of manifestations which are correlated to the natural growth of the society and the necessities of modern life, possible as long as they are within the circle of Islam. He saw no necessity for having a single Islamic nation, though he felt it very important for all Muslim nations to form one bloc.

> The Islamic system is not restricted solely to a replica of the first Islamic society, but is every social form governed by the total Islamic view of life. . . . The Islamic system has room for scores of models which are compatible with the natural growth of a society and the new needs of the contemporary age as long as the total Islamic idea dominates these models in its expansive external perimeter.[9]

While maintaining the eternality of the *shariah* as God-given and relevant for every time and place, Qutb affirmed during this period that the *fiqh* (law as it developed from man's application of the *shariah*) is the arena of change, the means through which Muslims can reinterpret the eternal prescripts in order to have them become relevant to modern life, its needs and problems. While the *shariah* is legislated by God, is eternal and unchanging, *fiqh* is made by man to deal with specific situations. Thus the original model of Islamic society "is not the final vision of this society . . . there are visions ever new." The uniqueness of the Islamic vision is that it is fashioned by the *shariah* which created it, while other legal and social systems are a response to local, temporary needs.[10]

The eternality and unchanging nature of the *shariah* guarantees that the new *fiqh* relevant to the events of the day be genuine and authentic. He warns against accepting modern culture and Islamicizing it. Law must be a barrier to human indulgence and desire. The necessity of keeping new interpretations in line with the *shariah* is to keep excesses out. For this he cites the example of the church in the United States where dancing is allowed in the church building. He talks about the colored lights and the sexually arousing music, he saw people dancing to the music and lyrics of "Baby It's Cold Outside."[11]

The Islamic vision is proposed because it is more authentic and will garner the support of the masses. "There is a permanent conflict between the spirit of legislation we borrow and the ethos of the masses for whom we legislate." People are alienated from laws promulgated by the national government that are borrowed from Western sources. Thus he notes that unless the people can respond to and appropriate the laws as their own, society is doomed to disintegration and anomie. In order to have a moral society, the ideology must be grounded in the Qur'an and follow the design of God for humanity.[12]

Qutb says that there are two ways of understanding the meaning of civilization. Muslims could either claim that we have a unique civilization and have the right to have our share in providing for an authentic civilization, or we could "borrow ready made models . . . to copy indiscriminately everything we see without thought or assessment." The first meaning, he says, is one understood and followed by human beings, while the second is understood by monkeys who emulate everything they see.[13]

Besides providing a sense of dignity, of self-worth, and of participation in the shaping of human society, an Islamic ideology provides also for the respect of those who have no value for us at present, by which he means both the West and the communist nations. For Qutb, both what he calls the communist West and the capitalist West are the same. They are two systems that have acted as one bloc of "enmity toward us." Palestine is a witness to this enmity.[14]

Communism showed us the value of the principles it preaches the day it armed Israel. Israel is the only nation established on earth based on religious affiliation. The religious element is the first thing communism denies as a constituent of nationhood. It would be the last thing it would embrace or defend. However, communism has no principle except its own interest. It tramples the principles it advocates.[15]

The United States also has given arms and support to Israel. It is obvious that capitalism has no respect for the Arabs. The experiment of capitalist rule in Egypt under colonial supervision left the people in an oppressed condition. It divided the country into classes of the oppressors and the oppressed.

Who will dare to claim that those million of hungry, naked, barefoot peasants whose intestines are devoured by worms, whose eyes are bitten by flies and whose blood is sucked by insects are humans who enjoy human dignity and human rights [as the Capitalist slogans claim?]. . . . Who will dare to claim that the hundreds of thousands of disabled beggars, who search for crumbs in garbage boxes, who are naked, barefoot, with faces crusted with dirt. . . . Who will dare to say that they are the source of authority in the nation, based on democratic election?[16]

Thus the political institutions devised by those emulating the West are not only alien to the people, they are a fraud. For instead of fostering dignity, they perpetuate want; in place of sufficiency, poverty and subservience to those in power. They continue the myth that the nation is the source of authority. Since the nation is made up of "millions of emaciated, ignorant, hungry people who toil night and day in search of food and who can spare no time in exercising what is called "the right to vote" and "freedom of choice,'" they follow the bidding of their masters who control their source of livelihood.[17]

The masses may be attracted to communism precisely because they have experienced the evils of capitalism. "Communism in itself" says Qutb, "is an insignificant idea which deserves no respect from those who think humanely, above the level of food and drink."[18]

It is out of the disgust with both capitalism and communism that a third alternative becomes necessary. The idea of the Islamic bloc was inspired by a speech given to the American Congress by Liaqat Ali Khan of Pakistan. As a bloc, Islamic countries would be strong and therefore respected by the two other blocs.[19]

This Islamic alternative is the proposed response to the exclusively appropriated significance that East and West ascribe to themselves:

> There are two huge blocs: the Communist Bloc in the East and the Capitalist Bloc in the West. Each disseminates deceptive propaganda throughout the world claiming that there are only two alternative views in the world, communism and capitalism, and that other nations have no alternative but to ally themselves with one bloc or the other. There is no other way out. . . . It is clear that both the Western Bloc and the Eastern Bloc are fighting over the world, manipulating battles for their own interest at the expense of the nations and peoples who are in their orbit. . . . As for us, what is our stake in this struggle? We have recently experienced in Palestine that neither the Eastern Bloc nor the Western Bloc give any credence to the values they advocate, or consider us ourselves as of consequence. . . . We will receive no mercy from either bloc. We are oppressed strangers in the ranks of both. We are therefore the tail end of the caravan regardless of the road we take. . . . Have the existing social conditions rendered us as a nation of slaves, not only to our resident masters, but to any authority that may hover from the West or the East thousands of miles away?[20]

THE ISLAMIC WORLDVIEW

The Egyptian revolution of 1952 brought enthusiastic support from the Muslim Brotherhood. The Free Officers had provided arms and training for members of the Brotherhood prior to the revolution. Upon assuming power the officers sent for Sayyid Qutb. He functioned as a consultant for six months during which he is reported to have eaten, slept, and voted on matters of policy with the Officers trying to influence their plans for the country. He left disappointed because they did not opt for his ideas of instituting an Islamic state and assigning the positions of leadership to committed Muslims from the membership of the Muslim Brotherhood.[21]

It was during this period that he wrote several books dealing with the Islamic view of reality and the world as he perceived it. These writings are less tentative in nature. They articulate in absolute terms the nature and scope of the Islamic vision, attempting to deal with such questions as the source, authenticity and function of such a worldview. Affirming its divine source, its originality and applicability to the modern world, Qutb appears throughout to be aware of the contending ideologies he was challenging. He identified the essential characteristics of this vision.

1. Lordship [of God] *(rabbaniyyah):* The primary characteristic of the Islamic vision is its divine origin. This distinguishes it from other ideologies posited by human beings in their quest to devise a comprehensive system that can give meaning to their lives, to the world in which they live and the relationship of both to the Creator, the source of all being.

> It is a divine vision that proceeds from God in all its particularities and its essentials. It is received by "man" in its perfect condition. He is not to complement it from his own [resources] or delete any of it; rather he is to appropriate it and implement all its essentials in his life.[22]

All visions other than the Islamic proceed from human arrogance which attempts by means of human whims and desires to devise a comprehensive worldview. This is true not only in those philosophical views that affirm idealism, pragmatism, or dialectical materialism,[23] but is also the case with polytheistic thought systems which are grounded in human emotions and fears, and in other revealed religions which have been corrupted and falsified by their adherents. The scriptures of the last are now supplemented by ideas of human origin. "Islam alone has remained preserved in its principles. Its sources have not been polluted, nor has its truth been superimposed with falsehood,"[24] a fact attested to by God, Himself: "Lo, Verily We have revealed the Reminder and that We are its Guardian" (S. 15:9). Thus the validity of this claim is verified in the Quran which affirms its own authenticity. (See S. 42:52–3; 53:1–4; 69:44–7; 5:67; 28:56; 6:125.)

While the Islamic vision applies to the realm of human existence and action, man is incapable of comprehending its totality.

> He is limited by his creaturehood. . . . He is not perfect or eternal. His ability to know is limited by his nature and function, which is vicegerency on the earth through which the meaning of worship is fulfilled. He has been granted the capacity to comprehend what is necessary for his role as vicegerent, no less, no more.[25]

2. Constancy *(thabat):* This characteristic of the Islamic worldview, like all others, proceeds from the Lordship of God and provides the basis on which change and progress are to be understood. Qutb sees the Islamic vision as a dynamic force that can be implemented in a variety of social structures and that can manifest itself in different forms of society. However, there is a constancy in its essential core which neither changes nor develops. This does not require the ossification of life and thought, rather it makes room for dynamism "within a constant perimeter around a constant axis."[26] The steadfastness is the characteristic of all of God's creation which is evident in matter, in the atom as well as the universe.

The constant axis for man is his humanity, endowed through the divine breath and thus placing him above other creatures. Although he grows and develops from sperm into old age, these developments do not alter his constant humanity. Man's elevation or degradation is in direct relation to the proximity or distance from the source of his humanity.[27]

The existence of steadfast constancy at the core of all reality, Qutb believes, protects against rampant deviation from the truth. "It controls human activity and change so that it may not proceed without guidance, as occurred in Europe when it severed its bond to belief, leading to its miserable condition."[28] This constant core provides a criterion of judgment that avoids aimlessness and lack of direction, and functions as a corrective to the human tendency to follow its own whims.

The doctrine of constancy contradicts that of unrestricted progress. Developed in the West to combat the tyranny of the church, its openness to all ideas led to corruption since it grants the right and justification for the existence of every concept, value, condition or system as long as it is new. Innovation and newness are a superficial and accidental justification which should not be the criterion by which the validity of values is determined.

The doctrine of constancy in the Islamic worldview is proposed by Qutb as a dam against Westernization and the appropriation of the European values, ideas, customs, and fashions.[29] It also functions as a refutation of the basic intellectual premise of Darwin's theory of progressive evolution, as well as that of dialectical materialism.

The doctrine of constancy in the Islamic worldview, as Qutb saw it, both guarantees the integration and harmony of Muslim life with that of the order of the universe, and also provides assurance in the order of society and an awareness of the permanence of the orbit within which one lives and moves. Thus, the Muslim can proceed knowing that his actions are leading toward progress, that his movement is forward and upward as willed by God, linking yesterday, today, and tomorrow.[30]

If Muslims persist in appropriating Western methods, values, and styles, says Qutb, they will harm not only themselves but all humanity since they will be falsifying and altering the only true source of guidance and revelation from God, the only true source of constancy.

> Those who attempt to alter this vision either under the name of renewal, reform or progress, or under the guise of eradicating the remnants of the Medieval age or under any other slogan are our real enemies. They are the enemies of humankind.[31]

Qutb then proceeds to fault the Westernizers because "they feed on the products of the nineteenth- or eighteenth-century European thought, not their own, and they have not as yet reached the products of the twentieth century."[32]

3. Comprehensiveness *(shumul)*: The third characteristic of the Islamic vision is its comprehensive nature. Man himself is never able to provide an equivalent comprehensive substitute, due in large part to his finitude and his limitation in time and place. Man is unable to provide a complete system that takes into account all considerations and aspects. "It is impossible that a human concept or a humanly devised system would ever personify comprehensiveness. It will always be temporary or fragmentary."[33]

The true Islamic vision has been corrupted by those who over the years have complicated it by mixing it with other ideas such as those of Plato or Aristotle as well as some Christian theologians. They are the "so-called" Islamic philosophers who incorporated these ideas into Islamic thought. This mixing is unacceptable because the Islamic vision is unique and does not accept ideas from other sources.

> This vision is of such comprehensiveness and breadth, of precision and depth, of authenticity and integratedness that it rejects every foreign element, even though it is merely a verbal expression which is currently fashionable in foreign [intellectual] circles.[34]

The comprehensive nature of Islam is reinforced by the unity that proceeds from the One Divine source. This unity is manifested in the areas of "thought and behavior, vision and initiative, doctrine and system, source and reception, life and death, striving and movement, life and means of livelihood, this world and the next. It does not divide into sections, seek various paths or horizons or march on different roads without agreement."[35]

When humanity is united in its obedience to the one source of all its vision, understanding, values, legislation, and law, then it will be at its best. In this way "the total human endeavor must become one movement, bent on the realization of the purpose of human existence . . . worship, the worship that is made evident in man's bondage to God alone in all that he undertakes as a vicegerent."[36]

Some Muslims have divided human activity into two spheres, *ibadat* (acts of worship) and *muamalat* (human relationships). This late interpolation into Islamic thought led some people to believe that a Muslim could continue to be a Muslim if he separates between the two and fulfills the acts of worship according to the Islamic injunctions while relegating the area of his relations to other human beings to legislative sources other than Islam. This to Qutb is unacceptable. To him the comprehensiveness of the system guarantees that "Islam is a unity that is indivisible. Any one who divides it into two sections is outside this unity, in other words, he is outside this religion."[37]

4. Balance *(tawazun)*: This characteristic has preserved the unique nature of Islam. It is evidenced in the harmony that exists between that which is revealed, which humans can grasp and apprehend, and that which is accepted by faith

since man has no capacity to comprehend it. Human nature feels comfortable with this vision since absolute knowledge rests with God in whom man places his total trust. "Any doctrine that is totally comprehensible to humans is no doctrine." It is the balance between the known and the unknown, the revealed and the hidden that is in accordance with human nature.[38]

5. Positiveness *(ijabiyyah)*: The Islamic vision emphasizes the positive relation of God to the world, life, and man. From obedience to God proceeds the positiveness in the believer's life. The Islamic vision is not a negative one that dwells in the world of the conscience, it is not idealistic or merely spiritual, but rather, "it is a 'prototype' for a reality to be implemented according to its plan."[39] There is not a single action in life which should not proceed as a witness to this religion, not only as an affirmation of faith through the tongue but one of action, evidencing to others that which makes a difference in the world.

6. Pragmatism *(waqiiyyah)*: This vision is not idealistic, but rather is grounded in the reality of life. Yet it is idealistic-realistic in that it aims at establishing the highest and most perfect system to which humanity can ascend.[40]

The role of man as perceived in Islam is within the limits of his capacity. Man is taken as he is, "one who eats, marries, procreates, loves, hates, hopes, and fears." Islam takes into account "human nature, his capacities, his virtues, evils, strengths, weaknesses." It does not portray man as inferior, nor does it denigrate his role on earth. It does not elevate him to the role of divinity, nor does it see him in angelic form. This is contrary to the Brahmanic vision of man which denies the body as unreal, and to Christianity which sees man as made of body and soul and determines that which pertains to the body as evil.[41]

7. Unicity *(tawhid)*: While *tawhid* is the essential comprehensive characteristic of the total Islamic doctrine and its primary basis, it is also one of its components.[42] *Tawhid* is the foundation of all the revealed religions given to the prophets by God. However, it is unique to Islam in that it is the only religion which has preserved it in its pristine condition, not falsifying it.[43] Islam affirms that there is one God to whom alone divinity can be ascribed and there is creaturehood of everything else.[44] The only relationship between Creator and creature is that of creaturehood. This assures that "there is no ruler save God, no legislator, no organizer of human life and of human relationships to the world, to living things or human beings save God. From Him alone is received all guidance and legislation, all systems of life, norms governing relationships and the measure of values."[45]

THE ISLAMIC IMPERATIVE

In 1954, Sayyid Qutb was arrested with many members of the Muslim Brotherhood. Accused of conspiring to assassinate Gamal Abdel Nasser, he was tried and sentenced to fifteen years of hard labor. During his incarceration he revised the first thirteen volumes of his interpretation of the Quran and wrote several books, including *Hadha al-Din* and *al-Mustaqbal li-Hadha al-Din,* in which his ideas acquired a radical bent and portrayed Islam as the Divine Imperative that must assume power in order to regulate all aspects of life.

After serving ten years of his sentence, Qutb was released from prison by Nasser as a result of the personal intercession of the president of Iraq, Abd al-Salam Aref. The physical and mental torture meted out by the prison authorities to members of the Muslim Brotherhood left scars on him. Upon his release he wrote *Maalim Fi al-Tariq,* his most controversial book. This resulted in his arrest in 1965. He was condemned to death on August 22, 1966, executed, and buried in a secret plot in an unmarked grave. To many he became the martyr of the Islamic Revival.

In this last phase of his writings, Qutb rejected all forms of government that did not follow what he believed to be the true Islamic system. They were condemned not only for their oppression but because he felt that they had usurped the role of God by providing legislation to govern people's lives.

The ideology he proposed in the early fifties as a guidline, a "tentative blueprint," by 1965 acquired a dogmatic nature, an absolute given. The variety of possibilities and visions were reduced to one which was mandated as the divine imperative that must command the total allegiance of the believers, summoning them to strive with all available means, not only to implement Islam in their own lives but also to eradicate all other forms and systems.

Reform was no longer sufficient since it did not deal with the root of the evil that permeates society. Only a radical transformation, a totally new beginning, what he in one place called the new birth, the categorical destruction of the old system, can guarantee the flourishing of God's system. Only then can the utopian society take root, the "Kingdom of God on earth."[46]

To struggle in the path of God, for Qutb, demands the willingness of the believers to renounce egotistical achievements and individual goals. The primary goal should be the corporate benefit, the *ummah* living in righteousness under the law of God. Only then can they recapture the ascendancy they were destined to have.

In this endeavor religion is the source of true sustenance. It not only provides the *mujahid* (one who strives to realize God's will; soldier) with the courage to speak out, to prescribe the good and forbid evil, but it also endows him with equanimity, with peace and the willingness to lay down his life for the cause of God. "All people die; he is a martyr. He departs this world to the Garden while his opponent goes to the Fire."[47] Thus he faces death not out of resignation but with the full assurance of his fulfilling the will of God, through the ultimate obedience, the essential meaning of what it means to be truly human.

Religion is also the final arbiter of all that is. It is not a fact of culture or separate from it. It provides both the framework within which all aspects of life are to be designed and the measure by which they are judged. Religion moulds and shapes culture. It is the active ingredient in all that man undertakes.

Thus articulated, the religion of Islam assumes an exclusive role. It no longer functions as one alternative among others. Rather, grounded in the teachings of the Quran which is affirmed as the only preserved true revelation of God it stands in judgment over all posited systems, norms, values, and ideologies. As God's vision for humanity it alone commands obedience and commitment.[48]

Jews and Christians have at one time received the vision from God, but they have distorted it. They have allowed their religious leaders to interpret the scriptures, legislate norms and values. In this they have usurped the role of God who alone is in possession of the power of governance.[49] The role of Muslims is not to legislate but to adhere faithfully in obedience to the way that God has charted for humanity. Muslims know that their victory and supremacy in the world are established by their faithfulness to the true guidance. To veer from such a vision would lead to dissipation, victory turning to defeat.[50]

The Islamic vision is realized in the world through human endeavor.[51] For "the truly chosen people of God are the Islamic *ummah,* that which dwells under God's banner regardless of race, nation, color or region."[52]

> Islam came to elevate man and save him from the bonds of earth and soil, the bonds of flesh and blood. . . . There is no country for the Muslim except that where the *shariah* of God is established, where human relations are bonded by their relationship to God. There is no nationality for a Muslim except his creed which makes him a member of the Islamic *ummah* in the Abode of Islam. The Muslim has no relatives except those who proceed from faith in God. . . . The relatives of the Muslim are not his father, mother, brother, wife or tribe unless the primary relationship is to the creator; from there it proceeds to blood relations.[53]

It is clear that Islam in this context assumes a liberating role. It turns conventional relationships and traditional roles upside down. It has its own definition not only of reality and the world but of how things ought to be—the goal toward which all humanity must strive.

> This religion is a general proclamation for the liberation of "man" on "earth" from bondage to creatures. . . . The proclamation of the sole Lordship of God over the worlds means: a comprehensive revolution against the governance of humans in its various shapes, forms, systems and conditions and total rebellion against all conditions in the world where government is [controlled] by humans.[54]

Islam frees man from subservience to any human institutions, forces, and attitudes that are destructive to the human being and the community. Man ceases to be passively responding, awaiting in dejection the next move of those who seek to oppress him; rather he initiates, sheds his inertness and assumes the reigns of his own destiny and that of the *ummah* through streamlining their wills and goals to those of God and His order.

From this stance and with the absolute assurance of the exclusive possession of the only truth, Qutb called on fellow Muslims to reject the West and the Westernizers because they are patterning their life styles and the norms of the society after those of the People of the Book. God prohibited Muslims from receiving guidance from any source save the Quran. "He proscribed inner defeat before any other people on the earth . . . which leads to the imitation of their society. The Muslim community was established for the role of leadership of humanity. It must derive its customs as well as its ideology from the source that chose it for leadership."[55]

The Quran had clearly warned the Muslims not to have contacts with Christians and Jews because they always seek to turn Muslims away from their faith. Perceived from the scope of the Quranic vision all relations, controversies, and issues between the West and Muslim countries are reduced to a religious struggle in which Christians and Jews attempt in a variety of methods to undermine the Muslims' commitment to Islam.

> It is the eternal doctrine which we see verified in every time and place. . . . This is the reality of the battle which the Jews and the Christians initiate in every land and at all times against the Islamic community. . . . It is the battle of doctrine that is raging between the Islamic camp and these two armies who may [at times] fight among themselves . . . however, they always cooperate in the battle against Islam and the Muslims.

> It is the battle of the doctrine in its essence and reality, yet the two veteran camps of enmity to Islam and the Muslims color it in various ways and raise different banners over it in calumny, cunning and concealment. They have experienced the Muslims' zeal for their religion and their doctrine when they faced them under the banner of doctrine. After that, the enemies turned around and changed the signs of the battle. They did not announce it a war in the name of doctrine—as it is in reality—fearing the zeal and emotion of the doctrine. Rather, they announced it in the name of land, of economics, of politics, of military bases . . . whatever. They proclaimed to those who were gullible among us that the issue of doctrine is an old story that has no meaning. It is no more advisable to raise its banner nor to wage war in its name. That is the sign of the fanatical reactionaries! That is in order to allay the outpouring of zeal for the doctrine . . . while in themselves: international Zionism, International Crusaderism—in addition to International Communism—all of them enter the battle primarily and above all else to destroy this mighty rock which they have long butted and which has bloodied all of them.

> It is the battle of the doctrine. It is not a struggle over land, produce or military bases nor is it any of these false banners. They falsify it to us because of a secret

purpose they keep to themselves in order to deceive us about the nature and essence of the battle and if we are deceived by their treachery we can blame only ourselves.[56]

Meanwhile, it is necessary for Muslims to assume their role of leadership through Islam, not only because it is the only thing they possess as a contribution to society. Nor is it because Islam provides a unique vision of the world as he asserted during the second phase. But Islam must assume the leadership because it is mandated to do so, to liberate all humanity from allegiance to any system or law save that of the Quran.

> The Kingdom of God on earth will not be established when religious leaders supervise sovereignty on earth as was the case under the power of the church, nor by men who pontificate in the name of Gods as was the case under "theocracy" or divine rule; rather it is established when God's law has sovereignty and all matters are judged in the light of God's will as evident in His *shariah*.[57]

Some Aspects of the Islamic Imperative

Several concepts developed during the last phase of Qutb's Islamic writing deserve closer attention due to their great impact on the current ideas of Muslim revivalists. In a certain sense, a great deal of what is being published at present is either inspired by his writings, plagiarized from his books, or is a commentary on his ideas.

Islam and Liberation

As noted above, the Islamic imperative was articulated as a commission for liberation. This was explained by Qutb in ways reminiscent of Latin American and Afro-American liberation theology.

> This religion is a universal declaration of human liberation on earth from bondage to other men or to human desires. . . . To declare God's sovereignty means: the comprehensive revolution against human governance in all its perceptions, forms, systems and conditions and the total defiance against every condition on earth in which humans are sovereign, or to put it in other words in which divinity belongs to humans . . . . in which the source of power is human . . . . making some the masters of others with disregard to God. This declaration means the extraction of God's usurped sovereignty and its restoration to Him.[58]

From his intimate experience of persecution and jail came the new militancy which saw the naïveté of proclamation, and the futility of declarations and preaching in the face of organized police repression and opposition. Noting that Islam teaches that there is no compulsion in religion, Qutb insisted that this freedom of choice comes only after the forces of oppression have been removed and in places where it is possible for people to adhere to and appreciate the benefit of God's vision for humanity. He felt that if there are obstructions in the way of the fulfillment of this vision, it becomes necessary that "they be eradicated first by force that it may become possible to address the human heart and mind after being freed from chains."[59]

Thus the jihad is crucial if the *dawah* ("call" to Islam) is to proceed unimpeded. For this he notes the precedent in the life of the Prophet Muhammad which he proposes as the prototype of the means of operating the *dawah* in order to bring it to a fruitful end. . . . For while the Muslims restricted their activities to preaching in Mecca, it became necessary for them to fight once they established the community in Medina.

> Truth and falsehood cannot coexist on earth. When Islam makes a general declaration to establish the lordship of God on earth and to liberate humanity from the worship of other creatures, it is contested by those who have usurped God's sovereignty on earth. They will never make peace. Then [Islam] goes forth destroying them to free humans from their power . . . this is the constant situation. The liberating struggle of jihad does not cease until all religion belongs to God.[60]

This reiteration of the necessary militancy against the forces that try to impede the way of Islam appears in several sections of his interpretation of the Quran.

> Islam is not a theological system that is realized when appropriated as an ideology . . . and then its mission ceases. Islam is a pragmatic activistic system of life. It withstands other systems which are based on power and is supported by material power. For Islam to establish its divine system, it is inevitable that these material powers be destroyed and the powers that administer the systems that resist the divine way be annihilated.[61]

Qutb defends the concept of liberation as an imperative to set humans free, to bring about the kingdom of God on earth. He sees the jihad for the realization of the righteous society ordained by God as a liberating force, not as an oppression.[62] He defends its militancy as necessary rather than coercive. "It has never been the intent of Islam to coerce people to believe in its ideology.[63] However, in the same paragraph he rules out the possibility that liberated people would choose by their own free will to re-establish systems thus eliminated.

> This freedom does not mean that they will [be able to] make their desires their Gods or that they would choose by themselves to be slaves of other creatures, or

that they would take others as sovereign over them, and not God. The system which rules humanity in the world must have as its foundation the worship of God alone and that is by accepting legislation from Him.... Anyone who grasps the nature of this religion—as discussed above ... understands the imperative for the dynamic movement of Islam by jihad with the sword—side by side—with the jihad through admonition—and would understand that it is not a defensive movement.[64]

Islam as a liberating force is universal in scope, not restricted to any people-hood, national or geographic boundaries. Its arena is the whole world which must at times strive to implement God's will on earth. "Whenever there is oppression, Islam is commissioned to eradicate it, to combat it, whether this oppression is against Muslims, against protected people or others with whom Muslims have no treaties."[65] In his interpretation of the Quran, Qutb wrote:

This religion is not a declaration for the liberation of the Arab man! It is not a message restricted to the Arabs!.... Its object is "man," the "human" genus—its scope is the "world" ... the whole world. God is not the Lord of the Arabs alone not even those who believe in the Islamic doctrine alone.... God is the "Lord of the worlds" and this religion seeks to restore "the world" to its lord and to extricate people from bondage to anyone save Him. The greatest bondage—in the view of Islam—is subservience to human laws legislated by humans.[66]

The attack on man-made systems and the insistence that the law of God must predominate are not pleas for lawlessness but pleas that are responding to the laws governments make in order to perpetuate their rule and impose their will on people. These laws, Qutb felt must be removed that true justice can exist in the world.

Jihad works to realize the idea of universal revolution not aimed at rule, control or booty. In this revolution peace in all its aspects is realized: the peace of conscience, peace in the home and peace in society ... finally, the peace of humanity.[67]

Jihad

Sayyid Qutb wrote a book on Islam and Peace in which he affirmed that peace is the essential character of Islam. It proceeds from the integration of creation with the law of life and the laws governing humans.

Peace is the eternal principle; war is the exception which becomes a necessity when there is a deviation from the integration exemplified in the religion of the one God [resulting] in injustice, oppression, corruption and discord.[68]

Islam rejects all the justifications for war in the world such as nationalism, racism, greed, and economic expansion. Under the rule of Islam all people will be co-operating together as "one close family" making "all creation a unity with no contradictory purposes."[69] The only legal war in Islam is one that is fought while striving to secure the dominance of the word of God in the world. Since His word is the expression of His will, Islamic wars seek to establish God's system, affirming His Lordship over all the world.[70]

Islam insists that there is no compulsion in religion; however, the compulsion comes into being "against those who oppose its way by force."[71] In this manner, Islam has placed a certain responsibility on Muslims. These include the following: 1) It is the duty of Muslims to protect the believers that they do not stray from the religion, permitting the use of force to repel force. 2) Islam must be guaranteed freedom of propagation, otherwise it becomes incumbent on Muslims to "eradicate" any oppressive powers on the earth which impede the *dawah* of Islam. 3) Muslims must be able to affirm God's sovereignty on earth and remove those who usurp this sovereignty by legislating laws. 4) Muslims must be free to establish the great justice that all people may enjoy its benefits. "This means that Muslims must combat oppression and injustice wherever they are found, even though it is the oppression of the individual against himself, the oppression of society against itself or the oppression of the government against its constituents."[72]

Islam confronts the forces that attempt to impede its progress in three ways: 1) People are invited to join Islam, the final religion, the way of truth, the law that realizes justice for all people. 2) If they refuse, they are asked to pay *jizya* (poll tax) as a symbol of the cessation of hostilities and their affirmation of the freedom of Muslims to propagate their faith. 3) If they refuse, then the only option left is war since the enemies of Islam would be fighting God's will, keeping humanity from enjoying the benefits that accrue from the Islamic order such as "light, justice and comprehensive peace."[73]

Mawdudi's works which were published in Arabic after 1951 appear to have had a great influence on Sayyid Qutb's writings on *jihad*. He quotes him as he accuses the West of exaggerating and embellishing the word jihad that it has come to mean savagery and bloodletting. It conjures up "for them" images of "savage hordes with burning eyes, yelling Allahu Akbar . . . killing kafirs" [nonbelievers]. The West on the other hand has "spent centuries and generations fighting and struggling to fulfill their base desires and quench their burning greed. That is their [unholy war] which they have waged against weak nations in both the East and the West seeking markets for their products and land to colonize."[74]

Jihad for Qutb is a practical matter which should not be renounced. He attacks the modernists who wrote extensive apologetic on jihad insisting that it was defensive in nature. Qutb calls them "spiritual and intellectual defeatists" who believe that they are providing a service to Islam by separating it from its method which he affirms is the destruction of all the existant unjust sovereign political systems.[75]

Jihad is an essential characteristic of Islam commanded in the Quran. That Muslims of his day were not fighting is due to the fact that "they do not exist."[76] Most Muslims have compromised with oppressive powers. Meanwhile, he affirmed that a study of the Quran and the history of the early believers reveals that "when God restrained Muslims from jihad for a certain period it was a matter of strategy and not of principle."[77] Thus Muslims should not be embarrassed and renounce force. If they are incapable of fulfilling the injunction, it is a temporary situation.

Jahiliyyah

One of the concepts that Qutb popularized has come to refer to all cultural aspects of the modern world. Used in the Quran to refer to the period of ignorance in which the Meccans lived prior to the revelation, *jahiliyyah* is currently being used by many authors and preachers as a pejorative term to designate all that one considers to be alien to Islam. Qutb concedes that he has borrowed this definition from Mawdudi's *Mabadi al-Islam.*[78] "*Jahiliyyah* is not a period in time. It is a condition that is repeated every time society veers from the Islamic way whether in the past, the present or the future."[79]

The difference between the historical *jahiliyyah* and the one prevailing in the world today is that the latter is more sinister since it is created willfully by men who usurp the role of God. The older *jahiliyyah* was based on "ignorance, naïveté, and youth. As for contemporary *jahiliyyah* it is grounded in knowledge, complexity and scorn."[80] Furthermore, it is established on the principle of "aggression against God's governance on the earth" under the rubric of the right to create visions and values and to legislate laws disregarding God's Path.[81]

> Today we are in a similar or darker *jahiliyyah,* than that contemporaneous to early Islam. All that surrounds us is *jahiliyyah,* people's visions, beliefs, their habits and customs, their source of knowledge, art, literature, rules and laws, even what we consider as Islamic education, Islamic sources, Islamic philosophy and Islamic thought—all of it is the product of *jahiliyyah.*[82]

The list of disciplines and intellectual endeavors that are relegated to *jahiliyyah* include all areas of the humanities and the social sciences including "philosophy, history, psychology (except the experimental branch), ethics, comparative religion, sociology (except statistics). . . . Most of it, if not all of it bears implicit or explicit enmity to the general religious understanding of life and in a specific way to the Islamic worldview."[83] The only aspects of culture that are universal and therefore could be learned from other societies are science and technology. This is restricted only to the area of technical know-how and does not include the "philosophical and metaphysical interpretation of scientific findings."[84]

The concept of *jahiliyyah* as developed by Qutb projects a Manichean view of the world. The believers are to be made aware that there is a constant struggle between the Islamic worldview and that of *jahiliyyah:* a struggle between faith and disbelief, faith in the one God and polytheism.[85] In essence, it is an ideological conflict.[86]

> There are two kinds of culture: Islamic culture based on the fundamentals of the Islamic worldview and the *jahili* [ignorant] culture which manifests itself in a variety of systems, all of which can be explained by one principle . . . that of elevating human thought [to the status] of a God not necessitating recourse to God's guidance.[87]

The *jahili* systems which humans adopt for themselves in disregard for God's guidance bear the evident imprint of human ignorance, weakness, and desire. They are contrary to human nature and can only provide partial solutions to human problems inevitably resulting in harm to some segments of society.[88]

Confined to the role of *jahiliyyah* is any system that relegates God and religion to the personal sphere. God must be in command of all life. *Jahiliyyah* is any society that is subservient to its own rulers and is obedient to its visions, values, concepts, feelings, traditions, and customs.[89] In a sense that Islamic concept of the creaturehood of man is affirmed as bondage to God. Thus any act of obedience to any system is dismissed as an act of worship. To obey anyone save God is to dwell in *jahiliyyah*.

Muslims must be wary not to accommodate the *jahili* system on any issue since that would lead to compromising the whole. The only proper relation to such a system is total rejection.[90] The systems Qutb defined as *jahili* include the communist nations because of their atheism that ascribes the moving power in the world to matter or nature and perceives human activities in terms of economics and production. They are in error also because they have established systems where allegiance is to the party, where the collective leadership usurps the role of God in determining human welfare. They limit human reality to the realm of the animal by focusing on food, drink, clothing, housing, and sex.[91]

Jahili systems include all the polytheist systems that exist in India, Japan, the Philippines, and Africa. It also includes Christian and Jewish nations because of their deviation from the truth in allowing their religious leaders to compromise with existent political orders legislating for them what is right and wrong, a matter which is the exclusive domain of God.[92]

The *jahili* systems include all societies that claim to be Muslim. They accept alien ideas and incorporate them into the Islamic framework in areas such as government, law, values, customs, and traditions. Some of these Muslim societies openly admit their adherence to secularism. They claim a respect for religion but ignore the laws of God as revealed in the Quran. They are *jahili* systems because they choose to operate outside the divine injunctions. They ignore the reality that God is the only source of knowledge. "He rules. His religion is the way of life." They fail to understand that "the source of power is God, not the 'people,' not the 'party' nor any human being."[93]

Muslims must also be alert that those who develop Islamic jurisprudence do not include alien ideas, Islamizing them.[94] That can only provide half-solutions due to their human source. Only when an Islamic order is devised based on the law of God and the teachings of the Prophet Muhammad can a comprehensive system come into being, one that is attuned to the reality of humanity and one that is capable of transforming people from *jahiliyyah* into Islam.[95]

The only effective means of eradicating a *jahili* society is the existence of a dynamic Islamic social organism with its superior strategy, ideology, and integration.[96] Muslims have a record of the only effective method that can replace *jahiliyyah*. The Meccan experience in which the Quranic message confronted the *jahili* forces directly, challenging the very existence of their society was not a theoretical, theological, or scholastic approach[97] but one that was frank, open, and constant.

Jamaah

For Qutb, Islamic society is "not a mere historical form that is hidden in the memories of the past, it is the demand of the present and the hope of the future."[98] Although it is grounded in eternal historical values, it is not a fixed historical entity. It can take a variety of shapes and forms as long as it adheres to the basic eternal values which include the total subordination of all things to God, the adherence to the ideology, the affirmation of the humanity of man over materialism, the domination of human values over animal instincts, the inviolability of the family, the vicegerency of man on earth according to God's covenant and prescription, the governance and supremacy of God's system and laws in the affairs of the world.[99]

The suppression of the Muslim Brotherhood and the imprisonment of its leaders led Qutb to define the process *(manhaj)* through which an Islamic society can be realized in a world where *jahili* systems prevail. He advocated the necessity of the *jamaah,* the coalition of committed individuals who become a vital organic cell of Muslims dedicated to the materialization of the true Islamic society, one in which the teachings of the Quran and the Prophet Muhammad impact all aspects of life: political, economic, legal, as well as cultural.

The necessity of the *jamaah* as the dynamic nucleus of the Islamization process is based on prophetic precedence, the method employed by the Prophet

Muhammad in organizing the first Muslim community. Qutb points out that for thirteen years the Quran was revealed in Mecca as a confrontation, challenging the very existence of Meccan society, addressing itself to the daily interaction of members of the society. At the same time, the Quran concentrated on the ideological nurture of the *jamaah,* providing them with the assurance of divine support and the strength to persevere in their struggle against the oppression of the *jahili* society in which they dwelt.[100]

The Islamic society is therefore a coalition of believers bonded together in their commitment to a specific system. It comes into being by necessity when three individuals believe in this ideology. They form an independent entity separate from the one they live in.[101] This separation is inevitable in view of the struggle that ensues between them and the *jahili* systems. This proceeds from the dynamic nature of Islamic society that seeks to convert all people to its own unique world view of life, history, values, and goals, rejecting all those advocated by others.[102] Commitment to these ideals is guaranteed to bring forth a utopian system where social justice is the essential core of the comprehensive ideological vision.

For Islam to be a reality in this world, unencumbered by human modifications to accommodate human demands, the existence of the *jamaah,* the vanguard of committed Muslims willing to separate themselves from the allurements of society, is crucial.[103] For unless faith is realized in a dynamic *jamaah,* it is incomplete.[104] This is not brought about through hasty action, but by a deliberate gradual inculcation that transforms the individuals as they translate the ideology into life itself. The Islamization of the *ummah* can only proceed from the *jamaah* whose total existence is focused on the mission it has assumed. Its membes become the nucleus, the agents, the life, the organization, the action as well as the evidence of Islam itself.

Hijrah

Historically used in reference to the emigration of the Prophet and his followers from Mecca to Medina in 622, hijrah was reified by Qutb to designate a necessary phase in the process of Islamizing society. From this vantage point, the goal of the historical hijrah was not the establishing of the Islamic society in Medina; rather, it was the eradication of the *jahili* system in Mecca and its environs. Thus the formation of the *jamaah* in Medina as a community governed by God's law in all aspects of life was an essential stage that must be realized before the transformation of the rest of *jahili* society can proceed. This for Qutb became the Islamic method as revealed by God.

Islam is not a mere theory to be believed and practiced by its adherents while they continue to live in a *jahili* society. Should they continue to dwell in such a system they will compromise Islam's very existence by consciously or inadvertently defending it against outside threats. Islam and *jahiliyyah* cannot coexist; Muslims must consciously separate themselves from the prevailing social order and seek to eradicate it.[105] Those who do not appropriate the Islamic vision and heed its method by organizing their existence on the basis of an organic dynamic coalition with one commitment and one leadership are responsible for the corruption and chaos in the world. The *hijrah* is necessary until restoration of the divine order is implemented.[106]

> It is important that anyone who wants to be a Muslim needs to know: he cannot practice his Islam except in a Muslim milieu, where Islam is sovereign. Otherwise he is misguided in thinking that he is able to realize Islam while he is a lost or persecuted individual in a *jahili* society.[107]

Hakimiyyah

Among the key terms utilized by Qutb to elaborate his ideas concerning the Islamic Imperative is that of *hakimiyyah* (sovereignty, governance). Unlike the others discussed above, it is not a Quranic term but one that is derived from the term *hukm* (to rule, or govern). It appears to have come into Arabic use in the writings of Mawdudi.

For Qutb, the term *hakimiyya* designated divinity, which was synonymous with ultimate sovereignty. For him the confession of faith reiterated daily by Muslims, "there is no God but God" is a revolution against human sovereignty of any shape or form, whether that be of priests, tribal chiefs, princes, or governors—in matters of conscience, rituals, wealth, or justice.[108] "There is no governance except for God, no legislation but from God, no sovereignty of one [person] over the other because all sovereignty belongs to God."[109]

Thus while the concept of *hakimiyyah* insists on God's absolute sovereignty, it also affirms man's "total bondage to God alone." This means that Muslims have to operate within the confines of the Quranic revelation as it was taught by the Prophet Muhammad, whose "role as instructor concerning this bondage" is affirmed in the second half of the *shahadah* (confession of faith): "Muhammad is the Messenger of God."[110]

A truly Islamic society can only be established according to the tenets of the *shariah* which alone can guarantee freedom and justice to all believers. "As long as there is a group of people legislating for others, equality and absolute dignity cannot be realized." In the final analysis Lordship must belong solely to God.[111]

The *shariah* is not restricted to legal injunctions or to principles of government. "The *shariah* of God means everything that God has decreed to organize human life. This includes the principles of faith, the principles of the administration of justice, the principles of morality and human behavior as well as the principles of knowledge." It also includes instructions concerning all social, economic, political, ethical, intellectual, as well as aesthetic aspects of life.[112]

It should be noted that the ideologies of the Islamic revolutionary groups in Egypt, al-jamaat al-Islamiyyah, have been inspired by Qutb's writings. The polemics by and against the most famous among them, al-Jamaah al-Muminah, nicknamed Ahl al-Takfir wa-al-Hijrah is full of references to *hakimiyyah, jahi-liyyah, jihad, hijrah,* and *jamaah.* It highlights the necessity of absolute commitment to the way of God superseding any kinship allegiances.[113]

Manhaj

Thus for Qutb, the Quran and the experience of the first Islamic community under the guidance of the Prophet Muhammad in Mecca and Medina provide the Muslims with guidelines for the present as well as the future. This Islamic *manhaj* (process, method) as well as the content of the faith cannot be separated. They were revealed not only to transform perceptions and ideological commitments, they were to provide the means by which God's nation can be built in the world. This method is authentic.

> It is not the product of a special period, environment or a particular situation relevant to the development of the first Muslim *jamaah.* It is the method without which this religion cannot be established at any time.... It is a divine program which by its nature invalidates all human systems which are [innately] deficient.[114]

This Islamic *manhaj* can be divided into four phases. The first phase is the one in which the *jamaah* is formed.

The second phase is one in which the *jamaah* becomes persecuted for its faith. Its summons to the *jahili* system in which it lives to turn to the way of God, elicit a reaction of *zulm* (oppression). This leads to a detachment from the system. This soon precipitates into an awareness that "there are two parties in all the world: the Party of God and the Party of Satan. The Party of God which stands under the banner of God and bears his insignia and the Party of Satan which includes every community, group, people, race and individual who do not stand under the banner of God."[115]

The third phase is the *hijrah,* the conscious separation from the *jahili* system, a period for the integration of the *jamaah* into an organic unity, based on mutual support and brotherhood. During this period the group is strengthened through additional consciousness raising.

The final stage is that of victory and consolidation of power. Its proof is the conquest of Mecca and its restoration to Islam. Thus Islam is realized as a new vision for life, humanity, and society. It affirms the sovereignty of God implementing a new political order, one governed by the will of God.[116] God himself grants and consolidates the victory.

ISLAM AND GOVERNMENT

Islam must have control of the government in order to ensure an equitable distribution of wealth as well as provide guidance in matters of public policy and must seek to implement its vision and values.

The governments based on the ideology of Arab nationalism have failed.[117] This was due mainly to the apeing of European institutions by attempting to separate religion from society with the total disregard of the fact that Europe had no other alternative since Christianity failed to provide adequate legislation for everyday life. It concentrated its efforts exclusively on spiritual matters, faith and prayer. Islam, on the other hand, is aware that an ideology cannot be realized in life unless it is embodied in a specific social system and is transformed into laws that govern life and organize its changing relationships.[118]

Political leaders in the Arab world, Qutb believes, have been aided by professional religious men who sanctioned and perpetuated the ideas of Arab nationalism. Such religious men are the enemies of Islamic government because they are aware that Islam has no professional clergy. "If Islam were to rule, the first act would be to banish the indolent who do not work" but make "a living in the name of religion."[119]

As for those "whose spirit is colonized by Europe and America" and who claim that it is reactionary and old-fashioned to establish a nation on the basis of religion, Qutb offered the example of Israel as a nation "founded on religion—and religion alone—Judaism is not a nationality but a religion. It includes the Russian, the German, the Pole, the American, the Egyptian and the Yemeni ... everybody and his brother on the face of the earth, of all nationalities," yet it is supported by the British, funded by the Americans, and accepted by the Russians.[120]

Thus for Qutb, given the example of Israel, Western objection to the formation of an Islamic government in the Arab world is not based on the objection to a nation based on religion per se; rather, it stems from the inadequacy of Christianity for such a task and the fear of Islamic success. "It is inevitable that Islam must govern because it is the only positive, constructive ideology which formulates from Christianity and communism a perfect mixture which encompasses all their goals adding balance, integration, and equilibrium."[121]

In all of his writings, Qutb did not offer any specifics about the form of an Islamic state. He emphasized that it must be democratic based on the Quranic principle of *shura* (consultation) (S. 3:159). However, since the *shariah* did not specify a particular method—whether that was to be the opinion of all Muslims or that of the informed leadership—he left the method of arriving at such a consensus to be determined by the needs of the age. The principle that Muslims should participate in managing their affairs is inviolable.[122]

As for the ruler, he receives his power and authority from "one source, the will of the governed." His role is not to legislate or improvise new ways of government; rather he is restricted to the "supervision of the administration of the *shariah*." Only then is he to be obeyed. That is a covenant with those governed—obedience contingent on the faithfulness of the governor to the *shariah*. If he deviates, their duty of obedience ceases. The Quran insists that anyone who does not govern by God's relevation is a kafir (S. 5:44) to be disobeyed and fought by committed Muslims.[123]

In this manner Islam guarantees individual dignity by ascribing governance to God. He is the master and the only ruler. He alone legislates. There can be no other despot since all men, ruler and ruled, are equal before Him. Thus a nation based on religious law grants complete freedom from all bondage on earth.[124]

Equity in the Islamic state is not limited to the political sphere. It operates on all levels and aspects of human relations. While offering no specific blueprint, Qutb insists that Islam provides for a comprehensive social system that guarantees the means of earning a livelihood to each person.[125] He affirms that Islam is for private property; however it places limits on the means of accruing wealth. It prohibits gambling, usury, deceit, hoarding, and monopolizing of resources.[126] Capital in Islam should not be restricted to the rich. The right of ownership of personal property is tempered by the right of the Islamic government to redistribute wealth according to the needs of the time. Thus if it appears to be in the public interest and in order to establish justice, the government may appropriate from the rich not only their profits but part of their capital. Furthermore, Islam insists that natural resources such as "fire, grass and water" must be in the domain of public ownership.[127]

Qutb affirmed that Islam also employs two means for recycling wealth. For him, *zakat* is not a benevolence; it is a tithe that assures that the poor participate in the bounty of the rich. The other instrument utilized is the principle of "where did you acquire this?" which places the onus on the rich to justify that what they possess was acquired through legitimate means; otherwise, it is subject to confiscation and redistribution.[128]

Qutb spells out in one of his books what can be categorized as the Islamic work ethic.

Islam is the enemy of idleness that proceeds from the accumulation of wealth. There is no recompense except for effort and no wages except for work. Those who are indolent who do not work, their wealth is unlawful. The government must utilize that wealth for the benefit of society and must not keep it for the lazy unemployed. Islam is the enemy of idleness that proceeds from laziness, the love of lowliness, making a living through the easiest means such as begging. It warns those who beg and are capable [of work] that on the Day of Judgment they will have no flesh on their faces! Islam is the enemy of idleness in the name of worship and religion. Worship is not an occupation of life. It has but its appointed time. The Quran says: When the Salat [daily ritual prayer] is done, dispense in the earth and seek the benefit of God.

The expending of life in hymn singing and praying with no beneficial employment that enhances life is not Islamic.

If matters were in the hand of Islam it would enlist all men to work. If they can't find employment the government will provide it for them. The right to work is like the right to eat.[129]

CONCLUSION

In his writings on the nature, function and mission of Islam, Sayyid Qutb appears to have passed through several stages in which he became progressively radicalized. His ideas generally reflect a growing frustration with the inability of the nationalist governments to produce a comprehensive change in the social, political, and economic environment of Egypt that would be of benefit to all Egyptians. His various experiences and concerns precipitated in an intellectual journey that began by endorsing a liberal secularism, passing through a moderate transitional period, and culminating in the advocacy of Islam as revolutionism that seeks to eradicate all existent systems and to replace them with an Islamic order.

His starting point was his deep conviction that Western society (in its capitalist and Marxist versions) has failed to provide for the welfare and dignity of humanity. This precipitated the inward search for an authentic alternative that would put an end to the bewilderment and confusion that plagued the contemporary Arabs. The answer he found was in the Islamic tradition: the Islamic alternative was proposed as a response to the categorical claims of both East and West of the sole possession of truth and the insistence that all people must subscribe to one or the other system.

Qutb believed that the collapse of the West was inevitable because it was based on ideas and principles of human origin and therefore founded on misconceptions, errors, and considerations of self-interest. As such, Western systems are diametrically opposed to the Islamic foundation of life grounded in the revelation of God. By separating the social dimension from the fundamentals of religion, Western society became an enemy of the religious perception of being. Thus for Muslims to emulate social, political, or economic patterns of European society is an apostasy.[130]

Recognizing the appeal of Marxist thought to the poor and the dispossessed, Qutb consciously set out to design an Islamic vision that would supersede it. The Quranic verses that he highlighted projected an Islamic worldview that

accepted the struggle between a variety of social forces as a given. While realizing that oppressive forces are active in the world and must be combatted by
the believers, the Quran saw it as a struggle between the Party of God and the
Party of Satan. Communism failed to see that the underlying conflict in the
world is not economic but spiritual in nature. The arena of the struggle is not
over the possession and monopoly of wealth, but for the heart, soul, allegiance,
and commitment of human beings.

In this, religion is not the opium of the people utilized to reflect the ideas of
those in power, justifying and legitimizing their position; rather it is the active
ingredient that alters the consciousness of the individual who becomes a trans-
former of society.

From this vantage point, Islam, as the divine revelation, must organize all
aspects of life; and every committed Muslim is charged with the task of summoning the world to the truth. This is the way of God which has been made
manifest in the lives of the prophets. Muslims must pattern their lives according
to this precedent. This ensures that the method used for the rebirth of the
dynamic Islamic society follows the model in which God has consistently functioned, manifesting Himself in history. Those who seek to propagate Islam in
the world must aspire to purity and constancy of commitment; there can be no
compromise in the hope of gaining some transitory advantage. They should
reject anything that is un-Quranic. A period of separation *(hijrah)* for consciousness raising, nurture, growth, and strength is necessary for both the individual
and the group. Finally, persistence and patience will prevail if men but stream-
line their work with the laws of nature which is the divine order that governs
the world.

Notes

1. His book *hadha al-Din* has been translated into Urdu, German, and Swahili: *al-
Mustaqbal li-Hadha al-Din* into Turkish, and *Maalim fi al-Tariq* appeared in two French
translations. Those available in English include: *This Religion of Islam, Islam the Religion of the Future, Milestones, Islam and the Universal Peace, Social Justice in Islam,*
and *In the Shade of the Quran,* vol. 30.

2. Sayyid Qutb dedicated his *al-Taswir al-Fanni fi-al-Quran* (Cairo: Dar al-Maarif,
1963) to his mother. In the introduction he relates that his abilding vision was of her
sitting listening with visible pleasure to Quran recitation on the radio or during the rec-
itations she sponsored at home (p. 5). His *Mashahid al-Qiyama fi-al-Quran* (Cairo: Dar
al-Shurug, 1947) is dedicated to his father of whom he writes, "You planted in my consciousness while I was a small child—the fear of the Last Day. You did not preach to
me, nor did you reprimand me, but you lived an awareness of the Last Day." The image

that persisted of his father was when each night after finishing supper he recited the first sura of the Quran and dedicated it to his departed parents in the hereafter (p. 5).

3. For a complete list see Mahdi Fadlallah, *Maa Sayyid Qutb fi Fikrihi alsiyasi wa-al-Dini* (Beirut: Muassasat al-Risalah, 1978), pp. 57–61. Fadlallah divides them into several categories: (a) works a literary criticism—*Muhimmat al-shair fi-al-Hayat*, al-Taswir al-Fanni fi al-Quran, Mashahid al-Qiyamah fi al-Quran, Al-Naqd al-Adabi: Usuluhu wa-Manahijuhu, Naqd Kitab Mustaqbal al-Thaqafah fi Misr: (b) novels—*Tifl min al-Qaryah, Al-Atyaf al-Arbaa, Ashawk* (co-author), *al-Madina al-Mashurah*; (c) education (allco-authored)—*al-Qasas al-Dini, al-Jadid fi al-Lughatu al-Arabiyyah, al-Jadid fi al-Mahfuzat, Rawdat al-Tifl*; (d) religious—*al-Adalah al-Ijtimaiyyah fi al Islam, Maarakat al-Islam wa-al Rasmaliyyah, al-Salam al-Alami wa-al-Islam, Nahwa Mujtama Islami, Fi Zilal al-Quran, Khasais al-Tasawwur al-Islami, al-Islam wa Mushkilat al-Hadarah, Dirasat Isla-miyyah, Hadha al-Din, Al-Mustaqbal li-Hadha al-Din,* and *Maalim fi al-Tariq*. Several collections of his essays have appeared posthumously including: *Tafsir surat al-Shurah, Tafsir Ayat al-Riba, Qissat al-Daawah, Maarakatuna Maa al-Yahud, Islam Aw La Islam, Fi al-Tarikh Fikratun wa-Manhaj,* and *Afrad al-Ruh*. Other books announced but not published include: *Hulm al Fajr, Qafilat al-Raqiq, Lahazat maa al-Khalidin,* and *Amerika allati Raayt*.

4. Numerous articles in such magazines as *al-Liwa al-Jadid, al-Dawah, Majallat al-Shihab, Majallat al-Azhar,* and *Majallat al-Iman*.

5. Fadlallah, *Maa Sayyid Qutb*, p. 44. He reportedly suffered from ailments in his stomach and lungs, among others.

6. Sayyid Qutb, *Maarakat al-Islam wa-al-Rasmaliyyah* (Beirut: Dar al-Shuruq, 1975 (4th printing)), p. 36.

7. *Maarakat*, pp. 34–38.

8. Ibid., pp. 50–51.

9. Ibid., p. 66.

10. Sayyid Qutb, *Nahwa Mujtama Islami* (Beirut: Dar al-Shuruq, 1975 (2nd printing), pp. 47, 50, 64.

11. *Maarakat*, pp. 67–68.

12. Sayyid Qutb, *Maalim fi al-Tariq* (Cairo: Maktabat Wahbah, 1964) (English translation: *Milestones,* Cedar Rapids, Iowa: Unity Publishing Company, n.d.).

13. *Maarakat*, p. 29.

14. Ibid., p. 30

15. Ibid., p. 33.

16. Ibid., pp. 10–11

17. Ibid p. 11

18. Ibid., p. 21

19. Ibid., pp. 26–27.

20. Ibid., pp. 25–26

21. *Fadlallah*, p. 91.

22. Sayyid Qutb, *Khasais al-Tasawwur al-Islami wa-muqawwamatuhu* (Cairo: Issa al-Babi al-Halabi wa-Shurakauhu, 1962), p. 45.

23. Ibid., p. 66.

24. Ibid., p. 49.

25. Ibid., p. 53.

26. Ibid., p. 83.

27. Ibid., p. 84.

28. Ibid., p. 88.
29. Ibid., p. 92.
30. Ibid., p. 98.
31. Ibid., p. 105.
32. Ibid.
33. Ibid., p. 108.
34. Ibid., p. 115
35. Ibid., p. 127.
36. Ibid., p. 128.
37. Ibid., p. 130.
38. Ibid., p. 134.
39. Ibid., p. 183.
40. Ibid., p. 190.
41. Ibid., pp. 206–10.
42. Ibid., p. 311.
43. Ibid., p. 315.
44. Ibid., p. 321.
45. Ibid., p. 222.
46. The Nature of the Islamic method ... is the insistence on the establishment of the kingdom (*mamlakat*) of God on earth and to bring all humanity from the worship of created things to the worship of God alone." *Fi Zilal al-Quran* (Beirut: Dar al-Shuruq, 1973–74) vol. 10, p. 117.
47. *Maalim,* p. 226.
48. Sayyid Qutb, *Hadha al-Din* (Cairo: Dar al-Qalam, 1962), p. 19ff.
49. Ibid., p. 18.
50. Ibid., p. 20.
51. Ibid., p. 4.
52. *Maalim,* p. 196.
53. Ibid., pp. 185–6.
54. Sayyid Qutb, *Fi Zilal,* vol. 9, p. 1433.
55. Ibid., vol. 1, p. 128–9.
56. Ibid., vol. 1, p. 108.
57. *Maalim,* pp. 82–3; cf. *Fi Zilal,* vol. 9, p. 1434.
58. *Maalim,* p. 81; cf *Fi Zilal,* vol. 9, p. 1433.
59. *Maalim,* p. 90; cf *Fi Zilal,* vol. 9, p. 1436.
60. *Maalim,* p. 93.
61. *Fi Zilal,* vol. 10, p. 1544.
62. *Maalim,* p. 173.
63. *Fi Zilal,* p. 1435.
64. *Ibid.,* p. 1435.
65. Sayyid Qutb, *al-Salaam al-Alami wa-al-Islam* (Beirut: Dar al-Shuruq, 1974), p. 174.
66. *Fi Zilal,* vol. 9, p. 1434.
67. *al-Salaam,* p. 172.
68. Ibid., p. 21.
69. Ibid., p. 22.
70. Ibid., pp. 23–4.
71. Ibid., p. 24.
72. Ibid., p. 170.

73. Ibid., p. 175.

74. *Fi Zilal,* vol. 9, p. 1444.

75. *Maalim,* p. 78.

76. *Fi Zilal,* vol. 10, p. 1634.

77. *Maalim,* p. 112.

78. Ibid., p. 63.

79. Ibid., p. 224.

80. *Hadha al-Din,* p. 93.

81. *Maalim,* p. 9.

82. Ibid., p. 21.

83. Ibid., p. 171.

84. Ibid., p. 173.

85. Ibid., p. 213.

86. Ibid., 248.

87. Ibid., p. 173.

88. *Hadha al-Din,* p. 34.

89. *Maalim,* p. 63; cf. *Fi Zilal,* vol. 10, p. 1556.

90. *Maalim,* p. 24.

91. Ibid., pp. 119–21.

92. Ibid.. pp. 121–3; see also Yvonne Haddad, *Contemporary Islam and the Challenge of History* (Albany: State University of New York Press, 1982), pp. 89–96, 162–68.

93. *Maalim,* pp. 125–28.

94. Ibid., p. 59.

95. Ibid., p. 200.

96. Ibid., p. 64.

97. Ibid., p. 61.

98. Ibid., p. 159.

99. Ibid., p. 161.

100. Ibid., pp. 48–50.

101. Ibid., p. 157.

102. Ibid., p. 156.

103. Ibid., p. 11.

104. *Fi Zilal,* vol. 10, p. 1560.

105. Ibid., p. 1556.

106. Ibid., p. 1560.

107. *Hadha al-Din,* p. 33.

108. *Maalim,* p. 28.

109. Ibid., p. 31.

110. Ibid., p. 165.

111. *al-Salaam,* p. 63.

112. *Maalim,* pp. 166–67.

113. Qutb insisted that Islam does not demand that the Muslim refrain from having relations with relatives; however, it warns against any human relationship becoming dominant in the life of the individual at the expense of his undeviating commitment to God (*Fi Zilal,* vol. 10, p. 1615). For further information on the relation of the group to Sayyid Qutb see Yvonne Haddad, "The Quranic Justification for an Islamic Revolution," *The Middle East Journal,* 37:1 (Jan. 1982): 18. See also Salim Ali al-Bahnasawi, *al-Hukm*

wa-Qadiyyat Takfir al-Muslimin (Cairo: Dar al-Ansar, 1977) and Hasan Ismail al-Hudaybi, *Du'at la Qudat* (Cairo: Dar al-Tibaah wa-al-Nashr al-Islamiyyah, 1977).

114. *Maalim*, p. 54.
115. *Hadha al-Din*, p. 84.
116. *Fi Zilal*, Vol. 10, p. 1522.
117. *Maalim*, p. 59.
118. *Maarakat*, p. 55.
119. Ibid., p. 105.
120. Ibid., p. 97.
121. Ibid., p. 61.
122. *al-Salaam*, p. 123; *Maaraket*, p. 72.
123. *Maarakat*, pp. 73–74; *al-Salaam*, p. 123.
124. *al-Salaam*, p. 63.
125. Ibid., p. 144.
126. *Maarakat*, p. 40.
127. *al-Salaam*, p. 144.
128. Ibid., p. 144.
129. *Maarakat*, p. 52.
130. *Maalim*, p. 181.

FIVE

Mawdudi and the Islamic State

CHARLES J. ADAMS

No discussion of the demand for an Islamic state in Pakistan and no account of the contemporary resurgence of Islam would be complete without attention to the major role played by Abul Ala Mawdudi in these movements. By far the most powerful and effective factors that worked to create sentiment for an Islamic state in the years immediately after the partition of the Indian subcontinent and the creation of Pakistan were Mawdudi and the movement which he founded and headed, the Jamaat-i-Islami. Indeed, it would be difficult to think of any issue of religious significance that has arisen in Pakistani public life concerning which the same could not be said. Mawdudi was, until his death in 1979 but especially to the time of his resignation as amir of the Jamaat-i-Islami in 1972, the best known, most controversial, and most highly visible of all the religious leaders of the country. He poured his energy unstintingly into speeches, writings, and religious and political activities, leaving behind a rich heritage of literature and thought on most of the issues that have troubled Pakistanis over the years. The number, size, and range of the published writings from his pen in the periods both before and after the founding of Pakistan are truly remarkable.[1] They are evidence of an altogether unusual degree of devotion and great creativity. Although these works were produced originally in Urdu primarily for a Pakistani or Indian audience, many have been translated into other languages of both the Islamic and the Western worlds. Thus, Mawdudi has attracted attention outside the Indian subcontinent, especially in other Muslim countries where he is now revered as one of the foremost modern exponents and interpreters of Islam. Today Mawdudi must rank among the most popular and respected authors in the Islamic domains, if indeed he is not the single most widely read writer among Muslims at the present time. His writings give strong expression to the themes basic to the present-day Islamic resurgence. When the time comes for the religious history of Islam in the twentieth century to be written, Mawdudi's name will unquestionably have a prominent and an honored place in its pages.

HISTORY

Mawdudi began his public career as a journalist. At the early age of seventeen he served as editor of the weekly *Taj* in Jabalpur, and he continued in journalism for about ten years before turning to other pursuits. The peak of his career in journalism was the editorship of *al-Jamiah,* the newspaper of the Jamiyat-i Ulama, which position he held from 1924 until he resigned in 1927. This was a position of extreme importance and influence for so young and inexperienced a man. It brought him into close contact with some of the leaders of Indian Muslim life and thought, and it gave him occasion to express himself on virtually every subject of importance to the world-wide Muslim community anywhere in the world.

Mawdudi came from a family steeped in the religious tradition of Islam. On his father's side he was descended from the Chishti line of saints; in fact, his very name, Abul Ala, derives from the first member of the Chishti *silsisah* (a Sufi "order") to have settled permanently in India. His own disposition toward religion was quite marked throughout his life. From his childhood Mawdudi received religious nurture at the hands of his father and from a variety of teachers employed by him to ground his sons in the essentials of Islam, Islamic history, and in the literary heritage of the Arabic, Persian, and Urdu languages. Mawdudi had a minimum of formal education (three years), and such as he did get was given him in a *madrasa.* His instruction included very little of the subject matter of a modern school; and European languages, specifically English, were not among the courses he followed. He studied English only some years later when his editorial work made knowledge of the language imperative. In spite of the strictness of his upbringing and the father's determination to insulate the youngest son of the family against the influences of Western culture and education, as a young man Mawdudi had the reputation of independent mindedness and of being something of a rebel against traditional ways. Despite these tendencies in his youth, throughout Mawdudi's long life religion was the strong foundation upon which all else was to rest, and with the passing of time it became increasingly clear to him that he had a religious mission to fulfill among India's Muslims.

A significant turning point came for Mawdudi in connection with the murder of a certain Swami Shradhanand by a Muslim fanatic in 1925. Swami Shradhanand had been the principal figure of the Shuddhi movement, an effort among Hindus to reconvert to Hinduism members of the depressed classes of India who had become, at least nominally, Muslim. The murder provoked a great public outcry, and criticisms of Islam and the Muslims began to appear in the public press. There were accusations that Islam relies upon the sword for its propagation, charges of bloodthirstiness, and repetitions of the old slander that

Islam promises Paradise to those who kill an unbeliever. Mawdudi undertook to answer these charges in the columns of *al-Jamiah,* and the articles which he wrote were later collected into a book and published as *al-Jihad fil Islam.* These essays were his first serious full-scale attempt to write about an Islamic issue, and the effort of composing them apparently brought an insight of great vividness and intensity into the nature of Islam. Many years later he said that the composition of this book was the decisive factor in bringing him to a full understanding of the Islamic way of life.[2] Virtually all of the themes and emphases that characterize his later activity and more mature thought are discussed there. Indeed, the entirety of his subsequent career might be viewed as a working out of the implications of this seminal document.

A second turning point came for Mawdudi in the early 1930s. He had given up his journalistic work in 1928 in favor of literary pursuits and historical research. In 1932 he associated himself with a journal called *Tarjuman al-Quran,* in Hyderabad. This journal, which was originally founded and managed by another, became Mawdudi's sole responsibility in 1933. It has been regularly published from that time until the present with only occasional and brief interruptions. With the assumption of this burden Mawdudi began to see that a mission had been laid upon him: to invite the Indian Muslims to a renewed and purified commitment to Islam and thereby to save them from destruction by the malevolent forces sweeping over their society. He thereupon launched himself into a work of criticism, analysis, and exposition of Islam designed to capture the allegiance of the Indian Muslim leadership and to redirect it into the path of Islam.

Mawdudi professed to see a great flood about to sweep away the Muslims into oblivion. It was to warn them against this danger that he took up his pen in what was to become the central effort of his life. He explained his purpose as twofold: 1) to expose the nature of *jahiliyyah* and all the evil that it contains especially in its modern Western form; and 2) to present the Islamic way of life in a reasoned, argued, demonstrated, and systematic fashion.[3] In practical terms this meant criticism of Western civilization, examination of the various schools of Muslim thought and their shortcomings, and detailed discussions of certain basic issues in Islamic theology such as *aqaid* (beliefs) and *imaniyat* (faith), Islam's understanding of the nature of man, and the fundamental principles of the civilization it seeks to create. The discussion of Islamic doctrines led him to define his religious views very carefully and resulted in much controversy and counter-criticism by sections of the community on whose toes he had trod. Particularly strong were the ripostes he stimulated among those Muslim leaders he blamed for the fallen state of the community.

Mawdudi's efforts were aimed primarily at the leadership of Muslim India, at its educated and intellectually inclined segments, not at the common man.

The first task he felt to be that of capturing the minds of the leadership because they carried the greatest weight in the society and would determine its destiny. Concentration upon the leadership was the logical outgrowth of a theory of social change expressed in *al-Jihad fi-l Islam,* in which Mawdudi explains that the character of a social order flows entirely from the top down. Authoritarianism was not only the idea of any society in his view but was at the factual level the way in which all societies actually function. He believed that practical social change was impossible unless the theoretical views held by the leadership changed first. His was not a mass movement, nor was the Jamaat-i-Islami in later years ever to become one. The task then was one of education in the principles of Islam, of religious nurture, and of correction of the erroneous ways of thinking into which the Muslim upper classes had been seduced by the agents of *jahiliyyah.* Concentration fell upon the rectification of individual Muslim character and life but not yet upon organized social efforts to transform the society.

Yet another significant change of direction was effected for Mawdudi in 1937 when he began for the first time to concern himself specifically with the political problems then agitating Muslim India. The stimulus to the new orientation was the 1935 Government of India Act and the provincial elections of 1937, as well as certain actions of the Indian National Congress such as the Muslim Mass Contact Movement launched in March 1938. In his youth he had had some part in the Khilafah movement, the Swaraj movement, non-cooperation, etc., and as editor of an important newspaper had inevitably concerned himself with politics both inside and outside India. Now, however, the situation was different, and the involvement was both more intense and more direct. India, it appeared, stood on the eve of achieving independence from the British, who had effectively controlled it for 150 years, and the constitutional arrangements of the future independent India were even then being determined in the debates among the various parties of Indians who opposed the British. Mawdudi saw a great danger in this situation for Muslims. He was fearful lest the political order then being constructed would result in the loss of Muslim identity, culture, and religion by submergence in the civilization of the Hindu majority. Mawdudi's response to the threat was again to take up his pen to address the problems at issue. From 1937 to 1941 he published in *Tarjuman al-Quran* a series of essays dealing with these political matters and their implications for the Muslims. The essays were later printed in book form in the three volumes entitled *Musulmanon awr Mawjudah Siyasi Kashmakash* and in the volume called *Masalah-i Qawmiyat.*

The particular source of Mawdudi's apprehension was the stance of the Indian National Congress, which affirmed that all Indians constitute a single nation and that a future government in India must be both democratic and sec-

ular. Mawdudi simply did not believe that the Muslims of the subcontinent
constituted one nation along with all other Indians. He insisted that the Muslims had an identity or nationality of their own which was Islam; they were
bound together not by ties of race, geography, language, mutual interest, economics, or even culture, but by their commitment to follow the will of God in
their lives. There were no claims which Muslims could raise against the British
or anyone else on the basis of their common nationhood with other Indians; he
stated quite unequivocally, in fact, that Islam is the polar opposite of nationalism and all that nationalism stands for. Within a united India where all were
Indians together, it would be construed as traitorous for Muslims to attempt to
maintain their peculiar identity and sense of nationality. They would, in fact,
be constrained to accept and manifest the identity of the Hindu majority.
Although he shared the desire of other Indians for freedom from British rule,
independence from the British was not worthwhile in itself if the Indian Muslims were to exchange servitude to outsiders for servitude to the majority within
their own country. Hence, he urged the Muslims not to participate in the freedom struggle being led by the Indian National Congress and its nationalist
Muslim supporters.

Mawdudi's criticism and fear of democracy echo a similar line of thinking.
Democracy, he believed, is the kind of government in which the majority rules
whether its views be right or wrong, and in which a minority may hope to have
a voice in affairs only by transforming itself into the majority. No guarantees
of rights or other safeguards that might be built into a democratic constitution
could truly protect a minority in a democratic polity. Democracy, when reduced
to its bare bones, amounts only to the tyranny of the majority. Since the Muslims were clearly a minority in India and likely always to remain so, the creation
of democratic institutions in the country was nothing less than a deadly poison
for them, one that would destroy their culture, take away their identity, and
finally force them even to give up their religion.

A third plank in the Congress-led freedom movement was the desire to foster
a secular government in India. In Mawdudi's writings the term employed to
translate "secular" (la dini) in fact literally means "religionless," and it should
be evident that a religionless social system would be anathema to him. Theoretically, in a secular system the government would adopt a neutral attitude
towards all religious groups, treating them equally. What would actually occur,
according to Mawdudi, was that the government would be secularist only
toward the minority religious groups, neither helping nor restraining them, but
it would be necessarily partisan toward the religion of the majority. Congress
secularism he believed to be based on Gandhi's teachings about tolerance
toward all other religions; it was nothing but a drawing out of the implications

of a specifically Hindu point of view. Congress policy would, therefore, result in the imposition of Gandhi's religious views on the whole of India.

Mawdudi's answer to the situation of the Muslims in India was that they should become better Muslims. As the result of that very process they would achieve organization, discipline, and social effectiveness, enabling them to transform the whole of India into Dar al-Islam (haven of Islam). The basic cause of the perplexing circumstances in which the Muslims found themselves was the error of thinking of themselves merely as a nation and then struggling for the well-being of the nation in economic, political, and social terms. The Muslims were not, he held, a nation in the ordinary sense but rather a party of community, a group "based upon principles and upon a theory."[4] They were not like the English, the Germans, or the French, nations in the conventional and racial sense, but rather like the socialists or the communists, a party ruled by a system of ideas. If the community, instead of striving for its mundane interests in the Indian situation, would seek to advance its principles and realize its theory of human life, it would attain a peak of power that would allow it to make over the whole of India into the image of the Islamic ideal. The thing required to meet the exigencies of Indian politics was the emergence of a *Salih Jamaat*, a righteous party or community characterized by a clearly defined ideology, allegiance to a single leader, obedience, and discipline. Of such a nature were the fascist and communist parties of Europe which, though minorities in large populations, were able to dominate the majority in their respective countries.

Mawdudi's advice to the Muslims amounted to saying that they could not participate in the political struggle for the independence of India in any of the forms in which it was being waged. All of the parties on the Indian side of the struggle, whether Muslim or Hindu, were operating in terms of ideals that were not principally and genuinely Islamic. The Muslims had to be true to themselves, to become more fully and more steadfastly Muslim, even if this meant the postponement of independence until it could be achieved in the right way and on the right basis. The Muslims should stand aloof and nurture themselves on the ideals that Islam teaches. This was on the one hand a counsel of despair and on the other a strong call to a life centered upon religion for the entire community. This attitude of "you can't get there from here" is the basis for the frequently repeated accusations that Mawdudi gave aid to the British imperialists and that he opposed the movement for Pakistan.

In August 1940, meeting in the shadow of the great Mogul Fort and the Badshahi Mosque in Lahore, the Muslim League passed its now famous Lahore Resolution which called for the establishment of autonomous states in the Muslim majority areas of the subcontinent. From that point on, the great weight of Muslim opinion rallied behind the demand for Pakistan, using the same argument Mawdudi had employed, that the Muslims of India were a distinct nation, but claiming also that their nationhood gave them the right to a state and territory of their own. In Mawdudi's eyes the new thrust of Indian Muslim political agitation, like what had gone before it, did not meet the needs of the Muslims but posed a new threat to them, for its ultimate result was only to substitute Muslim nationalism for Indian nationalism, and nationalism in whatever form was bad. Both were fundamentally secularist conceptions of the Muslim destiny, and both were concerned with the mundane interests of people, not their ultimate orientation.

Mawdudi's response to the Lahore Resolution was to launch into a new phase of the work of Islamic reform. He now turned to organized activity at the social level. In August of 1941, again in Lahore, a group of some seventy-five interested persons met in response to Mawdudi's invitation, and the Jamaat-i-Islami was born, he being elected as its first Amir or leader.

The intention in founding the Jamaat-i-Islami was to give concrete realization to the concept of the *Salih Jamaat* which Mawdudi saw as the answer to the Indian Muslim political dilemma. In ideal terms the purpose of the Jamaat-i-Islami was "that the whole system of human life in all its departments be erected upon the worship of God and the guidance of the prophets (upon them all be peace)."[5] From a practical and short-range standpoint the purpose was to prepare an organized and disciplined group of sincere Muslims capable of achieving the victory of Islam in the subcontinent. Thus, were the efforts toward partition to fail, there would be a group to counter the results of the failure; and were the efforts to succeed, there would be a group to spread the knowledge of Islam in both India and Pakistan. The Jamaat-i-Islami was to train a class of leaders for the Indian Muslims who would build Muslim civilization and culture. In a speech delivered to the Jamaat-i-Islami in Lahore in December of 1944, Mawdudi said that in his opinion the greatest reason for the world's evils lay in the failure of righteous people rightly to understand what righteousness is. Their tendency is to live in isolation and to leave the affairs of the world in the hands of evil people. The cure for this regrettable state of affairs is to organize a group dedicated to righteousness. There is no political task nobler than this, and there is no greater degree of political success than to achieve such an organization. His Messianic vision became clearly apparent in the ringing declaration that such a group, once formed, would be able to control all aspects of the world's life and to effect a sweeping revolution among mankind.[6]

The period between the founding of the Jamaat-i-Islami in 1941 and partition of India in 1947 Mawdudi has characterized as the time of "organizing and training." His energy and that of his fellows was given to the production of a body of literature that set out the nature of Islam in greater detail and with more depth than had the writings of the earlier phase. At the same time the structure of the Jamaat-i-Islami was refined and strengthened. Neither the membership nor the influence of the Jamaat-i-Islami was large during these years, and its political stand was unpopular among the majority of Muslims, for the organization, following Mawdudi's lead as its Amir, held itself aloof from the fierce political fight raging in India. These years did, however, weld the Jamaat-i-Islami into a disciplined and responsive organization which, when its opportunity for action came shortly after partition, was able to act swiftly and effectively.

When partition was effected in August of 1947, Mawdudi was living with a group of his followers in a small religious community in East Punjab which he called Dar al-Islam. Mawdudi had left Hyderabad in 1938 to take up residence there as the result of a correspondence between himself and Allamah Muhammad Iqbal. Mawdudi's purpose in moving was to pursue the ideal of a community where the principles of Islam would be fully realized. When the violence and communal hatred that accompanied the partition threatened to overwhelm the tiny and defenseless community, he migrated with his companions to Lahore. A portion of the Jamaat-i-Islami, however, remained in India, and from this time on the Indian and Pakistani sections of the Jamaat were two separate organizations. Almost from the moment of Mawdudi's arrival in Pakistan the Jamaat-i-Islami threw itself into activity to assist the refugees pouring into the ill-equipped new country. The partition of India is beyond all question one of the most traumatic events of the entire twentieth century, resulting in the brutal deaths of hundreds of thousands of people and the displacement of millions of others, as well as suffering and economic loss on a colossal scale. In these tragic circumstances members of the Jamaat-i-Islami in different places, many of them refugees themselves, rallied to help those in need.

More important than the relief efforts, however, was the political activity of the Jamaat-i-Islami. Beginning in January 1948, less than six months after Pakistan's birth, the Jamaat launched a campaign for the creation of an Islamic state in the country. This effort depended heavily on the literature that flowed from Mawdudi's pen[7] but was also taken to the common people by every means at the organization's disposal. Its purpose was to bring as much pressure as possible upon the Constituent Assembly—charged with writing a constitution for the country—to found the polity upon Islamic principles.

Mawdudi was undoubtedly right in his analysis of the situation in Pakistan at the time when he said: 1) that there was great confusion in the national movement because of the diversity of groups and viewpoints that had participated in it; 2) that there was no clear conception of the nature of the new state; 3) that the leadership of the movement rested in the hands of a highly secularized and Westernized portion of the population; and 4) that popular sentiment was strongly in favor of an Islamic state. One of the first and essential tasks was to write a constitution for Pakistan, and the constitution-making process inevitably raised the question of the role of Islam in forming the institutions of the government and in determining its actions. Since the Pakistan movement as conducted by the Muslim League in pre-partition days was concerned largely with the mundane economic, social, and political interests of the Muslim population and since it was based on a conception of Muslim nationalism that apparently aimed at a secular and democratic state for Muslims much like that which the Indian National Congress sought to create in India, Mawdudi felt that quick action had to be taken to assure that the desires of the majority of Muslims for an Islamic system were not thwarted. Mawdudi saw the achievement of independence in 1947 as a revolution, and he called it by that name (*inqilab*); but it was, he said, merely a revolution in the external circumstances of the Muslims and did not effect the inward and essential changes that Islam demanded. The movement for an Islamic state sought to give the country a definite Islamic stamp before it settled into some other and unacceptable mould whose impression would be very difficult to eliminate.

Mawdudi and the Jamaat-i-Islami were not alone in agitating for the Islamic state. They were joined by a variety of other bodies and individuals, notable among them the ulama organization, the Jamiyat-i Ulama Pakistan, and had behind them the sympathies of the mass of the population. All parties concerned were in agreement that Pakistan was to be an Islamic state though their respective visions of such a state differed widely. Mawdudi himself had discussed the nature and requirements of an Islamic polity in his writings from 1939 onwards. The expectations that people entertained about the creation of an ideal Islamic order that would solve all their problems were strongly reinforced in the difficult days immediately following partition. Faced with the almost insuperable problems of organizing a state, of dealing with refugees, and of conducting the war in Kashmir, the politicians appealed to Muslim religious sentiments as a means of rallying, uniting, and pacifying the population. It was made to seem that Islam contained the resolution of all difficulties, the one possibility for a true paradise on earth. The result was a wave of enthusiasm for an Islamic polity that swept over Pakistan, leaving the authorities little choice but to accede.

From one perspective the leadership shared this enthusiasm because its generally liberal and modernist version of Islam also embraced the concept of an Islamic polity. For many conservatives, however, the conception of the Islamic order held by the leadership proved difficult to distinguish from outright secularism. There is, therefore, no doubt that the Islamic state agitation was a source of great concern for the political leaders and the bureaucracy of the country who viewed it as a threat both to their own power and to the ideal of liberal democracy that inspired most of them. The government was in an uncomfortable dilemma; it could not afford to oppose the idea of an Islamic state, but neither could it allow conservative Islamic opinion to prevail.

The essentially religious question of the Islamic state was the most visible issue in Pakistani public life in those early days, but it was not necessarily the most important one. There were other and, in the final analysis, more telling practical considerations as well—such things as the distribution of powers between the center and the provinces, the relations of the two wings of the country, the problem of a national language—and a host of specific local and provincial issues where the power and influence of individual members of the Constituent Assembly—which it must be remembered was also the federal legislature—were at stake. The greatest obstacles to securing agreement on a constitution arose from such matters as these and not from religious issues; but in the public mind the religious questions occupied the foremost place. Given the depth of public response to religious questions and their potential explosiveness, it is not surprising that the government should have been unhappy about Mawdudi's activities. The suspicion, hostility, and fear that the successive governments of Pakistan have exhibited toward Mawdudi and the Jamaat-i-Islami date from this early time in the country's history. Before the end of 1948 Mawdudi and two of his associates were arrested and the newspapers of the Jamaat-i-Islami closed down. The incident that provoked Mawdudi's arrest was statements made in a mosque in Peshawar in which he denied that the war in Kashmir fulfilled the conditions of an Islamic jihad.

An important new stage in Pakistan's development toward becoming an Islamic state was reached for Mawdudi with the passing of the Objectives Resolution by the Constituent Assembly in March 1949. The Resolution, which was very general and quite ambiguous in its provisions, represented a compromise between the liberal modernist and the more conservative factions in Pakistan. The Resolution began with these words:

> Whereas sovereignty over the entire universe belongs to Allah Almighty alone, and the authority which He has delegated to the State of Pakistan through its people for being exercised within the limits prescribed by Him is a sacred trust . . . .

In a later passage it speaks of Pakistan as a country

> Wherein the principles of democracy, freedom, equality, tolerance and social justice as enunciated by Islam, should be fully observed;

> Wherein the Muslims of Pakistan should be enabled individually and collectively to order their lives in accordance with the teachings and requirements of Islam, as set out in the Holy Quran and Sunna . . . .

Those portions of the Objectives Resolution, especially the first and last clauses quoted, as well as its general tone amounted to a declaration by the Constituent

Assembly that Pakistan was to be an Islamic state, at least as Mawdudi under-stood them. A state that was previously non-Muslim and where there were *shar-iah* injunctions against Muslim service to the state or participation in its polit-ical life now became Muslim by, in effect, the recitation of a kind of collective *shahadah* (confession of faith). The state was made entirely different from what it had been. It was now lawful to serve the state of Pakistan, its laws were wor-thy of acceptance, there might be resort to its courts, and it was now proper to take part in its elections and to serve in its Parliament. The Jamaat-i-Islami adapted its policies accordingly, began to gear itself to participate in elections and continued agitating for provisions in the still unformed constitution that would reflect the character of an Islamic state. As Mawdudi said: "Now that this has become a regularized Islamic state, it is no longer the country of the enemy against which it is our duty to strive. Rather, it is now the country of friends, our own country, the strengthening, construction, and progress of which are our duty."[8]

Mawdudi's attitude toward the Objectives Resolution was, to say the least, surprising. Before partition he had rejected Pakistani nationalism, indeed, all nationalism, and condemned the leadership of the Muslim League for not fol-lowing Islamic principles or having Islamic goals before it. The Objectives Res-olution changed nothing of substance in Pakistan; it did little more than give vague expression to a desire for an Islamic order, and it left unclear and indef-inite far more than it specified. Pakistan was to remain a distinct national entity separate from other Muslim states; its state institutions, essentially British, were in no way changed; there was no significant shift in state policies; even the lead-ership remained the same. Perhaps most significant of all, the Objectives Reso-lution did not so much as mention the Islamic *shariah,* much less its being the law of the land. Yet Mawdudi felt that the Objectives Resolution transformed Pakistan into a "regularized" Islamic state. The explanation of Mawdudi's stand is probably to be found in the fact that his approval of the Objectives Resolution provided him personally and the Jamaat-i-Islami generally with a legitimate the-oretical basis for participating in Pakistani political life.

Pressure for the creation of institutions and other arrangements in accord with Islamic injunctions continued in Pakistan after the passing of the Objec-tives Resolution. The ulama in particular stepped up their contributions to the discussions.[9] Religious pressure on the government and the constitution makers reached a new high in 1952 and early 1953 in connection with the agitation against the Ahmadiyah sect which broke out in parts of Punjab. Begun by rep-resentatives of the Ahrar party in an effort to regain the public support they had lost by their opposition to the creation of Pakistan, the agitation demanded that the Ahmadiyah be declared a minority and that Chawdhri Zafrullah Khan, a prominent Ahmadi, be removed from his post as Foreign Minister. Virtually all religious parties supported these demands as did the majority of the general public. Violence soon began with the loss of Ahmadi lives and destruction of property. Because of delays by both the provincial government in Punjab and the federal government in taking steps to deal with the situation, it had finally to be controlled by the imposition of martial law in March 1953 as things were getting out of hand. Among other actions of the military authorities were the arrest of prominent ulama and of the leaders of the Jamaat-i-Islami. Mawdudi himself was brought before a military court and sentenced to death for his part in what had happened—specifically for the publication of a pamphlet entitled "The Qadiani Question,"[10] Qadiani being another name for the Ahmadiyah. The summary decision of the court was greeted with a great public outcry, especially in religious circles, and the sentence was commuted to fourteen years' rigorous imprisonment in May of the same year. The sentence was not carried out, however, and Mawdudi was released after twenty months' confinement.

Although Mawdudi had not personally participated in the agitation against the Ahmadiyah nor was the Jamaat-i-Islami officially committed to the "direct action" of the agitators,[11] he clearly had sympathy for the movement. He saw the agitation as an opportunity for advancing some of his own constitutional proposals for the Islamic state and for strengthening his hand in the political game. In consequence he joined with the ulama in discussions of the Ahmadi issue and for a time even acted as their leader and spokesman. The period of the anti-Ahmadi agitation represents the peak of Mawdudi's influence and prestige among the members of the religious class, and, as well, the peak of his influence in the affairs of Pakistan. That he was able to gain so high a standing among the ulama is somewhat astonishing in view of his strong cricicisms of their conservatism dating back to the 1930s and in view of his unwillingness in his constitutional proposals to accord to these venerable religious authorities the role of final arbiters in all matters Islamic. Mawdudi, however, was a very persuasive man, one not given to extremes in his manner of expression, and with a strong bent toward logic. In his qualities of leadership he stood head and shoulders above most of the ulama, and it was perhaps only to be expected that he would come to the fore as their spokesman. In any event, his role in drafting some of the documents which the ulama issued in regard to the constitutional issues in Pakistan was decisive.

When the first constitution of Pakistan was finally promulgated, in 1956, it was not the result of open public debate either in the new Constituent Assembly (the first one had been dissolved by the Governor General in 1954) or elsewhere. Rather, it was the outcome of some assiduous backroom work by the Prime Minister, Chawdhri Muhammad Ali, and was promulgated suddenly with very little advance notice or preparation of the public. Nonetheless, it was welcomed enthusiastically in the country, and among those who acclaimed and accepted it were Mawdudi and the Jamaat-i-Islami.

If Mawdudi's attitude toward the Objectives Resolution passed by the first Constituent Assembly was surprising, his approval of the 1956 Constitution was even more so. The constitution envisaged a government for Pakistan that was plainly modeled upon British parliamentary democracy. To be sure, it contained elements of a specifically Islamic nature, but many of these were vague, and the most important of them, namely, the provision that no law would be enacted or allowed to continue in force that was contrary to the Quran and Sunna, was specifically declared to be non-justifiable, thus depriving it of real force. The constitution was a compromise between the views of the modernist liberal political leadership, Westernized intellectuals, and the bureaucracy on the one hand, and more conservative religious groups on the other. On balance, however, the content of the constitution and the kind of state that it aimed to create were strongly tilted in the direction of the modernist preferences. In accepting it Mawdudi not only seemed to deny much of what he had previously insisted upon as characteristic of an Islamic state but, indeed, left intact very little that would distinguish him from the liberal constitutionalists he had previously so bitterly criticized for their un-Islamic ways.

The promulgation of the 1956 Constitution effectively brought to an end widespread discussion of the role of Islam in the constitution of Pakistan. Not long afterward, in early 1958, the country came under military rule, and with the exception of the interregnum of the Bhutto era, has remained under military control until this day. Both Mawdudi and the Jamaat-i-Islami continued to be active politically when permitted to do so by government, and they continued to see their ultimate purpose as the establishment of a genuine Islamic order in Pakistan. Many of the issues which they raised were of relevance to constitutional law, but the atmosphere of general public concern for the Islamic state and of interest in its nature and the means of achieving it was not to return. Only to a limited extent did some of these questions resurface in connection with the constitution promulgated by Ayub Khan and at the time of the Ahmadi issue in 1974. The role of Mawdudi and his movement from this point onward became specifically political in the sense of fighting on particular issues and of trying to achieve some degree of political power. His most important contributions to the understanding of the Islamic state belong, therefore, to the pre-partition period and to the period of Pakistan's history leading up to the ill-fated 1956 Constitution.

UNDERSTANDING OF THE ISLAMIC STATE

We may now consider the content of Mawdudi's conception of the Islamic state.[12] The need and justification for an Islamic state follow for Mawdudi from the nature of the universal order. The Islamic state, therefore, is part of a broad,

integrated theology whose cardinal principle is the sovereignty of nature's creative Lord. There is, Mawdudi reasoned, basing himself on the Quran as well
as his own observation, a law that governs everything that exists. That law is
nothing other than the will of the Creator who ordained that things should be
as they are, that the heaven should be above the earth, that the night should
follow the day, and so forth. Most of nature—all of it, in fact, except the human
race and they only in respect to some social and moral matters—necessarily
conforms to the divine law. Some men may entertain the illusion of their own
independence, but there is no independence; all in reality is ruled by God. In
this sense the natural order respects the divine will and obeys it and may for
that reason be said to be Muslim, or in other words to be among those who
submit themselves to the overlordship of God. It is not necessarily so with men,
however, who alone among all creation have been endowed with free will or
the capacity to choose whether in their behavior they shall follow the will of
their creator or not.[13] There is no question, however, that the divine will has
laid down a law (shariah) for human conduct just as it has ordained a law for
everything else. One's attitude toward that law is the central issue of human
life; upon it turns the decision whether one shall submit to the divine will for
the way in which life should be lived or whether he shall rebel against it and
go astray into error. Submission (islam) brings in its train earthly blessing and
heavenly reward while rebellion and refusal to submit produce only evil, unhappiness, and eternal punishment. Thus, the historical controversy that Islam has
awakened has not had to do with whether God is the creator or not but with
man's willingness or refusal to recognize him as Lord; the issue is not the control of nature but rather who shall claim the allegiance of men.[14]

The law that God has prescribed for men to follow is readily accessible to
all[15] who may be interested to learn its provisions; it is set forth in the Book of
God, the Quran, and in the lives of those through whom God has revealed His
book, the Prophets; but especially in the practice of the last Prophet, Muhammad. Prophecy is the means chosen by the divine to give concrete expression
and exemplification to its will. These two, the Quran and the Sunna of the
Prophet, therefore, are the ultimate authorities for all true Muslims in every
question that may concern either their individual or their collective lives. When
the Quran and the Prophet speak on an issue, there is no higher court of appeal,
for to displace or impugn them would be an offense against the awesome majesty of God, to commit the unpardonable sin of associating others with the
prerogatives that are exclusively His. There is one true and unimpeachable
source of law, one rightful law-giver and only one, who has chosen to make his
shariah known through the agencies of revelation and prophecy. Everything
that men enact or observe as law in their societies is to be measured against the

dictates and the spirit of the ultimate law found in the two great sources of all Islamic inspiration.

Now, the *shariah* in both its broad objectives and its specific provisions envisages more than the fostering of good and the avoidance of evil in the lives of individuals. To be sure, the *shariah* prescribes the modes of worship for the individual and gives guidance for personal morality and action along with many other things of purely individual concerns, but it also prescribes directives for collective life as well. These directives touch such matters as "family relationships, social and economic affairs, administration, rights and duties of citizens, judicial system, laws of war and peace and international relations. In short it embraces all the various departments of life.... The *Shariah* is a complete scheme of life and an all-embracing social order where nothing is superfluous and nothing lacking."[16] The *shariah* is also an organic and integrated whole whose many aspects and provisions all flow logically and ineluctably from the same basic principles. The organic and all embracing nature of the divine law Mawdudi believed to have been forgotten or neglected by Muslims for most of their history since the time of the Rightly Guided Caliphs. What is presently known as Islamic law, he said, is only part of the larger whole. It has no independent existence and can neither be understood nor enforced apart from the total system to which it belongs.[17] The establishment of the Islamic system in its entirety was the goal toward which he strove; then alone could the provisions of Islamic law be properly implemented.

One of the implications of the organic understanding of the *shariah* that is repeated over and over again in Mawdudi's writings, almost like a refrain, is that the Islamic *shariah* does not recognize any division between religion and other aspects of life,[18] and most specifically between religion and the state. There is, he insists, no area of man's activity and concern to which the *shariah* does not address itself with specific divine guidance. Thus the cultivation of private piety, worship, and the ordering of the individual's relationship with God, the matters that are normally identified as "religion" in popular parlance, do not satisfy the demands of the *shariah*. True Islamic faith must issue into social actions and attitudes, must strive for the creation of an Islamic society as well as for personal righteousness. Secularism which Mawdudi equated with the separation of religion and state or with religionlessness, he considered to be the very contrary of Islam since it opened the way, as he saw it, to the exclusion of all morality, ethics, or human decency from the controlling mechanisms of society. This, he thought, was precisely what had happened in the Western world whose governments and social bases he never tired of condemning as unutterably and irredeemably corrupt. In his mind, morality of any kind was simply inconceivable without religion and the sanction of eternal punishment to support it. When religion is relegated to the personal realm, men inevitably give way to their bestial impulses and perpetrate evil upon one another. In fact, it is precisely because they wish to escape the restraints of morality and the divine guidance that men espouse secularism. The evils that arise from the domination of men over man cannot occur in the Islamic system because it will not permit the life of the state to be carried on in isolation from the dictates of religion and the divine law. From the perspective of the *shariah*, life is a seamless whole that must be lived in its entirety under the perspective and within the limits set by God.

A state or some other instrument that will exercise political power is the necessary consequence of this conception of a universal divinely ordained pattern for the life of men in the world. Not only would the realization of the objective of the *shariah* to foster good and interdict evil in society be impossible without the agency of the state and the power it commands,[19] but the *shariah* itself specifically prescribes the creation of a state as witnessed in certain verses of the Quran but above all in the examples of the Prophet and the Rightly Guided Caliphs.

> ... the reforms which Islam wants to bring about cannot be carried out merely by sermons. Political power is essential for their achievement ... the struggle for obtaining control over the organs of the state when motivated by the urge to establish the *din* (religion) and the Islamic *shariah* and to enforce the Islamic injunctions, is not only permissible but is positively desirable and as such obligatory.[20]

Accordingly, in Mawdudi's understanding, *shariah* also provides the basic outline of the state's nature and characteristics. Guidance for Muslims about the state which they are obligated to establish, or in other words, materials for the constitution of an Islamic state, are to be found in four principal sources: the Quran, the Sunna of the Prophet, the conventions and practices of the Four Rightly Guided Caliphs, and in the rulings of the great jurists of the Islamic tradition.[21] A careful study of these four sources all of which are written down, readily accessible, and well known is, according to Mawdudi, sufficient for the implicit and unwritten state constitution set out in the *shariah* to be reduced to systematic written form. For any careful student of these basic documents the necessity of an Islamic state will be inescapably clear, and it will also be abundantly evident precisely what an Islamic state is. The criticism of the many individuals—mostly liberal and Westernized modernists—who ridiculed the idea of an Islamic state in saying that the basic sources of Islamic faith offer no guidance about the practical aspects of establishing and forming a state, he rejected as ignorance or deliberate mischief-making. Pakistan's constitutional problem he saw as relatively simple: to bring to explicit expression what had so far been only implicit, to transform an unwritten constitution into a written one.

What then is an Islamic state? There are different ways in which this question might be approached and Mawdudi principally used two: 1) through discussion of the basic principles on which the state is erected; and 2) through consideration of its institutions and specific characteristics. We may consider these one by one.

Basic Principles

The first principle of the Islamic state is its recognition of the sovereignty of God. The practical meaning of this recognition is that God and not man is the source of law in a Muslim society.[22] God must be the legal sovereign as well as the Lord of nature. No man, therefore, should be allowed to pass down orders in his own right, and no one should be obligated to obey such orders if they are given, for the prerogative of command belongs only to God.[23] Neither any individual, although he be a king, nor any class or group of people, nor the state, nor even the people as a whole has the right to make law. God is the unique lawgiver and authority. There can be no legislation independent of His will in the Islamic state, and no one can change what God has decreed. The Quran denies the right of men to exercise any discretion in matters decided by God and the Prophet.[24] The Islamic state must, therefore, be founded on God's law as delivered through the Prophet. Prescriptions or proscriptions laid down by rulers or governments will bear authority and be legitimate only to the extent that they rest directly upon what God has decreed or follow from it. If a government disregards the law revealed by God, its authority will not be binding upon Muslims.

Mawdudi acknowledged that the concept of sovereignty is difficult to comprehend and that it has caused great confusion for political theorists. Sovereignty is, he says, "the most disputed issue of political science."[25] The entire problem arises, however, because men try to locate sovereignty in the wrong place; "the political philosophers have tried to place the cap of sovereignty on man, a being for whom it was never intended and whom it, therefore, never fit."[26] True sovereignty can be ascribed only to God who is Creator, Sustainer, and Ruler of the universe. Basing himself on an analysis of two words used for God in the Quran, *rabb* (Lord) and *ilah* (master and lawgiver), Mawdudi traces the root cause of most human misery and calamity to the tendency of men to dominate over other men, either by claiming themselves to be *rabbs* and *ilahs* or by investing objects, idols, political parties, nations, ideologies, etc. with the qualities of *rabb* or *ilah* and then manipulating the credulity of other men for their own purposes.[27] These problems, both the theoretical issues and the evil consequences of misconceived sovereignty, are obviated in the Islamic state by the state's uncompromising submission to the sovereignty of God. Every issue of law in an Islamic polity must be referred back to the will of God by reference to the Quran and the Sunna as the ultimate authorities. Thus, the basic source of everything the state will do is the divine will, and in this sense God is the only lawgiver.

The second basic principle of the Islamic state is the authority of the Prophet. The Prophets, all of them, are representatives of God, and in that capacity they exercise the political and legal sovereignty of God Himself.[28] They are entitled to the obedience of those who have pledged themselves to accept the sovereignty of God. "Whoso obeys the Messenger obeys Allah," declares the Quran (S. 4:80) This role of the prophets is the basis for Muhammad's Sunna being considered one of the ultimate bases of law.

The third basic principle of the Islamic state is its status as the vicegerent of God. The state does not make or enforce law in its own name but acts as the agent of its suzerain. Again, the basis for this principle is Quranic, found in Sura 24:55 where God speaks of appointing caliphs or vicegerents in the earth. An Islamic state should properly, therefore, be called a caliphate for such is its nature. At the mundane level when it is considered alongside other states in the world, the Islamic state may be called a sovereign state because it exercises authority within the territory that it controls. This sovereignty, however, does not extend to disregard of the law of God and gives it no ability either to change that law or to go beyond it.

Further, the Quran vests vicegerency in the entire Muslim citizenry of the Islamic state. The right to rule belongs to the whole community of believers. There is no reservation or special prerogative in favor of any particular individual, family, clan, or class.[29] Such a society cannot tolerate class divisions, and it will not permit disabilities for citizens on the basis of birth, social status, or profession.[30] Instead it must give unrestricted scope for personal achievement, always of course, within the limits prescribed by God. Neither is there any room for the dictatorship of one individual or a group of persons. The ruler in an Islamic state is only one caliph or vicegerent of God among an entire community of caliphs, and he rules only because the other caliphs have delegated their caliphate to him. He is answerable both to them on the one hand and to God on the other, as indeed all individual Muslims are directly answerable to God. The ruler must enforce the all-embracing divine law, but he cannot legitimately go beyond its dictates to try to tell people what kind of dress they must wear, what script they must use when they write, or how they must educate their children.[31] His personal whims or preferences count for nothing since he is but the agent of the agents of God on earth. Thus, "'popular vicegerency' . . . forms the basis of democracy in an Islamic state while 'popular sovereignty' is its basis in a secular state."[32] The practical meaning of this popular vicegerency is that the government of the Islamic state can be formed only with the consent of all the Muslims, or at least a majority of them, and can remain in office only so long as it continues to enjoy their confidence.

The fourth principle of the Islamic state is that it must conduct its affairs by mutual consultation (*shura*) among all the Muslims. While Islam does not prescribe the institutional form in which consultation must occur, leaving it to the community to devise the best and fairest means as may suit the conditions of a particular time and place, it does insist that all people concerned in a decision must be consulted, either directly or through their designated representatives whom they trust. Further, this consultation should be completely free and impartial without duress of any kind; otherwise it is hardly to be considered a consultation at all. The rule of consultation applies in the very first instance to the choice of the head of state, and because consultation must occur, there can be no question of dictatorship, monarchy, or despotism in the Islamic context.[33] Another of the implications of consultation is to deprive the ruler under any circumstances of the right and the power to set aside the constitution at his own will, for had he that power, he would be virtually uncontrollable.

The requirement that Islam lays down for mutual consultation and consent among the Muslims is the basis for the claim that the Islamic state is a democratic state. Mawdudi says the most appropriate title for the Islamic state would perhaps be to call it the "Kingdom of God," a notion that is rendered in English as "theocracy." This English word, however, according to dictionary definitions, carries the implication of rule by a priestly order who govern in the name of God. The word, therefore, will not do, and Mawdudi ventures to invent his own term to express the character of the Islamic polity. It is, he says, a theo-democracy,[34] something that is not to be compared with any other system of government that the world has ever known. It rests upon the twin principles of the sovereignty of God and the caliphate of man. It may be called theocratic in a sense because it bases itself upon God's command and will not depart from it. At the same time it is also democratic because it makes every Muslim the agent for the realization of God's will on earth and demands their constant mutual consultation in the community. The Muslims, Mawdudi says, have a limited popular sovereignty, expressed principally in their right to depose the head of government and their right to express themselves on every public issue.

All administrative matters and all questions about which no explicit injunction is to be found in the *shariah* are settled by the consensus among the Muslims. Every Muslim who is capable and qualified to give a sound opinion on matters of Islamic law, is entitled to interpret the law of God when such interpretation becomes necessary. In this sense the Islamic polity is democratic.[35]

Mawdudi was consistent with this principle in his constitutional proposals; he firmly resisted the desire of the ulama to be given the decisive say in what would be accepted as Islamic or not by refusing to support the demands for a board of ulama with review and veto power over proposed legislation.

These principles pose a number of difficulties. In the first place there is a failure to distinguish between the locus of sovereignty at the theoretical level and sovereignty in the more immediate sense of who actually exercises power. Mawdudi is concerned here, as almost everywhere else and in all of his thought, with the theory and not with practice. As his attitude toward the Objectives Resolution and the 1956 Constitution has shown, he was apparently satisfied when the theoretical principle of God's sovereignty was affirmed. Many of Mawdudi's opponents, however, especially the political leadership, were more concerned to grapple with the institutional forms of government and to attempt to settle the issue of where power would actually reside, how it would be exercised, in what ways it would be limited, how those limits would be enforced, etc.—i.e., they were dealing with down-to-earth issues of constitution making and politics, the kinds of problems that interest the political scientist. The statement that the Muslims have a limited popular sovereignty in the Islamic state— the term "limited popular sovereignty" is itself a contradiction in terms—is a vague and partial recognition of this problem. While sovereignty may belong to God, God does not Himself intervene directly in the life of the Islamic state to give orders, decide policies, or render decisions; there must be a human agency to do those things on His behalf and in His name. Again in theory that agency is the entire Muslim people acting as vicegerents of God, but practically speaking it is the ruler, whoever he may be and however he may be selected, who performs these functions in consultation with the Muslim populace. If the fault of theocratic governments lies in the fact that some human agency attains unrestricted power by acting in the name of God, thereby opening up the possibility of tyranny, then one is hard pressed to understand how the Islamic theo-democracy that Mawdudi proposed would escape this fault.

The contrast which Mawdudi drew between Western "secular" democracy and Islamic "theo-" democracy also is open to question. The comparison turns upon these two adjectives, one which indicates the primary role of rationality in all human affairs and the other which indicates the primacy of the divine will in the political process. In each case, however, the substantive "democracy" is the same. First of all, it may be questioned whether the conception of democracy in the Western world is as devoid of religious elements as Mawdudi implied. More important, however, is the fact that the comparison is made between elements of different orders. Secularism is not the name of one kind of polity while democracy and theocracy are other types of polities. If there is a legitimate comparison to be made, it can be drawn between the latter two, for that is where the issue lies. What is the source and the legitimization of law and the state, man's will or God's will? For all the attention he gave it elsewhere, Mawdudi ignores this basic problem at this point; he wants instead to distinguish between good democracy and bad democracy, claiming good democracy as the prerogative of the Islamic state. Retention of the word "democracy" to describe the Islamic state inescapably implies a major role for the will of the people in deciding matters. In effect, Mawdudi was claiming that both the will of God and the will of the people were effective loci of sovereignty since the latter would necessarily conform to the former. The rationale reflects a desire to have things both ways: to reject the very foundation of the concept of democracy as it is normally understood while at the same time claiming for oneself its appeal and its advantages. In a situation of controversy such as Mawdudi faced, the use of such arguments is perhaps understandable, but they did not contribute either to clarity of thought about the constitutional problem of Pakistan or to the strengthening of his own case.

Specific Characteristics and Institutions of the Islamic State

Among the numerous special characteristics that Mawdudi attributed to the Islamic state we may single out two for special consideration: the universal and all-embracing nature of the state and the ideological character of the state.

The purposes of an Islamic state are positive as well as negative, Mawdudi says.[36] The object of the state is not merely to prevent tyranny, to put a stop to evils of various sorts, and to protect its territory but, more basically, to foster a balanced system of social justice and to encourage every kind of virtue. To accomplish these ends requires political power and justifies the state in using all of the means at its command, propaganda, public education, etc., for the task. A state with these purposes cannot permit itself to ignore important segments of the lives of its people on the ground that they are beyond the scope of its authority. Its approach has necessarily to be all-embracing and universal. "Its sphere of activity is co-extensive with human life. . . . In such a state no one can regard any field of his affairs as personal and private."[37] In short the state is totalitarian, seeing it not just as the state's right but as its divinely ordained duty to exert control, based on proper moral and religious principles, over literally everything. To retreat from this position by permitting a large area of existence to remain beyond the state's authority would be equivalent to denying God's sovereignty over these excluded sections of life. In the controversy whether the best government is the least government or the most, Mawdudi was clearly on the side of those who favored the maximum of government control. He admitted that there was a resemblance between the Islamic state which he described and the fascist and communist states of the modern world in their mutual espousal of totalitarianism,[38] but as in the case of good and bad democracy he distinguished between good and bad totalitarianism. Islamic totalitarianism, he assured his readers, did not suppress individual liberties just as the limitations placed on popular sovereignty by Islam did not suppress human freedom but rather protected it. There also could be no hint of dictatorship in the Islamic state; it would, presumably, be a totalitarian theo-democracy. In comparison with the democratic states with their emphasis upon freedom on the one hand and the modern totalitarian states with the suppression of the individual on the other, Islam represented a balanced middle way that captured for itself the virtues of both of these extreme expressions of the political order while at the same time avoiding their excesses and shortcomings.

Individual liberties, it would appear, have to do with such things as styles of dress, the script to be used, the modes of the education of children, things mentioned above in connection with the limitations on the power of the ruler. Or alternatively, they may fall within the great category of acts that in Islamic law are classified as neutral or permitted, neither mandatory, recommended, hateful, nor forbidden; the neutral type of acts is by far the largest category of all. In connection with the rights of citizens Mawdudi also indicated some other restrictions on the power of the totalitarian state. It may not deprive its citizens of life, honor, or property unless Islamic law specifically justifies its doing so.[39] It may deprive no one of personal liberty in the sense of incarcerating him without a just cause in law and due process.[40] Mawdudi's own experience with the preventive detention statutes of Pakistan gave him good reason to qualify the totalitarian state in this regard. The state also must allow freedom of opinion and belief, permitting people even in organized groups, to hold such views as they will and peacefully to practice them so long as they do not disrupt the life of the state or attempt to impose their ideology on others by force.[41] Nowhere does Mawdudi enter into a detailed discussion of the precise limits of freedom in the Islamic state or explain how a state may both control everything and yet be limited in its power in certain respects, or leave a large area of conduct, indeed, the greater part of it, to individual discretion.

Another basic feature of the Islamic state consists in its being an ideological state. "All those persons who . . . surrender themselves to the will of God are welded into a community and that is how the 'Muslim society' comes into being. Thus, this is an ideological society—a society radically different from those which spring from accidents of races, colour, or country."[42] The cementing factor among the citizens of the Islamic state is the ideology that they all hold in common. This ideology aims at the reform of human society, and the state is its instrument for that purpose. It follows that the state must uphold its ideology and protect it against every effort to subvert it. Every other ideological state, Mawdudi argues, does precisely the same thing, drawing the line at those activities which are calculated to destroy the very foundations of the system itself. The Islamic state does not insist that everyone living within its territories subscribe to its ideology, for it does permit the existence of minorities that are not Muslim and acts to protect them, but it clearly cannot permit the system to be attacked with impunity either from within or without.

Two important consequences follow from the Islamic state being an ideological state. The first is that the state must be controlled and run exclusively by Muslims. It is of particular importance that the head of the state, the locus of all power and authority, should be Muslim, and others are rigorously excluded from that most important of all positions. Of almost equal weight is the need to have faithful Muslims in those other posts of responsibility where state policy is formed and the general orientation of the state's affairs determined. It is illogical in Mawdudi's eyes to expect people, non-Muslims, who do not believe in the Islamic ideology to uphold it and work out its consequences in the life of society. "It is a dictate of this very nature of the Islamic state that such a state should be run only by those who believe in the ideology on which it is based and in the Divine Law which it is assigned to administer."[43] People of other religious persuasions may hold non-sensitive posts in an Islamic order, including fairly high ranks in the civil secretariat and even in the military, but they must be rigorously excluded from influencing policy decisions. Mawdudi held the same view with regard to the electoral system, his principal argument for the retention of the pre-partition separate electorates in Pakistan being the necessity to preserve the purity of expression of Muslim opinion without its being influenced or swayed by outside and alien factors. In British India separate electorates had been a political device to protect the rights of the Muslim minority and give it a voice against the majority; in Mawdudi's thought it had become a means of ensuring the continuing dominance of the majority and of ensuring that the minorties would have no real say in the life of the nation.

In this connection even more important for Mawdudi than the necessity for key officers and administrators to be technically Muslim was the need for them to be true and good Muslims as well. To uphold the Islamic ideology, they should be personally committed to everything that Islam enjoins and practice it in their individual lives. "The administrators of the Islamic state must be those whose whole life is devoted to the observance and enforcement of this Law, who not only agree with its reformatory programme and fully believe in it but thoroughly comprehend its spirit and are acquainted with its details."[44] Mawdudi's vision of the government personnel of an Islamic state was that of a uniformly indoctrinated, disciplined, and cohesive cadre. Not only did he believe in a monolithic set of basic principles that would be fostered by a totalitarian government, but he apparently also saw no real room for disagreement or genuine debate on basic matters within the ranks of government at any level. Ideology, unity, and discipline were the keys to the ideal society that Islam seeks to create.

The second consequence of the Islamic state being an ideological state is worked out in its conception of citizenship. Since Islam is straightforward and truthful, it plainly prescribes two kinds of citizenship in the Islamic state,[45] one kind for Muslims who are domiciled within the territory of the state and the other kind for all those non-Muslims who agree to be loyal and obedient to the Islamic state in which they live. Upon the Muslims falls the full responsibility for the conduct of the state, for they alone fully believe in it. It is they who must assume the obligations that Islam imposes, including defense, and in return they have the right to be members of its Parliament, to vote in choosing the Head of State, and to be appointed to key posts where state policy is laid down. The non-Muslim citizens or *zimmis (dhimmis)* are guaranteed protection of life and limb, property and culture, faith, and honor.[46] What they are not guaranteed is either full political expression or full equality with their Muslim fellow citizens. The Islamic state will enforce upon them only the general law of the land while leaving them free to use their own community personal law to regulate affairs in that sphere. They have a number of other guarantees and protections extended to them as well, including the guarantee of the state to provide the basic necessities of life, food, shelter, and clothing to all of its citizens without distinction. Islam, Mawdudi says, does not wish to abolish or destroy its minorities but to protect them, and this policy stands in the starkest contrast, he argues, with state policy toward minority groups in every other political system in the world. Nonetheless, non-Muslims are clearly a category of second-class citizens in the Islamic state; the very recognition of two types or kinds of citizens and of two sets of rules to govern the two types has made them so. Their special and inferior position is justified by their non-adherence to the Islamic ideology.

> That this is the standpoint of Islam is proved by the utter absence of even a single instance in the days of the Holy Prophet (peace be on him) or the Caliphs where a *Zimmi* [*dhimmi*] (non-Muslim citizen) may have been made a member of the Parliament, or the Governor of a province, or the *Qadi,* or the Director of any Government department, or the commander of the Army or a Minister of the Government or may have been ever allowed to participate in the election of the Caliphs. . . .[47]

Mawdudi defends the Islamic stance on this matter as being humane and equitable, saying that Islam has been the most just, the most tolerant and the most generous of all political systems in its treatment of national minorities that disagree with the prevailing ideology.

We may now consider two of the institutions of the Islamic state as Mawdudi presented them, the Head of State and the Legislature, for the further light that they will throw upon his conception of a proper Islamic polity.

The key official in an Islamic state is its head or leader, who is called Imam, Caliph, or Amir. His is the major responsibility for the conduct of the state, and he is the real locus of power[48] since he acts as *khalifah* or representative of God on earth on the one hand and as representative of the Muslim people on the other. The ruler does not hold his position in his own right or because of the claims of his family or tribe to special status but rather as trustee of the divine law and the community's affairs. In consequence, there are limitations on his powers and his actions. He must first of all act according to the dictates of the *shariah;* and to enjoy the physical strength for the enormous burden he must bear. The Islamic state would have neither political parties nor a political opposition; its policies would be calculated to meet the real needs of the population and to keep it satisfied. Hence, there would be no reason for elections at regular intervals or for a change of administration.

In accordance with the general principle, that government must be managed through mutual consultation, the ruler is to be selected, appointed, or elected (all three words are used) through a consultative process. Mawdudi says that Islam does not limit the scope of its possibilities by attempting to lay down exactly how the choice of leader will be made.[49] Different methods may be appropriate to different times and circumstances as is evidenced by the lack of uniformity in the ways of deciding the succession of the first four caliphs after the death of the Prophet. What is important is that the ruler chosen should have the full confidence of the nation, and this will happen so long as three principles are observed: 1) the choice of the head of state shall depend on the general will with no one having the right to impose himself by force as ruler; 2) no clan or class shall have a monopoly of rulership; and 3) the selection shall be made without coercion.[50]

As for qualifications of the ruler, they have principally to do with his moral and religious character. The object of the selection process in the Islamic state is to find the best man for the task, and by "best" is meant not only the person most knowledgeable of affairs of state and most capable of running them but also the person of most upright character and greatest piety. If personal devotion to Islam be basic for administrators of the state at large, it is doubly so for the ruler who holds the reins that direct the entire social enterprise. For this reason any person who actively seeks an office of leadership, whether as ruler or as member of the legislative-cum-consultative body, is automatically disqualified from holding the post. The desire for public office represents a degree of greed and self-aggrandizement in an individual that is incompatible with true fear of God or with trustworthiness of character. Thus, though the Islamic state may choose to elect its public officials, there cannot be political campaigns or competitions for public favor; the personal characteristics of potential officials as well as the qualifications demanded of anyone holding office in an Islamic state would have to be made known through the agency of an Elections Commissioner or similar officer, not as a private undertaking. In legal terms the candidate for leadership must meet four criteria: 1) be a Muslim; 2) be male; 3) be of adult age and sane; and 4) be a citizen of the Islamic state. These four, however, merely mark out the formal legal bounds to eligibility for the rulership of the Islamic society; far more important is the quality of the ruler's commitment to Islam and the depth of his knowledge of what the Islamic system demands.

Many of the considerations that govern the choice of a ruler also apply in the establishment of the legislative or consultative body which is among the basic institutions of the Islamic state. The purpose of the body is to carry out the consultation about their affairs enjoined on Muslims. This body is chosen by some kind of reference to the general will, but the precise means is unspecified.[51] In the time of the Four Rightly Guided Caliphs the consultative body was not elected, and Mawdudi attributes this fact to the circumstances of the time.[52] The important thing about the selection process is that it should result in the choice of the best people by whatever means that result may be achieved. Like the ruler the members of the Majlis-i-Shura, as this body is called, must be trustworthy, good Muslims, male, adult, etc., and must not be active seekers of the office. In connection with a discussion of the scope of legislation in the Islamic state, Mawdudi goes into the qualifications of members of the Majlis-i-Shura somewhat more fully. What is said there, presumably, may be understood also to apply to the Head of State but in a superlative degree. One who acts as representative of the Muslim nation in its legislature must, he says,[53] first of all have faith in the *shariah* and an absolute determination to observe it. He must also have a good knowledge of the Arabic language in order to understand the Quran and to be able to derive the authentic Sunna. Sound insight into the Quran and the Sunnah, both in respect to detailed injunctions and the general principles of the *shariah* is required. Also important is an acquaintance with the opinions and views of *mujtahidin* (experts in Islamic law) in previous generations. This Islamic knowledge which is the foundation of all else must be balanced on the other hand by a solid understanding of the problems of our time. But by far the most fundamental of all the qualifications for a legislator, however, is a commendable character and a record of good conduct, for laws made by corrupt individuals will not inspire confidence in people. Also of basic importance is the fact that members of the Majlis-i-Shura are not to be the hand-picked men of the ruler but rather persons who enjoy the full confidence of the masses.

The fundamental matter in connection with the establishment of a legislature or consultative body in the Islamic state is the question of why there should be a legislature at all. According to the Islamic ideology as Mawdudi has described it, sovereignty and the right of making law belong to God. The law which He has laid down is all-embracing with complete guidance for every phase of human activity. No man shares in the divine prerogative of command, and no man can, therefore, be the originator of law. Such a position would seem to rule out both the need and the very possibility of a legislature in the normal understanding of the term. Even the trusted representatives of the Muslim people, elected though they may be, have no power to create law or to impose their views on people beyond the limits sanctioned by the *shariah*. As we shall see in what followed, in addition to providing a means for the ruler to fulfill the duty of consulting, the function of the legislature is really that of law-finding, not of law-making, and even that function is confined within quite strict limits. Properly speaking, the word legislature should not be employed for the kind of body that Mawdudi had in mind, and his use of the word is another instance of a general tendency, such as we have seen in connection with his conception of democracy, to use a broadly accepted modern term in a new and peculiar way that sharply distorts its usual meaning. This way of proceeding is motivated by apologetic concerns; it implies that all the positive aspects of representative government and of expression of the general will are respected and preserved in the Islamic state, even though the most basic principle from which these things arise, the idea of the sovereignty of the people, has been discarded.

Mawdudi himself puts the problem in this way:

> ... one is apt to think these fundamental facts [i.e., God's sovereignty and the necessity of obedience to the Prophet] leave no room for human legislation in an Islamic State, because herein all legislative functions vest in God and the only function left for Muslims lies in their observance of the God-made law vouchsafed to them through the agency of the Prophet. The fact of the matter, however, is that Islam does not totally exclude human legislation. It only limits its scope and guides it on right lines.[54]

The legislation envisaged takes four forms, the first of which is interpretation. Although the legislature cannot in any way go against what God has laid down, a great deal that is presented in Quran and Sunna requires to be understood more fully, and to this the members of the Majlis-i-Shura should turn their attention. In Mawdudi's view the consultative body is engaged in legislating when it investigates such issues as the precise nature of the law and its extent, the law's meaning and intent, the conditions in which the law was intended to be applied, the minor details of laws stated too briefly for straightforward application, and the applicability or non-applicability of a law in exceptional circumstances.[55] All of these functions depend upon the prior existence of the law that is to be studied and have more to do with what most people would consider the task of the courts than with legislation in the strict sense.

The second form of "legislation" has to do with situations where the *shariah* has not laid down specific injunctions but has made provision for analogous situations in which the same principles are in operation. In these circumstances the task of the legislature would be to determine the causal connections that are operative in the original instance and to apply them to the new situation. What Mawdudi has in mind here is the application of the traditional Islamic jurisprudential principle of *qiyas* which is one of four sources of law recognized by most Sunni Muslims following the opinion of the great jurist, al-Shafii.

A third form of "legislation" takes the form of inference from general principles to derive guidance for situations where the *shariah* has provided nothing specific. Here the job of the legislature is to penetrate into the spirit of the *shariah* and the intention of the Law-Giver and to formulate specific rules in accordance with these two. This kind of "legislation" as well as the preceding one plainly fall into the category of a law-finding process which is, indeed, the principal activity of the Islamic consultative body.

The fourth and final mode of "legislation" Mawdudi characterizes somewhat astonishingly as the "province of independent legislation." The "independence" of the legislature in this sphere derives from the fact that " ... there is yet another vast range of human affairs about which Shariah is totally silent."[56] Where God has said nothing, he has left it to the discretion and judgment of men to make the laws which they see fit. The alleged "independence" of the legislature is more apparent than real, however, for Mawdudi immediately proceeds to say that any "legislation" of this kind must accord with the spirit of Islam, follow its general principles, and fit appropriately and naturally into the great scheme of the Islamic ideology. All four of these modes of "legislation" represent instances of the well-established Islamic legal principle of *ijtihad* in Mawdudi's view.

The legislature or consultative body in the Islamic state in the final analysis, therefore, comes down to a body of pious men with expert competence in the tools and the subject matter of Islamic law, who will work together to understand the *shariah,* to spell out what it has left unclear or unstated, and to extrapolate from its principles rules to cover what it has not touched at all. This group of men will be at the disposal of the ruler for him to consult, but in Mawdudi's presentation of the matter its opinions and judgments are not binding either upon the ruler or the people of the Islamic state. Complete power remains with the ruler who, so long as he is right, may act in disregard of legislative opinions. Mawdudi plainly expected that people would act and think in accord with the decisions or "legislation" of the Majlis-i-Shura once an ideal Islamic society had been established, but his expectation was based more on confidence in the desire of the Muslims to do the right thing than upon institutional arrangements built into the structure of the state. There is no anticipation of conflict or of deep, genuine, and irreconcilable disagreement and, therefore, no provision of effective machinery for resolving conflict. What is also striking about the description of both the Majlis-i-Shura and the Head of State is the extent to which one can see Mawdudi's own kind of training, background, interests, and work reflected there: he might have been describing himself in setting out the qualifications for those who must hold the most important positions of authority in the Islamic state.

Mawdudi's discussion of the operation of government in the period of the Prophet and the Four Rightly Guided Caliphs, which was his norm in respect to everything said about the Islamic state and its constitution, also casts some light on the way in which the ruler and the legislature should work. He envisaged a closeness and lack of friction between the two that is utopian, but this expectation is justified by their mutual devotion to the same ends through the implementation of the same ideology. The amir in the time of the Four Rightly Guided Caliphs always attended the sessions of the Parliament and presided over its sittings. He took full part in its discussions and personally accepted all responsibility for his own decisions and those of his government. There existed neither a party of the government nor an opposition party in the Parliament. The entire Parliament was the party of the amir so long as he did what was right, and the entire Parliament became the opposition party when he deviated from the right. There was freedom to oppose him both on the part of his ministers and the members of the Parliament, but since the spirit of cooperation reigned in all, there were no instances of resignation from the government in protest against the policies adopted. The amir was answerable to the Parliament and to the people for what he did, not simply in respect to state policy but also in regard to his personal life.[57] Sadly, however, this kind of government, otherwise unknown in the world, can exist and flourish only in the conditions provided by an ideal Islamic society. It is because such a society has not existed from the time of the Rightly Guided Caliphs until now that this type of government has disappeared from the world. The purpose of the Islamic movement in our time is to restore the unity and righteousness of such a system of government, and in order that this may be possible four principles at least must be observed: 1) those who bear responsibility should face the representatives of the public and the public itself, being accountable for what they do; 2) the party system should be reformed to abolish loyalty to parties; 3) the government should not operate with complex rules; and 4) the people elected to office should have the proper qualifications.[58]

The two institutions of government that we have discussed here, the Head of State and the Majlis-i-Shura, are the only institutions Mawdudi considers in any detail in his discussions of the Islamic state, and the attention given even to them is minimal. From time to time he also mentions the judiciary as a third fundamental institution, but his remarks on this subject are limited to a bitter attack on the "ugly" legal profession as it now exists and the demand for its utter abolition, some comments on the training of future Islamic jurists, and the general stance that the judiciary in an Islamic state must be independent of the executive. The material available is not sufficient to construct a clear picture of the judicial organs of an Islamic state. Certain other institutions are also referred to in passing, for example, the Bayt al-Mal or State Treasury, but nothing is said about their nature, powers, or functions. There is no merit, therefore, in attempting to pursue the discussion of institutions further.

CONCLUSIONS

As we have seen in the foregoing section Mawdudi gave but little attention— far too little—to the more practical and mundane aspects of the Islamic state. His discussion is notably lacking in any serious thought devoted to the institutional arrangements in the state that he hoped to see come into existence in Pakistan. At almost every point his views raise more questions than they answer because of the failure to consider the working out of principles in their concrete applications. Constitution making, to be sure, is concerned with the expression and preservation of certain broad principles, values and ideas, but the test of the value of any constitution is its capacity to find the ways of making these principles actually effective in the life of society. It is never enough simply to state principles in order to have them observed. Would it were true that justice, equality, peace, brotherhood, etc., could be attained by our mere espousal of them! Unfortunately, human life is more complex than the ordering of a set of abstract ideas, and one has taken only the first halting step toward the achievement of the good in the social realm when he decides upon the principles that shall guide his actions. Principles must be exemplified and put into action in a host of situations where the measures that best embody the principles are far from clear. In the case of the working of a polity the effectiveness of principles is to a large degree dependent upon the machinery and the policies devised for implementing them. A poorly thought out or self-contradictory way of pursuing a noble principle will result in its neglect as surely as will outright rejection of the principle; it may, in fact, result in disillusionment about the value and truth of the principle. Mawdudi seemed not to appreciate how much the life of society from day to day depends upon the specific structures it may evolve for governing itself. His concern—and this seems to be true of Islamic revivalist movements in the twentieth century in general—was always with abstract philosophical or religious considerations that would form the ideological basis of an Islamic constitution. Mawdudi himself admits the visionary and ideal nature of much that he had to say about the Islamic state. At several places he speaks of characteristics of the Islamic state that are realizable only in the context of an ideal Islamic society which does not now exist. Thus, he was not speaking of the urgent and immediate problems of the real—and far from ideal—Pakistan but of a grand concept of a perfect society that he thought once to have existed for a short time and that might, only might, exist again in future. His real interest and the subject to which he actually addressed himself was moral philosophy or perhaps in a somewhat narrow sense of the word, theology. To the extent that politics according to the old saw is the art of the possible, Mawdudi was not talking in the realm of politics at all but on the level of general ideas.

Unfortunately, when Mawdudi's views were criticized for their inadequacy to solve the real day-to-day problems of building a stable and acceptable government in Pakistan, he tended to interpret the criticism as rejection of the principles he upheld and, therefore, as equivalent to an irreligious or non-Islamic stand. His replies to criticism came in the form of defense of the truth of Islam, a defense that he had no need to mount with most of his opponents who also considered themselves Muslims and even upholders of the Islamic state as they saw it. Mawdudi and his modernist liberal opponents in particular were operating on two different levels of discourse, one in terms of fundamental religious commitment and the other in terms of a series of down-to-earth practical issues. At numerous points in his writing Mawdudi speaks of the details of such things as the method of choice of the ruler being left to the genius of the Muslims to work out. The details, however, are what count if one wishes to ensure that the general principles about proper and fair electoral processes are actually carried out. In a serious constitutional discussion to dismiss the details of governmental institutions as something of lesser importance or something that may be decided in some way or the other at some convenient future time according to whatever exigencies may then exist is simply to remove oneself from the real political battle and to accept defeat without striking an effective blow. The real issues about the nature of a polity are joined only when the specifics of institutions, how many and what they shall be, their structures, their powers, the limitations upon them, etc., come to be talked about.

It is regrettable that Mawdudi seemed unable to disentangle consideration of such matters from what he saw as the acceptance or rejection of an Islamic position altogether. One must remember, however, that he viewed Islam as a monolithic whole, a vast, integrated system of ideas, which, he insisted, must be taken in its entirety or not at all. If something was derived from what he thought to be a genuinely Islamic position, it had to be accepted, and there could be no possibility of disagreement about it. This understanding of Islam as a monolithic ideology is the source of the rigidity and the authoritarianism in Mawdudi's thought that made him so much feared and so much disliked by many people in Pakistan. His theologically oriented mind, preoccupied as it was with normative truth, could not accommodate itself to disagreement and diversity. Regrettably perhaps, the very essence and stuff of politics is disagreement.

Mawdudi's lack of interest in the details of Pakistan's Constitution and the limited scope of his contribution to discussions about it can be better understood if his theory of the nature of social control is also taken into account. As we have mentioned briefly above, he considered that everything in the life of a society depends upon its leadership, that a society will go exactly where the ruler as the center of power determines that it should go. He seemed not to recognize limitations of any kind on a ruler's effectiveness in achieving what he might want, nor did he acknowledge other forces in a society that might deflect it away from the ruler's intentions. Neither in his thinking about the Islamic constitution nor in the political campaigns he conducted to achieve power in Pakistan did he show recognition of the variety of physical, social, economic, and other difficulties that afflict the country as being in themselves genuine obstacles to overcome. For one with his point of view the sole matter of importance was the character of the person in charge. If the ruler is a good man, a pious, moral Muslim, with the intention of ordering society in the Islamic manner, the society must become what it should be. In such a social philosophy all problems can be reduced to issues of the moral character of leadership, and all political discussions are nothing but consideration of the merits of personalities. Institutional arrangements and other such things, in other words, are simply not important, for they are not the determinants in the social scene. There were no intractable social problems in Mawdudi's understanding; where inequity, injustice, and suffering exist in a society, they are inevitably the result of the lack of moral orientation in the leadership. Such problems exist because the leadership either wishes things to be that way or because it does not care about the well-being of the people. Change bad leadership for a good one, un-Islamic leaders for true Muslim ones, and society will become what it should be. The perspective is moralistic through and through with the realization of the Islamic ideal for society contingent upon the existence of a body of true Muslims who should seize political power. The Jamaat-i-Islami was conceived precisely to be such a body. It was the *salih* (righteous) *jamaah* (party or group) whose ideological purity, unity, discipline, and personal devotion would act as the leaven in the loaf of Pakistani society. Mawdudi in short invested his efforts at the place where he thought the real key to social change lay—in the formation of a leadership that would be capable of instituting the Islamic order. In his lecture to the Law College in Lahore he affirmed:

> I am sure that if a righteous group of people, possessing vision and statesmanship, wields political power and, making full use of the administrative machinery of the government, utilizes all the resources at its disposal for the execution of a well conceived plan of national regeneration, the collective life of this country can be totally changed within a period of ten years.[59]

Or again when speaking of the enforcement of Islamic law in Pakistan, he said:

> What we need is a group of people—a leadership—which is imbued with the spirit of Islam and which is determined to establish Islam, come what may. We all know that if a building has to be constructed, the objective cannot be achieved if the architects who *know* the design of the building and have the *will* to construct it and possess the *requisite resources* are not available. On the other hand if they are available anything can be built—be it a temple or a mosque.[60]

As Amir of the Jamaat-i-Islami, Mawdudi stood at the head of precisely the kind of group of men, organized on a truly Islamic basis, that Pakistan needed for its realization of the Kingdom of God.

Notes

1. A list of Mawdudi's writings may be found in the memorial volume dedicated to him after his death. The book, entitled *Islamic Perspectives,* edited by Khurshid Ahmad and Zafar Ishaq Ansari, gives the bibliography of Mawdudi's writings in chapter 2, pp. 3–14. It should be pointed out that many of the writings listed have been published more than once, sometimes in revised versions, and sometimes under titles different from the original titles.

2. Abul Ala Mawdudi: *Jamaat-i-Islami, us ka maqsad, tarikh, awr laihi aml* (Lahore: Markazi Maktabah Jamaat-i-Islami, 4th printing, 1953), p. 22, in a footnote.

3. *Laihi aml,* pp. 19, 20.

4. Ibid., p. 27.

5. Ibid., p. 5.

6. The speech was entitled, "The Invitation to Islam and Its Demands" and was published in the annual report of the Jamaat-i-Islami.

7. See the writings entitled *Islam ka nizam-i hayat, Islami qanun awr Pakistan mayn us ka nifaz ke 'amali tadabir, Islami riyasat mayn zimmion ke buquc, Azadi ke Islami taqade,* and *Mutalibah-i nizam-i Islam,* all from this period.

8. *Laihi aml,* p. 74. Mawdudi was apparently insensitive to the implications of this statement for his attitude toward Pakistan prior to the passing of the Objectives Reso-

lution. The statement casts a strong light on the government's actions against Mawdudi in 1948 and on its subsequent suspicion of him.

9. For a detailed study of the various constitutional proposals and counter-proposals and the groups who made them see Leonard Binder: *Religion and Politics in Pakistan* (Berkeley and Los Angeles: University of California Press, 1961).

10. The pamphlet was issued prior to the ban on publications dealing with the Ahmadi question. Mawdudi was condemned, therefore, for publishing something that was not against the law at the time he composed and distributed it.

11. Some parts of the Jamaat, however, took an active role in the disturbances, especially in Karachi, as was brought out by the court of inquiry that investigated the anti-Ahmadi agitation.

12. Fortunately much of the relevant material has been assembled within the covers of a single volume and translated into English by Khurshid Ahmad under the title, *Islamic Law and Constitution*. A collection of Mawdudi's speeches with this title, the most important being two addresses to the Law College in Lahore in early 1948, was published originally in 1955, but in 1967 Khurshid Ahmad produced a revised and corrected edition that also included materials absent in the first edition (Lahore: Islamic Publications, 1967). It is this enlarged, revised edition that we have used.

13. Ibid., p. 48.

14. Ibid., p. 138.

15. Ibid., p. 172.

16. Ibid., p. 53.

17. Ibid., p. 57.

18. Ibid., p. 165.

19. Ibid., p. 175.

20. Ibid., p. 177.

21. Ibid., pp. 217–19.

22. Ibid., p. 50.

23. Ibid., p. 145.

24. Ibid., p. 75.

25. Ibid., p. 177.

26. Ibid., p. 178.

27. Ibid., p. 135.

28. Ibid., p. 276.

29. This stand brought Mawdudi some criticism in view of the traditional insistence that leadership of the community must always be vested in Quraysh, the tribe of the Prophet. See *Rasail o Masail*, vol. I, p. 76.

30. *Islamic Law and Constitution*, p. 158.

31. These examples have reference to issues that Mawdudi discussed in pre-partition times in the political debates with the Indian National Congress.

32. *Islamic Law and Constitution*, p. 278.

33. Ibid., p. 280.

34. Ibid., p. 148.

35. Ibid.

36. Ibid., p. 154.

37. Ibid.

38. Ibid., p. 155.

39. Ibid., p. 266.

40. Ibid., p. 267.
41. Ibid., p. 268.
42. Ibid., p. 50.
43. bid., p. 155.
44. Ibid.
45. Ibid., p. 263.
46. Ibid., p. 265.
47. Ibid., p. 264.
48. " . . . the Amir was the only person to whom obedience and loyalty were enjoined." Ibid., p. 257.
49. Ibid., p. 252.
50. Ibid., p. 252.
51. Ibid., p. 281.
52. Ibid., p. 255.
53. Ibid., p. 80.
54. Ibid., p. 77.
55. Ibid., p. 78.
56. Ibid.
57. Ibid., p. 258.
58. Ibid., pp. 259–60.
59. Ibid., p. 109.
60. Ibid., p. 126.

SIX

Qaddafi's Islam

LISA ANDERSON

The regime inaugurated by a coup d'état in Libya on September 1, 1969, is often considered one of the earliest manifestations of the political revival of Islam. The new government, led by Colonel Muammar al-Qaddafi, quickly departed from the path of its military counterparts elsewhere in the Arab world in adding to their nationalist formulas of legitimacy frequent reference to Islamic precepts. Both symbolic and substantive reforms in the early days of the Libyan revolution—the banning of alcohol, the closing of churches and nightclubs, the reinstitution of Quranic criminal penalties—led many observers to conclude that this was indeed an Islamic government.

Until the Iranian revolution a decade later and the development of sizeable fundamentalist movements elsewhere in the Middle East, Qaddafi's rule was portrayed in the West (and in many ruling circles in the Muslim world) as a transitory atavism. Qaddafi himself was considered eccentric at best, psychotic at worst, and his government unworthy of serious scholarly attention.[1]

Qaddafi was not without admirers, however, for the dismay and disappointment which followed the 1967 Arab-Israeli war in the Muslim world had prompted a search for new leaders and new purposes. Qaddafi's proud announcement of his attachment to Islam distinguished him from other Arab political figures and seemed to answer the search. Qaddafi's supporters—in Libya and more importantly outside the country—were hardly more discriminating in their assessment of his government and goals, however, than were his detractors. Although his interpretation of Islam became increasingly idiosyncratic during the 1970s, it was not until the revolution in Iran that he lost his position as the best-known advocate of Islamic reform in power. In the meantime he had profited from the indulgence of many Muslims who had nowhere else to turn for an apparent example of political success during the 1970s.[2]

The failure seriously to assess Qaddafi's claims to a political role as a Muslim leader said more about the context in which he operated than it did about the claims themselves. Nonetheless, widespread ignorance of his positions, whether based on disdain or wishful thinking, permitted him to portray himself as an important figure in Muslim reformist circles—and to subsidize religiously based political opposition in a number of Muslim countries—without encountering significant disagreement. By the early 1980s, however, religious opposition within Libya coincided with the heightened consciousness of Islamic movements in both the Muslim and Western worlds to subject Qaddafi's Islam to closer scrutiny.

Qaddafi's view of Islam, like much else in his political philosophy, reflected the specific historical circumstances in which his worldview took shape. Twentieth-century Libyan history provides a backdrop as essential as his own biography for an understanding of Qaddafi's philosophical outlook. Libya's experience of European rule in the twentieth century served to reinforce rather than weaken the Islamic inclination to refer to religious legitimation of political power. At the same time, however, competition between orthodox and reformist religious establishments within the country undermined the credibility of conventional religious interpretation and traditional religious organization.

Qaddafi's interpretation of Islam reflected both a desire for what might be called extra-political or spiritual legitimation and simultaneously a profound distrust of independent religious organization. His distrust was widely shared by many contemporary political leaders in the Muslim world, including Egypt's Nasser, and like them Qaddafi tried to control the political activities of the religious authorities. In his religious activism he distinguished himself from his counterparts elsewhere in the Islamic world, however, by his continued personal intervention, at first mediating among various religious interpretations and eventually dictating the path Libyans were to follow.

As he matured from his late twenties into his early forties at the helm of the Libyan state, Qaddafi's perspective changed; Islamic precepts became more a set of political symbols and less a systematic guide to political action. Thus, although he never abandoned his chosen role as a proponent of Islamic formulas for political legitimacy, the substance of his religion became increasingly unorthodox. In proclaiming the need to purge Islam of historically inaccurate accretions, of specialized classes of jurists, of tradition and the tradition-bound, he was undermining the political power of the competing religious establishments in Libya. As he did so, however, his personal interpretation increasingly set him apart from the mainstream of Islamic thought and at odds with both the religious establishment and the fundamentalist reformers in the wider Muslim world.

QADDAFI'S LIBYAN ROOTS

Unlike most philosophers of Islamic government, Qaddafi was not trained in Islamic theology or jurisprudence. His appreciation of Islam and Islamic politics did reflect, however, the particular circumstances of life in his home country, Libya.

The government which was deposed in the military coup of 1969 was a monarchy.[3] King Idris had ruled since Libya became independent in 1951, when it was among the poorest countries in the world. The population of approximately one million had a per capita income of about fifty dollars a year and literacy was about 20 percent among adult men. The country was, for all intents and purposes, a ward of the United States and Britain, which subsidized the operating budget of the monarchy.

Despite appearances to the contrary, however, Libya was not a sleepy desert backwater. Its career during the first half of the twentieth century had been marked by almost constant upheaval, and the accumulated residue of its successive turns of fortune continued to shape the political and religious life of the country in the 1980s.

Libya had been an Italian colony, and a most unwilling one. Although the Italians first claimed sovereignty in 1911 they were forced, in one of the most brutal colonial wars of the twentieth century, to capture control of the North African territory kilometer by kilometer, facing fierce resistance well into the 1930s. Among the organizations which coordinated the resistance to the Italians was a religious brotherhood, the Sanusiyyah. The founder of the Sanusiyyah was born in Algeria in 1780 to a family whose ancestry is traced to the Prophet's daughter. He had settled in Cyrenaica, or eastern Libya, in 1843, and established the brotherhood's first *zawiyah* (lodge; pl. *zawaya*) there. By the 1880s, when the fraternity reached its height, it had gained adherents throughout the lands of Cyrenaica, the Fazzan in southwestern Libya, Chad, and western Egypt. It was an austere reformist movement, not unlike the Wahhabi brotherhood in the Arabian Peninsula, by which it was influenced and with which it retained contact.[4]

During World War I, the then newly designated head of the order, Idris, contacted British authorities in Egypt, and they gave him moral if not material support in the struggle against the Italians. He eventually fled into exile in Cairo, where he remained until the end of World War II, while his followers continued the resistance in Libya.

By the time Italian control of their North African colony was finally uncontested, the Libyan population had been halved by famine, war casualties, and emigration. Almost the entire educated elite and much of the middle class had been lost and agriculture and domestic trade completely disrupted. Nonetheless, during his visit to the colony in 1937 the Italian fascist ruler Benito Mussolini claimed to be the "protector of Islam." To counter the popularity and break the resistance of the Sanusiyyah—whose lands were confiscated for Italian settlement—the Italian administration encouraged non-Sanusi Islamic education. According to one analyst, "under the Italian occupation, contrary to what might have been expected the religious element preserved its status and felt stronger than ever before since it constituted the only autonomous Muslim authority within the government."⁵ In 1935 a Superior Institute of Islamic Studies was established, and a number of its students were later to hold political and religious positions under the monarchy; almost no other education was available to the Libyans, who had seven university graduates at independence.

Italian rule proved short-lived; the North African campaigns of World War II left Libya in British and French hands after a series of long and destructive battles. During the war, the British promised Idris, still in Cairo, that Cyrenaica would not be returned to Italian control if he would provide troops from among his followers to fight alongside the Allies. After the war, this promise proved decisive in the debates over Libya's future. The newly established United Nations was unable to agree on a suitable mandatory power and so Libya was granted independence in 1951 under Idris as king.

The monarchy's administration was very simple, reflecting the poverty of the country and its lack of educated bureaucrats. Most genuine political and administrative power was delegated to locally prominent families or members of the King's immediate circle, an economical and efficient—if not always equitable— arrangement. For the eighteen years during which Libya was ruled by the Sanusi King, official symbolism was largely limited to religious justifications of the monarchy, to which were added in the late 1960s a few concessions to Arab nationalism. Political power was similarly limited to the King's entourage, with occasional concessions to ambitious sycophants and cooperative technocrats. There was, as one observer put it, "an inevitable association between family prominence and religious leadership."⁶

In the consolidation of Sanusi control of the state, the position of the non-Sanusi religious establishment which had been fostered under the Italians was undermined. Their independence was eroded by the integration of the *shariah,* or Islamic law, courts into a national judicial system and by the incorporation of significant religious positions, like that of the Grand Mufti, into the government bureaucracy. The ulama became salaried employees of the state, while the control of the Sanusi institutions, including the rebuilt *zawaya,* remained in the hands of the private royal household.

As if the upheavals of the previous half-century had not been enough, oil was struck in the late 1950s. Within a decade, per capita income rose to more than 1500 dollars a year, and despite efforts to revamp and strengthen the administration, the bureaucracy proved too fragile to withstand the pressures of the new wealth. It was virtually impossible to separate the public administration from the private patrimonies which had been permitted in the poverty-ridden 1950s. Development planning and even everyday administration faltered in the face of system-wide corruption.

The monarchy, designed as it had been for a small, poor, and ill-educated populace, was equally poorly equipped to accommodate the new demands of politically conscious students or a new and economically savvy middle class. Political parties had been banned at independence and politics had taken the form of conflict over patronage within the aging King's circle. By the late 1960s, as Nasser's Arab nationalism was beamed over the radio waves from Cairo, the monarchy appeared to many observers to be an anachronism on its way out.

The military coup which brought Qaddafi to power in September 1969 was therefore greeted with more relief than surprise. The monarchy had faced opposition from nearly all sectors of society, from the non-Sanusi ulama to the youthful Arab nationalists and the new middle classes. Many plots had been afoot and the only question on the morrow of the coup was the identity of the successful plotters. The King, who was out of the country, abdicated, the militia thought to be his loyal guard stayed in its barracks, and the country waited to hear from its new rulers.

The upheavals of the twentieth century in Libya had been accompanied throughout by efforts at religious legitimation of political power. The struggle against the Italians had been characterized by the Sanusiyyah and their allies as a jihad; the Italians in turn attempted to create a religious establishment to act as a cooperative counterweight to the brotherhood. The close association between Idris and the British, and between the orthodox ulama and the Italians, weakened the nationalist credentials of organized religion, but religious observance remained a powerful indication of political legitimacy.

QADDAFI: HIS PERSONAL PERSPECTIVE

Despite his early attention to Islam, Qaddafi, as the new ruler of Libya, made no claim to a special religious charisma to justify his government's accession to power. Although the military rulers made a marked effort to disassociate themselves from what they viewed as the moral corruption of the Sanusi regime, it was indicative of the new view of politics they brought to government in Libya that Qaddafi's own tribal background was consistently described in socio-economic rather than religious terms. The Qadadfa tribe of which he was a member was a *murabit* ("marabout," or saintly) tribe of some political consequence in the nineteenth century; they are said to be descendants of the Prophet, and Qaddafi himself noted that "the tribal people felt very proud of this."[7] Unlike the regime of the similarly descended Sanusi family, however, the rule of the Revolutionary Command Council was not claimed to be justified by its leader's saintly ancestry. The military officers were, as Qaddafi emphasized, men of the people:

... the officers have the conscience to recognize the people's claims better than others. This depends on our origin which is characterized by humbleness. We are not rich people; the parents of the majority of us are living in huts. My parents are still living in a tent near Sirte. The interests we represent are genuinely those of the Libyan people.[8]

Whether his humble origin did in fact provide him with special insight into the aspirations of most Libyans, Qaddafi rightly identified himself as reflecting many of the characteristics of the average man in the street.

Claiming to be about twenty-seven at the time of the coup in 1969—he may have been several years older—Qaddafi allied himself with the vast majority in a country where the average age was about fifteen, and he represented a sharp contrast to the eighty-year-old King. He came from a region between the major provinces of Tripolitania and Cyrenaica, Sirte, often identified with the neglected southern Fazzan. Without a strong regional affiliation and with an Arabic accent typical of the frontier between the major regions, his abhorrence of regionalism and his dedication to nationalism and unity—Libyan and Arab— was borne out in his very demeanor. A fervent admirer of Egyptian President Gamal Abdel Nasser and his version of Arab socialism, Qaddafi proclaimed freedom, socialism, and unity the goals of the revolution.

Qaddafi's admiration for Nasser had been long-standing. At the age of ten, and it is said at great sacrifice to his family, he had been sent to a Quranic school in Sirte where he received his only formal religious training.[9] Four years later he entered the preparatory school at Sabha, the provincial capital of the Fazzan, and began to listen to Nasser's radio broadcasts. He soon became known as a political militant and troublemaker. After an altercation with a scion of the Sayf al-Nasir clan, long the dominant family of the Fazzan and an ally of the Sanusi monarchy, he was expelled from school and his family forced to leave Fazzan.

Although he continued his secondary schooling in Misrata, a coastal town east of the capital Tripoli, Qaddafi had already decided that political change would not come through the civilian arena. As one observer has succinctly put it:

> In 1963 the first general meeting of Gadafi's movement bringing together followers from Sabha, Misrata and Tripoli decided that Gadafi and two others would enrol at the Military Academy in Benghazi specifically to form a nucleus of Free Unionist Officers whose long-term purpose was to make a coup possible by gaining sufficient support for it within the army.[10]

Qaddafi graduated from the Military Academy in 1965 and was sent to Britain for a six-month signals course. His only experience of life outside Libya was apparently not a happy one; his early reputation for a notably pious and austere life style was, however, strengthened.

Upon his return to Libya he attended courses at the university at Benghazi. It was announced soon after the coup that he had a bachelor's degree in history, although it appears in fact that he did not complete the graduation require-ments. He spent most of his free time gathering support for an eventual take-over of power. As he would later describe this period:

> We tired ourselves most over the meetings. . . . The reason for our exhaustion was that they were held outside the cities and on holidays. . . . We travelled hundreds of miles accompanied by sleeplessness and heat or cold, according to the sea-son. . . . However, by praising God and with his help we were successful. . . .[11]

By January 1969 the Free Officers had decided that the time was ripe for action. After several postponements through the spring and summer, the announce-ment that a group of young officers was to be posted to England for training courses on September 2 provoked the final plan. The Free Officers moved on September 1.

ISLAM IN THE REVOLUTION: 1969–1974

The revolution very early reflected Qaddafi's view that religious affairs were properly within the purview of government.[12] The early decrees of the Revo-lutionary Command Council on religion abolished the special privileges of the Sanusiyyah and restored to the non-Sanusi ulama the position of prominence the Sanusiyyah had begun to lose under the monarchy. Within a month of the September 1 coup, maintenance of the King's palaces was suspended and the use of Arabic and the Muslim calendar made mandatory in all public communica-tions. Long before even the membership of the Revolutionary Command Coun-cil was announced in January 1970, a Grand Mufti had been appointed, the Sanusi *zawaya* taken under government supervision, and projects for building new ones suspended. Soon alcohol consumption, forbidden by Islam but per-mitted under the monarchy, was banned, and churches and cathedrals, night-clubs and cafés, were closed. By October 1972, a number of criminal laws had been promulgated, requiring Quranic punishments *(hudud)*—the amputation of the hand for a theft, for example—qualified by the requirement that modern surgical techniques be used.

Although Libyans apprehended with alcohol were routinely jailed, there was no evidence that the harsher Islamic criminal penalties were ever applied. The new laws were, however, of major symbolic significance in demonstrating the commitment of the new government to its self-ordained role as protector of the public morality, and they gave increased responsibility and visibility to the ulama, whose support was particularly valuable in justifying the dismantling of the Sanusi establishment of the old regime.

In taking an activist stance, the revolutionary regime not only bid for the early support of the non-Sanusi religious establishment and undermined the position of the Sanusiyyah, it defined the boundaries of acceptable religious activity as well. Like many of his secularist counterparts, Qaddafi distrusted independent religious organization. In discussing the Muslim Brotherhood (al-Ikhwan al-Muslimin), a reformist group active in politics in Egypt and elsewhere since the 1930s, he identified what he viewed as the danger in religious politics. He commented that:

> the ikhwan al-muslimin in the Arab countries work against Arab Unity, against Socialism, and against Arab Nationalism, because they consider all these to be inconsistent with religion. Colonialism allies and associates with them because colonialism is against Arab Unity, against Arab Nationalism, and against Socialism. So the ikhwan al-muslimin movement cooperated with colonialism without being aware of this, or perhaps colonialism had to choose one group or another, and thus it chose them.[13]

Nationalism and socialism were clearly high among the priorities of the Qaddafi government, and although Islam was to be given a much more prominent role than it had in Nasser's Egypt, this was because of the potentially divisive and mischievous role independent religious groups might have in Libya. The history of competing religious establishments, both of which had been known to cooperate with European powers—the Sanusiyyah with the British, the orthodox ulama with the Italians—required, in Qaddafi's view, particular vigilance by the government.

Qaddafi warned the religious leaders in the early 1970s that they would no longer be the final arbiters on questions of religion. Theological disputes, like those between the Sanusiyyah and the orthodox ulama, which might have political implications, would not be tolerated.

> We no more follow the old tradition of the royal regime which says: this has to be in accordance with this sect or that ism. We do not want to be the followers of any particular theory, or limit ourselves to one religious interpretation.... We must not restrict ourselves to one independent judgment in a legal or theological question.[14]

It would be, as it turned out, the secular leadership, in the person of Qaddafi himself, that decided which religious interpretations Libyans were to follow.

THE GREEN BOOK: THE REVOLUTION ELABORATED

By 1975, the first volume of Qaddafi's *Green Book,* in which is outlined his Third International Theory, was published. This volume, titled "The Solution to the Problem of Democracy," was his treatise on politics. Significantly, there was no mention of Islam, or indeed of religion, except oblique references to the potential divisiveness of sectarian organization and to "the negative and destructive effects on society of the tribal and sectarian struggles."[15] Qaddafi explained the lack of attention to Islam by suggesting:

> ... the Third International Theory is based on religion and nationalism—any religion and any nationalism. ... We do not present Islam as a religion in the Third Theory. For if we do so, we will be excluding from the Third Theory all the non-Muslims, something which we evidently do not want. *In the Third Theory, we present the applications of Islam from which all mankind may benefit.*[16]

Volume II of the *Green Book,* which followed several years later, was devoted to the "Solution of the Economic Problem: Socialism," and once again Islam did not figure in the discussion. The third volume, issued in the middle of 1979, outlined the "Social Basis of the Third International Theory." Here Qaddafi observed that "every nation should have a religion," but he identified the "national factor" as the "driving force of human history." In fact, he argued that a state established on any other basis, even that of a common religion, is a "temporary structure which will be destroyed."[17]

By the middle of the decade, the military government had consolidated its position as the successor to the Sanusiyyah and had apparently been successful in outbidding other claimants to religious legitimacy by winning the cooperation of the orthodox religious establishment. Although the Islamic prohibitions against alcohol consumption remained in force, and the nightclubs and cafés stayed closed, the regime had turned its attention elsewhere. Public pronouncements about religion dropped off perceptibly as the implementation of the political and economic dictates of the Third International Theory began in earnest. The value of maintaining the atmosphere of austerity and sacrifice which the Islamic laws imposed was considerable; a socialist revolution to benefit the toiling masses in a country where the per capita income of eight thousand dollars a year was the product of very little individual toil meant that a spirit of revolutionary discipline and sacrifice would have to be instilled through non-socialist ideology.

POPULAR AUTHORITY AND THE ECLIPSE OF THE ULAMA

Qaddafi formally resigned from his official government positions to become Philosopher of the Revolution with the declaration of Popular Authority in March 1977. The people were now to rule themselves—hence there was no need for a government—through the mechanisms outlined in the *Green Book.* This change was symbolized in the change of the name of the country to the Socialist People's Libyan Arab Jamahiriyyah, or "state of the masses."

Implementation of the revolutionary institutions outlined in the *Green Book* did not go as smoothly as its author seems to have expected. The failure of the people to appreciate fully the revolutionary system of popular committees and congresses through which they were to rule themselves and guide the economy appears to have been a source of frustration to the Libyan leadership. Among the groups that fell out of favor as a consequence was the religious establishment, which was held to account for some of the popular foot-dragging in the revolution. Qaddafi soon began addressing questions of religion again.

Early indications that Qaddafi was going to take on the religious authorities came in an article published in the official daily newspaper, *al-Fajr al-Jadid*, in October 1977. The article, signed by one Ibn al-Tayyib and said to have been inspired if not written by Qaddafi himself, was titled "No mufti, no marabits, no shaykhs." In it the author argued that representation of the people by religious functionaries is inadmissible and that the powers of the mufti are incompatible with popular authority. In the ensuing polemic Ibn al-Tayyib reminded his readers of a *mufti* of the old regime who had failed to declare a jihad against the Italians and had opted for Italian citizenship in the 1930s. Although the writer claimed to be criticizing the position, and not its incumbent, Shaykh Tahir al-Zawi, who had been appointed by Qaddafi, nonetheless resigned as Grand Mufti in the aftermath of the debate.[18]

The discussion continued, however, as Qaddafi himself took up the issue in public at an international colloquium on Volume II of the *Green Book* held in Benghazi in early April 1978. At that meeting a number of ulama objected to the economic socialism of the Third International Theory, saying that its declaration that "land is not private property" contradicted Islamic tradition and threatened *waqf* (the endowment of private property to the benefit of religious purposes), notably the upkeep of mosques and their personnel, including imams. Qaddafi's response, that his interpretation of social and economic justice was consistent with Islam because land belongs to God and men can only exploit it, reassured few religious leaders.[19]

Within barely a month the fears of the religious establishment proved to be well founded, as popular committees were instructed to "seize the mosques" to rid them of "paganist tendencies" and of imams accused of "propagating heretical tales elaborated over centuries of decadence and which distort the Islamic religion." These ulama were said not "to have remembered Islam until after the socialist measures limiting landed property." In fact, the law of May 6, 1978, which brought the real estate regime in Libya into harmony with the provisions of Volume II of the *Green Book* forbidding private property had severely undermined the position of the ulama, depriving them, and their constituents, of private land ownership and going far toward the abolition of *waqf*.[20]

In July 1978 *al-Fajr al-Jadid* published the proceedings of a discussion Qaddafi held with ulama from throughout the Muslim world. Here his rejection of orthodox Islamic formulations became more explicit. He acknowledged the authority of the Quran as providing binding precepts for Muslims; it is the Word of God and he agreed that the text is authentic. The Sunna—the Prophet's practice as recorded in the *hadith* (traditions about his words and deeds)—is not, however, necessarily binding. Qaddafi did not reject the notion that the Prophet's example ought to provide a guide to virtuous behavior; he argued instead that the historical disputes about the validity of the traditions suggest that inaccuracies and errors have crept in over the centuries. Moreover, as he had said earlier that year:

> If the Prophet had said: the *hadith* is mine, follow its path, that would have meant that he was working to replace the Quran, but he continually insisted on taking the Quran alone. . . . These words may seem strange. The reason is that we have strayed far at this stage, very far from Islam.[21]

Qaddafi thus rejected both the Sunna and the jurisprudence, or *fiqh,* which entailed its elaboration in Islamic law.

As al-Assiouty describes it in a discussion of the implications of Qaddafi's position for the law of marriage,

> . . . just as the Quran . . . is stable, the *fiqh* is changeable, the [Quran] represents the original Islam while the *fiqh* personifies the historical Islam; thus, the reformers of our days envision the re-examination of *fiqh* and the return to the original Islam.[22]

Using Qaddafi's own words, al-Assiouty goes on:

> As the Muslims have strayed far from Islam, a review is demanded. The [Libyan revolution] is a revolution rectifying Islam, presenting Islam correctly, purifying Islam of the reactionary practices which dressed it in retrograde clothing not its own. Because Islam is progressive, it is a universalist revolution at the height of the left. The Islamic revolution in the Libyan Jamahiriyah is neo-scientific socialism.[23]

Should there have been any doubt that Qaddafi felt that the ulama were both wrong and expendable, he dispelled it on the occasion of the Muslim new year, December 1, 1978. In a speech he illustrated his new approach to Islam by calling for a revision of the Muslim calendar. For almost 1400 years it had dated from the hegira, the Prophet's emigration from Mecca to Medina. In Qaddafi's view, this tradition should be abandoned, since another date—the Prophet's death ten years later—is much more significant for Islam, marking the end of prophecy and ranking in importance with the birth of Jesus for Christianity. Unlike the Gregorian calendar and the conventional Muslim calendar, which are of human origin, the lunar calendar beginning with the end of prophecy is the work of God. Thus scientific, not traditional, methods of determining time must be used. In 1979, official Libyan stationary adopted the Prophet's death as the beginning of the Muslim era.[24]

This eclectic reliance on science, Islamic forms, and personal reflection typified Qaddafi's approach to religion in the second decade of the revolution. With this revision of the calendar, he ended, at least for the time, the open debate about the role of religion in Libya. The ulama had failed to convince him of the error of his ways, as he had failed to convince them, and they joined many of their countrymen in opposition to the regime. Qaddafi did not appear particularly sorry to see them go, since he had other more important projects. In an interview with the Italian journalist Oriana Fallaci in December 1979, he gave an indication of his aspirations:

FALLACI: Tell me, Colonel, do you really think that this philosophy of yours, this little *Green Book,* will change the world?

QADDAFI: Without any doubt. Yes, without any doubt. The *Green Book* is the product of the struggle of mankind. The *Green Book* is the guide to the emancipation of man. The *Green Book* is the gospel. The new gospel. The gospel of the new era, the era of the masses. . . .

FALLACI: Well, then you're a kind of messiah. The new messiah.

QADDAFI: I don't see myself in those terms. But the *Green Book* is the new gospel, I repeat. In your gospels it's written: "In the beginning there was the word." The *Green Book* is the word. One of its words can destroy the world. Or save it. [American President] Carter can wage any war against us: to defend itself, the third world only needs my *Green Book.* My word. One word and the whole world could blow up. The value of things could change. And their weight. And their volume. Everywhere and forever.[25]

QADDAFI'S ISLAM: CONCLUDING THOUGHTS.

Qaddafi grew up in a world where religion and politics were inextricably entwined. His family and those around him could, and did, refer to religious heritages, to saintly and heroic ancestors, to historical battles fought in the name of religious righteousness. Both support for and opposition to European colonialism in the twentieth century had been cast in religious terms, and the post-independence monarchy had rested its case for political legitimacy upon its religious tradition and observance. The temptation, perhaps even the necessity, to refer to religion as an element of politics was therefore very strong in Libya, more so than elsewhere in the Muslim world where European influence had done much to secularize government if not politics.

Thus Qaddafi's references to Islam represented less a religious revival for Libya than continuity in the country's tradition of the political use of religious legitimacy. Unlike the supporters of the Iranian revolution or the movements associated with the Muslim Brotherhood, Qaddafi had no intention of establishing a state based on renewed, reformed, or rectified Islam. His goals were nationalist and socialist—he remained faithful to the spirit if not the letter of Nasser's legacy[26]—but he perceived and presented these goals in terms consistent with religious legitimacy. Whether his reliance on Islam grew out of personal conviction or political expediency is of little import, although there was probably an element of both in his actions. As Bleuchot and Monastiri have suggested:

> To abandon all reference to the Sunna is, for Qaddafi, to free him from a number of juridical contraints all the while permitting him to remain the champion of Islam, a situation which is very advantageous on the international plane.[27]

What was most marked about his interpretation, however, was his simultaneous distrust of organized religion and concern for extra-political legitimacy.

Qaddafi rejected the reformist tradition exemplified in Libya by the Sanusiyyah on political grounds: the Brotherhood's leadership in the person of the King had been neither egalitarian nor responsive to the needs of the people. Such criticism is easily cast in the evocative language of religion; the monarchy was not just or compassionate, as the rulers of the faithful ought to be, but rather corrupt. The difference between political and moral corruption was not one Qaddafi felt any need to elaborate.

The orthodox religious establishment lent him its support in the early days of the revolution. Pleased by their improved status and flattered no doubt by the attentions of the new government, the ulama allowed themselves to be used as one among the many sources of legitimacy upon which Qaddafi drew in the first years. In doing so they followed a well-trodden path in Islamic history, preferring to cooperate with the mundane powers rather than risk anarchy.[28] Qaddafi only courted the favor of the ulama as long as he felt the need for a counterweight to the Sanusiyyah, and they permitted him to do whatever he wished. When they and their jurisprudence interfered with his increasingly ambitious plans for the Libyan revolution, he no longer had any use for them.

Qaddafi's distrust of organized religion—orthodox and reformist—grew out of his conviction that the religious establishments could be manipulated, as they had been by European imperialists and as they had been by indigenous secular rulers throughout Islamilc history. In abandoning reliance on a religious establishment, however, Qaddafi did not abandon hopes of religious legitimacy. He strained the credulity of most Muslim and non-Muslim observers alike with his claim that the *Green Book* was the gospel. His rejection of the Sunna and hadith was predicated on that claim, however, for he never denied the need for a human elaboration of the word of God in the Quran. He merely saw the traditions of Islamic jurisprudence as inherently conservative and therefore contrary to the revolutionary spirit of Islam in its early days. That spirit could be recalled in a new human elaboration and a new set of laws; as Qaddafi put it, "in the Third Theory we present the applications of Islam from which all mankind may benefit."

To the extent that the *Green Book* represented only the worldview and aims of its author, Qaddafi's claims were merely those of an individual, idiosyncratic and—in the context of the debates on Islam and Islamic reform—insignificant. His visibility was due to his having captured political power in a wealthy oil-producing country, not to the sophistication, utility, or representativeness of his philosophy as an example of modern-day Islamic thought. His was not a religious reformation; it was, in terms of religious history, a heresy, and as such it is not likely to represent much more than a footnote to the worldwide debate on Islam and Islamic reform.

Qaddafi's example is important, however, in one respect, for his education and experience were not unlike those of many Muslims today. A smattering of religious training, technical education, and exposure through the mass media to Middle Eastern history and politics with its local disputes and international grievances provided the basis for the analysis and solutions outlined in the *Green Book* and in Qaddafi's pronouncements on world affairs. His eclectic mixture of religion, science, and politics was his own but his desire to find a synthesis of the competing logics and norms which today confront all Muslims was widely shared. The upheavals of the twentieth century in Libya in its tortuous path from Italian fascist rule to a British-supported monarchy to Qaddafi's own revolution, from colonial devastation to undreamt-of wealth, left many questions unanswered. Libya's experience was singular, but these same questions cast in different terms—about the meaning of history, the elements of identity, the nature of justice—were widespread in the Muslim world. Although Qaddafi's answers in his Third International Theory reflected both his Libyan roots and his personal experience and were therefore unlikely to satisfy most Muslims, the moral and political dilemmas they were designed to address were very real to many in the Islamic world.

Notes

1. The first decade of Qaddafi's rule was remarkable for the paucity in the West of scholarly work on his regime. Among the few scholars to follow Libyan affairs throughout the 1970s, particularly Qaddafi's Islamic policies were Hervé Bleuchot, whose work is available in, among other places, *La Libye nouvelle: rupture et continuité* (Paris, 1975), and Ann Elizabeth Mayer, who studied legal reform; see her "Islamic Law and Islamic Revival in Libya," in C. K. Pullapilly (ed.) *Islam in the Contemporary World* (Notre Dame, 1980).

2. The flattering and adulatory literature on Qaddafi and his regime is voluminous, much of it subsidized by the Libyan government. The article by al-Assiouty, cited below, is the best sympathetic discussion of Qaddafi's religious policy in a Western language.

3. On the Italian tenure and the monarchy see John Wright, *Libya: A Modern History* (Baltimore, 1982), which also includes an excellent account of the first decade of Qaddafi's rule.

4. The Sanusiyyah brotherhood is the subject of a famous, if increasingly disputed, monograph by British anthropologist E. E. Evans-Pritchard, *The Sanusi of Cyrenaica* (Oxford, 1949).

5. Salaheddin Hassan Salem, "The Genesis of the Political Leadership of Libya, 1952–1969," Ph.D. dissertation (George Washington University, 1973), p. 38.

6. Omar I. El-Fathaly, and Monte Palmer, *Political Development and Social Change in Libya* (Lexington, Mass., 1980), p. 26.

7. Muammar Qaddafi, *Thus Spoke Colonel Moammar Kazzafi* (Beirut, 1974), p. 24. This volume is a useful compilation of newspaper interviews published in Beirut and Cairo in the early 1970s.

8. Among the few full-length biographies of Qaddafi is Mirella Bianco, *Gadafi: Voice from the Desert* (London, 1975).

9. Meridith O. Ansell and Ibrahim Massaud al-Arif, *The Libyan Revolution: A Source Book of Legal and Historical Documents* (Stoughton, Wis., 1972), vol 1, p. 204.

10. Wright, *Libya,* p. 126.

11. Cited in Ruth First, *Libya: The Elusive Revolution* (Baltimore, 1974), p. 103.

12. Parts of this discussion appeared in a somewhat different form in my "Religion and Politics in Libya," *Journal of Arab Affairs,* 1:1 (Autumn 1981).

13. Qaddafi, *Kazzafi,* p. 61.

14. Ibid., p. 49.

15. Muammar Qaddafi, *The Green Book,* vol. 1, p. 35.

16. Emphasis added. Qaddafi, *Kazzafi*, p. 12.

17. Qaddafi, *The Green Book*, vol. 3, pp. 24-26.

18. This debate is reported by Hervé Bleuchot and Taoufik Monastiri, "L'Islam de M. El Qaddhafi," in Ernest Gellner and Jean-Claude Vatin, eds., *Islam et politique au Maghreb* (Paris, 1981), p. 215. Shaykh Tahir al-Zawi, one of the foremost chroniclers of modern Libyan history and an active opponent of imperialism in his country, was in his nineties when he resigned. He was not replaced.

19. Ibid., p. 216.

20. Cited by H. Mammeri, "Libye: Islam at idéologie," *Maghreb-Machrek*, 82 (Jan.–March 1979).

21. Bleuchot and Monastiri, "L'Islam," p. 215.

22. S. A. al-Assiouty, "Le Coran contre le fiqh: A propos du marriage d'apres le Livre Vert de M. Al Qaddhafi," in Christiane Souriau (ed.) *Le Maghreb musulmane en 1979* (Paris, 1981), p. 14.

23. Ibid., p. 17.

24. Bleuchot and Monastiri, "L'Islam," p. 217.

25. Oriana Fallaci, "The Iranians Are Our Brothers: An Interview with Col. Muammar el-Qaddafi of Libya," *The New York Times Magazine,* Dec. 16, 1979.

26. Daniel Crecelius has suggested that the appearance of a different policy toward religion in Nasser's Egypt may obscure fundamental similarities. As he writes, in discussing Egypt:

> Perhaps the most telling charge leveled against the ulama [by the Nasser regime] was that their inability to reform their own institutions or to make religious ideals compatible with modern science or conditions was turning the nation away from Islam and bringing into question the validity of the Prophet's revelation. Herein lay the seeds of the regime's evolving activist religious policy, for implicit in this criticism is a rejection of liberal-nationalism for its heavy reliance upon a belief system derived from the Christian West and its banishment of religion and religious principles to the domain of private concern. The military leaders were moving toward a religious solution which had eluded the ulama, Islamic reformers such as Muhammad Abduh, Rashid Rida, the Ikhwan, and the secular liberal-nationalists. The state itself would assume responsibility for the revival of Islam.

This is, of course, precisely the solution explicitly adopted in Libya. See Crecelius, "The Course of Secularization in Egypt," in John L. Esposito (ed.) *Islam and Development: Religion and Sociopolitical Change* (Syracuse, 1980), p. 65.

27. Bleuchot and Monastiri, "L'Islam," p. 218.

28. On the various historical relations between the ulama and political authorities see, among others, John Obert Voll, *Islam: Continuity and Change in the Modern World* (Boulder, Colo., 1982).

SEVEN

Imam Khomeini:
Four Levels of Understanding

MICHAEL M.J. FISCHER

I

Your vocal chords are silenced like anger in a fist
Your soul boils like a chained lion
. . .
You shouted at Iraq, Mashhad, and Shiraz
You warned Hejaz, Egypt, and Samarkand
You shouted at the whole world and to the free people
Through the heart of this imprisoned and repressed people
For the agression of Zahak, the soul of the people of Iran
Is just like esfand on fire
The masses rose like the chest of the Oman Sea
And they raised their fists like the peak of Alvand Mountain
. . .
The throne is yours in the whole Islamic world
From the Nile Valley to the banks of the Shatt al-Arab
You are the Imam among the ulema
. . .
Your thought is victorious by the glory of the Quran
And your name is everlasting, we swear by your name

> M. Azarm (Nemat Mirzazadeh),
> *Be Nameto Sogand* (We Swear by Your Name), 1965;
> a well-known ode to Khomeini, used to open
> his biography.[1]

II

It is quite clear to revolutionaries—be they Stanford and Sorbonne educated or
mullahs (religious leaders) from Qum and Najaf—that what seems to be the case
can be far more potent than the actual facts of the matter. The Ayatullah Khomeini's life, for example, is itself a revolutionary instrument, a legendary corpus

to be utilized. The facts of the matter are vague and contradictory, and largely irrelevant. Both personality and program are malleable devices. To lose sight of this is to self-delude. Our vision must thus be quadrascopic: the biography of the man, but also the projected persona; the stated program, but also the different interpretations and the context of competing figures. The persona focuses attention on issues of charisma, mobilization, and legitimacy. The competing figures and contested interpretations ensure that the stated program not be taken at face value, that rhetorical red herrings be distinguished from what is politically advocated, that revolutionary masques (and their moments of greatest impact) be differentiated from millenarian or mystical masques (and their more encompassing claims).

What, after all, is biography that it can inform, if not viewings from multiple angles, portraits in the round, or wider social relations and cultural forms refracted through one living? Four sections follow in approximate order of gnosis: biography, persona, politics (with the aid of negatives or semiotic-like definitions through contrast with competitors), gnosis (with its politics).[2]

III

Ruhullah Musavi Khomeini was born on the birthday of Fatima, the daughter of the Prophet Muhammad (20 Jummada Sani 1320) 1902, in the provincial town of Khomein. His grandfather, Sayyid Ahmad Musavi, had come to Khomein from Najaf at the invitation of Jusef Khan Kameri (whose daughter he married). The family claims descent from Mir Hamed Husain Hindi Nishaburi, the India-resident author of *Abaqat ul-Anwar* (Containers of Light), the first major effort in the Shiite genre of books attacking Sunni beliefs on the basis of Sunni hadith (i.e., turning their own documents against them). Ruhullah's father, Sayyid Mustafa, was killed shortly after he was born, in 1902; his mother and father's sister died when he was sixteen.[3]

At age seventeen, he went to study in Arak with Shaikh Muhsin Iraqi,[4] a close associate of Shaikh Fazlullah Nuri. Nuri had been the leader of the conservative clerical faction during the Constitutional Revolution (1905–11). He had been instrumental in having a clause inserted in the Constitution giving a panel of five *mujtahids* the right to veto proposed legislation they felt inimical to Islam. Nuri argued that the fad for constitutions be restrained to those which were "conditioned" by the Quran, punning on the Arabic root in the word for "constitution" (*mashruteh mashrueh*), a slogan echoed in Khomeini's 1970 lectures on *Islamic Government*.[5] Such conditions included rejection of Western notions such as equality of all citizens before the law (Muslims and non-Muslims should be treated separately), the freedoms of speech, press, and education (nothing inimical to Islam must be allowed), and taxations systems different from the old Islamic taxes, *zakat* (for the poor) and *khums* (in Shiah Islam, a religious tax).[6]

In Arak, Khomeini attached himself to the circle around Shaikh Abdol-Karim Haeri-Yazdi and followed the latter to Qum in 1920. Haeri-Yazdi was the modern founder of the theological center in Qum. Later one of Khomeini's sons married a granddaughter of Haeri-Yazdi. Haeri-Yazdi died in 1935, and after an interregnum by a troika leadership (including Sayyid Sadruddin Sadr, whose son became a prominent Shiite leader in Lebanon in the 1970s, and whose granddaughter married Khomeini's second son) was succeeded in 1944 by Ayatullah Hosain Borujerdi. Khomeini served as an aide to Borujerdi. He also taught in the Qum seminary system. He was somewhat unusual as a teacher in that he taught speculative mysticism, a subject often frowned upon by the orthodox as a threat to true faith, rationality, and orthopraxis. Khomeini, however, also wrote a defense of Shiite orthodoxy, including the popular customs of worshipping in shrines, invoking saints as intermediaries with God, and various forms of mourning the martyrdom of the imams, as well as the right of clerics to instruct others, to veto proposed legislation, and to live off donations and Islamic taxes. This defense, entitled *Revealing the Secrets* (1943), was a response to a book called *Secrets of a Thousand Years* by a disciple of Ahmad Kasravi. Kasravi, one of the leading Iranian intellectuals of the 1930s and 1940s (until he was assasinated by the Fedaiyyan-i Islam in 1945), had originally been trained as a cleric, but then turned against what he saw as the superstition, obscurantism, and ignorance foisted upon lay believers by the clergy. Khomeini also took the opportunity to attack Reza Shah in bitter terms for arbitrary tyranny and failing to govern in a manner which would foster Islam.

In this attack on Reza Shah, he always referred to the monarch with his pre-royal title, "Reza Khan." There are some claims that Khomeini had participated in the 1924 anti-Reza Khan march led by Nurullah Isfahani, that he had befriended Mirza Sadiq Aqa after the latter helped lead an anti-Reza Shah march in Tabriz in 1927, and that his classes on morals were peppered with anti-Pahlavi innuendoes so that Reza Shah had them first harrassed (by sending secret police among the students) and then closed. However, in the 1940s and 1950s, although part of the sullen opposition of the Pahlavis, Khomeini politically followed Borujerdi. Borujerdi in 1949 convened a meeting of clerics and urged withdrawal from the political arena. Fearing anarchism and leftists in the recovery period after World War II, Borujerdi cooperated with the monarchy to preserve law and order. Both Khomeini and Borujerdi were critical of the day to day involvement in politics of Ayatullah Abul-Qassim Kashani, a major figure in the National Front led by Dr. Muhammad Mosaddeq. Borujerdi argued that the moral power of the clergy would remain more effective if not dragged into ordinary wheeling and dealing. In the early 1960s, shortly before he died, Borujerdi began to engage this moral power against a number of proposals of the Shah's government which were to become the White Revolution.

When Borujerdi died, the struggle between conservatives and anti-Shah activists among the clergy flared into the open. Borujerdi's designated successor, Sayyid Abdullah Shirazi, died within months of Borujerdi, and many conservatives drifted toward the leadership of Sayyid Muhsin Hakim in Iraq. Activists, however, began to propagandize the name of Khomeini. There were rumors that Khomeini had broken with Borujerdi shortly before the latter's death, a rumor which was to be exploited in 1982 by radio broadcasts from Kurdistan of Borujerdi's alleged will, ending in the sentence: "Do not follow Ruhullah, lest you find yourselves knee deep in blood."[7] These activists included those who had privately soured on Borujerdi when he had in effect welcomed the Shah's return after the overthrow of Mosaddeq; they also included members of the Kashani faction which had first supported Mosaddeq and then abandoned him. In the provincial town of Yazd, for instance, Ayatullah Mahmud Saduqi hung a large portrait of Khomeini in the Hazireh Mosque; the poet and writer Muhammad-Reza Hakimi went around telling people that not to follow "Ruh-e Khoda" (the Persian form of Ruhullah, literally, "the spirit of God") was like committing adultery in the sacred precincts of the Kaaba in Mecca; and the preacher Muhammad-Taghi Falsafi dramatically interrupted his series of lectures to return to Tehran when Khomeini delivered a major speech. Saduqi had come to Yazd originally to run an unsuccessful parliamentary electoral campaign for a son of Shaikh Abdul-Karim Haeri-Yazdi; he had stayed and married into the mercantile elite of Yazd; later he would become part of Khomeini's entourage, an official of the Islamic Republic, and the ayatullah who would declare (in April 1981) that Bahais were *mahdour-e damn* ("those whose blood may be shed").[8] Falsafi was a popular preacher who had been allied with Kashani and led the nationwide hysterical campaign against the Bahais in the 1950s. Muhammad-Reza Hakimi wrote a poetic article supporting Khomeini ("*Ava-yi Ruzha*" or "Voices of the Days" in a collection by the same name[9]) and was a vigorous opponent of the idea that religious leadership be exercised collegially (the idea of a *shura fatwa*): there should be only one imam, and he is Khomeini.

The dramatic confrontation between Khomeini and the Shah's regime in 1963 secured Khomeini's leadership of the religious opposition to the Shah, although not necessarily of the religious institution itself (he became recognized as one of seven top rank *maraje-i taqlid* (a supreme authority on law). At issue were the enfranchisement of women, land reform, rigged elections, loans from the U.S., capitulations exempting American officials from Iranian courts, and in general, a modernization program perceived as political and economic subordination to the West. In March 1963, paratroopers attacked the Faisiyeh semi-

nary in Qum, killing a number of students. Khomeini responded on the fortieth
day anniversary of this event with an emotionally and rhetorically powerful
speech, in which he drew parallels with the killings and desecration of the shrine
of Imam Reza in Meshad by soldiers of the Pahlavi regime in 1935 firing upon
protestors against Western dress codes and general tyranny; he charged that the
regime was intent on destroying the ordinances of Islam for the sake of oil and
Israel and that it was attempting to place the affairs of Muslims in the hands of
"Jews, Christians, and the enemies of Islam." Khomeini continued his attacks
through the spring, delivering another powerful speech on the tenth of Muharram (3 June 1963), the most emotionally intense day of the Shiite ritual year.

He began with a *rawzeh,* a rhetorical form, normally occurring at the end
rather than the beginning of a sermon or preachment, which elicits weeping
and is intended to instill in listeners a stoical determination to re-dedicate themselves to the principles of Islam no matter what the odds and external pressures:

> I seek refuge in Allah from the pursuing Satan. In the name of God, the most
> merciful, the most compassionate. It is now the evening of Ashura. Sometimes
> when I review the events of Ashura, I confront this question: If the Ummayyids
> and Yezid, the son of Moaviyeh, were waging war only with Husain, why then
> the savage, inhuman behavior towards the helpless women and the innocent chil-
> dren of Husain? What had the women and children done? What had the six month
> old baby of Husain done? [The audience cries.] I think they wanted to destroy the
> foundation [of the family of the Prophet]. The Umayyids and the regime of Yezid
> were against the family of the Prophet. They did not want the Bani Hashem to
> exist and they wanted to uproot the sacred [family] tree.[10]

The metaphor of the arch-tyrant and destroyer of Islam, Yezid, standing for the
Shah, used throughout the sixties and seventies in preachments, is made explicit:

> I ask the same question here: If the brutal regime of Iran is engaged in a war with
> the ulama, why did it tear the Quran apart while attacking the Faisiyeh Seminary?
> What did it have against the Faisiyeh Seminary? What did it have against the stu-
> dents of theology? What did it have against our eighteen year old sayyid [Sayyid
> Younes Rudbari who had been killed in the March assault]? [The audience cries.]
> What had our eighteen year old sayyid done to the Shah? What had he done against
> the government? What had he done against the brutal regime of Iran? [The audi-
> ence cries.] Therefore we must conclude that it wanted to do away with the foun-
> dation. It is against the foundation of Islam and the clergy. It does not want this
> foundation to exist. It does not want our youth and elders to exist.

Israel is then invoked as the root of all satanic evil and humiliation:

> Israel does not want the Quran to exist in this country. Israel does not want the
> ulama of Islam to exist in this country. Israel does not want the laws of Islam to
> exist in this country. Israel does not want the well-informed to exist in this coun-

try. Israel, through her black agents, devastated the Faisiyeh Seminary. She is destroying us; she is destroying you. She wants to control your economy. She wants to ruin your commerce and agriculture. She wants to possess the property of this land. Through her agents she wants to remove every obstacle to her ends. The Quran is an obstacle; it has to go. The clergy is an obstacle; it has to go. The Faisiyeh seminary is an obstacle; it must be ruined. The religious students are future obstacles; they must be murdered; they must be thrown from the rooves; their heads and hands must be broken. Just because Israel must succeed, the government of Iran, following the blueprints and goals of Israel, must humiliate us.

Anger is expressed at the charge that the clergy are parasites; quite the contrary, it is the rich who are the parasites. And he admonishes the Shah:

I advise you Mr. Shah, Shah sir, I advise you to change your ways. If one day your masters decide you should go, I would not want the people to have cause to celebrate your departure. I do not wish for you the same destiny as your father.... God knows that the people rejoiced when Pahlavi left.... Listen to the advice of the clergy.... Do not listen to Israel.... I hope when you said that the reactionaries are impure animals, you were not referring to the clergy. Otherwise our duty will be most onerous and you will have a difficult time. You will not be able to live. The people will not let you continue. Are Islam and the clergy black reactionaries? But you black reactionary, you have created this white revolution. For what is this white revolution?

He charges that a group of preachers (vaezin) in Teheran were detained by the secret police and were threatened and forced to promise not to talk about three subjects: nothing against the Shah, nothing against Israel, and not to say that Islam is in danger. And he counter threatens:

Why does SAVAK say, "Do not speak about the Shah or Israel?" Does SAVAK mean the Shah is an Israeli? Is it the opinion of SAVAK that the Shah is a Jew? Mr. Shah! They want to portray you as a Jew so that I might declare you a kafir (unbeliever), so that you might be kicked out of Iran, so that you might be punished. Don't you realize that if one day you falter, none of these will stand by you. They are loyal only to the dollar. They do not have any faith; they have no loyalty; they try to blame you for everything. That little man whose name I will not mention [the audience cries] came to Madraseh Faisiyeh, blew his whistle, and the commandoes gathered around him. He ordered: "Forward, smash and ransack all the rooms; destroy everything." When he is asked, "Why did you do that?" he answers, "It was the order of His Imperial Majesty to destroy the Madraseh Faisiyeh, to kill and destroy."

And he ends:

Our country, our Islam are in danger. What is happening, and what is about to happen worries and saddens us. We are worried and saddened by the situation of this ruined country. We hope to God that things can be reformed.

Early the next morning, Khomeini was arrested. Thousands of people in cities all over Iran protested. They were met with military force, and thousands were martyred. The 15 Khordad (5 June 1963) became a day of infamy. Khomeini was saved from execution by several ayatullahs, led by Ayatullah Muhammad-Kazem Shariatmadari, certifying his status (for the first time) as a grand ayatullah (ayatullah al-uzma), the top rank of the clergy, thereby putting the state on notice that his execution would have the most serious consequences. Upon his release, Khomeini again delivered a blistering public speech, denying that he had compromised with the regime while in prison, as had been reported in the Etelaat newspaper. He began with the Quranic verse, "From God we come and unto Him we shall return," i.e., I cannot be intimidated. Again he utilized rawzeh techniques, eliciting tears and emotional responses:

> Never have I felt incapable of speaking, but today I do, for I am incapable of expressing my anguish, anguish caused by the situation of the Islamic world in general, and Iran in particular, the events of the past year, and especially the incident in Madraseh Faisiyeh. I was not aware of the incident of the 15 Khordad. When my imprisonment was commuted into house arrest, I was given news from the outside. God knows the events of the 15 Khordad devastated me. [Audience cries.] Now that I have come here from Qeytariyeh, I am confronted with sad things: little orphans [audience cries], mothers who have lost their young ones, the women who have lost their brothers [much crying], lost legs, sad hearts—these are the proofs of their "civilization" and our being reactionaries. Alas we do not have access to the rest of the world; alas our voice does not reach the world. Alas the world cannot hear the voice of these mourning mothers. [Much crying.]

He turns his anger against the charge that the clergy are reactionary; that they want to return to the Middle Ages; that they oppose electricity, cars, or airplanes. He claims for Islam the legacy of the Constitution. Islam is the source of all freedoms, of independence, of greatness. It was the clergy who brought about the Constitution, which guaranteed freedom of expression and free press. He criticized the begging of dollars (loans), the elaborate reception of foreigners, the bureaucracy, the misspending of the money of the poor, the use of radio and TV to drug people into acquiescence, the alliance with Israel, and the subordination to colonial powers. He objects to using Israeli advisors and sending students to Israel; better they should be sent to England or the United States, lest Sunnis begin baiting Shiites as Jew-lovers. He urges that the Constitution be put into practice. He mocks the claims that the government wants to establish an Islamic university and compares their misuse of Islam with Muawiyeh's trick of placing Qurans on his soldiers' spears so that Ali could not fight him. He speaks of an insult to any cleric (himself in this case) as an insult to Islam and says that all must stand united in the defense of Islam. He ends with a somewhat backhanded expression of gratitude to the clergy for having stood by him.

On 4 November 1964, Khomeini was exiled first to Turkey and then was allowed to go to Najaf in Iraq, where he spent the next decade and a half. He maintained his ties in Iran by serving as a *marja-i taqlid,* one to whom religious tithes (the *sahm-i imam,* one-half of the *khums* tax) are made for redistribution to students of religion and other purposes and by sending back missives, tape-recorded speeches, and writings. In 1971, for instance, he inveighed against the Shah's elaborate celebrations of 2500 years of continuous monarchy, reminding his followers that Muslims had nothing in common with the pre-Islamic heritage of Iran, and Islam had come to destroy the principle of hereditary monarchy. He appealed to his fellow clerics to protest, to the heads of state invited not to attend, and for all Muslims to refrain from participation. He charged that Israelis were arranging the festival, the same Israelis whom he charged with burning the al-Aqsa mosque, with attempting to pass doctored copies of the Quran from which verses critical of Jews had been excised, and with penetrating all economic, military, and political affairs of Iran, turning it in effect into a military base of Israel and by extension for America.[11]

This was also the period in which he delivered the lectures in his *dars-i kharej* (the highest level of classes in the seminary system) which were published as *Islamic Government: Guardianship by the Clergy.* These lectures apparently began in a dispute with Ayatullah Abul-Qassim Khoi.[12] The latter responded to students' questions about whether the formula "guardianship by the clergy" (*vilayat-i faqih*) included the obligation or right of clerics to participate directly in the political process and indeed to govern. Khoi responded that no such guardianship existed. Khomeini thereupon devoted two weeks of classes to a rebuttal and defense of a maximalist interpretation of clerics as the only legitimate supervisors of politics.

He candidly admits that a textual demonstration from the hadith literature is not conclusive,[13] but argues that supervision of politics, or even rule by religious scholars is logically self-evident from the nature of Islam. It can be supported by the examples of the Prophet and the imams and through the joint consideration of a series of hadith, none of which individually is unambiguous but taken together constitute a clear stand.[14] Indeed, he says at the very beginning, it would never have occurred to anyone to question that religious scholars should supervise politics had it not been for the attempts of the Jews and the imperialists to suggest otherwise. It is they who have taught false religious teachers (now ensconced even in the very heart of the Islamic seminaries) to say that religion and politics should be separated, that Islam is not a comprehensive system of social regulations covering every possible topic[15], that Islam demands no specific form of government, and that while Islam may have a few ethical

principles it is mainly concerned with ritual purity. Many ulama have descended
to this false view of Islam. But what kind of faithfulness is it to Islam to treat
its penal provisions as merely a text for recitation?

> For example, we recite the verse: "Administer to the adulterer and the adulteress
> a hundred lashes each" (S. 24:2), but we do not know what to do when confronted
> with a case of adultery. We merely recite the verse in order to improve the quality
> of our recitation and to give each sound its full value. (Algar translation, p. 75)

So too, what sense would it make for the Prophet to have brought the divine
law and not provided for successors to implement it?

> The major portion of the argument is devoted to establishing that those learned
> in the law, who are also just (i.e., not enmeshed in personal worldly ambition), are
> the only ones who ultimately can judge what in society is according to Islam, and
> what is not. After all, a major traditional Shiite argument that the first three caliphs
> were usurpers is that they often did not know the law and its procedures.

As to specifics about what an Islamic government might look like, there is
precious little. Islamic taxes are invoked as sufficient to run a government.
These include the *khums,* defined as one-fifth of all surplus income of all enter-
prises from the farmer to the industrialist, the voluntary *zakat* (dismissed as a
minimal amount), the *jizya* tax on non-Muslim "protected minorities," and the
kharaj (on state held land). But the argument about taxes is mainly used as evidence that such enormous sums as could be generated by the *khums* in particular were intended to support a state government and not just a minor parochial
religious institution within society.

Legislatures are dismissed as unnecessary, since all laws have already been
provided by God. Instead there need only be planning boards to set agendas and
supervise ministries (Algar, p. 56). The executive and judiciary are distinguished
(both in modern governments and in logical principle) (Algar, pp. 88, 96). Judicial functions are divided into civil disputes between individuals and crimes
against society prosecuted by a state prosecutor (Algar, p. 91). Rulers are defined
by their knowledge and morality, but any further specification of executive or
administrative problems is dismissed by acknowledging that

> the acquisition of knowledge and expertise in various sciences—is necessary for
> making plans for a country and for exercising executive and administrative func-
> tions; we too will make use of people with those qualifications. But as for the
> supervisions and supreme administration of the country, the dispensing of justice
> and the establishment of equitable relations among the people—these are precisely
> the subjects that the *faqih* [pl. *fuqaha*] has studied. (Algar p. 137)

The possibility is considered that a non-scholar ruler may consult scholars, but the issue is then mooted as to who is really the ruler:

> In such a case, the real rulers are the jurisprudents and the sultans are nothing but people working for them (JPRS translation, p. 20) or This being the case, the true rulers are the *fuqaha* themselves, and the rulership ought officially to be theirs. (Algar, p. 60)

The possibility is also considered that supervision of politics be in the hands of an individual jurisprudent or alternatively be collectively the responsibility of a number of jurisprudents (Algar, p. 62, 64). The principle is affirmed that no jurisprudent has precedence over any other (Algar, p. 64). And a jurisprudent who acts against Islam will be dismissed (Algar, p. 79), though it is not said according to what procedure.

Non-Muslims are only mentioned in passing to affirm that a society with both Muslims and non-Muslims must be under Muslim control (Algar, p. 89), "with the utmost force and decisiveness and without exhibiting the least trace of feeling" (Algar, p. 89). The annihilation of the Jewish tribe Bani Qurayza by the Prophet is given as a salutary example.

The final section of the lectures is devoted to bringing about an Islamic government. It is thought here that the effort will be a long, slow one, over perhaps two centuries, involving first propagation and teaching of true Islam, utilizing communal forms of worship as political forums (communal prayers, pilgrimages, Friday prayers), reforming the seminaries, purging false clerics, and adhering to an ascetic dedication which shuns the goods of this world.

Amid the attacks on imperialism, monarchy and Jews, and the calls for political engagement and economic redistribution ("For that is your Islamic duty, to take from the rich and give to the poor," Algar, p. 74), there are scattered hints that the goals of Islamic government are transcendental and not merely concerned with justice in society: "a just society that will morally and spiritually nourish refined human beings" (Algar, p. 80); the interpretation of a hadith attributed to Imam Sadeq—scholars are the heirs of the Prophets since prophets bequeath not wealth but knowledge—as meaning not that the Prophets bequeathed only learning and traditions, but that they were men of God and not materialistic (Algar, p. 106); and the repeated reference to the hadith relating Ali's evaluation of rulership as being worth less than a goat's sneeze, it being a duty extracted from scholars by God to prevent the decay of Islam.

During the 1970s Khomeini was a clear reference point for militant religious opposition to the Shah. His *Islamic Government* and occasional other missives circulated clandestinely. In the fall of 1977, his elder son mysteriously died or was killed, and in January 1978 a newspaper attack on Khomeini helped spark

demonstrations which provoked government violence and helped fuel the revolutionary process. During the 1977–79 revolution, Khomeini was expelled
from Iraq, denied entry to Kuwait, and was persuaded to center himself in Paris
where he had access to the international media as well as printing and tape
recording facilities. On 1 February 1979, Khomeini returned triumphantly to
Iran to preside over the creation of an Islamic republic and to demonstrate his
authority over all other potential leaderships: the more liberal constitutionalist
leadership of Ayatullah S. Muhammad-Kazem Shariatmadari, the more social-
ist-leaning S. Mahmud Taleghani, the lay leadership of Engineering Professor
Mehdi Bazargan, or the would-be heirs of Dr. Ali Shariati.

I V

Part of the appeal of Khomeini must be analyzed in terms of his persona, the
image he projects, rather than either his personality per se or his program and
tactics alone. The latter were often vague and changeable; in any case, people
placed faith in Khomeini far above and beyond enunciated programs. There are,
I have suggested elsewhere at greater length,[16] five dimensions to the legendary
figure of Khomeini, which taken together compose an emotionally powerful
configuration.

First, and least distinctive, is a play upon the tension between Shiism as
Iranian nationalism and Islam as universalistic. Khomeini's persona has an aura
of ethnic marginality upon which people continually comment. His great
grandfather moved from Khorasan to India (popular versions usually specify
Kashmir); his grandfather returned to Khomein. These ancestral peregrinations
allow a labeling that somehow Khomeini is "Indian." An elder brother took the
name "Hindi"; and Khomeini himself as a young man used that surname to sign
his poetry. It has been pointed out before that many nationalist leaders—the
Corsican Napoleon, the Austrian Hitler, the Georgian Stalin—have had per-
sonae which resonate with tension between nationalist and universalist ideologies. Khomeini himself rejects Iranian nationalism insisting on Islamic (albeit
Shiite) universalism. The story is told that great efforts had to be exerted in Paris
to persuade him to speak of Iran, a sine qua non if he was to appeal to a wide
spectrum of Iranians. During the drafting of the new constitution, again the
issue arose, and Khomeini's phrase of a supreme *faqih* (to excercise the *vilayat-
i faqih* or guardianship of the clergy) to serve as head of state had to be modified
to make sure that he would be an Iranian, something unimportant to Khomeini,
though quite important to most Iranians.

More important is that Khomeini's persona cultivates a legend of distress,
connecting him with the martyr of Karbala. There are several parts to this con-

struction, beginning with the death of his father at the hands of—depending on the variant—a bandit, a mayor, a civil servant, or a landowner, but whichever, an agent of Reza Shah. This deprivation is said to have occurred either when Khomeini was six months old or a year and a half. This would place the event around 1900, but Reza Shah did not come to power until the 1920s. The legend continues that his mother sought and obtained some revenge, either the execution of the murderer or the removal of the governor; but in any case, the theme is established that obstinacy in pursuit of justice is part of the family tradition and is ultimately rewarded. The second important component of the legend of distress is Khomeini's exile from Iran in 1964, made emotionally more compelling by the (apparently true) story that he narrowly escaped execution thanks to the intervention of Ayatullah Shariatmadari and others. Like the imams, Khomeini was denied his rightful position. Analogous to the theme of the eventual return of the twelfth imam, the Mahdi, there is also a legend that Khomeini performed a divination before moving to Qum in 1920 and learned that he would die in Qum; this was taken by his followers throughout his long exile in Iraq to mean that he would return to Iran in triumph. The third component of the legend of distress is the loss first of an infant daughter and, more importantly, in the fall of 1977, the death of his elder son, many Iranians believe, at the hands of SAVAK, the Shah's secret police. The themes of this persona of enduring distress and injustice include a father unjustly killed, a son deprived of rightful possessions (father, land, position, children), and the need to pursue justice in the face of overwhelming odds. These are the themes of Ali and Husain and of the imams. According to the Shiite account, all the imams were either slain or poisoned (except the last, who will return); the theme of poison—Westernization and colonialism as a poison—is one that Khomeini plays upon.

More interesting yet, a distinctive feature of Khomeini's persona is that he dabbled in mysticism, a subject that the orthodox fear can easily destroy faith. Part of the defense of Khomeini's supreme position and the attribution to him of the title Imam (which in Persian until the revolution was reserved for the twelve Imams alone) is the suggestion that he can control dangerous esoteric knowledge as well as power, both of which can easily destroy lesser men.

Closely allied to this mystical component is Khomeini's asceticism, his eschewing of humor and positive affect, the studied monotone in which he speaks. The contrast is striking here with the style of other ayatullahs, who cultivate humor as a way of engaging followers. Gnosticism or mysticism is dangerous, and the pursuit of the enlightenment it can yield requires much self-control. Islamic asceticism (*zuhd*) is not withdrawal from the world, but a refusal to be seduced by materialist concerns. Asceticism is a technique to avoid the madness (either manic ecstasy or depression) mystical pursuits can induce;

it is also a technique to avoid corruption in a corrupt world. Less profound, but of equal public relations importance, the ascetic style serves to ward off the suspicion that whoever exercises power must be self-seeking.

Finally, unlike the other top-rank ulama, Khomeini cultivates a populist language of confrontation and a propaganda style of comic-book-like hyperbole. Whereas other ulama speak in scholarly, considered language, Khomeini speaks the language of the ordinary man, attacking intellectuals and eggheads, the rich and the elite. He plays a politics of trusting the masses as well as occasionally intervening to balance factions of central political actors. When the Iran-Iraq war broke out, rather than turning to the army, Khomeini called for arms to be given to the people: if the young men cannot save the country, it is not worth saving; we have not fought a revolution just for security and economic well-being, but for Islam, for a just society, for non-alignment, for a society responsive to the common man, not one subservient to a professionalized army dependent on foreign arms, advisors, and control.

The total configuration of Khomeini's persona is one which draws on traditional images in a forceful way none of the other top ulama or lay leaders can match. Like Husain, he represents perseverance for justice against all odds, with an ability to endure injustice and suffering. Like Ali, Khomeini represents combined political and religious leadership, utilizing all means at hand, including force and cunning on behalf of Islam, the Muslim community, and the just society. Like the imams, Khomeini represents access to wisdom and ability to control the dangers to ordinary men of dabbling in esoteric knowledge or in power. It is an emotional configuration which stresses stoicism and determination in a tragic world where injustice and corruption all too often prevail. It is a continuation of the emotional configuration of the Karbala Story, which forms the central symbolic core of popular religion in Iran. It is a configuration which ought to appeal to the sub-proletarian populations of rural migrants to the cities as well as to the traditional petit bourgeoisies and some (if not all) of their sons educated in the modern university system.[17]

V

There are, of course, social strata who are less than enamoured of Khomeini, the man or his persona. Peasants of a village near Shiraz could skeptically dismiss Khomeini as another Shah and his clerical minions as so many capricious and corrupt bureaucrats.[18] Many close to the clerical establishment recognize Khomeini's place within it and, consequently, are too close to allow any validity to his claims of sole supreme leadership. Outside detractors speculate about a new nepotistic elite around Khomeini bonded by kinship and filial ties. Angry cartoonists, testing impolitic juxtapositions and Rabelaisian puncturings of pretension, portray him as the owl of death perched above a field of human bones, in the uniform of the Shah or counting a rosary of skulls.[19]

The sociologist, Said Amir Arjomand, charges that Khomeini in the early 1960s "set out to create . . . a traditionalist political movement," and that he has succeeded through the 1979 constitution in becoming the first Caesar-Pope in Shiite history.[20] Arjomand argues on organizational grounds, citing Max Weber, that with the emergence of mass politics, clerical establishments claiming political influence must also organize as parties. How much of such Weberian intuition or strategy is attributable to Khomeini himself and how much to the evolving dynamics of the Islamic Republican Party leadership, remains unclear. What is clear is that by 1970–71, Khomeini had given up his traditionalist language of urging the Shah to reform and engaged in an effort to formulate a justification for maximalist control of the clergy in the political sphere. By 1979 he was slowly shedding the veils of constitutionalist rhetoric by which he had engaged the alliance of such men as Mehdi Bazargan, Ibrahim Yazdi, and Abul-Hassan Bani-Sadr.

How much of this shedding was calculated deceit on his part (justifiable in terms of *taqiyya,* dissimulation in defense of Islam) and how much was self-delusion on the part of his allies may perhaps be illustrated in an anecdote from the time when he first led prayers in Paris. The prayers were held in a tent, and several women complained about having to remain outside while the men disappeared inside. Khomeini responded that their complaint would be heeded, that prayers should be done as the Prophet did early in his career, with men and women intermingled. The women were impressed, and a number may have taken this as a sign of Khomeini's relative liberality. To those who thought about the reference to Muhammad, however, it should have been clear that this was but a temporary device: when surrounded by unbelievers, one does not leave women outside unprotected.

Muslim religious opponents of Khomeini (excluding secularists) comprise an interesting set: former Prime Minister Mehdi Bazargan (who complained of Khomeini's deceit to Oriana Fallaci shortly before being squeezed out of power), Sayyid Mahmud Taleqhani (the leading cleric sympathetic to the left), Ayatullah Muhammad-Kazem Shariatmadari, and in general, those who see themselves as heirs to Dr. Ali Shariati (including especially the "Islamic leftist" Mujahheddin party).

Shariatmadari is the most prominent of a group of conservative to liberal ayatullahs (including the late Ayatullah Bahaeddin Mahallati of Shiraz, Sheikh Ali Tehrani of Meshad, and Ayatullah Abdullah Shirzi-Qumi of Meshad) who have warned and protested against the autocratic style of Khomeini and of the Islamic Republican Party. In the first phase of the 1977–79 revolution, Shariatmadari was the most important religious leader inside Iran. Throughout the 1970s he had adopted the strategy of the good shepherd, attempting to protect his followers, to tacitly negotiate with the government, to maintain a posture of moral critique of Iranian society. This strategy was in conscious contrast to Khomeini's confrontation style. It was thus a major signal that something revolutionary was occurring when Shariatmadari in January 1978 publicly condemned the Shah's regime for killing religious demonstrators in Qum. Throughout the first phase of the revolution, Shariatmadari exercised a leadership role, attempting to pressure the government while simultaneously urging his flock not to provoke unnecessary violence from a vastly superior military machine. Upon Khomeini's return, Shariatmadari quietly invoked his seniority, having Khomeini come to him to pay his respects first. He warned that Khomeini's acquiescence in the use of the title "Imam" was close to blasphemous.[21] He reminded people that political decisions invoking Islamic authority should be made, if not collegially, at least through the consensus of the top ranked clergy. He objected to the railroading through of the referendum which established an Islamic republic. He objected to the proposal to have a small group of people around Khomeini draft a new constitution which would only then, if at all, have popular input through a similarly managed referendum. He objected to the insertion of the phrase *vilayat-i faqih* into the constitution, and to the referendum which ratified it. In general, until he was silenced, he served as the religious leader of the conservative-liberal forces of the revolution.

Ayatullah S. Mahmud Taleghani had, together with Mehdi Bazargan, led the Freedom Movement of Iran. Both had been involved with the group of clerical and lay reformers in the period 1960–63 which had held discussions and lectures, and had published a journal, *Goftar-e Mah* (Monthly Speeches) as well as the important volume, *An Inquiry into the Principle of Marjaiyyat* (clerical leadership) *and the Clergy*. The central concerns of this group were how to reform the clergy and revitalize the religious institution. Such innovations as collegial decisions (*shura fatwa*) by top clerics, and the apportioning of technical areas of responsibility so that different religious leaders might acquire a degree of specialization in matters affecting a modern economy and polity were discussed. From 1965 to 1973 this group of reformers was centered in the buildings called the Husainiya Ershad. Similar institutions had been established earlier in Meshed by Sayyid Abdol-Karim Hashemi-Nejad and Sayyid Mahmud Abtahi, and subsequently in Shiraz by the Mahallatis. The leading light in Teheran was Dr. Ali Shariati who galvanized the youth by proposing to fuse the latest in Western social theory with Islam, thereby making possible a renewal of understanding of Islam for the contemporary world and a cleansing of Islam of decayed and corrupted scholasticism. Shariati argued against the scholasticism of the traditional clergy, arguing that since the Safavid period the clergy had overseen a religion shot through with superstition, shrine worship, mediation between man and God, meaningless ritualism, and above all appropriation of authority by ignorant old men. This hierarchical, fossilized and superstitious religion he tagged "Safavid Shiism." Muslims needed a Protestant reformation, a cleansing and renewal that insisted upon each Muslim undertaking responsibility for his own actions and for helping to think through the moral, social and political meaning of Islam in a fashion relevant to a modern, technological society. Such an understanding of Islam, he tagged the original and true "Alavi Shiism." Naturally enough, the traditional clergy did not much like Shariati. They wrote some tracts against him, pointing out errors of doctrinal scholarship. But they tread carefully, recognizing in him not merely an ally against the Shah, but more importantly a generational hero: too open an attack would lose them much of the youth.

Shariati died in 1977. The Mujaheddin, who see him as one of their heroes, had earlier broken away from Bazargan's Freedom Movement over the issue of the use of violence. In the 1970s they began a small guerilla movement. They too experienced a split (in 1975) between those who wished to remain Islamic marxists and those who opted for a secular path. A son of Taleghani, Mujtabai, led the secular faction. At the time of the first phase of the revolution, the father, S. Mahmud Taleghani, led the massive street demonstrations on 9 Muharram 1979, a month after having been released from prison. When Khomeini returned from Paris, Taleghani (like Shariatmadari) refused to join the clerical greeters; he was at the airport, but sat apart, allegedly responding ironically to invitations to join the other ulama by saying: that is the place for the ulama (literally "the learned"), I belong here with the *jahil* (street toughs, the ignorant). Just a few months later, he dramatically went underground in protest against the efforts of the Khomeini forces to monopolize the revolution, against the escalating rate of executions, and against the attempt to round up the Mujaheddin (including two of his own children). After a meeting with Khomeini, he was silenced for a few more months, but then returned to public criticism shortly before he died, warning that there was danger of a dictatorship worse than that of the Shah: dictatorship by religious students *(inhizab-i tulab)*. He reminded Muslims that it was contrary to Islam to deprive people of the right to criticize, to protest, and to express grievances; that consultation in Islam did not mean decision-making by an oligarchy, but democratic councils at all levels of society.[22]

It is important to stress that Khomeini's voice or the voice of the Islamic Republican Party are not the only Islamic voices in Iran. It is important to listen to those other voices to see where the limits are of Khomeini's claim to represent Iranians, to embody the values of freedom, transcendence of class divisions, authenticity, and social justice. These limits help define the line between a people voluntarily struggling to live up to an Islamic ideal and imposing a tyranny in the name of Islam. But above all, in terms of evaluating Khomeini, the man and the persona, it provides a means to see where and why so many Muslims misunderstood him, and mistook his mystical vision for a revolutionary one. For these now disillusioned former allies and followers, who bitterly complain of deceit, revolution was the goal: a government to arrange social affairs in a more just way. For Khomeini, such a government is "not the ultimate aim; it is merely the means for advancing man toward that goal for the sake of which all the prophets were sent."[23]

V I

The transcendent goals of Khomeini's Islamic Republic may be explored by (1) juxtaposing his lectures on Sura Fatiha with the work of the great seventeenth century Mulla Sadra; (2) tracing the evolution of his political pronouncements since the 1940s; and (3) considering those acts of the current regime clearly motivated at his direction in the light of the logically possible relations between rulers and the ruled. All three considerations confirm millenarian or mystical, rather than revolutionary, intentions and trajectories, in the dual senses of being transcendental (and having all the tyrannical dangers of forcing utopias on this world, dangers analyzed clearly by classical Muslim scholars), as well as being counter-revolutionary (traditionalist, invoking mediational levels of access to God, insisting upon hierarchical religious authority) over against the "Protestant" reformation goals of Shariati, of the Husainiye Ershad, and of the Freedom of Movement in the 1960s and 1970s.

Two sets of polar arguments about the relation between ideals and actualization are often debated in Muslim scholarship:

1a—Once each individual becomes truly Muslim, all need for social coercion and oppressive state structures will wither away; versus

1b—The Quran speaks of justice and iron (the sword) in Sura Hadid (Sura on Iron), i.e., force may be required to establish the social conditions to foster the development of true Muslims and a true Muslim society.[24]

2a—Knowledge is accessible to all reasonable men, and so society can rely on consultation among men; versus

2b—Divine knowledge is the privilege of the few (an imam or amir; a body of ulama) and so society must be ruled by a tutelage dictatorship/oligarchy. Khomeini's writings have increasingly stressed the second of each pair.

He began in his 1943 *Revealing the Secrets* with a traditional advisory stance toward government: "Bad government is better than no government. We have never attacked the sultanate; if we criticized, it was a particular king and not kingship that we criticized. History shows that *mujtahids* have aided kings, even kings who did wrong: Nasir-ud-Din Tusi, Mohaqqiq Sani, Shaykh Bahai, Mir Damad, Majlisi" (p. 187). Or again:

> Some say that government may remain in the hands of those who have it, but they must get approval [*ijaza*] from the legal experts [*faqih*]. Yes, but a *mujtahid* can give such approval only under condition that the law of the country is the law of God. Our country does not meet this condition since the government is neither constitutional nor the law of God. Yet bad government is better than no government, and *mujtahids* do not simply attack it, but if necessary help it (p. 189).

Indeed he goes so far as to argue (inaccurately[25]) that despite the fact that the Umayyids were the worst government to date in their hostility to the family of the Prophet, nonetheless the fourth Imam composed a long prayer for their protection. One should remember that it was the clerics who prevented Reza Shah from declaring a republic in 1924. Fearing republicanism would also mean Attaturk-style secularization, they insisted on a monarchical form of government. In *Revealing the Secrets,* Khomeini complains about the materialistic and selfish motives of politicians and kings. His solutions are: taking advice from the ulama, allowing the ulama to appoint a just man as king, allowing the ulama to serve as a kind of parliament. In any case, he denies any desire to see ulama as kings or direct rulers.

By the 1960s, as we have seen, Khomeini is claiming the legacy of the Constitution for the ulama. It was they, he claims, who brought it about; it is they who are advocates of the liberal values of freedom of expression. This, of course, is an adversary stance, and can be interpreted as an argument: if not a fully Islamic government, then at least a constitutional one. By 1970, Khomeini is arguing that monarchy is incompatible with Islam, at least in the sense that any form of government must be subordinate to the law of Islam. The crimes of monarchs throughout Iran's history are recited, and gradually by the end of the 1970s the call is made to overthrow not only the particular monarch on the throne but monarchy as well. The argument over *ulil amr,* the Quranic formula in Sura Nesa: 62 ("Oh you who have faith, obey God, obey the Prophet of God, and obey the *ulil amr* [the issuer of orders]") was merged with the discussions over the formula *vilayat-i faqih.* The latter in traditional jurisprudence primarily referred to guardianship over persons not competent to look after their own financial affairs (orphans, widows, the mentally deficient, communal religious property lacking a designated administrator); occasional references in the literature hint at extending this meaning to political guardianship. It was Khomeini's purpose in *Islamic Government* to try to build a case for this expansion.

After the revolution, Khomeini's speeches became filled with calls for unity and steadfastness of purpose. There is an ambiguous fusion between pragmatic necessity to defend the revolution and more long term efforts to reorganize social consciousness. There are his defenses of summary execution and dismissal of due process procedures: criminals need no lawyers, he insisted on several occasions. There are his calls for unity of expression (*vahdat-e kalam*), and his exhortations to parents to turn in children who seem recalcitrant to the new regime. There is the insertion in the preamble to the new Constitution of 1979 (which sees the history of the regime in terms of the career of Khomeini) of the term *maktabi*: once *maktabi* meant merely "bookish"; now it means "according to the Book, the Quran" and is a device used to exclude anyone who does not adhere to the interpretations of the regime.[26] It has been argued that Khomeini has thus for the first time turned the *shariah* into a tool for moulding consciousness, for invading man's private relationship with God.[27] Traditionally there was no *taqlid* (following of a scholar's example, instruction or advice) in matters of faith, but only in matters of practice (and even then one should not follow blindly).[28] What one does is a matter of social concern, a matter between men; what one thinks is to be judged by God alone. Now, however, what one thinks, or at least what one says, is to be judged and sanctioned by the state. Rose points out that "Ayatullah"[29] Muhammad Beheshti, architect of the Islamic Republican Party, divided clerics by their ideological purity rather than their skill in traditional learning, and that Khomeini's overriding concern in all his speeches has been for long-term, difficult, reorganization of mass consciousness. One of Khomeini's more eloquent statements of concern for Iranian self-respect is his 1979 speech on the anniversary of the Black Friday (8 September 1978) Jaleh Square massacre:

> ... our problems and miseries are caused by losing ourselves. In Iran until something has a Western name it is not accepted. . . . The material woven in our factories must have something in the Latin script in its sleeve edges. . . . Our writers and intellectuals are also "Westoxicated" and so are we. . . . We forget our own phrases and the word itself. Easterners have completely forgotten their honor. . . . As long as you do not put aside these imitations, you cannot be a human being and independent. . . .
>
> An enlightened heart cannot stand by silently and watch while traditions and honor are trampled upon. An enlightened heart cannot see its people being drawn towards baseness of spirit or watch in silence while individuals around Tehran live in slums.
>
> The second commandment which God gave to Moses was "remind people of the Days of God" . . . some days have a particularity. The day that the great Prophet of Islam migrated to Medina . . . the day that he conquered Mecca. . . . The day of Khawarej . . . when Hazrat Ali unsheathed his sword and did away with these corrupt and cancerous tumors . . . the fifteenth of Khordad (5 June 1963) when a people stood against a force and they did something which caused almost five months of martial law. But because the people had no power, they were not consolidated, they were not awake, they were defeated. . . . The seventeenth of

Shahrivar (8 September 1978) was another one of the Days of God when a people, men, women, young people and older people, all stood up and, in order to get their rights, were martyred.... A nation which had nothing broke a force in such a way that nothing remained of it.... Empty-handed, a monarchical empire of 2500 years, 2500 years of criminals was done away with.

Note that the speech utilizes themes generally identified with non-clerical revolutionary spokesmen: the phrase "Westoxification" comes from a famous essay by Jalal Al-Ahmad; the theme of imitation/alienation was popularized in the 1970s by Shariati, drawing on Sartre and Fanon. The rhetorical device of iterated Days of God is a powerful cosmogenic image derived from both preaching skills and literary metaphorizations (which also provided power and popularity to Shariati's formulations). The themes of alienation, Westoxification, and false understanding of Islam mean to Khomeini that Iran is faced with a deep-seated problem beyond any simple political or economic reconstruction.

Thus, as we have noted, when Iraq attacked Iran and President Bani-Sadr suggested releasing military personnel from prison to fight, Khomeini reminded the country that the revolution had not been fought merely for economic well-being, a different political system, or territorial integrity, but for Islam. If the country could not be defended without giving the army the hegemony of force it had previously used to oppress the people, then Iran was not worth saving. As he put it elsewhere:

Once someone asked Imam Ali a question concerning the divine unity just as a battle was about to begin, and he proceeded to answer it. When another person objected, "Is now the time for such things?" he replied, "This is the reason that we are fighting Muawiya, not for any worldly gain. It is not our true aim to capture Syria; of what value is Syria?" (Algar, p. 400–401)

Such transcendent and long-term attitudes towards Iran's problems have provided practical politicians and interpreters of Khomeini (Prime Ministers, Presidents, leaders of the Islamic Republican Party) with contradictory instructions at times, as well as with a certain inflexibility towards pragmatic issues. Economics, Khomeini is alleged to have said at one point, is for donkeys. Legislation, we have seen, is an unnecessary activity: the role of parliament is merely to set agendas and to oversee implementation; the laws themselves are divine or deducible from the Quran and the hadith. This is not senile obtuseness but an insistence that details of administration are inconsequential, can be handled in any number of ways, as long as over-all policy is rightly guided, and a faith that right-guidance is either intuitively obvious or is simply decided by consulting with a few people who know the basic facts of a case.

Thus, Khomeini was first influenced to kill a land reform proposal which had been approved by the Revolutionary Council in 1979; and more recently in

1981, after renewed interest in Parliament, he overrode the objections of the Council of Guardians and approved the same proposal.[30] Or more starkly, Khomeini's response to the public outcry at the early pace of executions and the range of crimes for which people were executed, led him initially to direct that only those who killed and tortured for the Shah be executed. But the directives were ignored, and his, at minimum tacit, acquiescence since indicates that he still believes as he wrote in *Islamic Government*, "Islam is prepared to subordinate individuals to the collective interest of society and has rooted out numerous groups that were a source of corruption and harm to human society" (p. 89). The legal procedures and civil rights protections of Islamic law, on which the example of Imam Ali is often cited with pride by Shiites in contrast to the arbitrary rule of the Caliph Omar apparently do not apply in a society not yet Muslim (although Ali's example would deny this as his was also a period of struggle to create a Muslim society).

That Khomeini ordered a return to customary folk techniques of mourning the martyrdom of Husain during Muharram 1981 is a further indication of his transcendental rather than revolutionary concerns. In 1978 Khomeini had invoked the distinction between passive weeping and active witnessing and fighting for Husain's cause, and so he called for suspension of flagellations, processions and passion plays in favor of political marches and mobilization against the Shah. By 1981 the revolutionary moment has passed for him, and he is concerned with passive order, obedience to the regime, consolidation and stabilization, and has returned to his 1943 defense of all the psychological devices which aid people in their belief. His television defense of mysticism (the lectures on Sura Fatiha) suggested that while all Muslims should strive toward spiritual advance, certain people are already further along and can serve as leaders to the rest.

It is perhaps too easy to point out that there is nothing in this vision that remotely compares with a notion of politics as give and take between conflicting yet just group interests within society. There is nothing in this vision that considers the possibility that the business of administering society is anything more than a technical detail. Khomeini's program, when it comes down to it, consists of critique (of colonialism, imperialism, monarchy, bureaucracy, coercion based on economic inequality, alienation through erosion of cultural authenticity and self-confidence), of abstract moral vision (constructed from traditional parables, mystical philosophy, scholastic argumentation, and faith in the righteousness of Islamic jurisprudence), and strategic defenses (the construction of such legalisms as *maktabi, vilayat-i faqih,* a Council of Guardians, revolutionary courts). It is a valid expression of (especially petit bourgeois) exasperations, and it has claims to universalistic values (anti-imperialism, social

justice, cultural authenticity). As the example of the Imams so vividly and trag-
ically demonstrated so long ago, this is not enough.

Such Western critique may frame the tragic struggle of Khomeini for us. But
there is also a tragedy from an Iranian philosophical point of view as well, as
can be appreciated by juxtaposing Khomeini's lectures on Sura Fatiha with the
work of Mulla Sadra.[31] Khomeini's philosophy draws deeply on Mulla Sadra.
Both are inspired by a vision of simultaneous progress in social justice and spiritual consciousness. Both see the role of philosophical mysticism to be to integrate social norms (a stage of ethical agreement among men) with higher philosophical values, and thereby to give society a direction toward developing
greater justice, equity, and fulfillment. Both maintain a creative tension between
transcendent and ordinary perception. Both spoke out at critical historical junc-
tures when there seemed to be a possibility of guiding public interpretations and
symbols of man's destiny. Both deride literalist clerics, and defend the language
of mysticism. Mulla Sadra, however, attacks the notion that *mujtahids* or
fuqaha should serve as interpreters for the ignorant masses, whereas Khomeini
has adapted it as the cornerstone of his state policy. The difference is not
resolved if one considers that Khomeini's distinction between false clerics and
those who understand Islam might parallel Mulla Sadra's distinction between
fuqaha and *urafa* (enlightened mystics). Mulla Sadra keeps attention focussed
on the goals, the understanding, and the striving towards man's highest potential. The tragedy of Khomeini is that he has averted the gaze to the relative
strength or weakness of one man (or at best a council of particular men), the
faqih. Khomeini unintentionally has fulfilled Shariati's charge of practicing
Safavid Shiism, which would institutionalize the power of a clerical profession
and find justifications for traditional folk practices used to subordinate the
masses to that power. As Imam Ali put it many centuries ago:[32]

> The people are dead except the ulama; the ulama are dead except those who prac-
> tice their knowledge; all those who practice their knowledge are dead except the
> pious ones, and they are in great danger.

Notes

1. Translation by Mehdi Abedi from the text in *Zendigi-Nameh Iman Khomeini*
(Teheran: Fifteenth of Khordad Publishers, n.d.), volume 2, p. 1.

2. This essay complements arguments already laid out in 1) "Becoming Mullah:
Reflections on Iranian Clerics in a Revolutionary Age" (see especially part three, "The
Ayatullah as Allegory: A Walter Benjaminite Interpretation of Khomeini's Mesmerism"),

Iranian Studies 13:1/4 (1980); 2) "Islam and the Revolt of the Petit Bourgeoisie" *Daedalus* 111:1 (Winter 1982); and 3) *Iran: From Religious Dispute to Revolution* (Cambridge: Harvard University Press, 1980).

3. *Nahzat-e Imam Khomeini,* vol. I, The anonymous author is probably Shaikh Mahmad Razi. The work has been republished by the Houston chapter of the Islamic Students Association of North America.

4. Gregory Rose, "Vilayat-i Faqih: Alienation, Ideology and the Recovery of Islamic Identity in the Thought of Ayatollah Khomeini," Paper presented to the Society for Iranian Studies, November 1981, p. 15.

5. "Islamic government . . . is constitutional . . . not constitutional in the current sense of the word, i.e., based on the approval of laws in accordance with the opinion of the majority. It is constitutional in the sense that the rulers are subject to a certain set of conditions . . . set forth in the Noble Quran and the Sunna. . . ." Hamid Algar translation, *Islam and Revolution: Writings and Declarations of Imam Khomeini* (Berkeley: Mizan Press, 1981), p. 55.

6. Compare again Khomeini in 1970: "What connections do all the various articles of the Constitution, as well as the body of Supplementary Law concerning the monarchy, the succession, and so forth, have with Islam? They are all opposed to Islam; they violate the system of government and the laws of Islam." Ibid., p. 31.

7. The broadcast explains that at the time of Borujerdi's death, people interpreted "Ruhullah" to refer to "Isa Ruhullah," Jesus in his manifestation at the end of time; and that this had confused people (one should follow not reject prophets) and had alienated people from Borujerdi.

8. "They are irretrievable apostates (*mortad-e fitri,* apostates by nature) and [thus] their blood may be shed (*mahdur-e dam,* whose blood may be wasted) [by anyone]." *(Inha mortad-e fitri va mahdur-e dam hastand.)* Apostasy is a capital crime. The phrase *mahdur-e dam* implies that there need be no trial or decision by a constituted authority, but that anyone may perform the act on his own initiative.

9. Meshad: Tus Publishers, Esfand 1344.

10. Translation by Mehdi Abedi from the text in *Zendigi Nameh Imam Khomeini,* pp. 38–43.

11. See his declarations to the Hajj pilgrims of February 6, 1971, and his missive on the 2500 year celebrations of October 31, 1971.

12. Rose, "Vilayat-i Faqih," p. 11.

13. "If the only proof I had were one of the traditions I have been citing, I would be unable to substantiate my claim." Algar translation, p. 99.

14. Rose points out that in the long rehearsal of the argument from the hadith, Khomeini selects hadith in collections from the late Safavid period (especially from the *Wasail al-Shia* of Amili) in preference to earlier collections, and that by so doing he can salvage a crucial sentence not given in an early hadith, and can drop the last part of a hadith which he uses in a central way (the *maqbulah* of Umar ibn Hanzala). The abbreviated version in the *Wasail al-Shia* does not raise the issue of the fallibility of even the most pious and most learned, an issue centrally posed by the full version in the classic collection *Usul al-Kafi.* Rose thus provides a nice demonstration of Shariati's charge that the clergy, including Khomeini, tend to practice a Safavid Shiism. Said Amir Arjomand further points out that Khomeini's citation of Mullah Ahmad Naraqi as a precursor is not quite just, "The State and Khomeini's Islamic Order," *Iranian Studies* 13:1/4 (1980).

15. "There is not a single topic in human life for which Islam has not provided instruction and established a norm." (Algar, p. 30). See also the paragraph beginning, "First the laws of the shari'a embrace a diverse body of laws and regulations, which amounts to a complete social system." (Algar, p. 43).

16. "Becoming Mullah."

17. See "Islam and the Revolt of the Petite Bourgeoisie" for a fuller statement of this analysis of the social base of Khomeini's appeal.

18. Mary Hooglund, "One Village in the Revolution" MERIP Reports No. 87 (May 1980).

19. See the June 25 and July 26, 1981 issues of Iran Times.

20. "The State and Khomeini's Islamic Order" Iranian Studies 13:1/4 (1980): 153.

21. In pre-revolutionary Iranian Persian, "imam" was generally reserved for the twelve Imams. In Arabic, in Iraq, "imam" served as a title equivalent to ayatullah. Shariati provided leftists a rationale for using the title in Iran by comparing it to the Weberian definition of charismatic authority. In older philosophical usage, as in Mulla Sadra, it referred to a state of spiritual achievement. Khomeini initially carefully captioned his official portraits, "Nayeb-e Imam" (Aide to the Imam), a nineteenth-century title.

22. His television lectures on Sura Nazeat have been published by the Mujaheddin under the title, Ba Quran dar Sanah (With the Quran in the Battlefield). In them he distinguishes metaphysical interpretations of the Quran from their everyday social meanings. He had previously published a somewhat different interpretation of the same Sura in Partoi az Quran (Rays from the Quran) and says he modified his opinions while he was in prison. The Islamic Republican Party refused to publish these talks and instead issued a book by Khomeini using the same title.

23. Lecture 5 on Sura Fatiha (1980), in Algar translation, p. 415.

24. This verse has interesting populist implications which the Islamic Republican Party would like to deny: "We sent down with [our Messengers] the Book and the Balance so that men [nas, the people] might uphold justice. And we sent down iron, wherein is great might. . . ." (Arthur J. Arberry translation, The Koran Interpreted (New York: Oxford University Press, 1964), p. 567.

25. Ironically, the dua or prayer of Imam Sajad does not mention the Umayyids but only prays for the soldiers of Islam. It is Khomeini who draws the inference that since the government at the time was an Umayyid Caliphate, the prayer was in their defense.

26. Indeed on 6 Khordad 1360, Khomeini issued a fatwa in the course of a public speech that those who make fun of maktabi Muslims are mortad-e fitri and mahdur-e dam (see n.8): "their wives shall be forbidden (haram) to them, their property shall be seized and distributed, and their blood may be wasted" (Anonymous, Munafeqin-i Khalq Ru Dar Ru-ye Khalq (Teheran: Political Office, Revolutionary Guards, 31 Shahrivar 1360), p. 48).

27. Rose, "Vilayat-i Faqih."

28. The chapter on taqlid in Usul-i Kafi (the first of the four canonic collections of Shiite hadith) gives but two hadith (one with two different chains of transmission), both censuring blind taqlid. Imam Sadeq is asked in one about the Quranic verse which charges Jews and Christians with raising their rabbis and priests to the level of divinity. Asked if this is true, Imam Sadeq replies: not in the sense that they prayed to these leaders or fasted for them, but in the sense that when these leaders allowed what God had forbidden and forbade what He had permitted, the Jews and Christians had followed them. (Implication: the misled is as guilty as the misleader; you who practice taqlid, beware.)

The other hadith condemns the Morjeeh (a Muslim group which believed that faith alone would bring salvation) for practicing excessive *taqlid*.

29. A title acquired thanks to the revolution.

30. Drafted by Reza Esfahani, then in the Ministry of Agriculture, it would 1) distribute land confiscated by revolutionary courts; 2) distribute uncultivated land; and, 3) distribute farms above a certain size according to local conditions determined by a council of seven. The third is the controversial provision.

31. See especially the new introduction and translation by James W. Morris, *The Wisdom of the Throne: An Introduction to the Philosophy of Mulla Sadra*. Princeton University Press, 1981.

32. The first poem in *Divan-i Ali ibn Abi Taleb*.

EIGHT

Muhammad Iqbal and the Islamic State

JOHN L. ESPOSITO

Muhammad Iqbal (1873–1938) poet, philosopher, lawyer, political thinker, and Muslim reformer is a dominant figure in twentieth-century Islam. Some forty years since his death, Muhammad Iqbal continues to be important not only in South Asia but also in the Middle East.[1] Arab writers from the late Sayyid Qutb to the contemporary Sadiq al-Mahdi acknowledge his influence. Since he wrote in Persian as well as Urdu and English, his writings were also accessible to Iranian reformers such as Ali Shariati, a hero and ideologue of Iranian youth and the Islamic left during the Iranian revolution.

Writing during the early decades of this century, Iqbal showed his perceptiveness and genius in identifying and addressing many of the problems and concerns that characterize the contemporary Islamic revival: disillusionment with the West tempered by a recognition of its scientific and technological accomplishments; awareness of the pressing need for the renewal of Muslim society through a process of reinterpretation and reform; affirmation of the integral relationship of Islam to politics and society; espousal of an Islamic alternative; and reaffirmation of the transnational character of the Islamic community.

Iqbal's poetry has moved millions; his life and work have inspired literally thousands of books and articles as well as Iqbal societies and journals. Because of his stature as spiritual father of Pakistan and the popularity of his poetry among educated and uneducated alike, political activists and Muslim intellectuals of every persuasion have sought to proclaim him as their source and master. Indeed, because of Iqbal's widespread influence upon such divergent groups, it becomes necessary to return carefully to his writings in order to distinguish his thought from that of those who claim his influence. This study will demonstrate the relevance of Muhammad Iqbal's thought to the contemporary revival of Islam, focusing on his understanding of the nature and purpose of Islamic society and how such a society might be realized today.

Like many of today's Islamic reformers, Iqbal, in his education and experience, reflects both Western and Islamic influences. He was among the first Muslims to do so. Born in Sialkot in the Punjab, Iqbal received an early classical Islamic education and studied at the Scotch Mission College in Sialkot. In 1895, he went to Lahore where he pursued graduate work and taught philosophy at Government College. There he met and studied with T. W. Arnold, noted British Orientalist. With the encouragement and support of Arnold, Iqbal traveled to Europe in 1905 where he studied at Cambridge with R. A. Nicholson, a specialist in Sufism, and the Neo-Hegelian, John M. E. McTaggart. Iqbal then studied in Heidelberg and Munich, where he completed his doctorate in 1908 with a dissertation entitled *The Development of Metaphysics in Persia*.

After returning to Lahore in 1908, Iqbal taught briefly. However, for most of his life, his profession was the law, and his passion, writing prose and poetry.

Iqbal's writings, spurred by his deep concern for the crisis of Islam in contemporary society, were indebted to two principal sources: his Islamic heritage and the Western philosophy he studied at Cambridge, Heidelberg, and Munich. His writings reflect the influence of the Quran, hadith, and Muslim thinkers like the great jurist Ibn Taimiya, the Indian reformer Wali Allah, and the renowned Sufi sage Jalal ud Din Rumi. His selective, eclectic use of Western materials reflected the influence of Bergson and McTaggart. Iqbal's synthesis of East and West may be seen in his dynamic concept of the self which is central to his teaching and has been described by M. Mujeeb as

> ... an integrated concept of the Self, fusing together the sufi's passion for union with God, the idea of dynamism expounded by Bergson, the groping for self-assertion which was the philosophy of Nietzsche, and the Shariah of Islam.[2]

Islamic Society

Drawing upon his Islamic heritage and Western studies, Muhammad Iqbal responded to the weakened condition of Indian Muslim society, which he viewed with deep concern. Iqbal lived amidst a Muslim minority which had once ruled India but which now faced co-existence not only with a Hindu majority but also with British colonial rule. The proud days of Islamic ascendancy were no longer. Furthermore, he believed that Hindu intellectualism and Sufi pantheism had severely lessened the Muslim community's capacity for action. He viewed the quietism of the Indian Muslims as a radical departure from the true spirit of Islam, that of dynamic movement and creative evolution. Rejecting the static universe of Plato[3] and those aspects of Muslim mysticism which denied the affirmation of the self in the world, Iqbal, basing himself on the Quran, developed a dynamic *Weltanschauung* in his theory of selfhood (egohood) which embraced all of reality, self, society, and God.

The individual self, the basic component of Muslim society, enjoys a special, exalted status. Following the Quran (S. 2:30), Iqbal emphasized man's chief end or mission as God's vicegerent. It is the Muslim's God-given task to carry out His will on earth:

> . . . this world of colour and scent is your empery—grain by grain gather the jewels from its soil, falcon-like seize your prey out of its skies, smite your axe against its mountain ranges, take light from yourself and set it all afire . . . hew out a new world to your own desire.[4]

Man must mould the matter of the universe in space-time to shape and direct the forces of nature.[5] In this sense, man shares in an ongoing process of creation, " . . . inasmuch as he helps to bring order into at least a portion of the chaos."[6] For Iqbal, then, man is the committed Muslim believer *(mumin)* who assumes his Quranically mandated responsibility for the world and endeavors to produce the model society which is to be emulated by others, Muslim and non-Muslim alike. Self-realization and personal fulfillment necessitate the Muslim's societal involvement. In *Rumuz-i Bekhudi (The Mysteries of Selflessness)*, Iqbal describes the self's relationship to society:

> All his [man's] nature is entranced
> with individuality,
> Yet only in Society he finds security
> and preservation.[7]

And again we read:

> The link that binds the Individual
> To the Society a Mercy is,
> His truest Self in the Community
> Alone achieves fulfillment.[8]

Due to his strong need and desire for association, the individual forms the basic unit of the *millat* ("community," nation). An interdependence exists between the two: the individual is elevated through the community while the community is organized by individuals. In mystical language, Iqbal spoke of the individual losing his "self" in the community and thus discovering that his personality had become an embodiment of past traditions and a bridge between his past and future:

> Tis like a drop which, seeking to expand,
> Becomes an ocean. It is strong and rich

> In ancient ways, a mirror of the Past
> As to the Future, and the link between
> What is to come, and what has gone before.[9]

THE ISLAMIC STATE

The human need for society is satisfied by Islam. For the Muslim, Islam is more than a creed: it is his community, his nation, the locus in which he will attain his true individuality (selfhood).[10] The Islamic community (*ummah*) is a society based upon common belief. However, it encompasses more than the notion of religious community as understood in the Judeo-Christian tradition for it includes the notion of the state as well. There is no bifurcation of the spiritual and the temporal. It is not correct to speak of Church and State as two sides or facets of the same thing, for Islam is a single unanalyzable reality "which is one or the other as your point of view varies."[11]

The purpose of the Islamic state is to take Islamic principles and endeavor to realize them in a definite human organization in history. Basing himself upon the Prophet's saying, "The whole of this earth is a mosque," Iqbal could assert that in Islam: "All that is secular is therefore sacred in the roots of its being" for "All this immensity of matter constitutes a scope for the self-realization of spirit."[12]

The twin pillars of Islamic state and society are the prophethood of Muhammad and, most importantly, the doctrine of *tawhid*. Muhammad came as the final messenger or "Seal" of all the prophets and taught the community that faith which gives it unity. Thus Iqbal wrote in his *Rumuz-i Bekhudi*:

> ... through his wisdom flows the lifeblood of the whole community.... His was the breath that gave the people life ... his Apostleship brought concord to our purpose and our goal.[13]

Muhammad was not only God's messenger but also the model or exemplar for the Muslim community. Indeed, his Sunna had become normative. Traditions (hadith) about the Prophet's words and behavior from earliest times had been preserved and collected and, with the Quran, had provided the material sources of Islamic law. Moreover, it was Muhammad who had served as the Prophet-Statesman of the early Islamic community at Medina. As such, he reflected the union of religion and state in his life. Muhammad, who came to a world of men subject to temporal and spiritual tyrants, rejected the privileged class, priesthood and caste alike, and founded a society based upon freedom, equality and brotherhood.[14]

Tawhid, the "Unity of God," affirms the radical monotheism of Islam. God is one; there are no other gods and nothing else should be valued in His place. The Islamic doctrine of *tawhid* extends to all of creation, for the Creator sustains and governs all of His creation. Therefore, God's will is to be realized in every area of life. For Iqbal, *tawhid* is the principle that brings the community together, the source of its equality, solidarity, and freedom: *tawhid* "is the soul and body of our Community."[15] Such is its force that the community of believers is as a brotherhood of equals (regardless of race, national or geographic origin): "Sharing in one speech, one spirit and one heart."[16] This very unity of thought should serve as the motivating force for action leading to the advancement of God's will in space-time.

The constitution of the Islamic state, reflecting the doctrine of *tawhid*, rests upon two basic propositions: the supremacy of God's law (the *shariah*) and the absolute equality of its members. Islamic law is a comprehensive law which provided the blueprint for Muslim society. The law encompassed all areas of life: duties of God (e.g., worship, fasting, pilgrimage) and duties in society (civil, criminal, and family laws).

From the nineteenth century on, Muslim countries, under the influence of colonial rule, adopted Western (European) inspired legal codes, and thus with the exception of family law, Islamic law was displaced. In the Indian subcontinent, the interaction of British and Islamic law in the nineteenth century produced Anglo-Muhammadan law. Again with the exception of Muslim family law, British-based codes in civil, criminal, and penal law were enacted. Iqbal, like Islamic revivalists today, recognized the need to reaffirm the centrality of Islamic law to the unity and life of the Muslim community:

> When a Community forsakes its Law
> Its parts are severed, like the scattered dust.
> The being of the Muslim rests alone
> On Law, which is in truth the inner core
> Of the Apostle's faith.[17]

In 1937, in a letter to Muhammad Ali Jinnah, the leader of the Muslim League and the founder of Pakistan, Iqbal stressed the importance of Islamic law as fundamental to the survival of Islam and the Muslim community's role as a political and moral force in Southeast Asia. Enforcement of the law required a Muslim state: " . . . endorsement and development of the Shariah of Islam is impossible in this country without a free Muslim state or states."[18]

Iqbal's second basis for Islamic state and society is absolute equality, rooted in the doctrine of *tawhid* (unity of God) and the mission of the Prophet and based upon the Quran (S. 49:13), "The noblest among you are those who fear

God most." Any notion of aristocracy is inimical to Islam. Rather, Islam is a unity without class distinctions established through a common faith or conviction. Iqbal saw this principle of equality, which gave the individual Muslim a sense of his "inward power," as the source of Muslim political power. The early history of Islam which saw the Muslim community emerge as "the greatest political power in the world" provided validation for this belief.[19]

Surveying contemporary Indian Muslim society, Iqbal maintained that it was this same "elevation of the down-trodden" that should be the secret source of Muslim power. However, he found just the opposite to be the case. The Muslims of India had, in fact, "out-Hindued the Hindu himself" by developing a double caste system: religious (sectarianism) and social. The remedy for this situation, then, must be a return to the true egalitarian spirit of Islam which transcended all distinctions, Wahhabi, Shia, or Sunni in Islam.

Iqbal's central emphasis upon equality and brotherhood led to his conclusion that democracy was the most important political ideal in Islam. For this form of government (rooted in the Islamic principle that the interests of Islam are superior to those of the Muslim) allowed man the necessary freedom to develop all the possibilities of his nature while limiting his freedom only in the interests of the community.

This democratic ideal, which existed for the first thirty years of Islamic history, had disappeared with Islam's political expansion. The fostering of this democratic spirit is one of the duties of the Islamic community which historical circumstances had prevented. Iqbal praised England for embodying this "Muslim" quality:

> Democracy [which] has been the great mission of England in modern times . . . it is one aspect of our own political ideal that is being worked out in it. It is . . . the spirit of the British Empire that makes it the greatest Muhammadan Empire in the world.[20]

However, Iqbal's recognition of democracy as an ideal form should not be equated with a wholesome acceptance of democracy as it existed and functioned in the West.[21] He believed that the success of a democratic system was contingent upon the preparedness of its members. A democratic system might be less than ideal given the constituents of the society. Thus, Iqbal did not accept the absolute democracy of undeveloped individuals. This is at the heart of his criticism of modern Western democracy: "Democracy is a system where people are counted but not weighed."[22]

The existence of a society whose members are undeveloped individuals necessitated for Iqbal the guidance of great leaders (supermen): "The ethical training of humanity is really the work of great personalities, who appear, from time to time, during the course of human history."[23]

The idea of a superman or Perfect Man is not a totally new concept in the history of thought. It was a favorite theme of Nietzsche in the West and had also been taught by Muslim mystical metaphysicians, as the "perfect man" *(insan-i-kamil)*, like ibn Arabi, Rumi, and Jili. All were men who influenced Iqbal's thought and were praised in his poetry.[24] However, Iqbal did not simply follow their thought uncritically. Rather a new synthesis resulted: "The perfect and godly man of Rumi embraces the superman of the unbelieving Nietzsche and becomes the Iqbalian man."[25]

For Iqbal, the ideal Muslim is the Quranic "man of belief" *(mard-i-mumin)* or the "perfect man" *(insan-i-kamil)* called to realize his full potential in Muslim society. Iqbal's goal was a democracy of "more or less unique individuals, presided over by the most unique individual possible."[26] Speaking of democracy as the most important aspect of the Islamic state on the one hand and yet ruled by supermen on the other created an apparent inconsistency as when Iqbal wrote:

> Keep away from Democracy: Follow the Perfect Man,
> For the intellect of two hundred asses cannot bring forth a single man's thought.[27]

However, as previously noted, for Iqbal the functioning of a true democratic system was contingent upon the preparedness of individuals and was always subject to God's law. Given the decay of the Muslim community, the democratic ideal in Islam was an ideal yet to be realized. Thus, the need for the guidance of a great leader. Unfortunately, Iqbal does not suggest how in a modern state that leader would gain power. The "perfect man" of Islamic mysticism applied to the prophets as well as the Sufi saint *(wali,* "friend" of God). How this concept is to function effectively regarding the political leadership of the Muslim community remains unanswered.

WAR AND PEACE

The preservation and protection of the Islamic state and a desire to respond to Western perceptions of Islam as militaristic necessitated Iqbal's consideration of the question of jihad. He denied the claim that jihad represented an offensive attack of the Muslim community for self-aggrandizement. Returning to the sources of Islam, he argued that all the wars waged under the Prophet Muhammad's leadership were defensive.

Moreover, while defensive war is permitted, aggressive warfare is contrary to the Quran.[28] The only justifiable excuse for warfare is the exaltation of God, not the acquisition of land or any other end:

> War is good if its object is God.
> If God be not exalted by our swords,
> War dishonours the people. . . .
> Whoso shall draw the sword for anything except Allah,
> His sword is sheathed in his own breast.[29]

Contrary to the Western caricature of Islam as a "religion of holy war" Iqbal maintained that according to the Quran it is a religion of peace: "All forms of political and social disturbance are condemned . . . the ideal of Islam is to secure social peace at any cost."[30] He concluded that any attempt at social change through the employment of violence is impossible and approvingly cited Tartushi, a Muslim lawyer from Sapin, who had written: "Forty years of tyranny are better than one year of anarchy."[31]

Iqbal did not discuss the criterion for implementing his Islamic ideal of a just war. Since governments often use religion to justify waging war, how does the Muslim determine that the real motive is Allah? More importantly, if "war is good if its object is God," then how justify "social peace at any cost"? The answer may lie in Iqbal's intention to respond to the distorted picture of Islam presented by its European critics. He was responding to the needs of Muslim community at that time. One can only wonder what he would say to those Islamic movements today in Afghanistan, Iran, Pakistan, Egypt, Syria who argue that the establishment and/or preservation of Islamic society requires political and social upheaval.

IDEOLOGY AND THE MODERN ISLAMIC STATE

Iqbal's understanding of the Islamic state as a community whose membership is based on common religious belief and whose purpose is to realize freedom, equality, and brotherhood in history led quite logically to his rejection of territorial nationalism as contrary to the universal brotherhood established by Muhammad:

> Our Master, fleeing from his fatherland,
> Resolved the knot of Muslim nationhood.
> His wisdom founded one Community
> The world its parish—on the sacred charge to civilize.[32]

Iqbal rejected any understanding of the nation-state as a foundation of the Islamic community. Nationalism was the tool used by colonialism to dismember the Muslim world: "to shatter the religious unity of Islam in pieces."[33] Its results are the estrangement of man from his fellow man, the disunity of nations, and the separation of religion and politics that had led to the downfall of Christianity.

In "Political Thought in Islam," Iqbal wrote that the "political ideal of Islam consists in the creation of a people born of a free fusion of all races and nation-alities."[34] The inner cohesion of this community issues not from geographic or ethnic unity but from the unity of its political and religious ideal. Membership or citizenship is based upon a declaration of "like-mindedness" which termi-nates only when this condition has ceased to exist. Territorily, the Islamic polity is transnational, embracing the whole world. Though the Arab attempt to estab-lish such a pan-Islamic order through conquest failed, its establishment still remains an ideal to be realized. The ideal Islamic state does, in fact, exist in germ form:

> The life of modern political communities finds expression, to a great extent, in common institutions, Law and Government, and the various sociological circles . . . are continually expanding to touch one another.[35]

Meeting the objections of those who fear the loss of individual states' sover-eignty, Iqbal pointed out that this need not occur since the structure of the Islamic state will be determined not by physical force but by the spiritual force of a common ideal.

Although Iqbal had devoted a good deal of his thinking and writing to his understanding of the political theory of Islamic society and had expressed a pan-Islamic spirit, he realized that the exigencies of his times necessitated adaptation and patience:

> In order to create a really effective political unity of Islam, all Moslem countries must first become independent, and then in their totality they should range them-selves under the Caliph. Is such a thing possible at the present moment? If not today, one must wait.[36]

Thus, for Iqbal, the Muslim community must pursue an immediate as well as a long-range goal. First, each Muslim nation must gain its independence, turn in on itself and put its own house in order. This would bring each to the strength and power necessary to realize the second goal, to come together and establish a living family of republics whose unifying bond would be their com-mon Islamic spiritual heritage:

> It seems to me that God is slowly bringing home to us the truth that Islam is neither Nationalism nor Imperialism but a League of Nations which recognize artificial boundaries and racial distinctions of reference only and not for restricting the social horizon of its members.[37]

The poet/philosopher, applying the logic of his thought to his own Indian/ Muslim situation, concluded that the Muslims of India were in danger of losing the freedom necessary for development. As noted earlier, Iqbal maintained that every Muslim needed the Islamic community for his development. While many advocated a secular Indian state to incorporate Hindu and Muslim alike, Iqbal rejected any notion that Islam could be reduced to a private ethical code separated from the socio-political sphere:

> The religious ideal of Islam, therefore, is organically related to the social order which it has created. The rejection of the one will eventually involve the rejection of the other.[38]

Iqbal saw the displacement of Islamic solidarity as a real possibility facing the Muslim minority in India.

Reviewing the history of India, Iqbal recognized that the Hindu and Muslim communities had guarded their collective existence and identities jealously and had shown no inclination toward absorption into a larger whole. Moreover, all attempts at discovering a principle of internal harmony had failed. Therefore, for Iqbal, communalism seemed to be absolutely necessary for Muslims to preserve their identity and way of life: "the Indian Muslim is entitled to full and free development on the lines of his own culture and tradition in his own Indian Homelands."[39] He distinguished this from a narrow communalism which deprecated other communities and their customs. Since he viewed the units of Indian society as communal and not territorial (as in Europe) he could agree with Muslims' demand for the creation of a Muslim India within India. However, Iqbal went beyond this resolution of the All-Parties Muslim Conference of Delhi and in his now famous "Presidential Address" of 29 December, 1930, called for the formation of a separate Muslim state:

> I would like to see the Punjab, Northwest Frontier Province, Sind and Baluchistan amalgamated into a single State. Self government within or without the British Empire, the formation of a consolidated North-West Indian Muslim State appears to me to be the final destiny of the Muslims, at least of North-West India.[40]

ISLAM AND WESTERN IDEOLOGY

Using his Islamic perspective, Iqbal sought to assess capitalism and socialism, the two major ideologies dominating the twentieth century and vying for power in the Muslim world. His criticism of Western democracy followed from his belief that the Western capitalist system suppressed the individual and his growth and made true democracy an impossibility:

> The Democratic system of the West is the same old instrument
> Whose chords contain no note other than the voice of the Kaiser,

> The Demon of Despotism is dancing in his democratic robes
> Yet you consider it to be the Nilam Peri of Liberty.[41]

and again in *Persian Psalms (Zabur-i-Ajam)* we read:

> Of the hireling's blood outpoured
> Lustrous rubies makes the Lord,
> Tyrant squire to swell his wealth
> Desolates the peasant's tilth.[42]

In *The Pilgrimage of Eternity* (the *Jabid Nama*), Iqbal ultimately finds the fundamental faults of capitalism and communism to be the same:

> Both fail to recognize the Lord, deceive
> Mankind. The one for revolution thirsts,
> The other for tribute: they're two millstones
> That pulverise the human kind.[43]

He condemns the gross materialism and godlessness of both systems:

> The soul of both is impatient and intolerant, both of them know not God and deceive mankind. One lives by production, the other by taxation and man is a glass caught between these two stones.[44]

Iqbal was attracted by several Marxist teachings insofar as they exemplified Islamic social principles. This explains his seemingly naïve enthusiasm for the Russian revolution and his citation of the Soviet Union as proof that some Islamic social principles could be applied in practice in modern times:

> From the behaviour of nations it appears to me
> That the rapid progress of Russia is not without gain . . .
> Perhaps at this time it demonstrates the truth
> That is hidden in the words "Say: The Surplus."[45]

It is important to remember that Iqbal was not well versed in Marxist theory. His socialist tendencies are best understood within his own religious tradition; his socialism was rooted in Islam's social teachings based on Islamic principles such as the equality and brotherhood of believers and the social welfare obligation of all Muslims to their fellow believers exemplified by the *zakat* (tithe, wealth tax). Such beliefs, coupled with an awareness of the poverty of many of his fellow Muslims, moved him to employ S. 2:29 often in his poetry:

> Allah said to the Muslims "Let the soul use your hands,
> Whatever you have over needs give!"[46]

TRADITION AND CHANGE

Iqbal's underlying concern, which motivated and informed all of his thought, writing, and activity was the revival of Islam. He saw himself as standing in the great tradition of Islamic renewal and reform (*tajdid* and *islah*) which stretched across the centuries and was epitomized by men such as Muhammad Ibn Adb al-Wahhab, Shah Wali Allah, and modern reformers like Jamal al-Din al-Afghani and Muhammad Abduh. These Islamic revivalists reformed their Muslim community through the reapplication of the pristine principles of Islam to the needs of their age. As a result the dynamic, creative spirit of Islam was reaffirmed while preserving that which was essential, immutable. Iqbal's life-long intention was to call for and contribute to the development of a new Islamic synthesis for his age. The title of one of his last works, *The Reconstruction of Religious Thought in Islam*, summarizes his purpose quite clearly.

Iqbal asserted the need for both permanence and change in a living, developing Islamic state, a belief which originates in his interpretation of the Quranic view of God and its relationship to Islamic society. God or Ultimate Ego has creative, dynamic life which is both permanent and changing. Iqbal understood creation to be the unfolding of the inner possibilities of God (Ultimate Ego) in a single and yet continuing act: "The Ultimate Ego exists in pure duration wherein change ceases to be a succession of varying attitudes, and reveals its true character as continuous creation."[47]

If this element of permanence and yet change is true of God, the "ultimate spiritual basis of all life," then it must be true at every level of His creation. Thus, the Islamic way of life as found in the *shariah*, the blueprint for Muslim society, is itself dynamic and open to change. Iqbal rejected the centuries-long tendency of the majority of Muslims to view law as fixed and sacrosanct. The Quran's legal principles were not comprehensive and thus "the early doctors of law taking their cue from this groundwork evolved a number of legal systems. . . . But with all their comprehensiveness these systems are after all individual interpretations and as such cannot claim any finality."[48] Although the eternal, immutable principles of the *shariah* are necessary for the regulation of its collective life, yet the Islamic state includes a principle of change by which it can adapt itself to all the possibilities arising from that which is "essentially mobile in its nature."[49] This principle of movement is *ijtihad*. The failure to appreciate and utilize *ijtihad* was judged by Iqbal as the cause for the immobility of Islam during the preceding 500 years. While acknowledging the role of ulama (religious scholars) in the past, he blamed them for the conservatism which had characterized Islam since the fall of Baghdad (1258). With their acceptance of the dictum: "The door of *ijtihad* is closed," these self-proclaimed scholar-guardians of Islam, who had developed the schools of Islamic law and the system of education, stopped a dynamic process of reinterpretation and reapplication of Islamic principles to new situations. They were content to serve simply as the protector—perpetuators of established traditions. Indeed, while *ijtihad* had been accepted in theory by the Sunnis, "in practice it has always been denied ever since the establishment of the schools, inasmuch as the idea of complete *ijtihad* is hedged round by conditions which are well-nigh impossible of realization in a single individual."[50] Iqbal aligned himself with men like Ibn Taimiya, ibn Hasm, Suyuti, and especially Muhammad ibn Abd al-Wahhab—whom he viewed as the father of "all the great modern movements"—and called for the opening of the gates of *ijtihad*.

Furthermore, Iqbal extended or developed the function of *ijtihad*. Noting the growth of the republican spirit, he accepted the importance of modern legislative assemblies and advocated the transfer of the right to interpret and apply the law from the domain of individual ulama to that of the legislatures.[51] This collective or corporate *ijtihad* would then constitute the authoritative consensus (*ijma*) of the community. Traditionally, *ijma* referred to community consensus or agreement, one of the four sources of Islamic law. In fact, the consensus was that of religious leaders/scholars of the community. However, given the needs of modern society, Iqbal called for the transfer not only of legal interpretation (*ijtihad*) but also of community authority (*ijma*) from the ulama to a Muslim legislative assembly, the vast majority of whom, he believed, possessed the requisite knowledge of modern affairs: "In this way alone we can stir into activity the dormant spirit of life in our legal system and give it an evolutionary outlook."[52]

While acknowledging the ulama's creative contribution during the early Islamic centuries, he stressed that "a false reverence for past history and its artificial resurrection constitute no remedy for a people's decay."[53] Undue dependence upon the ulama's traditional education could lead to inadequate understanding of and response to the demands of modernity. In addition, Iqbal argued that the complex nature of many modern problems required wisdom derived from the polling of experts representing various disciplines—traditional and modern.

CONCLUSION

Muhammad Iqbal lived during the period between two epochs, the old feudal society and modern capitalism. Given the station of his birth, his education, and his travel in Europe he could appreciate the pluses and minuses of both systems. The poet—for certainly he was first and foremost a poet by temperament—saw and responded to the quietism of the Muslim community and the internal crises which faced Islam. He could admire the achievements of the West—its dynamic spirit, intellectual tradition, and technological advances. However, he was equally critical of the imperialism of European colonialism, the moral bankruptcy of secularism and the economic exploitation of capitalism. Therefore, he advocated a return to Islam in order to construct an Islamic alternative for modern Muslim society.

Like most Muslim revivalists, Iqbal attributed the weakening of Islam to the Muslim community's departure from Islamic principles. His political theory, like all of his thought, is characterized by a conscious turning to the past to rediscover those principles and values which could provide a model for the present as well as the future.

Iqbal's great contribution was his rekindling of an awareness of the dynamic spirit of Islam. He represented to the community those Islamic ideals that could bring new life to the Islamic polity. He reconstructed fundamental principles in a poetry that could move his fellow Muslims, literate and illiterate, to an intuition of what ought to be and fire their minds with a desire to find ways of realizing such ideals.

It is possible to speak of an earlier Pan-Islamic ideal in Iqbal's political thought which would have necessitated a caliphate. However, political events during his lifetime called for some modification. This did not mean a total abandonment of a Pan-Islamic ideal. It was the goal of his counsel, that each Muslim nation should look within and strengthen and rebuild itself so that the Muslim nations might enter into a "League of Nations"-like relationship. Such a "League" would be rooted in the common ideal of its members. This common "like-mindedness" would spring from their Islamic traditions with their common ideals of equality, fraternity, and solidarity and their common law—the *shariah*. Thus, Muslim nations could avoid the divisive pitfalls of nationalism with its tendency toward the disintegration of society into rivaling tribes.

Iqbal, like most men, was limited by his temperament. A poet draws heavily upon his feelings and emotions as he attempts to convey his intuition of reality. He could write of social injustice or political ideals while at the same time moving his reader to an experience which enabled him to empathize with the victim of injustice or to be aroused by the nobility of the ideal. However, neither poetic temperament nor the poem itself is concerned with the practical implementation of social reforms or the realization of the ideal.

Muhammad Iqbal articulated those Islamic political principles which he believed were fundamental for a rejuvenation of the Islamic community while leaving the practical implementation to the politicians, sociologists, economists, etc. He expressed the need of the Muslim community when he called for the formation of Pakistan but its practical implementation was to fall to Jinnah and others. Still there is a place in our world for the idealists. To have clothed his insights in poetic form and thus to have fired the hearts and minds of millions to pursue and implement these ideals is an extraordinary achievement, one which more than justifies the great esteem that Muhammad Iqbal had enjoyed.

Notes

1. See, for example, pp. 337 and 446 of this volume.

2. M. Mujeeb, *The Indian Muslims* (London, 1967), p. 454.

3. Muhammad Iqbal, *The Secrets of the Self* (London, 1920), pp. 56–59.

4. Iqbal, *Javid Nama* (London, 1966), p. 63. See also *The Secrets of the Self*, p. 78ff, and *The Pilgrimage of Eternity* (Lahore: 1961), p. 57ff.

5. Iqbal, "Knowledge and Religious Experience," *The Reconstruction of Religious Thought in Islam* (Lahore, 1968), pp. 10–12; idem, *Javid Nama*, pp. 59–61.

6. Iqbal, *The Secrets of the Self*, p. xviii.

7. Iqbal, *The Mysteries of Selflessness* (London, 1953), p. 8.

8. Ibid., p. 5.

9. Ibid.

10. Iqbal, "Islam as a Moral and Political Ideal" in S. A. Vahid (ed.), *Thoughts and Reflections of Iqbal* (Lahore, 1964), pp. 35–38, 50.

11. Iqbal, "The Principle of Movement in the Structure of Islam," in *The Reconstruction*, p. 154.

12. Ibid., p. 155.

13. Iqbal, *The Mysteries*, pp. 20–21.

14. Iqbal, "Islam," p. 53. See also *The Mysteries*, pp. 21–23, and *The Reconstruction*, p. 154.

15. Iqbal, "The Principle of Movement," p. 154.

16. Iqbal, *The Mysteries*, pp. 12–13. See also *The Reconstruction*, p. 147.

17. Iqbal, *The Mysteries*, p. 37.

18. Jamil-ud-Din Ahmad, ed., *Historic Documents of the Muslim Freedom Movement* (Lahore: Publishers United Ltd., 1970), pp. 207–8.

19. Iqbal, "Islam," pp. 53–54.

20. Ibid., p. 52.

21. Iqbal had some strong criticism for European democracy. See, for example, his *Javid Nama*, pp. 62–63; and also A. Anwar Beg, *Poet of the East* (Lahore, 1940), p. 257.

22. Iqbal as quoted by Fazlur Rahman in "Some Aspects of Iqbal's Political Theory," *Studies in Islam*, vol. 5 (New Delhi, 1968), p. 165.

23. Iqbal, "Islam," p. 43.

24. B. A. Dar, *A Study in Iqbal's Philosophy* (Lahore, 1944), p. 90ff.; S. A. Vahid, *Iqbal, His Art and Thought* (Lahore, 1964), pp. 132ff.; and especially Khalifa Abdul Hakim "Rumi, Nietzsche and Iqbal" in *Iqbal as a Thinker* (Lahore: 1944), pp. 128–202; and Subhash Kashyap, "Sir Mohammad Iqbal and Friedrich Nietzsche," *Islamic Quarterly*, 2 (1955), pp. 175–92.

25. Hakim, "Rumi, Nietzsche and Iqbal," pp. 196–97.

26. As quoted in Iqbal Singh's *The Ardent Pilgrim* (London, 1951), p. 243.

27. Iqbal as quoted by Beg, *Poet of the East,* p. 257.

28. Iqbal, "Islam," p. 46.

29. Iqbal, *The Secrets of the Self,* p. 119, 121.

30. Iqbal, "Islam," pp. 48–49.

31. Ibid., p. 49.

32. Iqbal, *The Mysteries,* p. 30.

33. Shamloo, ed., *Speeches and Statements of Iqbal* (Lahore: al-Manar Academy, 1948), p. 224.

34. Iqbal, "Political Thought in Islam," *Thoughts and Reflections,* p. 60.

35. Ibid.

36. Iqbal, "The Principle of Movement," p. 159.

37. Ibid.

38. Muhammad Iqbal, "Presidential Address," in *Thoughts and Reflections,* p. 167.

39. Ibid., p. 169.

40. Ibid., pp. 170–71.

41. Iqbal as quoted in Beg, *Poet of the East,* p. 257.

42. Muhammad Iqbal, *Persian Psalms (Zabur-i Ajam),* trans. A. J. Arberry (Lahore, 1961), p. 86.

43. Iqbal, *Javid Nama,* p. 57.

44. Ibid.

45. As quoted in Jan Marek, "Perceptions of International Politics," in *Iqbal,* ed. by H. Malik (New York: Columbia University Press, 1971), p. 171. "Say: The Surplus" refers to a Quranic verse (S. 2:219) which Iqbal often cited: "And they ask thee what they should spend. Say: The Surplus."

46. Iqbal, *Javid Nama,* p. 91.

47. Muhammad Iqbal, "The Revelations of Religious Experience," *The Reconstruction,* p. 60.

48. Iqbal, "The Principle of Movement," p. 168.

49. Ibid., p. 148.

50. Ibid., p. 149.

51. Ibid., p. 174.

52. Ibid., pp. 173–74.

53. Ibid., p. 151.

NINE

Ali Shariati:
Ideologue of the Iranian Revolution

ABDULAZIZ SACHEDINA

The 1960s in modern Iranian history was the period in which the Shah's government was determined to undermine the practical religious culture of Islam and its sense of moral responsibility toward social, economic, cultural, and political conditions. This devitalization was directed more particularly toward the younger generation who were being driven to self-alienation, and, in turn, to a superficial and, at times, distorted comprehension of their role in the society. While the leaders among the religious class, the ulama, realized the urgency to communicate with the youth, they found themselves ill-equipped methodologically to direct the younger generation—confused by false messages of modern living—to a meaningful reorientation of their role vis-à-vis contemporary social conditions. This helplessness was due, most probably, to their "traditional" approach to the teaching of Islam. By characterizing their method as "traditional," I do not wish to suggest that their approach was "unpragmatic" or "backward" looking; nor do I consider their method to be based upon long-held traditions which remained unaltered throughout their history. Rather, religious leaders needed to convey the Islamic ideas to the new generation of Muslim youth, who were demanding and exerting pressure on the religious class to *reinterpret* Islam and apply it to their conditions of life in the face of modern challenges. However, any attempt to shape the response to meet the needs and demands of the people was held to give rise to a doctrinal schism. As a matter of fact, such an attempt to shape a response to modern living was perceived as requiring a "rethinking" and "reapplying" of "independent reasoning" *(ijtihad),* to solve the socio-political complexities produced by the process of modernization in traditional Iranian society. In the past, "independent reasoning," as practised by Muslim jurists, had made it possible to maintain a smooth interaction between the demands of the original teachings of Islam and the new contingencies underlying the social, political, and economic conditions of the time. However, in the course of history, Muslim jurisprudents had abandoned their practical role of providing expedient guidance to their followers, with the result that modern Iranian youth needed to be delivered by someone who could understand their predicament and provide a viable and reassuring alternative to the alien concepts of society.

The secularly educated Iranian intellectuals, who could perhaps have stepped in to provide the crucial practical guidance to Iranian youth, were, for the most part, during this period, too self-complacent, self-centered, and preoccupied with materialism even to perceive the existing predicament of the youth. Moreover, their general lack of understanding or even appreciation of their own traditional values, which continued to nurture the majority of the rural, industrious youth, resulted in their inability to communicate effectively within the cultural framework in which they themselves had grown up. For them, "traditional culture" connoted "primitive culture" which was transcended as man moved into an age of rationality and scientific self-consciousness. They overlooked the truth that the "traditional" in man could never be fully extinguished, not even in the most technologically advanced civilization.[1]

A truly intellectual elite, unalienated from Islam, deeply rooted in the cultural tradition of Islamic Iran, was needed, to apply a new scientific method in the understanding of the sociological fact of Islam, and explain the interaction of the Islamic message with society—the embodiment of the cultural life of the community. This was the place reserved for Ali Shariati, who had perfectly comprehended the predicament of the young generation. Shariati's call for a return to the original teachings of Islam, embodied in Shiism and best exemplified in the life and teachings of the Imams Ali and Husayn, was based on his sincere faith in Islam and his personal commitment to make others aware of it through his diverse speeches, lectures, and writings. Without such a faith and commitment, he would not have been able to create and move posthumously, a religious movement of the magnitude experienced by Iranian youth in the 1970s. The significance of Shariati's impact was not so much due to his thorough and systematic presentation of Islam, as to his ability to reformulate Islamic beliefs, relating them to social and economic conditions in order to reveal their practical implications. He saw Islam as a socially and politically committing ideology, open to reinterpretation in the light of modern contingencies. It is precisely this which led to the Islamic revival among Iranian youth.

FROM MAZINAN TO MESHAD[2]

Ali Shariati was born in Mazinan in eastern Iran, in 1933/1312. He received his early education in Meshad, and he was in high school when his erudite father, Muhammad Taqi Shariati, established the Center for the Spread of Islamic

Teachings. Those early formative years in Shariati's life, spent in the companionship of his father, left a substantial mark on his personality:

> My father fashioned the early dimensions of my spirit. It was he who first taught me the art of thinking and the art of being human. . . . It was he who introduced me to his companions—his books; they were my constant and familiar associates from the early years of my schooling. I grew up and matured in his library, which was for him the whole of his life and his family.[3]

It was during these years that Shariati was exposed to his father's relentless efforts to bring modern-educated youth back to the Islamic fold, by making the Islamic revelation the central means for teaching and by explaining the interaction between Islamic ideals and the contemporary social environment. It is no mere coincidence that his father and Shariati adopted the same method in their exposition of Islamic revelation, which, in the case of the former, marked the beginning of a special school of Quranic exegesis, based on critical examination of the circumstances of revelation, and re-interpretation of its historical setting.[4]

By the time Shariati joined the Teachers' Training College he had been recognized as an active member of his father's center, where he was frequently asked to speak. This brought him into close contact with students, most of whom belonged to the lower economic strata of Iranian society. Shariati embarked on his career as a teacher after having completed high school and Teachers' Training College. He taught in the vicinity of Mashhad for some years. He was enrolled in the undergraduate program at the newly established Faculty of Letters in the University of Meshad (1956). During these years through his writing and eloquent lectures he promoted religious awareness among the young participants at the center, which, in turn, nourished his own intellectual and religious development. His activities at this center and his enrollment at the Faculty of Letters, made him conscious of the importance of the college teacher's role as the intellectual in modern society, in shaping the future outlook of Muslim youth. Apart from some of his teachers in the university, whom he mentions as having influenced his intellectual development at this time, he found most of his colleagues to be imitative intellectuals who had very little originality and thus an inability to offer solutions to the decadence of the modern age.

The situation at the institutes of higher learning had worsened following the overthrow of Mosaddeq's government in August 1953. Furthermore, the *madrasas*—which had remained the nucleus of religious guidance for a long time in Iranian social history—were going through a period of reevaluation under the new educational system instituted by the government. This led to the retreat

of religious leaders from active participation in any kind of intellectual movement in Iranian society, and most particularly, in those connected with secularly
educated intellectuals. This negative attitude of the religious leaders became a
factor in the spiritual vacuum already experienced by the youth who were
exposed to modern Western thought. An additional factor that prompted Shariati to resolve to pursue the next stage in his intellectual development abroad
was the significance attached to obtaining a higher degree from a foreign university, which, somehow, augmented the credibility of a native scholar in his
own society.

PARIS

In 1960 Shariati had the opportunity to pursue graduate studies at the University
of Paris. Here, he was able to broaden his vision and direct his attention to the
analytical and critical school of French sociology. But, after examining the
works of French sociologists, he discerned the need to find categories that
would explain the social realities of people who had experienced a different life
under a distinct culture which was rooted in Islam. This realization was the
basis for his criticism of the methodology Iranian intellectuals had adopted in
analyzing their own distinctly Islamic society. The main problem with these
intellectuals had been their negligence in taking into account the hazards of
imposing Western socio-cultural categories in attempting to understand the
dynamics of their own society. For instance, Shariati firmly asserted that the
application of a time category such as "modern" was erroneous in the context
of a Third World society. Conclusions based upon simply categorizing such a
society as "modern" because it happens to exist in the twentieth century, without examining that society's history and the time period in which it actually
could be placed, would yield a fallacious thesis.[5] However, his conceptualization
of the sociological fact of Islam in Iran received proper expression only after
he returned to Iran.

Shariati completed his graduate work with a doctoral dissertation entitled:
Fadail al-Balkh (Les mérites de Balkh), an edition and translation of a medieval
Persian text.[6] His sojourn in France at a mature age gave him a rare opportunity
to perceive that Islam did have the socio-political framework to offer the Iranian Muslims, provided a new intellectual dynamism could be applied to elaborate this framework. It is precisely in this area that Shariati demonstrated his
originality and creativity, disregarding the nuances of official Western sociology, and clinging instead to his own observation and discernment of the social
trends in modern Iran. He avoided the pitfall of many modern Western sociologists who held rigorously to their conventional analytical norms of sociol-

ogy, and thus been unable to scan the true nature of the Iranian society. For Shariati, it was indispensable that a real harmony exist between the ideas of the so-called Iranian intellectuals and the social realities of Iran.

RETURN TO IRAN AND LAST YEARS

Shariati returned to Iran in 1964 and was immediately arrested and imprisoned for six months for having taken part in anti-government activities in France. On his release, he applied for a teaching position at the Faculty of Letters in the University of Teheran, but was turned down. Thereafter, he taught at various high schools and the College of Agriculture, until a teaching position in history became available at the University of Meshad in 1966. Within a short time, Shariati became the most popular teacher in the university and speaker at most of the significant religious festivals observed by the university community. He had a style that could best be described as innovative in the Iranian context, both in method and in substance. The latter element was bound to cause much trouble and distress for him, since he was taken to task by the religious leaders for his flaws in expounding Islamic doctrines, or more particularly, the Shiite interpretation of them. Shariati lacked a firm grounding in Islamic sciences and errors were noticed even in his citation of some well-known historical events. The incisive criticism of his work by some sympathetic members of the religious class helped him revise the content of his extremely influential lectures. At the same time, his father's presence and his frequent communication with him became an important factor in polishing the rough edges of his Islamic material. Nevertheless, Shariati's sociological approach to Islamic history, on the one hand, and his free methods of teaching, on the other, combined to bring him in conflict with the university administration. The University of Meshad was headed by conservative and pro-monarchy elements and Shariati proved to be a committed native intellectual, with an acute sense of social and moral responsibility, far more radical and popular than could be contained in the Iranian academic context.

Shariati's frequent lecture trips to Teheran led to the establishment of the Husayniya-yi Irshad in 1965, an institution which played a central part in Shariati's development as an independent Muslim thinker. His lectures there had an immeasurable nationwide impact. In Iranian religious life *husayniya* (in Shia Islam, center for religious education) has been a common feature of all large and small Iranian cities, where they have existed besides mosques for public commemoration of the martyrdom of Imam Husayn, the grandson of the Prophet, and the third imam of the Twelver Shiites, at Karbala (680 A.D.). It is essential to note that *husayniyas* in Shiite Iran had supplemented the religious observances provided by mosques, where mostly formal religious practices such as congregational prayers were held. In *husayniyas* popular preachers were called upon to inform the masses didactically about the events that led to the tragedy of Karbala, where Husayn, betrayed by his own supporters, received a martyr's death. As such, these religious edifices were crucial in arousing the emotional sympathy of the believers for the *ahl al-bayt,* the model family of the Prophet* who, in the Shiite tradition, upheld justice and hatred for their enemies, who symbolized tyranny. The choice of the name *husayniya* for the institution, the symbol of Imam Husayn's struggle against the oppressive rule of the Umayyads (660–750 A.D.), served as a model for the struggle of Iranian Muslim youth to transform their own oppressive circumstances into a just social order. It was this inherent character of the *husayniya* in Shiism, closely identifiable with the socio-political aspiration of the Islamic community, which was to underlie its confrontation with the Shah's regime.

Shariati devoted all of his time to teaching and preaching his interpretation of Islam. His lectures had such a political impact on Iranian society that the regime arrested him in the summer of 1973. The activities of the Husayniya-yi Irshad were suspended and although Shariati was released toward the end of 1975, he was not free to move about and remained in exile in Mazinan, his home town. In early June, 1977 he was permitted to leave Iran to travel to Europe. On 19 June, he died in England under mysterious circumstances that suggest the almost certain involvement of the Iranian secret police. He was buried in Damascus, next to the mausoleum of Zaynab, Imam Husayn's sister and heroine of Karbala. It is ironic that Shariati was possibly the target of a plot similar to that which he believed Moise Tshombe had masterminded when he set Patrice Lumumba free:

> We all remember that Tshombe released Lumumba from the prison so that he would not be held responsible for killing him while he escaped from the Katanga prison. Did you see how he got rid of him? This proves the point that one should ask: "Who is setting free whom? and why?" We should not speak about "those who are released"; rather, we should consider "acquiring freedom." Or, still better, we should think about recognizing and choosing freedom and becoming free.[7]

MAN AND SOCIETY

One of the unprecedented contributions in Shariati's approach to the understanding of Islam is his introduction of a fresh style of discourse and a new terminology to interpret and teach Islam in the Iranian milieu. The ideas were

---

*The *ahl al-bayt* is the family of the Prophet's cousin, Ali.

not original in themselves, as we shall see below; but they certainly appeared novel in the terminology that was used to express them for the educated youth, who under the pressure of modern living and modern thought, seemed likely to abandon their religious affiliation and adopt ideologies and values that were alien to their Islamic heritage. Young people were drawn to these lectures and infuenced by the use of Western sociological terms and famous Western social thinkers in Shariati's discourse on Islamic topics. Consequently, a speaker of Shariati's caliber, well acquainted with Western sources and remarkably versatile in utilizing them to expound the sociological fact of Islam, proved far more effective than any of the more profound traditional Muslim preachers. Personally, however, Shariati was ambivalent about the inclusion of Western jargon in his lectures. He, on more than one occasion, complained to the present author about the shallowness of educated Iranian youth who readily accepted the validity of their spiritual legacy if it was recounted on the authority of a Western scholar or with reference to a Western school of thought. Shariati was very conscious of the centrality of intellectual integrity in solving the problems of modernism in Iranian society, and hence, during his years at the Husayniya-yi Irshad, he devoted himself to developing a program which could utilize all the available resources in analyzing and explaining the causes behind the cultural crisis in Iran. The response to his program affirmed his conviction that Muslim youth in the Third World depended on a committed Muslim intelligentsia to address the pressing social issues confronting them. It was the intelligentsia who could come to grips with the society's inner contradictions and totally commit themselves to remedy the socio-cultural malaise and resulting crisis of identity experienced by an increasingly self-aware segment of the educated Iranian population. For Shariati, society needed a *mujtahid* (a person who would wage war in order to create such a society), an enlightened Muslim intellectual to provide a reinterpretation of Islam, to make it compatible with the aims of original Islam, namely, to create a just and progressive social order.

The other component of Shariati's methodology for a dynamic interpretation of Islam was his use of traditional Islamic material in proving his theses. His diverse exegetic approach to the Quran and Islamic traditions (*hadith*), which appeared to be radically innovative, was comparable to the method employed by *ashab al-ray* (the scholars who propounded their views, relying on their personal opinion) in the classical period of Islam (8–12th centuries A.D.). This group ventured to prove their exposition of Islamic teachings by quoting passages of the Quran and the traditions of the Prophet, sometimes out of their evident historic context. His citations from the highly prestigious sources of Islam, as far as the Muslim populace was concerned, were of primary significance to the success of Shariati's lectures, affording credibility to his pledge to perform his central task as a Muslim intellectual, namely, to increase Islamic consciousness in the youth. If he had not placed Islamic revelation at the center of his historical and socio-religious analysis, he would have estranged a large number of his listeners; they had had enough of the imitative Western material from secularly educated Iranian intellectuals, material which lacked an in-depth comprehension of the issues that confronted them. The 1970s in Iran had witnessed much religious revival, in the wake of the realization that "Western " or "modern" ideologies could not solve the variety of problems confronting Iranian society, both at the political and cultural levels. An essential characteristic of Islam is its emphasis on the indivisibility of spiritual and secular spheres of man's action. This became the core of Shariati's lectures and drew the drifting youth back to a reconsideration of the primary element of his practical culture, the Islamic message.

Shariati called upon his listeners to reconsider the proclamation of the Quran that man was God's *khalifa* on earth, and as such his excellence depended upon his being God's representative in the world. Intrinsic to this divinely mandated vocation was his being a two-dimensional creature. This is confirmed by the creation narrative in the Quran according to which God fashioned man out of clay and then breathed His spirit in the clay and man was created.[8] Shariati developed this into a symbolic story explaining the purpose of man's creation and the need for religion in human society. The bi-dimensionalism of man was a well-established subject of discourse for Muslim political thinkers as well as theologians who contended the necessity of the investiture of an imam ("leader," in the technical sense of the term) to ensure both the religious and worldly welfare of man at all times. For Shariati the theme contained profound truths concerning man's purpose on earth. In this respect he followed Muhammad Iqbal (d. 1938), whose Persian works he had read extensively, especially, his favorite theme regarding man's divine vicegerency. Unlike Iqbal, Shariati was not himself a poet. However, he had a firm grounding in Persian literature, without which it would have been impossible for him to communicate with his audience culturally.

Shariati maintains that the Islamic concept of man is based upon a symbolic interpretation of religious language. There are two basic reasons for this: first, religious language is addressed to different human types; and second, it is not intended for a limited period of time. In any religion there are concepts whose inner significations were not comprehensible at the time of their proclamation, and their profound meanings became apparent only when later generations of men had advanced in their thought and outlook. Shariati strongly believed that religion must speak in images and symbols that engage man's intellect in all times; religion that expressed its ideas in apparent meaning would become outmoded in later times. Symbolic religious language represents profound ideas in the form of images with inner connotations that man can discover in proportion to the depth of his thought and experience in the realm of meaning. The Quran employs symbolic language in delivering its message and, Shariati maintains, it is necessary that Muslims living in contemporary times attempt to discover the inner signification of a narrative like the one describing the creation of man. Such an awareness would enhance their understanding of their role in the society, and would enable them to shoulder the responsibility of fulfilling the Trust that they had accepted at the time of their creation.

The virtue and excellence of the two-dimensional man in Islam is revealed by the fact that when God completed His creation He offered the Trust (amanah) unto the heavens and the earth and the hills, but they shrank from bearing it and were afraid of it. And man assumed it. "Lo, he has proved a tyrant and a fool."[9] The Trust, according to major Quranic exegetes, means the divine sovereignty (al-wilayat al-ilahiyya), which God offered to all His creatures. It is only man who has the capability of accepting the divine sovereignty, because only he has the potential to attain perfection and perfect his environment. Furthermore, he alone is not afraid to bear the burden of the Trust, which, according to Shariati, must be interpreted as "free will," and accept the consequences of being a "tyrant" and "ignorant" because it is also only he who can acquire their opposite attributes and be described as "just" and "knowledgable." In fact, both "tyranny" and "ignorance" are primarily the correctors of his responsibility in accepting the divine sovereignty. It is indeed through the acceptance of this Trust that man acquires both the responsibility for his action as well as superiority over all other creatures in the world.

By breathing His spirit in man and offering him the Trust, God establishes a special relationship with him which is evident in the provenance of the most exalted concept of the Unity of God (tawhid) in man. The fundamental tenet of Islam is the affirmation of tawhid. In explaining his belief that Iranians must learn Islamic history, Shariati asserts that it is impossible to understand the Islamic spirit of Iran without understanding tawhid. The principle of tawhid, according to Shariati's teaching, is unique in Islam as compared to the previous monotheistic traditions. Evidence for this assertion is provided by a sociological principle that treats the "degree of signification." For instance, the words "revolution" and "freedom" connote the same meaning lexically as they did before or after the French Revolution; but, the degree of their signification certainly changed following the Revolution. Hence, when one speaks about tawhid in Islam, one is not signalling a new idea, initiated by Islam; rather, tawhid is an idea that has gained a new degree of signification, embodying a wider criterion, influence, and area in meaning. Tawhid says Shariati, is not merely a principle beside other fundamental principles of Islam, such as belief in the Prophecy and the Day of Judgment; rather, it is the foundation of all these other principles. Thus tawhid in Islam assumes an unprecedented signification and becomes the most sensitive tenet in Islam against which all social and individual behavior is measured to ascertain sincerity and commitment in religion. In other words, *tawhid* is the foundation of the individual and social life of a Muslim. All human activities and relationships, whether political, economic, literary, or artistic, ought to be firmly founded on *tawhid*. It provides one, single direction, and it guarantees a unified spirit for its adherents.[10]

Thus, Shariati points out that when he takes the question of belief in One God seriously, it is not in order to engage in a theological or philosophical argument about it; more correctly, it is an attempt to comprehend the spirit of history and existing sentiments regarding this affirmation in every age. Without a consideration of this subjective aspect in a historical study of a society, the study of history, more than likely, is a dry, boring, and wasteful examination of events chronologically. All historic as well as primitive societies have been saturated with the belief in a divine being or beings, and, it can be safely assumed that both individual and social conscience has been imbued with the idea of God. In Islamic history, *tawhid* not only gives man certainty and a sense of security and inner tranquility; it also makes him responsible for the welfare of his own self and the society in which he lives, giving meaning and direction to his existence. In other words, *tawhid* embodies all the manifestations of religious faith in the spiritual as well as material life of man.

According to Shariati, the cause of every corruption, distortion, and immoral behavior in man and his society is due to three elements in man: ignorance, fear, and greed. *Tawhid* eliminates all three of these elements from the depth of the spirit of a person who has affirmed *tawhid*. "Ignorance" is not used here as an antonym of "knowledge" or "science." It is used as the antonym of the word "wisdom" or "sagacity," as employed in the Quran. In the Quran "wisdom" connotes "right apprehension" and "comprehension of truth." "Wisdom" is a motive power which encourages man to move toward moral perfection, and restrains him from committing wicked deeds that would lead to his moral decline. It is a conscious power that cannot be found in science, which is essentially amoral. Hence, a man like the Prophet who established his social order on *tawhid*, thus creating *nizam-i tawhid* (system based on unity), actually established it on "wisdom." It is "wisdom" which makes him the great moral reformer of the world; and it is precisely the moral and spiritual change that he brought about in his society that makes him the great teacher and reformer. A scientist who employs his knowledge in creating a bomb; or, an historian or a sociologist who distorts his research to uphold and justify the unjust and cruel behavior of those in power and to mislead the ordinary people cannot be said to possess the "light" of knowledge which is a God-given gift. "Knowledge" and "wisdom" mean the salvation and perfection of man, not his destruction. Thus, "ignorance" connotes all that knowledge which leads to wickedness and corruption among men. It is, therefore, significant to keep in mind, concludes Shariati, that *tawhid* perfects the ethical conscious in man. It endows him with the hidden power of "wisdom" which nurtures and perfects him.[11] Further, it creates for him a worldview by which he reacts rationally to his environment, creating necessary responsibility in him to bring about a just social order. Man's existence and behavior in the society is subject to the quality of his thought and belief. Moral and human standards, various values attached to different things, goals set for life and followed through, all depend on the worldview created by an individual through his belief and religious commitment. The conviction that existence has meaning, value, and purpose—and as a consequence human life and mankind cannot exist futilely—lays the foundation for a clear, positive, broad worldview and a firm basis for individual and social moral life, thereby destroying ignorance.[12]

As for "fear" and "greed" in man, *tawhid* prevents a person who truly believes in One God from committing any shameful and degrading act resulting from the sense of danger and loss. A *muwahhid* (believer in *tawhid*) is not fearful of such elements and affirms the only source of danger or fear from God, who alone is Omnipotent and exercises absolute will in the world. Thus, a *muwahhid* is not afraid of death, poverty, and of various deprivations. All the ills in the society, says Shariati, are due to lack of faith in one God, which brings about a confused personality. A man without faith is preoccupied with numerous factors that generate insecurity and fear in him and as a result of this preoccupation he is never himself. He does not have his own color; it can be said that he is colorless. He is constantly concerned with "others" and this becomes the cause of "alienation." Alienation means that his "self," his personality, or his originality, does not exist anymore. "Fear" and "greed" have caused all other factors to be obliterated and he has become alienated from himself. He has become an expedient being rather than an actual being. It is in this light that one should examine dictatorship. Dictatorship is repugnant because except for the person and personality of a dictator, all other personalities are exterminated and absorbed into his personality. As a consequence, a society of a million "expedient" *(masalahati)* individuals is left with one "actual" *(haqiqi)* being and one single personality. It is this type of society which becomes poor and base.[13]

However, *tawhid* does not allow for such a social malaise to arise, because at least five times a day God requires man to stand in His presence and declare sincerely that "Thee alone we worship and Thee alone we ask for help." This is the essence of *tawhid,* which man ought to affirm with all sincerity and which can eliminate all fear and greed that exist in his spirit. By affirming *tawhid,* man becomes free, secure, fearless, and free from greed. He becomes capable of depending upon his personality at all times, in all places. When such individuals come together to form a society, that society will reflect the personality created by *tawhid*, namely, independent and fearless.

Islam, according to Shariati, based its message upon *tawhid* and called upon people to affirm the Unity of God, so that they would be saved. The idea of being saved is not simply soteriological; rather, it is a promise of salvation of man from all kinds of limitations and pressures, in both worlds, this and the next. To this end, besides requiring man to affirm *tawhid*, God teaches him "the names of all things,"[14] that is, he endows him with the faculty of rational discrimination, which empowers him to perceive and comprehend the scientific truths inherent in the world, and also learn through empirical observation about his responsibility toward himself and his fellow beings, in order to be "saved." The special relationship and affinity between man and God implies man's individual as well as social responsibility in his capacity as God's vicegerent for creating a new life, a just social order—*nizam-i tawhid*—that *tawhid* demanded. The two-dimensional man is the true reflection of the challenge of Islamic revelation which explicitly requires the creation of an ideal social order as the necessary outgrowth and context of the personal dimension of human responsibility. Shariati maintained that only Islam, the two-dimensional religion with orientation to this world and the next, could enable man to discharge his supreme responsibility.[15]

But man needs a model to follow in order to perform his responsibility; this model is provided by Muhammad, the founder of Islam. This exemplar is also bi-dimensional and is sent to all humanity with the message. The duty of a prophet is to show men the school and path of the truth. Once the Prophet has conveyed the divine message, his mission, according to Shariati, is completed, and then it is left to men to choose to follow the guidance or reject it.[16] In the final analysis, the people themselves are responsible for their decline or advancement, since they are acknowledged as one of the fundamental factors in determining the course of society. The other factors are: the personality of the leader, the tradition that has definite and immutable laws with it, and a certain form of accident.[17] The people have to "exert" themselves (i.e. practice *ijtihad*) in order to evaluate the impact (of the new forces in all their forms) on Islamic society. When the new forces—socio-economic, cultural-moral, or political— occur in or to a society, the destiny of that society obviously depends upon meeting the new challenges creatively. If society can react to these new forces with self-confidence by exercising the necessary assimilation, absorption, rejection and other forms of positive creativity, generated by *tawhid,* it can and will develop a new dimension for its inner aspirations, a new meaning and scope for its ideals. Should a society fail to face the realities of the present squarely, it must become a fossil. It is an immutable law of God that such fossilized societies do not survive for long: "We did them no injustice; it is they who did injustice to themselves."[18] Thus, Shariati regards *ijtihad* (independent estimation and reasoning) to be an absolute necessity in order creatively to interpret and elaborate Quranic revelation to meet the new factors that impact upon a Muslim society. *Ijtihad* can produce the creative response necessary if a Muslim society is to progress within the framework of Islam. Thus, he called for a re-evocation of *ijtihad* and a relentless process of hard, clear, systematic, and synthetic thinking, which, according to Shariati, was not visible among the practitioners of *ijtihad* in Iran.[19]

Ijtihad, then, is a continuous process and a fundamental principle of perpetual revolution in Islam.[20] It is *ijtihad* which can lead the *mujtahid* (jurisprudent) to recognize the conflict between the traditional interpretation of Islam and the demands of the contemporary life and to amend his opinion to arrive at a new one. For Shariati, the ordinary Muslim, though not a *mujtahid* in the technical sense of the term, and perhaps unable to do original thinking, is nevertheless capable—and indeed must exercise this capacity—of making up his own mind as to whose opinion to follow. He should follow *(taqlid)* opinions and not persons. "Imitation" tends to degrade the intelligence of the simple man and it leads him to commit the sin of "associationism" or "religious idolatry" *(shirk),* which nullifies *tawhid.* Thus, contends Shariati, a person who engages in merely identifying a *mujtahid* as "more learned" or "less learned" rather than assessing his opinions as "rational" or "irrational," then, commits a sin of "associationism." Such blind following contradicts the essence of *tawhid* which requires a person to trust in God alone and none beside Him. In the worldview of *tawhid,* man worships only Him, and is answerable before one judge, God.[21] However, *taqlid,* acceptance of mere authority, became so widespread in Muslim history that ijtihad, or reinterpretation for creative response to future developments, became practically non-existent. *Taqlid* was originally recommended for the common man although it was conceded that even the common man has sufficient power of discernment to exercise *ijtihad* in deciding between conflicting views. Later, however, *taqlid* enveloped almost all members of Muslim society. It is in view of this situation that Shariati, like Iqbal and other modern Muslim reformers, espoused *ijtihad* with a greater sense of urgency to meet the impact of new conditions created by modernity.

In a society founded on the principle of *tawhid,* its members ought to submit to God's will alone. His will is manifested in the norms that govern society. Man must conform his will to the Will of God by following the immutable and scientifically demonstrable laws of nature. Society, according to Shariati, is like a living organism and like all living organisms, it has laws. From a certain point of view, then, development and change in a society are governed by these immutable laws which form the very basis of social life. But, Islam goes beyond just determining the immutable laws underlying a human society. It makes the individuals who come together to form this society, separately and equally, responsible for their own destinies. The Quranic affirmation that "God does not change what is in a people, until they change what is in themselves"[22] implies social responsibility at both the individual as well as the collective level. Man has the responsibility of recognizing the norms of society and of improving those norms for the progress of his society. To achieve this end he needs to furnish himself with knowledge of the norms that predominate in society. The leaders in a society are those who have equipped themselves with more than merely adequate knowledge of these norms, and hence have greater responsibility for and freedom in changing and developing a society. Historically, then, the prophets have proven to be great teachers by virtue of their improvised, true knowledge about the divine order, as a result of which they could and did lead people to construct an ideal society. Muhammad's emergence as a prophet in Arabia in the seventh century had a fundamental purpose behind it and that was to transform the contemporary tribal structure of Arab society into a Muslim *ummah*—a religio-socio-politcal community—a transformation which changed the course of history. The social transformation envisioned and initiated by Muhammad was the logical outcome of his faith in and his comprehension of the divine norms, which required that the entire society and not just individuals must demonstrate just social behavior. The emphasis on the necessity for the Muslim community at large to live the new life led to a crucial prerequisite for the fulfillment of the *ummah's* social responsibility. The Muslim community always needs an imam who should be acknowledged by the people *(nas)*. Following the Prophet's death in 632, the institution of Islamic leadership was continued in the presence of a caliph/imam, who, at least in theory, was to be acknowledged by the people. In Shiism the imamate was seen as the continuation of Prophecy and as such an imam had to be invested with leadership by the clear designation of the Prophet himself. Subsequently, the imam was acclaimed as such by the adherents who were required to follow his lead in all matters pertaining to the conduct of life. However, the imam cannot become the active cause in the advancement of the *ummah* to establish an Islamic social order without the people's participation in bringing about fundamental change and development in a Muslim society. In short, the Muslim community has the ultimate responsibility not only for acknowledging the leader, the Imam, but also for sufficiently educating itself about the will of the leader, transmitted in the form of his teachings and their application for the improvement and advancement of human society. Present day Muslims need to acknowledge the Imams Ali and Husayn, and become the Abu Dharrs (activist and loyal adherent of Imam Ali, and paragon of Islamic struggle for social justice), so as to enjoy life and liberty, thought and learning, power and stability.

Such an *ummah* would be able both to defeat its enemies and to become the true adherents of *tawhid*.[23]

Yet, Shariati, fully aware of the predicament of Islam in the Iran of the Pahlavis, was bound to remark that Islam, with its unique conception of two-dimensional leadership and its contribution to man's social progress, had been misinterpreted and transformed into an ideology far removed from the everyday lives of the people. The traditional religious leadership had failed to stand by its obligation to provide model instruction for modern Iranian Muslims. Such criticisms of the religious leadership were not new in Iran because it was evident that religious leadership, in general, ignored the problems of the modern age, the comprehension of which would have directed their efforts in offering a new kind of religious instruction such as that which Shariati had begun in the Husayniya-yi Irshad.

At this point it is important to examine more closely the relationship between the religious class and Shariati in order to elucidate and clarify some misinterpretations of his views on the religious leadership.

SHARIATI AND THE RELIGIOUS LEADERSHIP

One can ascribe the "anti-clerical"[24] atmosphere in Iran, especially among the modern educated class, to the aftermath of Mosaddeq's downfall. The ulama had carried on the function of guiding the community of believers, in their religious as well as social affairs, from the early days of Shia history. They were recognized by the Shiites as the "general deputies" of their last imam, who went into the Complete Occultation in the year 941 and was to reappear as the messianic leader at the End of Time.[25] They were solely responsible for the guardianship of the Shia community, and had maintained its religious as well as its social structure throughout the vicissitudes of the Shia history for some nine centuries. Some of the prominent Shiite scholars in the last century were forerunners of the Ayatullah Khomeini in their opposition to the tyrannical rule of Persian monarchs and their capitulations to Western imperialist powers.

In the 1960s the Iranian government was determined to underplay the sense of moral responsibility toward social, economic, cultural, and political conditions which could be vitalized by adherence to the practical religious culture of Islam. The principal target of this devitalization program was the educated youth who would drift away from their faith under the pressure of modernization. Religious leaders, who were re-examining their own methods to find solutions to contemporary social issues, could not come to the aid of the youth, who were, for the most part, left to the secularly educated, imitative, and self-centered Iranian intellectuals, who lacked both preparation in and appreciation of their own practical culture.[26] It was these circumstances that gave rise to strained relations and estrangement between the religious class and the educated youth.

Some scholars unfamiliar with his thought or his cultural background have ascribed to Shariati a vision of Islam without institutionalized religious leadership. Shariati complained of the inability of the religious class to communicate effectively with Iranian youth. It is critical to review some of the events that took place during the years when I was a student both at the *madrasa* and the university in Meshad and saw a great deal of Sharati. These events shed some light on his subsequent attacks on self-interested members of the religious class. It is also relevant to remember that his criticism of the religious class begins during his involvement in the Husayniya-yi Irshad, more precisely, after Murtaza Mutahhari, a renowned member of the ulama, who was a professor at the Faculty of Theology, University of Teheran, had resigned from the managing board of that institution, because he felt that Shariati was deviating from the original goals of the institution by over-emphasizing the sociological fact of Islam at the expense of its intellectual dimension.[27]

Sharati's early lectures in Meshed, at the Faculty of Letters, as mentioned above, were not without historical or theological flaws. Sometimes, in order to make Islam intelligible, sacrifices in accuracy were made. For instance, the highly controversial and sensitive question concerning the succession of Ali after the death of the Prophet (632) was treated as merely a difference of opinion between the Shiite concept of *wisaya* (designation of Ali as the executor of Muhammad's will of testament), and the Sunnite concept of *shura* (election or selection of a leader through consultation). Both of these groups have arguments to support their theses, and both, according to Shariati, were logical and correct, because their contentions were derived from their understanding of the Prophet's role in the Islamic community. According to the Shiites, the power of the Prophet included both political and spiritual spheres, and as such, he alone was in a position to appoint a leader for his community. Such a person, explicitly designated by him, was the most worthy person to continue his mission and he had to be obeyed in all matters. On the other hand, the Sunnites contended that the very fact that the Muslims of Medina, immediately upon the Prophet's death, gathered in a place to elect their leader, supports the view that they felt it was their responsibility to select the Prophet's political successor themselves.[28] It is apparent to any student of early Islamic history that matters were not as clear-cut and simple as portrayed by Shariati. In addition, by regarding the Sunnite arguments as on a par with the Shiite ones, he was running into direct conflict with a long-established Shiite dogma concerning Ali's sole right to the Imamate. After all, the sole justification for the existence of the Shia was the Imamate of Ali and if that were reduced to one among several truths, then the entire devotional as well as theological edifice of Shiite Islam would crumble. Such an exposition by Shariati of the most sensitive issue of the Imamate was bound to cause much anxiety among the prominent religious authorities, who privately acknowledged the tremendous religious impact his lectures had on the Iranian youth.

Shariati's interpretation of some of the Shia doctrines prompted public criticism from some of the *akhunds* (popular preachers, belonging, as far as knowledge was concerned, to the lower stratum of the religious class). In reality, they magnified these flaws to arouse public condemnation of his lectures. Shariati proved to be overly sensitive to these attacks. On one occasion, during my theological session in the *madrasa,* I mentioned to one of the local theology teachers that I intended to translate into English parts of Shariati's major written work, *Islam Shinasi* (Islamology). He suggested that before I undertook the task, it would be advisable to have my theology teacher check those sections for doctrinal accuracy. Shariati, when informed about this conversation by a classmate, was enraged to the extent that when he wrote his brief work on Hujr b.~Adi al-Kindi (one of Ali's most loyal supporters, executed by Umayyad governor in 672), he recounted the whole incident in a footnote, fiercely criticizing the theologians for their claim to thoroughgoing knowledge. He became increasingly sensitive to these criticisms. In a series of lectures published later, *Alid Shiism and Safavid Shiism,* he overtly attacked the religious class and their mode of presenting Islam, their lack of Quranic comprehension, and so on. He went so far as to assert that a degree in *ijtihad,* which was the highest academic level that could be attained in the *madrasa* and which empowered a *mujtahid* to form his own independent opinion in matters pertaining to Islamic law, did not require the study of the Quran.[29] Probably, what he meant was that the Quran itself was far more liberal in its social message, and that the religious scholars had failed to interpret it to the advantage of the Muslim community.

In his lectures on early Shiism, he distinguished between the Shiism of Imam Ali and later Shiism, which he called Safavid Shiism, that is, "institutionalized" Shiism. He employed this distinction to make his Shia audiences aware that Shiism, and for that matter Islam in general, could not be used as a badge of identity without accepting the challenge of its message to create the just Islamic social order. Early Shiism had stood firmly for the procurement of this deal and the events of Karbala in the year 680 are a reminder to Muslims that "Everyday is the day of Ashura [a day of struggle for the realization of the Islamic ideal, even if that struggle culminates in martyrdom]; and every place is Karbala [a stage of struggle with the forces of opposition to such a realization]."[30] However, in the course of time, the humanistic aspects of the struggles of Ali, Husayn, and Zaynab (Ali's daughter and Husayn's sister who was present in

Karbala) became concealed beneath the dust of abstraction, which tended to elevate their human personalities to the level of supernatural beings. Two factions were responsible for this gross distortion of the true, original Shiism: first, the Safavid and, implicitly, the post-Safavid rulers of Iran, who made Shiism their political tool so as to control the people and keep them in subjugation; second, some of those religious leaders who cooperated with these opportunistic rulers and allowed vacillation and misinterpretation of the original teachings of Shiism.[31]

Shariati could not deny the positive role of religious leaders throughout the Shia history, being fully aware through his own family tradition that there was a real and practical need for the cultivation of expertise in religious sciences, so that the community should benefit from their guidance. However, he could not hold back his most severe, and sometimes unreasonable, criticisms of particular shortcomings of the religious leaders in social and political affairs during the last two decades. In his lectures, toward the end of his career, he was aware of his oversensitivity and overreaction to valid criticisms of his own shortcomings as well as those that he leveled against some of the religious leaders,[32] and had, accordingly, revised his stance. He was deeply concerned that some of his lectures were misconstrued as stemming from his personal dislike for an *akhund,* and to rectify this misconception he said:

> Disliking an *akhund* is not a matter of personal taste that one should declare his like or dislike for an *akhund.* One must document one's divulgence and produce a proof for one's position. So far as I know, under most of the documents that went to further foreign domination of this nation [i.e. Iran], the signatures of those who were educated among us, that is, doctors and engineers, and who had returned from the West, are to be found. If I had come across a signature of an *akhund* or the one who had come back from Najaf [the center for Islamic learning] [on those documents], then, I too would have declared, like you do, by saying: "I do not like *akhund.*"[33]

Shariati's main concern in his criticism of the religious class was their indifference to the modern situation, and in this he was not alone. Muhammad Iqbal had leveled similar criticism against the *mullahs* who had given up their role as *mujahidun* (strugglers in the path of Islam) and had confined their energies to the hair-splitting discussion about minor details of rituals. In Najaf, Ayatullah Khomeini had criticized his colleagues for the lack of social and political vision which had betrayed the dignity and true mission of their class.[34] The community needed religious scholars who could make Islam intelligible to the educated and raise the level of creative self-realization among the Muslim masses. In one of his communications Shariati, admiring the contributions of the learned Ayatullah Muhammad Baqir Sadr (executed in 1979 in Iraq), remarks that the Ayatullah in his two major works, *Our Philosophy* and *Our Economy*, had amply demonstrated his knowledge not only of the Islamic sciences but of the modern age as well. He had employed modern scientific methods and the language of contemporary times to express his thought: "Our age needs such an approach and such is the learned Islamic scholar [Muhammad Baqir Sadr], who is needed in this era."[35] Religious leaders were indispensable to the betterment of Muslim society.

However, to become a truly Islamic scholar (*alim-i islami*), a student of the *madrasa* system needed special training to enable him to serve Islam. According to Shariati, a religious scholar had in the first place to be a Quranologist, who could explain the essential elements of the new society envisioned by the Islamic revelation. Second, he had to be a Prophetologist, thoroughly acquainted with the biography, the traditions and custom of the Prophet, whose position in the Quran-oriented society was indispensable and unique. Third, an Islamic scholar must have an exhaustive familiarity with Islamic history and knowledge about the Imams and other members of the Prophet's household, as well as their close associates, all of whom should be models for personal devotion to moral purity and just social behavior. In the fourth place, a religious scholar was thoroughly acquainted with Islamic culture, and had a specialization in one of the sub-fields of Islamic studies such as Islamic philosophy, history, or law.[36] Most of these qualifications for an Islamic scholar were already recognized in the *madrasa* system. The method in that system, however, was drastically different from the one to which Shariati had been exposed and which he advocated. Undoubtedly, it was the method that was crucial in the presentation of Islam to modern educated youth. The backwardness of the Muslims, according to Shariati, had to be attributed to their methodology, according to which they endeavored to discover universals without any attempt at empirical observation of the natural phenomena. The "Hellenized" intellectuals among Muslim religious scholars were satisfied in classifying the Quranic verses into two kinds: 1) Those which *required* a person to perform its like, such as the daily *salat* (worship), fasting and so on; and 2) Those which *call on* a person to perform its like, without requiring it, such as traveling in order to empirically observe the outcome of a career of God-fearing and God-rejecting peoples. The second type, in Shariati's view, would have led to the modern methodology of direct observation and experimentation, so as to extract the particulars which would have led to an inference of the universals. Lack of concern to understand the particulars, including the underlying norms of the society and the individual, has led to an overall ignorance among the so-called ulama. In spite of their prolific literary output, they have remained out of touch with modern Muslim society.[37]

To Iranian youth, Shariati's approach to the understanding of Islam was scientific and originated from a deep-seated belief in the supremacy of Islamic revelation. They also felt an affinity with one who resembled them in their external as well as inner disposition. After his lectures, we used to tell each other that Shariati sounded very familiar and yet convincing. He was distinct from all other teachers and lecturers. He was like a brother, a person who dressed like us and aspired to what we all aspired. He inspired new interest and confidence in Islam and a total commitment to its norms in everyday life. Muslims under Islam had to face its fundamental revolutionary challenge—the challenge that was historical and which generated a profound sense of responsibility and concern for common human destiny. An incredibly large number of people were drawn to Islam as a result of Shariati's eloquence and sincerity—two qualities that do not always occur together.

Yet, with all that powerful vision of Islam that he was able to create in the minds of millions of Iranians, Shariati knew the limitations of a reformer such as himself: he sets out the best of theses and principles on paper, but is never able to change a society. What was the point of the distinction he drew between a reformer/teacher like himself and a prophet who is endowed with knowledge about the divine norms which exist in nature and who employs these norms to the advancement of his society? Was he alluding to the religious position that a prophet alone holds due to his claims to an extraordinary communication with God enabling him to move his society to a definite goal?

Shariati knew Iran too well not to acknowledge the cultural and religious aspirations of his people and not to realize the numerous obstacles to their achievement. The major impediment that he saw was the lack of creative self-realization and self-respect among the youth. They could be vitalized only by an Islamic revival. This was especially the case in the wake of the apparent failure of pre-Islamic Iranian cultural notions employed during the Pahlavi regime in an attempt to revitalize a sense of national and moral responsibility in youth. He recognized the extent to which the competently trained religious scholars were capable of correcting the situation with their prophet-like personalities and the legitimacy that was afforded to them in that position by the people. A mere lay reformer could not and did not possess a similar basis to attain his goal in improving society. Shariati, therefore, regarded the religious scholars as fulfilling a fundamental function in Iran. He did not hesitate to repudiate those among them who in no way contributed to the socio-political life of the Muslims, but merely prided themselves on a special status as *ruhani*, similar to the ordained priesthood, with ceremonial priestly duties.[38] In his last years of exile in Mazinan and his solitary life there before he left for Europe in 1977, it was evident that in spite of all the popularity that he enjoyed, his role as religious reformer in the Shia Islamic context was in question even among the youth. Some of his lectures on the topic of dialectics and historical development, which call for the establishment of social justice and equity—a theme shared by Marxism and Shiism—left much room for various contending groups, religious as well as non-religious, to claim him as their ideologue after his death.

This factor has led to the difficulty of assessing his actual contribution to the Iranian revolution in 1978–79. It must now be acknowledged that not all who rallied under his banner after his death, were truly his followers in any sense. Clearly, not all people in Iran had declared their allegiance to Islam following the departure of the Shah in 1979. Claiming to be the follower of Shariati was not only seen to be revolutionary and progressive, but it was also used as a cover for a latent anti-religious leadership stance. It is unfortunate that Shariati, who spent the best years of his short life expounding and revising his views on religion, which actually contributed to the Islamic revival among a large sector of modern educated youth, did not live long enough to modify his simplistically treated material on Islamic social history before it fell into the hands of opportunistic and religiously ill-informed persons to manipulate to the detriment of what he had worked for.

CONCLUSION

It is not simple to analyze personalities like Shariati, who appear multi-dimensional in their thoughts and deeds. It is a remarkable phenomenon in the history of great men that they leave so much unresolved in their careers that one always wishes that they had lived a little longer to solve these puzzles. Shariati set out to establish a discipline of "Islamology" (Islam shinasi), that is, to apply Islam to the needs of contemporary society, rather than further contribute to the perfection of traditional "Islamic studies" (maarif-i Islami). For him, Islam was a bi-dimensional religion which could meet the challenges of modern times. "Islamic studies," as taught in the madrasa and at the faculties of theology in modern Iranian universities, was a discipline founded on the "institutionalized" version of the original and dynamic message of Islam, and preoccupied with the abstraction and theorization which had engaged the energies of traditional scholars up to pre-modern times. However, "Islamology" was concerned with providing the necessary guidance to modern Muslim society at the practical level through the understanding of Islamic revelation based upon a reinterpretation of Islam. To achieve this latter goal, Muslims in contemporary times were in need of the husayniya-like religious institutions, capable of arousing them to transform their present circumstance to an ideal Islamic society, where Muslim intellectuals, committed to the discipline of "Islamology" could expound the true Islam. Shariati's contribution to the Islamic revival in the last twenty years should be viewed in connection with the transformation of a popular *husayniya* into an institute of "Islamology" and the change of an intellectual's role into that of a modern-day Muslim teacher-preacher-reformer.

Muslim youth in Iran, whose predicament was well understood by Shariati, found his fresh sociological approach to the teaching of Islamic history not only originating in a strong religious belief and upholding its practical implication in one's life, but also providing a direction for Islamic conduct and holding Muslim youth to it. His "Islamology" dealt with Islam as a new sociological fact, a new practical Islam, markedly different from the one a traditional preacher spoke about. Shariati's thought, as a consequence, has a remarkable appeal for the younger generation of men and women who found in his "Islamology" a viable and reassuring alternative to the Marxist and Western conceptions of society. His "Islamology" became far more popular with younger Iranians, who clearly understood the dynamic and revolutionary content of Shariati's lectures and writings during the Islamic Revolution in 1978–79. However, in the process of demonstrating the socio-political framework of Islam in vigorous lectures, Shariati's system achieved its impact in part at the expense of intellectual caution. In his brief analysis of *ijtihad,* for instance, where he assigned conscious and deliberate accommodation to new conditions and views, he failed to show how the principle of "independent reasoning" was to be maintained if the classical analysis in the works of "demonstrative jurisprudence" (*al-fiqh al-istidlali*) were abandoned. His interpretation of the classical Islamic period was more than often strained to achieve his purpose and his comprehension of the evolution of the modern West was shallow and, at times, one-sided. He never gave serious evidence to show that Islam would be better able than other systems to survive modernity without endangering its principle of continuity. Nevertheless, his lectures presented a more satisfying interpretation of Islam than the one Iranian Muslims were accustomed to finding in the discourses of the traditional Muslim preachers. The natural consequence of Shariati's sense of the high ultimate destiny of Islam was to regenerate the revolutionary and reformative aspect of early Islam, as became apparent in 1979.

Notes

1. Shariati in his lecture, *Ijtihad va nazariya-yi inqilab-i daimi* (Independent Reasoning and the Principle of Perpetual Revolution) (Houston, Tex.: n.d.), p. 18, alludes to this predicament of Muslim youth. He says that the greatest obstacle to a Muslim youth's comprehension of Islam is the fact that those who possess the knowledge of Islamic sciences (the religious class) do not have access to modern methodology to make it intelligible to modern youth; and, those who are trained in modern scientific method are alien

to Islamic learning. It is only by cooperation and coming together of these two types of scholars that the true Islam can be made available to the society.

2. In sketching his career, I have tried to follow his intellectual development as delineated in his book: *Kavir* (A Salt Desert) (Meshad, 1349/1970). This book is, more or less, an autobiography of an intellectual deeply rooted in the rural tradition of Iran, with a profound sense of responsibility toward his social environment, but, with numerous obstacles in the way of the fulfillment of that obligation. In his words, inscribed on the copy of the work he gave me: "It is an account of a distressed and confined soul, which should be read with patience. . . ."

3. Shariati, *Pasukh bi badi az sualat* (In Response to Some Questions), (n.p., n.d.), p. 89.

4. Muhammad Taqi Shariati, *Tafsir-i nuvin* (Teheran, 1968), is a good example of his brilliant efforts in this direction.

5. Shariati, *Ma va iqbal* (Iqbal and Us), part of his collected works entitled: *Majmua-yi athar*, 8 vols. (Teheran, 1977), vol. 5, pp. 92, 152. Hereafter referred to as *Majmua*. This issue was treated in his early major written work *Islzm shinasi* (Islamology) (Meshad, 1347/1978), p. 455ff. The ideas in this book should be regarded as the mainspring of his later lectures in which all the themes treated here, in the form of question-answer, recur.

6. See *Catalogue Thèse de Doctorat* (France: Ministére de l'Education), vols. 79–80 (1962–63), p. 381, which records the thesis under *Lettres*.

7. *Majmua*, vol. 5, pp. 67–68.

8. Quran, S. 55:14, 15:26, 6:2, 23:12.

9. S. 33:72.

10. Shariati, *Islam shinasi*, p. 75–76.

11. Ibid., p. 83–87.

12. Ibid., p. 87.

13. Ibid., p. 89.

14. Quran, S. 2:30. In *Islam shinasi* he discusses the dynamic sense of *tawhid* which he says he had derived from his father M. Shariati, pp. 74–114. See also fn. 53 on p. 123. For his discussion of *tawhid*, see below.

15. Shariati, *Islam shinasi*, p. 85.

16. Ibid. In his first chapter, pp. 27–129, in various places, he indicates this point. For Shariati it is the message of the Unity of God which is eternally generating the social responsibility.

17. Ibid., pp. 46–59.

18. Quran, S. 11:101, 16:33.

19. Shariati, *Ijtihad*, 11ff.

20. Ibid., p. 14–5.

21. *Islam shinasi*, p. 97.

22. Quran, S. 13:11.

23. *Islam shinasi*, p. 95–114

24. "Anti-clerical" is an inaccurate designation to describe the situation that occurred in 1960s in Iran. More appropriate description would require a phrase like "estrangement between the youth and the religious class."

25. See my *Islamic Messianism: The Idea of Mahdi in Twelver Shiism* (Albany: 1981), especially chapter 3.

26. Shariati, *Insan va islam* (Man and Islam), p. 237ff. where he delineates the responsibility of the Iranian intelligentsia in the improvement and advancement of their society.

27. Mutahhari was among the founding members of the Husayniya-yi Irshad. He and Seyyid Hossein Nasr, then Dean of the Faculty of Letters at the University of Tehran, had collaborated with Shariati in realizing this goal.

28. For detailed discussion of his exposition on the question of *wisaya* and *shura* see his *Ummat va imamat* (Community and Leadership).

29. *Majmua,* vol. 6, p. 14.

30. A famous tradition which is attributed to the twelfth Imam, who is reported to have told one of the high ranking *mujtahids* of the late Safavid era, namely, Muhammad Baqir Majlisi.

31. Shariati, *Tashayyu alavi va tashayyu safavi* (Teheren, 1971/1350).

32. He once confided to me that only Sayyid Fadil al-Milani, the grandson of the late Ayatullah Milani, among the religious class had offered constructive critique of his works, having first read them meticulously.

33. Shariati, *Ijtihad,* p. 26–29.

34. Khomeini, Ruhullah, *Hukumat-i islami* (Islamic Government) (Najaf: 1971), pp. 24–25.

35. *Majmua,* vol. 1, p. 181. Both these works have been published in Iraq and Iran.

36. Shariati, *Ijtihad,* p. 29.

37. Shariati, *Islam shinasi,* p. 58.

38. *Majmua,* vol. 7, p. 182.

III

MUSLIM PERSPECTIVES
ON A RESURGENT ISLAM

As material in Sections I and II illustrates, while a core of Islamic belief and practice exists, modern Islam has been going through a dynamic period. Islamic thought and practice have been conditioned both by historical circumstance and by Muslim interpretations. Although an abundance of Western analyses of the resurgence is increasingly available and useful, Muslim perspectives on the nature of their resurgence—its causes, problems, agenda, and prospects—are central to our understanding of this complex and multifaceted phenomenon. This section of the volume provides direct access to contemporary Muslim reflections on the nature and agenda of a resurgent Islam, its implications for political and economic development. The material that follows does not simply represent the statements of detached observers, but rather the opinions of Muslims who have been directly involved in the Islamic movement, within their own countries and internationally.

In the opening selection, "The Impact of the West on the Muslim World and the Islamic Resurgence," Professor Khurshid Ahmad, protégé of Mawlana Mawdudi, and trained economist, as well as a former minister of Planning and Development in Pakistan, maintains that the Islamic movement today seeks freedom from western dominance. Its goal is a "restructuring of society (individual life and collective life), the rebuilding of socio-economic life on the foundations of Islam." Amidst the conflict of western and Islamic cultures, the resurgence represents a third alternative to capitalist and socialist systems, a positive, creative response to the challenge of modernity.

A critical issue for twentieth-century Islam has been the question of change and adaptation. If the classical doctrine is that Islam is a total way of life, revealed by God and enshrined in Islamic law, then to what extent is change

215

possible? This question is especially poignant today as Muslim revivalists seek to establish more Islamically-oriented states and societies. Dr. Sadiq al-Mahdi, great-grandson of the famed nineteenth-century Sudanese Islamic revivalist, Oxford trained, and a former prime minister of the Sudan, responds to this question in "Islam and Social Change." For different reasons, Western analysts and conservative Muslims have shared a tendency to view Islam as antithetical to change. For the former, Islam is a literalist religion which is an obstacle to change. For the latter, it is the perfect, immutable, "straight path" to be followed without deviation. If law is the comprehensive, divinely mandated path, then substantive change or innovation *(bida)* is an unwarranted departure from tradition/law.

Sadiq al-Mahdi analyzes the causes of these false views of Islam and attempts to demonstrate how Islam fosters and accommodates change. While more conservative fundamentalist Muslims look to the past for their paradigms, Sadiq al-Mahdi argues that there is no particular Islamic political or economic system. Instead, there are immutable principles in light of which Muslims in the past and in the present must develop systems that are appropriate to their historical and social milieu. Thus, the task of contemporary Islam is to undertake a fresh interpretation of Islam.

Hassan al-Turabi is a Sorbonne-educated legal scholar, founder of the Sudanese Muslim Brotherhood, and currently Attorney General of the Sudan. As he notes, he is "directly involved in the political process that seeks to establish an Islamic state." Dr. Turabi presents some of the essential or universal characteristics of such a state, focusing on its nature and functions.

There are many issues surrounding the creation of modern Islamic states. The historical and social circumstances within which Islam developed have changed; what does this mean for Islamic political thought and practice today? How open is Islam to modern notions of state and society: nationalism, popular sovereignty, democracy, freedom and dissent, popular political participation and representation, modern law and economics? The remainder of this section presents selections which delineate the nature and purpose of an Islamic state and society. Given the ideology of an Islamic state, what place is there for nationalist or pan-Islamic identity and allegiance? What are the implications of an Islamic state regarding questions of sovereignty, elections, political parties, and the rights of non-Muslims?

A fundamental issue underlying attempts to establish modern Islamic states is the nature of authority and the role of democracy in Islam.

Justice Javid Iqbal (the son of Muhammad Iqbal), scholar, lawyer, and for many years, justice of the Supreme Court in Pakistan, addresses this important question. For Justice Iqbal, as for Dr. Turabi, while Islam is open to the development of new political and legal systems, the ideological commitment of the state does set certain limits or restrictions affecting such areas as candidates' qualifications for elective office, the conduct of elections, the legislative scopes of a national assembly or parliament, and the political party system. "Only such political parties which adhere to Islamic ideology can be permitted to function in a Muslim national state."

The establishment of Israel in 1948 was the fulfillment of Zionist dreams to provide a homeland for the Jewish people. However, for Muslims the loss of Palestine to the Israelis was and continues to be a major political and religious issue. As indicated earlier in this volume, the Arab-Israeli wars, in particular Israeli control of Jerusalem, make Palestine not simply a Palestinian or Arab problem but a worldwide Islamic issue. Ismail R. al-Faruqi, a Palestinian scholar and Muslim leader, articulates the perceptions of many Muslims in their distinction between a rejection of Zionism and recognition of Judaism. In addition, he suggests what an Islamic solution or alternative would imply.

A major theme of the Islamic resurgence is economic/social justice. Just as Western-based political systems have been found wanting so too have their economic systems—capitalism and communism. Poverty, illiteracy, and distribution of wealth have continued to plague most Muslim societies. Western economic systems and Arab socialism have not altered the situation appreciably. Muslim revivalists attribute this failure to continued reliance on imported economic models. Instead, an Islamic solution to economic development is advocated—one which is rooted in the beliefs, values, and experience of the people and is, therefore, better able to inspire, motivate, and assure Islamic social justice (adl). Khalid Ishaque is a jurist and scholar who has served as an expert member of Pakistan's Islamic Ideology Council in its efforts to formulate modern Islamic economic measures. In "An Islamic Approach to Economic Development," he summarizes the critique of Western economic models and presents an Islamic social framework for economic development.

As we have seen throughout this volume, religion has been part and parcel of Muslim history and politics, a religio-political movement with a universal mission to spread God's rule and His revealed way of life. Thus, Islamic history is the record of Muslim attempts at different times, in different places, and with varying degrees of success and failure, to carry out God's will. The period of Muhammad, the early caliphs, successive Muslim empires, and assorted movements to renew (tajdid) and reform (islah) the Islamic community are part of a continuum which extends to current and future movements in Islam. Kemal Faruki, lawyer and Islamic scholar, in his "Islamic Resurgence: Prospects and Implications" views current attempts at Islamization both in relation to recent Islamic movements in Libya and Saudi Arabia and contemporary experiments in Pakistan and Iran. Such an evaluation is important because of the issues and questions that arise from such experiments as well as their potential implications for the future direction(s) of Islamic revivalism.

TEN

The Nature of the Islamic Resurgence

KHURSHID AHMAD

Four important consequences directly related to the impact of colonial rule are relevant to an understanding of the contemporary Islamic resurgence in general and the emergence of the Islamic movement in Pakistan and all of the subcontinent in particular.

MUSLIM PREDICAMENT: THE IMPACT OF COLONIAL RULE

The first is secularization: secularization of the state, its political, economic and social institutions. Secularism tried to introduce and "impose" a new social ethics deriving inspiration from a worldview and a policy perspective diametrically opposed to the basis on which a Muslim society is founded. In a Muslim society individual morality and social ethics are both derived from the same divine source: the Quran and Sunnah. In secularism divine guidance becomes irrelevant and man's roots in the divine scheme of creation and his destiny in the life beyond physical existence are denied.[1] This produces a unique set of parameters for socio-political life, fundamentally different from the ones on which a faith-based society is established. This major change produced catastrophic consequences for Muslim society. The very moral fiber of the society was undermined.

Second is a new pattern of Western dominance, not merely by virtue of its political rule but through basic institutional changes within the colonized countries and their structural relationships with the outside world, particularly the colonizing countries. The result was a pattern of dependence upon the West, institutionalizing the dominance of the West.

Third, and a logical consequence of both the factors cited above, has been the bifurcation of education into two parallel mainstreams of secular and modern education, and religious and traditional education, resulting in the division of the society into two groups: the modern secular elites and the traditional leadership. The members of the new secular leadership, who were carefully groomed into power in different walks of life, are looked upon by the masses of Muslim people as mercenaries—as people who have taken the values and life-style of the colonial rulers and who would be prepared to act at the behest of a foreign power, or at least as people who identified themselves with Western culture and its values and became voluntary or involuntary instruments for the Westernization of the society. This has acted as a divisive force in society.

This led to the fourth consequence, a crisis of leadership. The traditional leadership of the Muslim society was systematically destroyed. A foreign political leadership was imposed and in its wake came the imposition of a foreign-oriented local leadership, a leadership which held the reins of political and economic power but which did not enjoy the trust and confidence of the people, a leadership alienated from its own people and identified with the alien rulers and their life-style.

STRATEGIES FOR REVIVAL

These were among the more important consequences of Western dominance and the whole of this scenario made the Muslims ask a very pertinent question: "Why has this happened—this situation of political dominance as well as the decay and deprivation of our past heritage?"

One group tried to answer this question by suggesting that the times have changed and that we must take to the values, the technology, and the institutions of the dominant power. This would be the way to rise up again. This was the strategy of modernism.

Another said that we have reached this stage because we are not true to our original position. We are not truly Muslim. Islam is not responsible for our present predicament; it is the departure from and non-abidance with Islam which is responsible.

This latter answer again produced two further responses—one which tried to fall back upon the Islamic tradition and grasp it tightly, which I will describe as a traditionalist position, which believed that any change would be a change for the worse. Therefore, hold fast to our tradition and its legacy, remain tied to our roots and history. The two aspects of this strategy were: (1) isolation and withdrawal from the processes of Westernization; and (2) concentration on preservation and protection of the Muslim legacy, cultural, intellectual, and institutional. This can also be described as a strategy of protective resistance, waiting for an opportunity to reassert itself for the achievement of some positive objectives.

There has also been a second response which emphasized that the preservation of the past was not enough if we are to face the challenge that is knocking at our doors. We have to put up a creative, positive response to this situation by trying to understand the nature of the Western challenge and offer an alternative to that. The challenge from the West was not confined to political domination. It was a challenge from a new civilization, having its own worldview and socio-economic institutions, seeking political domination over the entire world. As such, the response has to be more positive and comprehensive: to prepare for an all-out confrontation with the challenging power and offer Islam as the alternate basis for culture and civilization. This response called for the emergence of Islam as a socio-political movement which sought to go back to the original message of Islam; to discover its relevance to our own times and to strive to change the status quo; to rebuild the society and its institutions in the light of the Islamic milieu; and to inspire the individual with a new vision and a new destiny.

This response has been described as *tajdid* (renewal and reconstruction), a perennial phenomenon in Islamic history and therefore not particularly new or modern. Yet it is distinct in its contemporary manifestation to face the challenge of the twentieth century.

THE ISLAMIC MOVEMENT: ITS ORIGINS AND CHARACTER

The contemporary Islamic resurgence, and particularly the Islamic movements that constitute the sheet-anchor of this resurgence, must be understood not merely by examining them as reactions to colonal rule but in the context of the positive aspirations of the Islamic *ummah* to regain the position it lost because of the Western domination. As such, the contemporary Islamic upsurge deserves to be seen as a positive and creative response to the challenge of modernity. In this respect, in the subcontinent the very establishment of Pakistan, in a way, is symbolic of the Islamic resurgence. The Pakistan movement derived its inspiration from the idea that Islam has to be the decisive factor in building our individual and social life. This was not possible under foreign dominance or under the dominance of the Hindu majority and therefore, the need for an independent country where Islam is free, where Islam is able to determine the course of events. This was the thinking behind the Pakistan movement.[2] That is why the establishment of Pakistan, somehow, constitutes a watershed in contemporary Muslim history; it not only represents the beginning of the end of the colonial rule in Muslim lands but also heralds the beginning of a new era in the ideological life of the Muslim people. Their search for a future assumed a new dimension, an effort to rediscover their ideological personality and to seek for a new social order based on the ideals and values of Islam.

This urge has been articulating itself ever since the mid-forties, despite all the obstacles and deterrents within and without. This creative urge was never looked upon with sympathy in the non-Muslim world in general, and the West[3] in particular. There were genuine difficulties and impediments within Muslim society, particularly the ones generated by the impact of colonial rule on Muslim lands, but the situation was aggravated by the continuing efforts of the Western powers to "Westernize" the liberated Muslim countries and keep them tied to the politico-economic system of the West, to perpetuate some kind of center-periphery relationship between the West and the rest.

This is the background for the contemporary movement of Islamic resurgence. That such an upsurge is there at almost all levels of Muslim existence, intellectual, moral, social, cultural, literary, political and economic, is undeniable. But it would be too simplistic to assume that the movement is heading toward global success. The state of the contemporary Muslim society can at best be described as one of "creative tension." There are certain clear pointers toward the people's positive identification with Islam as a source for personal ethics and the dominant inspiration for the socio-economic order they want to establish in their lands, but the institutional obstacles and selective resistance from certain power-elites are also a reality. A new process has been inaugurated in most of the Muslim countries, but the process has yet to unfold itself fully. It is, therefore, important to identify some of the major factors and forces that are shaping the future of the Muslim world.

RESISTANCE AND RESURGENCE

The major forces of resistance to Islamic resurgence are, somehow, related to the four factors we have identified earlier as aspects of the impact of Western rule in the Muslim World. The forces that lie at the root of Islamic resurgence can be identified as two—first a general urge in the entire Islamic *ummah*, the Muslim people and particularly Muslim youth thrilled by an urge to carve out a new future and seek a place of respect and honour in the world. This is an all-embracing movement which cannot be classified in organization stereotypes. It can only be seen and felt and followed. It is made of two major strands, one negative and the other positive. The negative strand represents strong dissatisfaction with the experiments with secularism and secular ideologies of nationalism, capitalism and socialism in the Muslim World. The positive strand is represented by a rediscovery of Islam as an all-embracing system of life—as a faith as well as an ideology and a programme of life.

Contemporary Islamic resurgence is symbolized as much as it has been strengthened and fortified by the political liberation of the Muslim lands and some significant shifts in the balance of economic power in favour of some of the Muslim countries. But the most decisive influence in producing this upsurge has come from the contribution of the religious leadership of the Muslim countries, the Ulama and the Sufiah in general, and more specifically the Islamic revivalist movements.

ISLAMIC REVIVALIST MOVEMENTS

Islamic revivalist movements have their roots deep in the history of the Muslim people, medieval as well as modern. It would be naive to assume that these movements have emerged out of the blue. There is an almost continuous chain of Islamic movements operating amongst the Muslim people in all parts of the world.[4] These movements have mostly been conveniently ignored by the Western observers of the Islamic scene, who have confined their gaze to the ripples on the surface of the water, never caring to understand the currents and crosscurrents beneath the surface. Those who have tried to touch upon this phenomenon have done greater injustice by misrepresenting these movements as manifestations of militant Islam. The labels put upon them bear no relevance to the nature of these movements; they represent the bias or the fears of the vested interests. Therefore it is very important that the nature of these movements be understood in the light of their own perceptions of their role.

The Islamic movements, despite some local features and indigenous accents, have stood for similar objectives and displayed common characteristics. They have shown unwavering commitment to Islam and great capabilities to face the challenge of modernity creatively. Their intellectual contribution is matched only by their moral fervour and political consciousness.

The most important aspect of the mission of these Islamic movements has been their emphasis on Islam, not just as a set of beliefs and rituals, but as a moral and social movement to establish the Islamic order. And by emphasizing this, they have identified themselves with all the *tajdid* and jihad movements of history. The works of Dr. Muhammad Iqbal, and Mawlana Sayyid Abul Ala Mawdudi (Indo-Pak subcontinent), of Imam Hasan al-Banna Shahid and Sayyid Qutb Shahid (Egypt), of Malik bin Nabi and Shaikh Ibrahim al-Jazairi (Algeria), of Dr. Ali Shariati and Imam Kohmeini (Iran), of Said Nursi (Turkey), and others together constitute the most important influence in producing the contemporary revivalist movements in Islam. Only a close look at the mind and thought of these leaders and the movements they inspired can reveal the true nature of this phenomenon of *tajdid,* an effort to relate Islam to the contemporary reality of the Muslim life and society.

It also deserves to be noted that these Islamic movements seek for comprehensive reform, that is, changing all aspects of life, making faith the centre point. The relationship between the eternal and the temporal, the moral truth and the contemporary socio-political reality, is then a central issue. Mawlana Mawdudi and others have addressed themselves to this issue. They have shown the relevance of faith for individual morality as well as for social ethics, for political life, for economic relationships and for the establishment of a just social order. This all-embracing comprehensiveness of the Islamic movement is integral to the Jamaat-i-Islami Pakistan, the Muslim Brotherhood, as well as to other Islamic movements of the twentieth century. This comprehensiveness of Islam as an integrative principle is something which contrasts sharply with the West for it is not in keeping with the contemporary Western approach to human life and its problems, under whose influence problems are studied piecemeal and in isolation because they are not seen as interrelated and grounded in an integrated worldview.

Another important aspect of Islamic resurgence is that although socio-political struggles have taken place in the context of national situations, even highlighting local interests and problems, the thrust of the Islamic revivalist movement is not nationalistic in character. It is an ideological movement. Even if it is confined or its impact is confined to a particular territory, its approach is not nationalistic or parochial. It is ideological and then by definition international. Islam is a universal religion and all Muslims, regardless of regional or national ties, belong to a single community of brotherhood *(ummah).*

Yet, another important aspect of this movement is that it is non-sectarian. And this is very important in the context of Muslim history. This movement has tried to bring all sects, all the schools of Muslim thought to common ground. It is moving, neither on the pattern of the "ecumenical movement" in the Christian world, nor of that of a religious trade union. Its basic emphasis is that the essential area of agreement amongst all Muslim schools of thought is far greater than its fringe differences. When the basic laws and regulations of Islam are being threatened, we must concentrate upon the essentials in the areas of agreement, allowing for the freedom of each individual and each group to follow his or her own interpretation. Thus, the works of some of the Shia scholars, for example, the late Ayatollah Muhammad Baqir Sadr, Imam Khomeini, and Dr. Ali Shariati have been published by predominantly Sunni organizations such as Mawlana Mawdudi's Jamaat-i-Islami in Pakistan, the Muslim Brotherhood in Egypt and other Arab countries. On the other hand, the works of Mawlana Mawdudi, Sayyid Qutb, Hasan al-Banna and others have been published by the Shia communities of Qum. The Islamic revolution of Iran has been welcomed by all Islamic revivalist movements, and even when there are differences on many a point of strategy or tactics, the universalistic Islamic current is easily discernable in a world which had unfortunately taken to sectarian and group affiliations.

Finally, an important aspect which deserves to be kept in view is the division in Muslim society between modern and conservative, between the new and the old, the westernizing and the traditional. This Islamic movement represents a third alternative force. Without condemning any of these, it acts as a bridge between these two and derives its strength from both of them. Instead of expanding the distance between these, it seeks to reach a point of convergence and join together all their resources. In the Jamaat-i-Islami Pakistan[5] we find people from the old school, the ulama and the Sufiya (mystics) as well as highly educated people, students, professionals, and the working classes. The movement works among the labour force, among farmers, among all the various segments of society.

On the international plane too, the approach of the Islamic movement is to draw on the modern civilization as well as the original sources of Islam and to seek to modernize without compromising on Islamic principles and values. The movement clearly differentiates between development and modernization on the one hand and westernization and secularization on the other. It says "yes" to modernization but "no" to blind westernization. The Islamic movement seeks to provide a new leadership to society, a leadership which, although culled from the modern and the traditional hinterland of the society is not identified with any one of these two extreme groups but nonetheless preserves the best in both.

THE FAILURE OF THE WESTERN MODEL

This, I think, is extremely significant because a very important dimension of the present day crisis in the Muslim world is that the westernizing model as well as the westernizing elite have failed. The two classic examples of westernization in Muslim countries are Turkey and Iran. Whether we judge on the basis of the material results these experiments have produced or the moral havoc, the social ills and the psychological shock that have come in their wake, it is the profound feeling of the Muslim people that the Westernization experiment has decisively failed. Both its variants, the capitalistic as well as the socialistic, have been tried and found wanting.

The whole of the Muslim *ummah* has somehow passed through a trauma, becoming more and more conscious that the westernizing model cannot deliver the goods. They want to make a fresh start. They do not want to cut themselves off from the rest of the world. But they also do not want to be dependent on the non-Muslim world. They want freedom with strength; friendship with honour; cooperation without dependence. If the westernizing experiment has failed to achieve this, what next? The Islamic movement represents one such alternative.

If you look at the Islamic movements over the last two centuries, you will find that in the first phase the predominant challenge that the Islamic movement faced was invasion by foreign powers. It tried to resist threats to the freedom and political sovereignty of Dar al-Islam (Islamic territory) but it could not succeed. Nonetheless it made its impact. A second phase occurred when western dominance had consolidated itself. Again, the challenge to colonialism came from Islamic sources which informed the people of their Islamic identity and inspired resistance movements against foreign rule. The Islamic movement was the chief source of the independence movement, seeking liberation from the political dominance of foreign powers. And it succeeded. But in its success, there also was a failure. The new system that was established by the new regimes in most of the Muslim countries was not Islamic. It was still cast in the likeness of Western models. The new political, economic, and intellectual leadership of the Muslim countries was just a replica, a transplant implanted by Western powers. Now we have a third phase that Muslim countries are passing through. The third phase is the Islamic resurgence. The westernizing model has failed and now Islamic movements want to reconstruct society. They are in search of a new social order. They want new answers to the questions which have been agitating them. The Islamic movements have given Muslims a new outlook, a new hope, a new possibility. It is the restructuring of their society, individual and collective life and rebuilding socio-economic life on the foundations of Islam. They are not averse to the technology of the West; but are not prepared to have it at the cost of their own identity and ideology.

THE SPECTER OF FUNDAMENTALISM!

The West has failed to see the strength and potential of the Islamic movement. It has chosen to dubb it as fundamentalist, as fanatic, as anti-Western, as anachronistic, as what not. Nothing could be farther from the truth. It appears that the West is once again committing the fatal mistake of looking upon others belonging to a different paradigm, from the prism of its own distorted categories of thought and history.

Efforts to put the cap of "fundamentalism" on Islamic movements is one such example. Fundamentalism was a unique phenomenon produced in certain periods of Western Christian history. It tried to impose a literalist interpretation on a Book which claimed divine inspiration but was not the word of God, pure and simple. The fundamentalist groups in Christian history came up with many new interpretations and strange religio-political positions and are generally regarded as reactionary and unrealistic. By clamping the same term on Islamic movements great violence is being done to history. It is also bound to misinform the western people and policy-makers about the true nature of Islamic resurgence, as they are being forced to see them in the light of a particular unhappy chapter of their own history. Islamic resurgence is a future-oriented movement and has nothing in common with the fundamentalist approach of the Christian groups. It has shown great awareness of the problems of modernity and the challenges of technology, and its emphasis on the original sources of Islam, the Quran and Sunna, imparts to its approach a flexibility and a capability to innovate which is conspicuous by its absence in the approach of the conservatives who stick to a particular school of *fiqh* (law). All these possibilities are ignored by analysts who try to see the contemporary Islamic world in categories which are not relevant to it.

The present Muslim mind cannot be understood properly unless we realize that it is deeper than just a political anguish. Unfortunately, efforts to understand the Islamic resurgence are often simplistic. The theory that the Islamic resurgence is just a result of rapid developmental efforts, particularly in the case of Iran, is overly simplisitic. Yes, the development syndrome has its own problems, but it would be an oversimplification to assume that the Muslim peoples' overwhelming response to forces of resurgence is simply due to the tensions that have been produced by efforts to achieve quick economic development through technology transfer. Such diagnosis betrays abysmal ignorance of the ethos of the Muslim society.

Similarly, reducing the resurgence to just an angry reaction of people against Western imperialism is equally misleading. There is a reaction against imperialism; there is no doubt about that. However, more than a political fury is being expressed or articulated. A much deeper cause is dissatisfaction with the ideals and values, the institutions and the system of government exported from the West and imposed upon them. It is a dissatisfaction with their leadership which they associate with Western interests and believe has been instrumental in imposing Western models of development on the Muslim society. It is a multi-dimensional phenomenon. On the one hand, it is an historical expression of the concerns as well as the aspirations of the people, based primarily upon internal indigenous factors. On the other hand, it is also a response to an external challenge, the challenge of post-colonial impacts on Muslim society.

The movement of Islamic resurgence is a critique of the Muslim status quo. It is also a critique of the dominant culture of our times—the Western culture and civilization which is prevalent in many of the Muslim countries. And it is a critique from a different base, from a different point of reference; and that point of reference is Islam, the original sources of Islam—the Quran and Sunna of the Prophet Muhammad (peace be upon him).

It represents a reawakening of faith. This dimension is neglected in most of the Western writings; they assume that it is just a question of political and social rearrangements. The social order is definitely important but the starting point is reawakening and strengthening of faith, and rebuilding of the moral personality and the character of the individual. There is an upsurge of spirituality and idealism, generating a new sense of direction and a commitment to reconstruct their world, whatever by the sacrifice.

The model of leadership during the period of colonial domination and of post-colonial manipulation has been one which just looked after personal interests. That is why Muslim society has become so devoid of moral values and become rife with corruption. Corruption and exploitation have become a way of life in our part of the world. Muslims have their own weaknesses and they had faced many reverses as part of the global situation. But the explosion of corruption which is so visible in the present day Muslim World is a new phenomenon. We relate it to the impact of secularization and westernization resulting in loss of individual morality and of social ethics, which had historically been based upon *tawhid* (the unity of God) and loyalty to the Sunna of the Prophet (peace be upon him), and which were weakened under these alien influences. Muslim modernism which has been the secularizing spearhead of westernization in Muslim lands tried to super-impose the values of western liberalism on Muslim society with the result that the grip of traditional values was weakened; but no new morality could be developed to fill the gap. It is in this moral vacuum that personal aggrandizement and socio-economic exploitation have become rampant, mostly in the name of economic development and material progress. Islamic resurgence represents a rebellion against this state of affairs. It stands for a reaffirmation of Islamic morality and a rededication of the resources of the *ummah*—material as well as human—to the achievement of social justice and self-reliance. Muslim youth have been inspired by a new vision to rebuild their individual and social life in accordance with the ideals and principles given by Islam and to strive to establish a new social order, not only within their own countries but to see that a new world order is established ensuring peace, dignity and justice to the oppressed of the world.

ISLAM AND THE WEST

In conclusion, I would suggest that the Islamic resurgence is primarily an internal, indigenous, positive and ideological movement within Muslim society. It is bound to come into contact, even clash with forces in the international arena.

The close contact of the West, particularly through colonial rule is relevant but not the most decisive factor in producing the Islamic response.

Muslims constitute one-fifth of the human race, around 900–1000 million in all parts of the world. There are forty-nine independent Muslim states. If they want to reconstruct their socio-economic order according to the values of Islam, it is bound to come into conflict with the international status quo. So conflict is there. And to that extent, I would like to invite my western colleagues to understand that Muslim criticism of Western civilization is not primarily an exercise in political confrontation. The real competition would be at the level of two cultures and civilizations, one based upon Islamic values and the other on the values of materialism and nationalism. Had western culture been based on Christianity, on morality, on faith, the language and *modus operandi* of the contact and conflict would have been different. But that is not the case. The choice is between the Divine Principle and a secular materialist culture. And there is no reason to believe that this competition should be seen by all well-meaning human beings merely in terms of the geo-politic boundaries of the West and the East. In fact all those human beings who are concerned over the spiritual and moral crisis of our times should heave a sigh of relief over Islamic resurgence, and not be put off or scared by it.

Once the nature of the conflict as taking place on the level of values and culture is clarified, I want to underscore that there is a political dimension to the situation that we must not ignore. There is nothing pathologically anti-western in the Muslim resurgence. It is neither pro- nor anti-West regarding the political relationship between Western countries and the Muslim world, despite the loathsome legacy of colonialism which has the potential to mar these relationships. If China and the United States and Russia and India can have friendly relations without sharing common culture and politico-economic system, why not the West and the Muslim World? *Much depends upon how the West looks upon this phenomenon of Islamic resurgence and wants to come to terms with it.* If in the Muslim mind and the Muslim viewpoint, Western powers remain associated with efforts to perpetuate the Western model in Muslim society, keeping Muslims tied to the system of Western domination at national and international levels and thus destabilizing Muslim culture and society directly or indirectly, then, of course, the tension will increase. Differences are bound to multiply. And if things are not resolved peacefully through dialogue and understanding, through respect for each other's rights and genuine concerns, they are destined to be resolved otherwise. But if, on the other hand, we can acknowledge and accept that this world is a pluralistic world, that Western culture can co-exist with other cultures and civilizations without expecting to dominate over them, that others need not necessarily be looked upon as enemies or foes but as potential friends, then there is a genuine possibility that we can learn to live with our differences. If we are prepared to follow this approach, then we would be able to discover many a common ground and many a common challenge. Otherwise, I am afraid we are heading for hard times.

Notes

1. See, Eric S. Waterhouse, "Secularism", *Encyclopaedia of Religion and Ethics,* ed. by James Hastings (New York: Charles Scribners and Sons, vol. 11, pp. 347–50.

2. "The Muslims demand pakistan, where they could rule according to their own code of life and according to their own cultural growth, traditions and Islamic laws," Quaid-e-Azam Mohammad Ali Jinnah, Message to Frontier Muslim League Conference, Nov. 1945. See *Speeches and Writings of Mr. Jinnah,* ed. by Jamiluddin Ahmad (Lahore: Sh. Muhammad Ashraf, (1964) vol. 2, p. 2.

The Quaid-e-Azam has also stated succinctly in a speech at Aligarh in March 1944 that:

"Pakistan started the moment the first non-Muslim was converted to Islam in India long before the Muslims established their rule. As soon as a Hindu embraced Islam he was outcast not only religiously but also socially, culturally and economically. As for the Muslims, it was a duty imposed on him by Islam not to merge his identity and individuality in any alien society. Throughout the ages, Hindus had remained Hindus and Muslims had remained Muslims and they had not merged their entities—that was the basis for Pakistan". Ibid, vol. 2, p. 2. Similarly Pakistan's first Prime Minister and the former Secretary-General of the Muslim League, while moving the Objective Resolution in the Constituent Assembly of Pakistan declared that:

"The Muslim League has only fulfilled half of its mission (and that) the other half of its mission is to convert Pakistan into a laboratory where we could experiment upon the principles of Islam to enable us to make a contribution to the peace and progresss of mankind." *Constituent Assembly of Pakistan Debates,* Karachi, Manager of Publications, Govt. of Pakistan, vol. 5, no. 5, p. 96 (Mar. 12, 1949).

That is why the real issue for the Muslims in their struggle for freedom in India *was not simply liberation from foreign colonial rule but a liberation leading to 'free Islam in a free India.'*

3. "West" has been used here as a proxy for the dominant powers of our times, capitalist or communist, Eastern or Western, consisting of both the super powers and the forces dominant in Europe.

4. Syed Abul Ala Mawdudi, *A Short History of Revivalist Movements in Islam,* (Lahore: Islamic publications, n.d.).

5. The same is true of the Jamaat-i-Islami, Hind; Jamaat-i-Islami, Bangladesh, the Muslim Brotherhood in the Middle East and other Islamic movements.

ELEVEN

Islam—Society and Change

AL-SADIQ AL-MAHDI

The question of Islam's response to social change is much misunderstood both within the Muslim world itself and outside it. The purpose of this essay is to explain how that misunderstanding arose and to elucidate the ways and means by which Islam fosters and accommodates social change.

Three factors have colored the Western view of Islam. First was a heritage of fear and suspicion which lingered on after the three basically antagonistic encounters between Islam and Christendom which took place centuries ago: The Andalusian (Spanish) encounter, the Crusades, and the Ottoman encounter.

A second factor is an image of stagnation and despotism. Disenchantment with the political system which governed the Muslim world after the assassination of Ali (the fourth caliph) was expressed sometimes violently but by many Muslims mostly in terms of a quiet withdrawal from engagement in the current political system. Thus the founders of the schools of Muslim law distanced themselves from contemporary rulers and developed their ideas in an atmosphere of political abstraction. Shiite doctrine and practice represented a type of withdrawal within a cohesive shell. The Sufi orders may also be characterized as islands unto themselves. Those withdrawal stratagems have been reinforced by means of *taqlid* (the blind following of tradition) which in every way discouraged initiative and dynamic enterprise. This led to intellectual stagnation. Meanwhile the contemporary rulers proceeded to develop their systems along despotic lines. As a result, stagnation and despotism, more often than not, represented the position of Islamic society during its medieval period of decline.

A third major influence on Western perceptions of Islam is Orientalism, which began as a study of the culture of the East, sponsored by colonial governments to formulate policy toward the peoples concerned. Since then it has grown out of that mould and become more sophisticated. Nevertheless, that "original sin" is today responsible for the tendency not to appreciate Islam in itself and to give undue emphasis to its ultimate role in the East-West conflict. Some scholars, historians, and politicans, noting the atheism of Marxist philosophy, thought about Islam only in terms of its being a barrier against communism. Others believed that, on the contrary, certain structural similarities between Islam and communism are bound to make Muslim society prone to communism.

These three factors have in one way or another colored much Western opinion of Islam: the prevalent view was that Islam is fatalistic and encourages despotism and stagnation. Islam was held responsible for the type of society which existed in the Muslim world. Several authors, among them Max Weber, articulated such views.

This syndrome of fear and suspicion is responsible for that anxiety which greets any signs of revival in the Muslim world as a menace to be described by such inflammatory expressions as: militant Islam, the dagger of Islam and so on. These views are important in themselves, for their effects on international opinion, and on the views of Westernized authors, thinkers and statesmen in the Muslim world. Such views have not only discouraged international understanding, but they have also widened the ideological gap within Muslim society.

It is untrue to say that all Western views of Islam have been equally biased in the way described here. Many have been both sympathetic and objective, often supported by research and hard work. But the above mentioned views have continued for a long span of time because they supported and were in turn supported by an incompatible political, economic and strategic relationship between the West and the world of Islam.

However, from the mid-twentieth century onward, a number of factors have opened a new page in the understanding of Islam. These are:

1) After World War II, the West engaged in a high degree of self-criticism. Anthropology, Orientalism, and indeed all Western study of other cultures have relatively liberated themselves from former imperial policies and become more objective.

2) The ideas and designs of Westernized Muslim thinkers and statesmen which were so solid between the wars as represented by Kamalism (secularism) and its admirers in the Arab world and Iran, came to a sad disappointment. In fact die-hard Westernizers like Dr. Taha Husayn, Dr. Zaki N. Mahmoud, and others have reconsidered their views and come to see the truth in Islam.

3) The cause of Westernization was espoused by elites, leading "liberal" political parties and military regimes. The performance of those political parties and more particularly those military regimes was singularly wanting. The decline of the authority of those elites went hand in hand with the emergence of mass based movements which appealed to the masses' unquestioned commitment to Islam.

The masses have always regarded Islam as the basis of their identity, the source of their morality and the unchallenged inspiration for their past, present and future. Many sections of the elite fell prey to foreign acculturation not only in the positive sense of modernization but also in the negative sense of subservience. Elites hoped to effect a total blood transfusion, rejecting their heritage in favor of this or that imported "ism". They promised to transform their societies to become modern, independent and prosperous but did not deliver those goods. That disillusionment turned the eyes of many elites away from their foreign inspiration and confirmed the insight of the masses.

4) Islamic voices became increasingly vocal and eloquently expressed the essential universality and dynamism of Islam, for example, Jamal al-Din al-Afghani, Muhammad Iqbal and Ali Shariati.

5) This tendency was strengthened by the exposure of Western and Eastern "isms" (capitalism and communism): their role as vehicles of foreign domination and control, their satisfaction of the desire for freedom at the expense of social justice, or social justice at the expense of freedom, and in both cases their satisfaction of material needs at the cost of spiritual and moral starvation.

6) In the encounter between North and South, these factors have in various degrees produced a trend of self-awareness and self-assertion in the whole of the South—the Third World. The Muslim world being relatively more cohesive and having its self-consciousness enhanced by its strategic value and its natural resources (oil) has displayed a larger degree of self-awareness and self-assertion. Contemporary political literature shows that the developed world has got the message that peaceful international relations require them to change the pattern of their relations with the under-developed world so that the development gap between North and South is bridged. What they will do about it remains to be seen. The other message which must equally be heeded in this context is that Western cultural ethnocentricity has been a barrier to international understanding.

RELIGION AND CHANGE

The question of social change in Islam should be considered in the context of the wider issue of religion and change. Man is endowed with self-consciousness, intellect and imagination. Those faculties set him apart from the natural world in spite of the fact that he is part of it. Religion is a system of beliefs which addresses itself to this predicament and makes man at home in it. It gives meaning to life, explains the unknown and butresses social cohesion. Religion is a psychological, sociological and ecological necessity. That is why religion, widely defined, has been known to exist in all human society.

Social change is always a feature of human society. The Caliph Ali said "people are more akin to their generations than they are to their parents." It is an unfailing cause of tension when religiously held beliefs fail to accommodate social change. Some creeds like Hinduism put their metaphysical beliefs on the same level as their social norms. This leaves no room for social change, as happened with the caste system, and causes the tension to grow. When the authority of the church in medieval Europe bestowed religious sanctity upon the existing social system the resulting tension fueled the anti-clerical and later anti-Christian character of much modern European social thought.

In Islam, revelation affirms that religious belief is innate: a divine imprint (*fitra*) in the nature of Man. The inevitability of social change is also confirmed. The Prophet said: "The Apostles preached an identical spiritual message. They differed, however, in respect of the legislative codes they preached." Islamic social legislation in the Quran is sparse. Out of the 6000 verses of the Quran, only 245 are on diffrent aspects of social legislation: on personal affairs (70); on civil and financial matters (70); on criminal affairs (30); on witnessing and adjudication (30); on constitutional matters (10); on international affairs (25); and on economic affairs (10).

It is true that in addition to the Quran, the Sunna constitutes another source of Islamic legislation but it is itself governed by the Quran. The prophet said "Numerous sayings will be attributed to me; Whatever you hear judge it by reference to the Quran: If it agrees with it, then I have truly said it and if not then reject it." In addition to this there are many sayings of the Prophet which warned against giving his sayings parity with the Quran: He said in a hadith narrated by Um Salama: "On matters which are not explicitly revealed, I dispense matters on the basis of my opinion."

After the Prophet, Islam sanctioned no representative or representatives of God on earth who could establish a religious authority. It entitled no one to be exclusive interpreter of the sacred texts. The Quran recognized and cited all the known means of knowledge: revelation, intuition, reason and experience. It encouraged interest in the achievements of other civilizations. It cited the experience of other peoples. Thus the Quran took an open attitude to the adoption of useful ideas and institutions of foreign origin. The Caliph Umar adopted several such ideas and institutions, for example, the land tax called *kharaj,* and the bureaucratic system called *diwan.* Muslims have incorporated and digested the achievements of other civilizations. That dynamism in Islam was inspired by the Quran and shaped by the example of the Prophet and his companions. Abu Jafar al-Naqib had said: "The companions of the Prophet recognized that the spiritual message of Islam is fixed. To that they were faithfully committed. The social message of Islam is, however, flexible. Their experience amply demonstrated that flexibility" (*Sharh ibn Abi Hadid,* vol. 3, p. 160). Thus in Islam while religion is integral to politics and society, there is a distinction between that which is immutable and that which is subject to change and development.

THE TWO ASPECTS OF ISLAM

The distinction which I have described is best explained by Abdulla al-Maraghi in his book *Marriage and Divorce in All Religions:*

> Islamic injunctions are divided into two: The first group is concerned with regulating the relations between Allah and man in beliefs and worship. These are God given and fixed so that they may not be extended by analogy or any other means. . . . The second group deals with relations between men. Here the holy texts employ welfare criteria and injunctions have an explicit functional purpose. Change here is possible when circumstances change.

There are many examples from the Prophet, such as, "I have previously forbidden you to store meat to make it available for the temporary visitors of Medina, now you may store it."

Islamic jurists are unanimous about the welfare orientation of these injunctions. They differ, however, in that some like al-Shafii think that all the welfare there is, is already considered by the received holy texts, and therefore we are not justified in citing welfare considerations which are not explicitly supported by those texts. Abu Hanifa went further employing juristic preference *(istihsan)* to support legal formulations which were not based on the authority of a sacred text directly or by analogy. Imam Malik and ibn Hanbal maintained that welfare is a recognized principle in the *shariah* where there is no explicit sacred text. Al-Shafii's restricted attitude was cogently criticized. Ibn al-Qayyim approvingly quoted Ibn Aqil who said:

> al-Shafii said no policy is justified unless it is based on the revealed texts. This is wrong and would put the Companions of the Prophet at fault. Islam approves of all policy which creates good and eradicates evil even when it is not based on any revelation. That is how the Companions of the Prophet understood Islam. Abu Bakr, for example, appointed Umar to succeed him without precedent. Umar suspended the Quranically mandated punishment of hand amputation during a famine, he suspended it also when he discovered that the two thieves, the employees of Hatib, were under-paid. And so on.

That dynamic open-minded attitude in Islam has gradually disappeared. At the beginning, the Islamic system of government was a type of participatory populism. The economy was a compassionate sharing system, and the whole social set up was a fraternity of believers. That set up gradually disappeared and was replaced by a monarchic system of government, a class-based economy and a sharply stratified society emerged. This development did not go unchallenged. Reaction to it was pervasive and varied. In some cases it involved violent revolutionary uprisings. In some cases it led to rejection in the form of dropping out of the socio-political system. Some enterprising individuals found activity which abounded with intellectual and spiritual vitality but which kept a clear distance from the reigning dynasties. The would-be founders of the schools of Muslim law were "lay" individuals who pursued their activities at an arm's length from the governments of their day. Their activities, those of the emergent Shia community, and those of the initiators of the Sufi movement, may be described as attempts to engage in righteous pursuits within a sick body politic. Consequently many pious Muslims felt it necessary to protect those activities from unwanted government interference.

The process of deducing laws and regulations from the original texts of the Quran and Sunna—a process which involved a high degree of reasoning and interpretation—is known as *ijtihad*. Toward the end of the fourth century A.H. (eleventh century after Christ), many sections of the Muslim community, especially jurists, became more and more anxious about the ever present tendency of despotic rulers to manipulate *ijtihad* for their own purposes. They were also anxious about the corrosive effects of foreign concepts and ideas which *ijtihad* inevitably drew into Muslim thought. Further they dreaded the divisive effects of *ijtihad* on the unity of the Islamic community. Those anxieties caused the emergence of the reign of *taqlid* (to follow or imitate) which discouraged *ijtihad* and required succeeding generations of jurists and lawyers to recognize the authority of the deductions, interpretations and reasonings of the first generations of jurists as final. In the fullness of time, within the Sunni community of Islam, *taqlid* reigned supreme. Jurists and lawyers were no longer allowed any initiative. They were expected to accept the received opinions and formulations of the past expressed by preceding lawyers. That is how a monolithic partisan pattern of jurisprudence and law came about and reigned dominant. This development is not only alien to the teachings of Islam which we have described earlier and which are so flexible in accommodating social change, but it is also alien to the purposes of the founding imams.* Thus Imam Malik refused to allow Abu Jafar al-Mansur to make obligatory the formulations compiled in his book *al-Muwatta*. Imam ibn Hanbal said: "those who follow others in religious matters uncritically are feeble minded." Those imams were free from partisan attitudes.

Notwithstanding these facts, the regime or reign of *taqlid* pervaded the world of Islam. The phenomenon of *taqlid* was blamed by Imam ibn al-Qayyim for narrowing scope of *shariah*. He said "those who put *shariah* in a straight jacket are responsible for driving policy makers to seek extra-*shariah* improvisations." Along with despotism, social injustice and economic stagnation, the

---

*Iman: "leader," here it refers to the founders of the schools of Islamic law.

regime of *taqlid* is responsible for destroying the inner vitality and purposeful-
ness of the Islamic *ummah* and so preparing it for foreign domination. In the
words of Imam Malik "a domination accepting mind was created."

Kamalism (secularism) in Ottoman Turkey and its various versions in the
Arab world and Iran were movements which viewed Islam in terms of the phenomenon of *taqlid* (i.e., as unchaging) and advocated its total rejection in favor
of a total commitment to secular nationalist Western thought. Some religious
movements were so carried away with self-hate and reconstruction in the foreign image that they preached cults which went beyond the denounciation of
taqlid to the emptying of Islam itself. The Bahai, the Qaddiani, and recently in
the Sudan the Ikhwan Republican (Republican Brothers) movements have this
in common: a Prophethood after Muhammad, abrogation of the *shariah*, nega-
tion of *jihad* and an unconditional open door attitude to the influence of foreign
cultures.

The system of *taqlid* was instituted with the purpose of protecting the cause
of righteousness. It served that purpose at the cost of spiritual and intellectual
initiative and substituting rigidity for the flexibility of Muslim social teachings.
It is not necessary to wander outside the pale of Islam to restore that flexibility.
The case for social change in Islam is fundamental to it. It is authentically supported by the Islamic texts and the experience of the Prophet and his companions. When non-Muslim opinion refers to Islamic fundamentalism, it is the system or systems of *taqlid* that they have in mind. Those systems should be put
in perspective and seen as responses to certain historical circumstances. It is
accommodation of change, rather than its denial, which is fundamental to
Islam. I shall demonstrate that point and its contemporary relevance by reference to four fields of inquiry: political, economic, international and legislative
affairs.

THE CASE FOR SOCIAL CHANGE

1) *The Political Sphere:* There is no particular system of Islamic government.
All those who theorized about such a system have simply expressed historically
relevant means of applying Islamic political injunctions. An Islamic system of
government requires the fulfillment of two conditions: first, a set of general
principles—for example, the need to politically organize society, the need to
base that on popular participation, the imperative of justice, and so on; second,
the requirement to apply Islamic legislation. Any system which fulfills those two
conditions is entitled to be called Islamic. Contemporary Muslim political
thought may abide by these two conditions, inform itself with all the achievements of modern political thought and institutions, be fully aware of contem-

porary political problems and needs, and proceed to establish a political system of leadership and government which is both Islamic and modern.

2) *The Economic Sphere:* There is no particular Islamic economic system. Islamic economic injunctions require the fulfillment of two conditions: first, the application of certain general principles—for example, that wealth is collectively owned by mankind as vicegerent (representative) of God, that individual ownership is legitimate through effort, that it is a duty to develop and exploit natural resources, that society should provide for the needs of the poor and disabled and so on; second, the establishment of particular injunctions—for example, *zakat* (alms tax), inheritance regulations, and prohibition of usury and indeed prohibition of all unearned income—that obtained through gambling, frauds, the monopoly of profits, and so on. Abiding by those two conditions, contemporary Islamic economic thinking may study modern economic theories and institutions, inform itself of current economic needs, and design an economic system which is both Islamic and modern and which will be able to effect economic development as well as an equitable distribution of its outcome.

3) *The International Sphere:* The international system conceived by classical Muslim jurists reflects the imprint of their historical circumstances. The Quran and Sunna are explicit about the desirability of peaceful relations between peoples: "God forbids you not with regards to those who fight you not for your faith, nor drive you out of your homes, from dealing kindly and justly with them: for God loves those who are just" (S. 60:8).

War is justified to deter injustice: "You have been permitted to fight to deter aggression" (S. 22:39). Violence is not permitted as a means of promoting Islam: "There is no compulsion in religion" (S. 2:256). *Jihad* does not mean enforced Islamization. *Jihad* refers to the supreme effort expected of all Muslims to promote the cause of righteousness within themselves and in their social environment. It means going to war to protect the freedom of Muslims to promote that cause or to deter aggression. Those who claim that *jihad* is enforced Islamization cite Sura 9:5 for support: "fight and slay the pagans whenever ye find them. . . ." A careful study of the text of that chapter shows that this verse refers to a particularly treacherous group of pagans who betrayed the Prophet and initiated violence. Verses four and six of the same chapter indicate the particularity of verse five. Thus: "but the treaties are not dissolved with those pagans with whom ye entered into alliance" (S. 9:4). And: "If one of the pagans asks thee for asylum, grant it to him so that he may hear the word of God then escort him to where he can be secure" (S. 9:6). Five principles constitute the basis of international relations in Islam and they may be so considered by contemporary Muslim lawyers and statesmen who, aware of contemporary international law and present-day international needs and problems, could elaborate a system of international relations which is both Islamic and modern. These are:

i) A human brotherhood with an honored status among creation.

ii) The Supremacy of justice: "Be just under all circumstances" (S. 5:8).

iii) Continuous preaching of Islam by peaceful means and if fredom to do so is denied, or the Muslim community is attacked, war must be waged to deter aggression.

iv) Contracts and trusts must be honored under all circumstances and whoever the other party may be. As the Prophet said: "Three are equally binding upon you whether the other party is a believer or non-believer: contracts, Trusts, and family obligations."

v) Reciprocity in the conduct of relations when no agreements to regulate them exist.

4) *The Legislative Sphere:* Even the most specific injunctions, injunctions which have been explicitly specified by the holy texts are contingent upon conditions which permit a high degree of flexibility. Thus the canonical punishments known as *hudud* (e.g., amputation for theft) and the inheritance regulations known as *faraid* are associated with elaborate conditions which allow circumstantial considerations to qualify their application. Circumstances are also taken into consideration in the application of Islamic economic injunctions, for example, *zakat* and usury. The means employed by the learned jurists of Islam to deduce laws from the Quran and Sunna further demonstrate possibilities for change and development. For example, *ijma* (consensus) allows dominant trends in public opinion to influence legislation; *qiyas* (analogy) permits the extension of a rule into further horizons on the basis of analogy; *istihsan* (preference) makes it possible for rational considerations to override textual ones; *istislah* (utility) makes it possible for utility considerations to weigh in the scales; and so on. Those devices are numerous and the degree to which the different schools of law employ them varies. In addition to those already mentioned, other devices exist such as abrogation *(naskh)* of one revealed text by a later one, and custom *(urf)*.

Employing these means in different degrees, and employing different methodological systems, those trail blazers (the early jurists) have developed several schools of Muslim law, eight of which have become famous: Hanifi; Maliki; Jafari; Zaidi; Shafii; Hanbali; Zahiri; and Ibadi. Their work was a valuable testimony to the resourcefulness of the *shariah*. There is no basis, however, for the claim that any or all of them (the law schools and their law books) are entitled to a monopoly of legislative authority in Islam. The very fact that they genuinely differed proves the possibility of different interpretations in Islam. Further, it is evident that methodological and environmental differences reflected themselves in the views of the founders of the law schools.

A serious attempt at Islamizing the legal systems of Muslim countries today can only be undertaken by scholars familiar with the whole heritage of Islamic law, familiar with contemporary legal systems, familiar with contemporary social needs and problems and assisted in that by economists, sociologists, political scientists and statesmen. That workshop or think tank could base itself on the Quran and Sunna and proceed in the spirit of a new *ijtihad* interpretation of Islam to codify a civil, criminal, personal and international law.

CONCLUSIONS

A regime of "internal or indigenous colonialism" has paralyzed the world of Islam and resulted in a state of spiritual, intellectual, and social decay which sapped the vitality of the *ummah* and prepared it for the "domination complex" which it experienced in its encounter with an expansionist imperialist West. Until the period between the two world wars, it seemed that new intellectual and social forces within the *ummah* had turned away from Islam and prepared for a total restructuring of their societies in the image of the secularist, nationalist, dominant West. After World War II, communism constituted an alternative attraction to the new social and intellectual forces in the Muslim world. That intellectual and cultural aggression was never accepted unchallenged. Many reacted by reasserting the traditionalist thesis associated with the system of *taqlid*. This was assisted by the realization which gradually dawned in encounter with the West and the East (Soviet Union) that their ideological and cultural thrust was not merely a bid for modernization but was a Trojan horse within which lurked imperialist designs which aimed at subordinating the hearts and souls of the weaker party and the exploitation of its natural resources.

The reassertion of the traditionalist thesis or approach would never have gotten under way had it not been for the fact that it acted as a shield of protection against the invading designs of the West and a channel for the expression of "native" identity and dignity. Along with these two responses: rejection of traditionalism in favor of the acculturating designs and rejection of acculturation in favor of the traditionalist thesis, there was a third response, namely: separating Islam from the traditionalist thesis, separating modernization from the acculturation syndrome, and establishing a synthesis which is both Islamic and modern. Westernization is the West's version of modernization. It is embedded in Western culture and interests. Sovietization (or for that matter sinicization) are Soviet and Chinese versions of latecomers to modernization and are embedded in Russian and Chinese cultural views and interests. Modernization can and must be divorced from those cultural and historical expressions of it.

The traditionalist Islamic thesis is a historically conditioned understanding by Muslims of the teachings of the Quran and Sunna. To transcend that thesis (in its various forms) in favor of Islam in a modern context is both Islamic and rational. This itself is a supreme Islamic principle: that revelation and reason complement each other: "In the earth are signs for those of assured faith as also in your own selves: will you not then see?" (*Zariat* No. 20).

TWELVE

The Islamic State

HASSAN al-TURABI

Although I am directly involved in a political process that seeks to establish an Islamic state, I am not going to describe the forms that an Islamic government might take in any particular country. Rather, I will try to describe the universal characteristics of an Islamic state. These derive from the teachings of the Quran as embodied in the political practice of the Prophet Muhammad and constitute an eternal model that Muslims are bound to adopt as a perfect standard for all time. However, the diversity of historical circumstances in which they try to apply that ideal introduces a necessary element of relativity and imperfection in the practice of Islam.

An Islamic state cannot be isolated from society because Islam is a comprehensive, integrated way of life. The division between private and public, the state and society, that is familiar in Western culture, has not been known in Islam. The state is only the political expression of an Islamic society. You cannot have an Islamic state except insofar that you have an Islamic society. Any attempt at establishing a political order for the establishment of a genuine Islamic society would be the superimposition of laws over a reluctant society. This is not in the nature of religion; religion is based on sincere conviction and voluntary compliance. Therefore, an Islamic state evolves from an Islamic society. In certain areas, progress toward an Islamic society may be frustrated by political suppression. Whenever religious energy is thus suppressed, it builds up and ultimately erupts in isolated acts of struggle or resistance which are called terrorist by those in power or a revolution. In circumstances where Islam is allowed free expression, social change takes place peacefully and gradually, and the Islamic movement develops programs of Islamization before it takes over the destiny of the state because Islamic thought—like all thought—only flourishes in a social environment of freedom and public consultation (shurah).

The ideological foundation of an Islamic state lies in the doctrine of tawhid—the unity of God and of human life—as a comprehensive and exclusive program of worship. This fundamental principle of belief has many conse-

241

quences for an Islamic state: first, it is not secular. All public life in Islam is religious, being permeated by the experience of the divine. Its function is to pursue the service of God as expressed in a concrete way in the *shariah,* the religious law. The Christian West has been through an important historical experience of secularization. There has also been certain elements of secularization in the political conduct of Muslims. But the difference between Christianity and Islam is that Muslims are never fully resigned to such practices because the preserved sources of religious guidance (the Quran and the example of the Prophet) constantly remind them of any gap that develops between their ideal and their practice and inspire a process of revitalization that would completely integrate politics with religion. If one compares Christian secularism in France with Muslim secularism in Turkey the process would seem strikingly similar. All religious life is subject to these historical challenges to their identity. But once the Muslims experience the tension of an historical fall and become conscious of the fact that public life has moved away from the moral values and norms of religion, they rise to reform their political attitudes and institutions.

Second, an Islamic state is not a nationalistic state because ultimate allegiance is owed to God and thereby to the community of all believers—the *ummah.* One can never stop at any national frontier and say the nation is absolute, an ultimate end in itself. Islam does allow for limited allegiances either social, ethnic, or territorial. The state of Medina itself was, for some time, a regional state; the Muslims of Mecca were not citizens, and the duty to extend protection to them against any persecution was subject to the treaty obligations of the state. So there is an Islamic concept of a territorial state which is not coextensive with the whole *ummah.* But that state is not nationalistic. In modern times Muslims have adopted Arab-Turkish or other nationalities as a framework for development, but they were never enthusiastic about it, and always yearned for an open *ummah.* However, this does not mean that every Muslim all over the world should necessarily have immediate access to an Islamic state; it does mean though that the state would be much more open and less discriminatory in its domestic laws and foreign policies. It would develop institutionalized international links with other Muslim states and would work toward the eventual unity of the *ummah* and beyond. Ultimately there is nothing final even about the so-called Muslim world or Muslim nation, because Islam is open to humanity, is universal.

Third, an Islamic state is not an absolute or sovereign entity. It is subject to the higher norms of the *shariah* that represent the will of God. Politically this rules out all forms of absolutism. Legally it paves the way for the development of constitutional law, a set of norms limiting state powers. In fact, the Islamic tradition of rules limiting the power of the sovereign is much older than the concept of constitutional law in the secular West. Because the Islamic state is not absolute, Muslims have also known from the beginning the rules of international law which derive from the supreme *shariah* and bind the state in its relations to other states and peoples.

Fourth, an Islamic state is not primordia; the primary institution in Islam is the *ummah*. The phrase "Islamic state" itself is a misnomer. The state is only the political dimension of the collective endeavor of Muslims. The norms of Islam are only partly legal depending on the sanctions of state power. For most of it, the implementation of the *shariah* is left to the free conscience of believers or to informal means of social control.

States come and go; Islamic society can and has existed without the structures of a state for centuries. Of course society, if able to live religion in its integral, comprehensive manner, would have its political dimension in a government that seeks to fulfill some of the purposes of religious life.

The form of an Islamic government is determined by the foregoing principles of *tawhid*, entailing the freedom, equality, and unity of believers. One can call an Islamic state a republic since the *shariah* rules out usurpation and succession as grounds of political legitimacy. In early Islam the system of government was called a caliphate *(al-khilafa)* which emphasized succession to the Prophet and thereby subordination of all power to his Sunna or way. But whereas the Prophet was appointed by God, the caliph was freely elected by the people who thereby have precedence over him as a legal authority. Although the Prophet used to consult his companions systematically and normally would follow their consensus, he had the divine right to an overriding authority. The caliph, however, or any similar holder of political power, is subject both to the *shariah* and to the will of his electors. As reflected in Islamic jurisprudence this implies that, save for the express provision of the *shariah,* the consensus *(ijma)* of the community is paramount. A process of consultation that leads ultimately to *ijma* is mandatory for the resolution of all important public issues.

The caliphate began as an elected consultative institution. Later it degenerated into a hereditary, or usurpatory, authoritarian government. This pseudo-caliphate was universally condemned by jurists, though many excused its acts on the grounds of necessity or tolerated them in the interest of stability. The question arises whether the proper Islamic form of government—elective and consultative—amounts to a liberal representative democracy?

In a large Islamic state consultation would have to be indirect, undertaken by representatives of the people. This was practiced in early Islam and recognized by jurists in their reference to *ahl al-hal wal aqd* or *ahl al-shura* (those who resolve public affairs). In a parallel development *ijma,* which is the conclusion of a process of consultation, came to mean the consensus of the ulama. This was a practical adaptation of the original popular concept of *ijma* as the consensus of the community which had resulted from the Muslim expansion.

In effect, Muslims were then to be found all over the world, and there was no practical way of consulting everyone in the general *ummah* in those days. So the ulama posed as representatives of the people and maintained that their consensus was a form of indirect representation, of indirect, binding *ijma*. In different circumstances other formal delegates can lawfully represent the *ummah* in the process of consultation.

It follows that an Islamic order of government is essentially a form of representative democracy. But this statement requires the following qualification. First an Islamic republic is not strictly speaking a direct government of and by the people; it is a government of the *shariah*. But, in a substantial sense, it is a popular government since the *shariah* represents the convictions of the people and, therefore, their direct will. This limitation on what a representative body can do is a guarantee of the supremacy of the religious will of the community. The consultative system of government in Islam is related to and reinforced by similar features of Muslim society since politics is an integral part of all religious life and not simply a separate secular vocation. The fair distribution of political power through *shura,* whether direct or indirect, is supported by an equally just distribution of economic wealth. So an Islamic democracy may never degenerate to a formal system where, because of the concentration of wealth, the rich alone exercise their political rights and determine what is to be decided. Also, ideally there is no clerical or ulama class, which prevents an elitist or theocratic government. Whether termed a religious, a theocratic, or even a secular theocracy, an Islamic state is not a government of the ulama. Knowledge, like power, is distributed in a way that inhibits the development of a distinct, religious hierarchy. Nor is an Islamic democracy government by the male members of society. Women played a considerable role in public life during the life of the Prophet; and they contributed to the election of the third caliph. Only afterwards were women denied their rightful place in public life, but this was history departing from the ideal, just like the development of classes based on property, knowledge *(ilm)*, or other status. In principle, all believers, rich or poor, noble or humble, learned or ignorant, men or women, are equal before God, and they are his vicegerents on earth and the holders of his trust.

An Islamic government should be a stable system of government because the people consider it an expression of their religion and, therefore, contribute positively to the political process. In their mutual consultations, they work toward a consensus that unites them. The majority/minority pattern in politics is not an ideal one in Islam. That is not to say that decisions have to await a unanimous vote, because this could paralyze a government. But people can deliberate openly and argue and consult to ultimately reach a consensus and not simply assert or submit to a majority opinion. This raises the question of the party system. Can an Islamic government have a multiparty system or a single party system? There is no legal bar to the development of different parties or to the freedom of opinion and debate. Such was the case in the constitutional practice of the caliph. However, a well-developed Islamic society would probably not be conducive to the growth of rigid parties wherein one stands by one's party whether it is wrong or right. This is a form of factionalism that can be very oppressive of individual freedom and divisive of the community, and it is therefore, antithetical to a Muslim's ultimate responsibility to God and to *ummah*. While there may be a multiparty system, an Islamic government should function more as a consensus-oriented rather than a minority/majority system with political parties rigidly confronting each other over decisions. Parties should approach the decision-making process with an open mind and after a consensus adopt a mutually agreeable policy.

Finally, decisions should not be arrived at lightly. Parliament does not simply deliberate and come to a conclusion. Any agreement must be an enlightened decision with conscious reference to the guiding principles of the *shariah*. Because of this, the ulama should have a role in the procedure, not as the ultimate authority determining what the law is, but as advisors in the *shura* to enlighten the Muslims as to the options which are open to them. What do I mean by ulama? The word historically has come to mean those versed in the legacy of religious (revealed) knowledge *(ilm)*. However, *ilm* does not mean that alone. It means anyone who knows anything well enough to relate it to God. Because all knowledge is divine and religious, a chemist, an engineer, an economist, or a jurist are all ulama. So the ulama in this broad sense, whether they are social or natural scientists, public opinion leaders, or philosophers, should enlighten society. There should be an intensive procedure of hearings, research, and deliberations and thus a wider consultation than that which sometimes takes place now in modern parliaments where bills can be rushed through and policies resolved on arbitrary passion and prejudice.

What are the functions and frontiers of an Islamic government? The functions that fulfill the aims of Islamic life pertain primarily to society. Because Islam is comprehensive, one might conclude that an Islamic government, acting for society, is a totalitarian one. However, in many ways, an Islamic government is a very limited government. First, not every aspect of Islam is entrusted to government to enforce. It is in the nature of a unitarian religious order of society that the individual should enjoy a wide degree of autonomy. Moreover, not everything is practically capable of enforcement through government law. Classical jurists have developed the distinction between religious obligations and juridical obligation, the latter only being enforceable through formal, objective sanctions. Most aspects of Islamic life are subjective or private and outside the domain of law as applied by governments. Second, and this is a question which depends on history, where society can manage, government has no business intefering. This is similar to a liberal, minimal theory of government. In the past a Muslim government had a very limited function simply because the Muslims were spread over such a wide territory and the government could not reach them. Today, because of the revolution in communications, a government can easily take over functions which an Islamic government did not oversee so many centuries ago. But there are certain historical considerations which I would want to underline very strongly. The Islamic government historically has been, for the most part, illegitimate as far as the election of the head of a state is concerned. That explains why it was so severely limited. The jurists, realizing that the state was not a legitimate, consultative government, deliberately restricted its domain in favor of private social action. The jurists totally eliminated governmental authority as a source of law in their development of *usul al-fiqh* (the source of law). A very important arm of government, the legislative power, was actually assumed by the jurists themselves. They determined what the law was and the judges, who were appointed by the government, looked to the jurists to apply the law.

Another area where government was severely limited was in its power to tax. There is nothing in Islam which inhibits or forbids the government from imposing, from time to time, taxes other than *zakat* for the general welfare of the community. The power to tax is one of the most oppressive weapons in the hands of any government. Many constitutional conflicts in the West revolve around the slogan, "No taxation without representation." Although Muslim jurists have effectively deprived government of many means of exploitation, in a modern Islamic state the representative legislature would probably assume all political functions. A modern Islamic government could, subject to the *shariah*, establish and enforce further norms of law and policy derived from the *shariah*. It can establish complete legal codes. Such codes, as were known to Muslims in the past, did not emanate from the state but from the great jurists like Malik, Abu Hanifa, and Sahfii. There were mainly seven such operative legal codes throughout the Muslim world. It was the absence of an official organ of government charged with the unification of the legal system that led to the closing of the door of *ijtihad* (judicial research) for fear of the proliferation of laws and ensuing threat to order and legal security. Subject to the *shariah* and *ijma* it is up to a Muslim government today to determine its system of public law and economics.

An Islamic government is bound to exercise all powers necessary for providing a minimum of the basic conditions of Muslim life. The actual scope of government depends on society. Where society on its own manages to realize social justice, for example, then the government does not need to interfere. In Muslim history, governments were mostly illegitimate and did not or were not allowed to develop a macro-economic polity. Therefore, Muslims addressed questions of social justice within their private dealings. This was done especially through a wide, mutually supportive family system, through extensive charities and endowments, and through a system of private mutual insurance still operative in many parts of Muslim society today. Where this failed for any reason, the government was bound to step in and try to rectify the situation. This holds for other welfare services as well. Society can manage, for example, its own system of private education like that of Muslim Spain which was so widespread that it almost eliminated illiteracy through free education for all. Otherwise, the government is bound and entitled to promote education, health services, and what have you.

What are the frontiers of government vis-à-vis society and the individual? This question has not been posed very acutely in the past. Why? Simply because the Islamic government was not a totally alien institution superimposed upon society. To the extent that it was alien—in the sense that it was not legitimate—the jurists saw to it that it should be relatively powerless. But, on the whole, the aims and means of government correspond to that of society, being related to religion and based on the *shariah*. Furthermore, the individual was largely free because the lawmaking and financial powers were so limited; so there was not any intolerable oppression. Even though the particular caliph might be a usurper, he was not a totalitarian, absolute dictator. Certainly, where his security was threatened, he would impinge on freedom, but otherwise people were left alone.

It was only recently when secularized governments were introduced and established in Muslim lands and the protective shield of the *shariah* withdrawn and the forms of government regulation expanded, that Muslims really felt the bitter oppression of totalitarian government, and that the issue of fundamental rights and liberties was raised.

The freedom of the individual ultimately emanates from the doctrine of *tawhid* which requires a self-liberation of man from any worldly authority in order to serve God exclusively. Society, and particularly those in power, is inspired by the same principle and the collective endeavor is not one of hampering the liberty of an individual but of cooperation toward the maximum achievement of this ideal. To promote this cooperation, the freedom of one individual is related to that of the general group. The ultimate common aim of religious life unites the private and the social spheres; and the *shariah* provides an arbiter between social order and individual freedom.

I do not have to go into the various rights of man vis-à-vis the state or society in Islam. The individual has the right to his physical existence, general social well-being, reputation, peace, privacy, to education and a decent life. These are rights that the state ought to provide and guarantee for a better fulfillment of the religious ideals of life. Freedom of religion and of expression should also be guaranteed and encouraged. Thus, while a Muslim would not oppose the *shariah* because he believes in it, if he does not agree to a particular interpretation of the law, he is entitled to his view. Actually, these are not pure rights that the individual is free to exercise. He owes it to God and to his fellow Muslims to observe these as a social obligation as well. He should contribute to the political solidarity and well-being of the state. If government becomes so alien as to transcend the *shariah,* he has the right and obligation to revolt. This is the revolutionary element in Islam. A Muslim's ultimate obedience is to God alone.

What about representative institutions in an Islamic government? This depends on the particular historical circumstances. In the period of the Prophet all the functions of the state were exercised by him as teacher and sovereign. He wisely but informally consulted with his companions. Later this consultative process was almost developed into an indirect representative institution called *ahl al-shura* or *majlis-i-shura* (consultative council). The breakdown of the early legitimate political order did not allow the procedures and institutions of *shura* to crystalize. Today this could very well be formulated through a parliament, a council or a *majlis-i-shura.* People may directly, through referendum, exercise their *ijma* consensus or otherwise delegate power to their deputies. There would, however, be certain rules regulating the qualifications of candidates and election campaigns for the choice of deputies or other officers of the state. In Islam, for example, no one is entitled to conduct a campaign for themselves directly or indirectly in the manner of Western electoral campaigns. The presentation of candidates would be entrusted to a neutral institution that would explain to the people the options offered in policies and personalities. Factors of relative wealth or access to the communications media are also not allowed to falsify the representative character of deputies. The prevailing criteria of political merit for the purposes of candidature for any political office revolves on moral integrity as well as other relevant considerations. All this would, no doubt, influence the form and spirit of accession to positions of power.

The other central institution in an Islamic government is that which provides both leadership and effective execution of the general will: Caliph, Commander of the Believers, President of the Republic, or Prime Minister. As noted earlier, the word "caliph" was not originally chosen for any specific reason except to denote succession and compliance with the prophetic example of leadership. Most modern and contemporary constitutional theory tends to vest political leadership in one individual and not in a collegiate body—a presidency rather than a council of ministers. But neither a president nor a prime minister can be very powerful and representative of the unity of political purpose so essential to an Islamic polity. Whatever form the executive may take, a leader is always subject both to the *shariah* and to the *ijma* formulated under it. He enjoys no special immunities and can, therefore, be prosecuted or sued for anything he does in his private or public life. This is a fundamental principle of Islamic constitutional law, ensuing from the supremacy of the *shariah*. No rigid theory of separation of government functions can develop in a comprehensive, coherent system like the Islamic political order, except to provide some necessary checks and balances to safeguard liberty or justice. Besides those powers delegated by the *majlis-i-shura* or consultative council and subject to its control, the executive may derive powers both directly from the *shariah* and *ijma*.

The judiciary, although appointed as part of the administration, plays an extremely important role in an Islamic state because of the special legalistic nature of the political order which is organized in accordance with a strict hierarchy of norms. The *shariah* is the highest revealed law followed by popular laws based on *ijma* and by executive orders and regulations. Because of this, judges, as the guardians of the *shariah,* adjudicate in all matters of law. Early Muslims were very keen to provide judges with a generous income to protect them against temptation and to allow them a very large degree of autonomy with broad powers to administer justice. However, the legal systems of Islam did not know a lawyer's profession. The modern capitalist institution which requires the participation of solicitors and barristers in the administration of justice ultimately works in favor of the rich who can afford the expenses and the delays of justice in a system administered in this way. I realize as a lawyer, myself, that adjudication in a contemporary society is a very complicated, time-consuming process. Judges cannot listen to all the complaints and determine the issues. But such a difficulty was resolved in early Islam by the office of a counsellor to the judge: an assistant who first heard the parties, ascertained the matters in issue, marshaled all the relevant evidence, and researched the law in preparation for a decision by the judge. In an Islamic state there would be a tendency to do away with or to minimize the role of the legal profession by establishing an extended system of legal counsel and assistance, especially for the poor.

As far as public law for the administration of an Islamic state or government is concerned, one can draw upon early Islamic history and tradition regarding service for forms of achieving the political ideals of Islam. But due to the transformation of public life in contemporary societies, the Muslim would also draw heavily on comparative constitutional history and practice. This has a legal basis in Islamic jurisprudence. Any form or procedures for the organization of public life that can be ultimately related to God and put to his service in furtherance of the aims of Islamic government can be adopted unless expressly excluded by the *shariah*. Once so received, it is an integral part of Islam whatever its source may be. Through this process of Islamization, the Muslims were always very open to expansion and change. Thus, Muslims can incorporate any experience whatsoever if not contrary to their ideals. Muslims took most of their bureaucratic forms from Roman and Persian models. Now, much can be borrowed from contemporary sources, critically appreciated in the light of the *shariah* values and norms, and integrated into the Islamic framework of government.

Finally, I come to the inter-state and inter-faith relations of the Muslim state. I have remained quiet about the status of non-Muslims because I did not want to complicate issues. The historical record of Muslims' treatment of Christians and Jews is quite good especially compared with the history of relations between different religions and religious denominations in the West. The first Islamic state established in Medina was not simply a state of Muslims; it had many Jews, and many non-Muslim Arabs. Therefore, the problem of non-Muslim minorities within a Muslim state is nothing new. Muslims do not like the term "minorities." They call them the People of the Book *(ahl al-kitab),* the *dhimmi,* or protected people. These non-Muslims have a guaranteed right to their religious conviction, to profess and defend their own convictions and even to criticize Islam and engage in a dialogue with Muslims. Non-Muslims also have the right to regulate their private life, education, and family life by adopting their own family laws. If there is any rule in the *shariah* which they think religiously incompatible, they can be absolved from it. There can be a very large degree of legal and political decentralization under an Islamic government. The more important thing is that, morally, Muslims are bound to relate to non-Muslim minorities positively. It is more than a matter of tolerance and legal immunity. Muslims have a moral obligation to be fair and friendly in their person-to-person conduct toward non-Muslim citizens, and will be answerable to God for that. They must treat them with trust, beneficence, and equity. There may be a certain feeling of alienation because the public law generally will be Islamic law. However, the public law of Islam is one related rationally to justice and to the general good and even a non-Muslim may appreciate its widsom and fairness. Christians in particular who now, at least, do not seem to have a public law, should not mind the application of Islamic law as long as it does not interfere with their religion. It is a moral based on values which are common and more akin to Christian values than any secular law—Caesar's law.

As to the inter-state or international relations of a Muslim state, we have noted earlier the limitations on state sovereignty imposed by the *shariah* in favor of nationals of other states. The sanctity of treaty obligations and the vocation to world peace, except in situations of aggression, provide a basis for the development of extensive international relations. The international practice of Muslim states in history is well known. What is not as well-known is its contribution to the development of modern international law.

In conclusion, it is important to note that an awareness of the general nature and features of the Islamic state is necessary for an understanding of modern Islam as a resurgent force seeking to make up for a failure to realize Islam fully.

Muslims are presently focusing more on general ideals—ideals as standards for guiding their different attempts to implement Islam. Whatever diverse forms their practice assumes as these universal ideals come to be expressed in the light of differing circumstances of particular Muslim states, the clarity of the universal model is necessary on the one hand to guide Muslims toward a greater unity and, on the other hand, to enable them to grasp both the general and the particular in Muslim life. Otherwise, they run the risk of discerning nothing beyond the confusion of a multiplicity of Islams, determined purely by historical factors.

THIRTEEN

Democracy and the Modern Islamic State

JAVID IQBAL

The Islamic state is, in theory, Allah's state, or the Kingdom of God on earth, and the Muslims constitute Allah's party *(hizbullah)*. The mode of life which a Muslim is commanded to follow can only be followed if he is a member of a politically or economically free community. Consequently, the Muslim community must strive to establish a state wherever it is possible to establish a viable state. A state which is managed and administered in accordance with Islamic law is technically called *dar al-salam* (country of peace). If a *dar al-salam* or an Islamic state is politically or economically subjugated by a non-Muslim power, it will be transformed into *dar al-harb* (country of war), and the Muslims shall be left with only two alternatives: either to conduct a jihad in order to regain their independent status or to migrate *(hijra)* to some Muslim country.

Consequently, a Muslim is to render obedience firstly to God, then to the Holy Prophet, and lastly, to those members of the Muslim community who command authority over him provided that they are acting only in execution of the commands of God and the Holy Prophet. Thus, it is evident that rendering obedience to those who command authority over the Muslim community is conditional. This obligation ceases if the above condition is not fulfilled. In case they insist on obedience to that which does not come from God and the Holy Prophet, then any member of the Muslim community or the community as a whole is legally entitled to rebel against them and to replace them.

The Islamic state is based on a two-fold concept of happiness. It must provide for the realization of happiness for the Muslim community *(ummah)* in this world as well as prepare it for realizing happiness in the hereafter. These objectives of an Islamic state necessitate that the Muslim community be founded on the principles of equality, solidarity, and freedom.

Muslim jurists have emphasized three important components of an Islamic state: the Muslim community, Islamic law *(shariah)*, and the leadership of the Muslim community, the caliph *(khilafah)*. Since absolute authority or ultimate sovereignty vests in God, the Islamic state upholds the supremacy of His Prime

Will as expressed in Islamic law. Further, since the Muslim community is to be governed in accordance with the Islamic law, it must have a directing head to implement or execute the law. According to the Islamic faith, law has already been laid down by God in the Quran. The head of the Islamic state, therefore, is only an executive authority and has no inherent power to legislate. Wherever the law is clearly laid down in the Quran, he must implement or execute it. He is authorized to make subordinate legislation guided by these laws and principles. He can appoint a Council of Advisers *(majlis-i-shura)* which must be consulted in making subordinate legislation or for other administrative matters, but he is not bound by their advice.

The head of the entire Muslim community is called caliph *(Khilafah,* the successor of the Holy Prophet) or imam (leader). The judiciary has the power to interpret the Islamic law and to adjudicate in accordance with the same. According to the Sunni view, the appointment of the caliph as head of state is to be confirmed by the Muslim community through its consent, which is formally obtained by means of *baya* (a symbolic oath of allegiance). The *baya* is a contract in which two parties are involved. The Muslim community is to render obedience to the caliph in consideration of the caliph's promise to govern the Muslim community in accordance with Islamic law. If there arises any dispute between the parties, then according to the Quranic injunction, the matter may be referred to the judiciary for adjudication in accordance with the Quran and the Sunna. The judgment of the court shall be binding on both the parties (S. 4:49). If the dispute cannot be resolved through peaceful means, the Muslim community or any member thereof is entitled to rebel against the erring caliph and to replace him with another leader or imam.

In an Islamic state the people are not vested with ultimate sovereignty, nor does absolute authority rest with the head of the state or with parliament. Ultimate sovereignty and absolute authority only vest in God, and the only principle operative in an Islamic state is the supremacy of Islamic law. Using modern terminology, therefore, the Islamic Constitution has only two important organs: the executive and the judiciary. The third organ, i.e., the legislature, is not an important feature since all legislation has already been made by God in the Quran which is only to be implemented or executed by the caliph who in consultation with his Council of Advisers or otherwise may make subordinate legislation by way of ordinances.

There are two verses in the Quran with respect to consultation: "They conduct their affairs by mutual consultations" (S. 42:38) and "Consult them in affairs and when thou hast taken a decision, put thy trust in Allah" (S. 3:159). In the first verse, consultation is recommended and does not create an obligation. However, it is descriptive of the nature of the Muslim community which is expected to conduct all its affairs by mutual consultation. The second verse, which is addressed to the Holy Prophet and contains a command and the principle that "those who command authority" ought in all matters of importance to consult the Muslims, is undisputed.

Ibn Khaldun has pointed out the following important distinction between an Islamic state and a secular state: The Islamic state is governed in accordance with the laws of God as revealed in the Quran whereas a secular state is governed by laws made through human reason. There are other important differences between an Islamic state and a modern secular state. A modern secular state must have three features: it must be fully sovereign; it must be national; and it must have well-defined territories. When these three features exist, a state can legitimately claim to be a sovereign state. However, an Islamic state, although sovereign from this accepted standpoint, is not fully sovereign because according to the faith of Islam, ultimate sovereignty vests only in God. Strictly speaking, it is also not a national state because the Muslim community (ummah) is a community of faith and consists of peoples who may belong to different tribes, races, or nationalities, and may speak different languages and be of different colors, but who share a common spiritual aspiration, i.e., their faith is Islam. Consequently, an Islamic state is a multinational state. An Islamic state is not a territorial state in the strict sense of the term, because it aims and aspires to become a universal state. Nevertheless, it is not a utopia or an imaginary state. It has to be initially founded as a territorial state, although the territories are expected to expand.

The Quran has ordained that only the most suitable person is to be appointed head of state (S. 4:58), though this is even logically the duty of those making the appointment; but no specific method for the appointment of a caliph, i.e., universal head of the Muslim community, is laid down in the Quran. This was quite natural because the Quran is concerned mainly with matters relating to right and wrong or good and evil, and is not concerned with matters relating to planning (tadbir). That the best person ought to be appointed is a matter relating to right and wrong, but the question as to whether a particular process employed for determination of the best person will be successful or not is a matter relating to efficiency and wisdom in the light of prevailing conditions. Similarly, no procedure has been prescribed for the deposition of the head of state or caliph. According to the Sunni view, the Holy Prophet did not nominate or appoint any successor after him, nor did he lay down any rule or method for constituting or deposing his successor. These structures were to be evolved in the light of the good sense of the community as they were not meant to be permanent, but were subject to the law of necessity in accordance with the requirements of the Muslim community from time to time. Consequently, the real object of Islam is to establish a community of faith governed by Islamic law (the *shariah*), and for its enforcement, the Muslim community is at liberty to determine any mode of constitutional structure which suits its requirements.

During the normative period of the First Four Rightly Guided Caliphs (632 A.D. to 661 A.D.), different methods were adopted for the appointment of the caliph, and in all four cases the appointment was confirmed by the Muslim community's oath of allegiance *(baya)* which was formally obtained. Generally speaking, the methods adopted during this period had a common feature, i.e., the selection of the best man followed by the *baya* of the Muslim community. The majority principle, although not specifically disapproved, was not followed.

In the historical process of transformation from 661 to 1258 the interaction of numerous forces and events led to changes in the caliphate in substance as well as form. Nevertheless, the role of Muslim jurist had throughout been to bridge the gulf between the ideal and the real, theory and practice, by attempting to provide an Islamic rationale for every change in order to maintain the continuity of the Islamic character of the community. Therefore, if the period of the Rightly Guided Caliphs had provided an ideal Islamic polity, the development of later consitutional thought represented a rational justification of the formal and substantial departures from the ideal under the pressure of circumstances. During this period, according to the Sunni jurists, replacement of a caliph by another through force or coercion was considered as a legitimate method of change of government. It may be pointed out at this stage that according to some Sunni jurists—Shah Wali Ullah, for example—methods for constituting a caliph or imam are restricted only to those adopted by the Rightly Guided Caliphs or through coercion. According to al-Mawardi, the rule of a usurping leader (amir) is legitimate if he governs the state in accordance with Islamic law. This is similar to al-Ghazzali's doctrine of necessity: that the tyranny of a usurping amir is preferable to chaos. Since the source of strength of a usurping amir is his own power, some jurists are of the view that he does not require the consent of the Muslim community. However, others think that he too requires the approval of the Muslim community in addition to governing the state in accordance with Islamic law.

So long as the Muslim world remained one and united, theoretically it was managed and administered by a Universal Caliphate, even though it had been transformed into a hereditary or dynastic monarchy. There has been an instance in the history of Islam of the establishment of more than one caliphate at the same time in Baghdad, Cairo, and Cordova. But even during that period, two of the additional caliphates in Cairo and Cordova eventually disappeared, and only the one in Baghdad survived. After the sack of Baghdad by the Mongols when the Abbasid Caliph was put to death in 1258, there was for a period of three years (1258–61) no caliph in the world of Islam. However, in the later period of Islamic history when numerous rulers managed to acquire power or controlled specific territories in the world of Islam and the Universal Caliphate only existed in name, these rulers did not adopt the title of caliph or imam but remained content to call themselves amirs, sultans, or pashas.

The modern revival of Islam commenced from the eighteenth century onwards when gradually numerous independent or semi-independent Muslim national states emerged. In some of them, hereditary or dynastic monarchy was the order of the day, and in the others legislative assemblies were constituted. Thus, when Islam entered modern history, the question arose: since the Universal Caliphate had become a thing of the past, could different Muslim national communities manage their affairs by themselves? In other words, could the powers and obligations of a caliph or imam be shared by a body of persons as the elected representatives of the Muslim community in a particular Muslim national state? After the break up of the Ottoman Empire and the abolition of caliphate in Istanbul (Constantinople) in 1924, Turkey was the first country in the world of Islam to advance the legal reasoning that the power of the caliph or imam could be vested in a body of persons in the form of an elected assembly or legislature. This had been the viewpoint of the Khawaraj in the earlier history of Islam, who had held that it was not obligatory for the Muslim community to appoint a caliph, but the Muslims could manage their affairs themselves by mutual consultation as recommended by the Quran. Views were also expressed and adopted to the effect that in modern Muslim national states elected assemblies could constitute the advisory council (majlis-i-shura) of the Muslim community and make subordinate legislation on the basis of *ijtihad,* i.e., reinterpret Islamic law in accordance with the changing needs and requirements of the Muslim community in light of the principles laid down in the Quran and Sunna. In any case, no voice was raised against the transformation which had taken place in Turkey, and in due course even in the Muslim countries where legislative assemblies were formed, their establishment has not been considered repugnant to the injunctions of Islam.

Be that as it may, a Muslim national state does not become an Islamic state unless and until it adopts its characteristic features which still remain unalterable. The democratic method which has been adopted by some of the Muslim countries due to the influence of Western ideas is not a perfect method. An Islamic state is expected to be run by the best members of the community. The democratic method, although adopted by Western countries in order to achieve the same objective, ordinarily does not ensure the election of the best, because a really suitable or competent candidate may be defeated by an unsuitable or incompetent candidate only for the reason that the latter has obtained more votes, regardless of how they might have been achieved. Similarly, a vote is no substitute for *baya,* because *baya* is a bilateral contract whereas a vote does not have the implications of a contract. Furthermore, according to the Sunna of the

Holy Prophet, a person who offers himself as a candidate for any office abuses his position of trust and must be ignored. If this rule is usually adopted for the selection, for instance, of a "judge," then why should it not be adopted for the election of a so-called "legislator." Again, there is no obligation to follow the majority principle as the right of such a majority is not recognized in Islam. Supporters of this viewpoint also argue that since Muslims constitute Allah's party, an Islamic state must have a one-party government and that a multi-party system is repugnant to the Quran and Sunna. It is also pointed out that some Sunni schools of law do not acknowledge community agreement *(ijma)* as a source for the evolution of Islamic law. According to them, *shura* is merely a body of advisers or experts which must be appointed by the caliph or imam (through selection or nomination and not election). They serve in an advisory or consultative capacity and are not an independent legislative body.

There are a number of arguments advanced in favor of the democratic method. If the powers and obligations of a caliph or imam are to be shared by the Muslim community in a particular Muslim national state, it is necessary to create a body of persons to constitute an *ijma* or *shurah* which should conduct the affairs of the Muslim community through mutual consultation. Such a body cannot be constituted except through the elected representatives of the Muslim community. Although the majority principle was not followed during the historical experiment of the Rightly Guided Caliphs, its adaptation had neither been specifically forbidden nor disapproved by the Quran and Sunna. Admittedly, the Quran and Sunna insist on the sovereignty of Allah and the enforcement of His laws, but the evolution of the method for the realization of these objectives is left to the good sense of the Muslim community in accordance with its requirements from time to time. As the real object of Islam is to establish a community of faith governed by the *shariah,* the Muslim community is free to evolve any suitable method for the enforcement of Islamic law. The principle that a person who offers himself as a candidate for any office abuses his position of trust and therefore must be ignored cannot be made applicable universally. If all suitable or competent persons are to refrain from offering themselves as candidates, then the Muslim community, not being aware of their presence, may be compelled to select mediocrities for appointment to positions of trust. Furthermore, strictly speaking, a vote may not be a bilateral contract like *baya,* but it certainly is an indication of selection of a candidate among others, on the basis of his suitability or competency in the eyes of the electors, in order to represent them only for a fixed period of time. If he does not prove himself to be suitable or competent, he can be rejected at the next election. The establishment of a legislature is also necessary because subordinate legislation which is not repugnant to the Quran and Sunna is a very wide field due to the changing needs and requirements of the modern Muslim community, The successful working of the democratic method really depends on the conscientious electorate which is aware of its rights and obligations under Islamic law. It is likely to fail where the electorate is gullible. Therefore, it it necessary to educate and train the Muslim community in order to make it conscious of its rights and obligations under Islamic law, for only through education and training would it be in a position to elect the best members of the community. In addition, although the Muslim community is Allah's party, the formation of groups amongst Muslims for promoting good and suppressing evil is permitted, indeed recommended by the Quran. Only such political parties which adhere to Islamic ideology can be permitted to function in a Muslim national state. Furthermore, measures must be adopted to determine clearly as to who obtains an overwhelming (and not merely bare) majority of votes in his favor.

Today, many argue that the democratic method must be adopted because there is no other appropriate substitute for the time being which could yield better results as required by the Islamic standards. The conflict in viewpoints regarding Western and Islamic forms of democracy creates a problem which is faced by some Muslim national states at present, and it is probably the cause of occasional instances of political breakdown today.

However, as it has been pointed out, the fundamental principles on which an Islamic state is founded continue to remain the same. A Muslim national state can only claim to be an Islamic state if its constitution strictly adheres to two basic principles of ultimate sovereignty vesting in God and the supremacy of Islamic law. But it must be clearly understood that an Islamic state is not a theocracy. Islam does not recognize the distinction between the "spiritual" and the "secular," and it is incumbent on every Muslim constantly to endeavor to realize religious values while performing his temporal obligations. In this sense the Islamic state assimilates the qualities of an ideal secular state. In the positive sense, a secular state ought to guarantee religious freedom to every citizen and endeavor to promote the material advancement and welfare of all its citizens without distinction of religion or race. This is also one of the numerous duties of an Islamic state, which must protect the places of worship of citizens adhering to faiths other than Islam due to the Quranic injunction: "If Allah had not raised a group [i.e., Muslims] to ward off the others from aggression, churches, synagogues, oratories and mosques, where Allah is worshiped most, would have been destroyed" (S. 22:40). Similarly, it must guarantee man's inalienable rights, e.g., equality of status and of opportunity; equality before law; freedom of thought, expression, belief, faith, worship, association, assembly, movement, trade, business, or profession; and the right to hold and dispose of property, subject to Islamic law and morality. It must ensure the complete independence of the judiciary and uphold the supremacy of rule by Islamic law. Each of these principles can be directly traced from the Quran and Sunna.

Nevertheless, the legislature in an Islamic state has a restricted power of legislation for, technically speaking, its authority is delegated and can be exercised only within the limits presecribed by the Quran and Sunna. Consequently, it must enjoin that which is considered by the Quran as *"maruf"* (universally acknowledged moral values). There are three spheres of legislative activity in a Muslim national state: 1) To enforce laws which have specifically been laid down in the Quran and Sunnah; 2) To bring all the existing laws in conformity with the Quran and Sunnah; and 3) To make laws as subordinate legislation which are not repugnant to the Quran and Sunnah.

The establishment of such a legislature by means of election requires, firstly, an electorate which is aware of its rights and obligations under Islamic law; second, the recognition of only such political parties which adhere to the Islamic ideology and are in a position to put up candidates who are familiar with the legislative limits prescribed by the Quran and Sunna; and third, the adoption of measures which should clearly determine who has the overwhelming support of the voters. Due to historical circumstances, a modern Muslim legislative assembly, at least for the present, must consist mostly of members who possess no knowledge of the subtleties of Islamic law. Therefore, they are likely to make grave errors in their interpretation of Islamic law. Ideally speaking, if an elected legislative assembly is to be formed in an Islamic state, it should consist of experts in different fields and lawyers who are qualified in Islamic law as well as modern jurisprudence. This objective can be realized through the accomplishment of a reform in the present system of legal education in Muslim countries, by extending its sphere so as to combine the study of Islamic law with an intelligent study of modern jurisprudence. However, this is a long-term objective. For the interim period two constitutional devices have been adopted by some Muslim national states in order to reduce the possibilities of erroneous interpretations of Islamic law in a modern Muslim legislative assembly. These are making provision with the national assembly for a separate committee of ulama which has the power to supervise the legislative activity of the assembly and constituting a body of ulama outside the assembly as an advisory council which has the authority to advise the national assembly as to whether proposed legislation is or is not repugnant to the injunctions of Islam.

The Islamic state may be considered as an ideal, but it is an ideal which the Muslim community must aspire to realize. It is through the realization of this ideal that the attitude of Islam to authority can be really demonstrated to the world. There are three objectives which the world community is trying to achieve: peace of mind for the individual because without it no happiness is possible; peace amongst the nations and disappearance of the threat of destruction by war; and finally, respect for the rules of international behavior. All three objectives remain unattained, and it is evident that with the present materialist dimension of national objectives no further improvement in the world condition is logically possible. Politics divorced from religion and morality can only lead to the situation that exists at present. Human conduct cannot be expected to conform to standards of rectitude in the absence of belief in the ultimate accountability of man. Islam, with its organic relationship of religion to politics and society, provides the framework for a political development which can realize the objectives of the world community.

FOURTEEN

Islam and Zionism

ISMAIL R. al FARUQI

NOT JUDAISM BUT ZIONISM

Islam is not opposed to Judaism but regards it as the religion of God. It acknowledges the God of Judaism, i.e., of Ibrahim (Abraham), Ismail, Ishaq (Issac) and Yaqub (Jacob), as the God. It recognizes Musa (Moses) as prophet and the Torah as revelation from God. Islam questions not Judaism but the Jews, first as to their faithfulness to the Torahic laws and second, as to the total integrity of the Torahic text. In doing so, Islam is at one with most Jews in history as regards the first point, and with those Jews (Reform, Conservative and Reconstructionist) who have accepted Biblical criticism as regards the second. Rather, Islam is opposed to Zionism, to Zionist politics and conduct.

Zionism is a movement launched by Theodor Herzl following his disillusionment by the Dreyfus Affair. It is designed to transform Palestine and its adjacent territories into a Jewish state, "as Jewish as England is English." Its pursuit of this objective is thoroughly Machiavellian. Its single-minded purpose is given absolute priority over all considerations, including the moral.

Having obtained the Balfour Declaration, Zionism played its power to the hilt to acquire land. It stopped at nothing in this effort, including the application of pressure, blackmail, bribery, speculation and forced eviction of Palestinian farmers from lands which they had inherited from their ancestors through the millennia.

For its crimes against the individual Palestinian men and women, against the corporate existence of the Palestinians, against the individual Arabs of the surrounding countries as well as the *ummah,* Islam condemns Zionism. Islam demands that every atom's weight of injustice perpetrated against the innocent be undone. Hence, it imposes upon all Muslims the world over to rise like one man to put an end to injustice and to reinstate its sufferers in their lands, homes and properties. The illegitimate use of every movable or immovable property by the Zionists since the British occupation of the land will have to be paid for and compensated. Therefore, the Islamic position leaves no chance for the Zionist state but to be dismantled and destroyed, and its wealth confiscated to pay off its liabilities. This obligation—to repel, stop and undo injustice—is a corporate religious obligation *(fard kifayah)* on the *ummah,* and a personal religious obligation *(fard ayn)* on every able adult Muslim man or woman in the world until the *ummah* has officially assumed responsibility for its implementation. Defense of the *ummah,* i.e., of every province over which the banner of the Islamic State has once been raised, is jihad, or holy war, and it is a prime religious duty. Fulfillment of this duty is *falah* (felicity) in this world and the next, i.e., victory in this world, martyrdom and paradise in the other (S. 3:169). Moreover, God commands the Muslims "to avail themselves of all means and instruments of force in order to overwhelm the enemy and bring the war to a quick end" (S. 8:60).

However, dismantling the Zionist state does not necessarily mean the destruction of Jewish lives or of properties. Such destruction will, however, be regarded by Islam as a necessary evil if Zionist forces resist the dismantling and seizing process. It is a first Islamic principle that aggression and injustice be met with an identical proportion of same (S. 2:194). Excess is absolutely forbidden. Moreover, hostilities must, according to Islam, be immediately stopped as soon as resistance stops. To continue them beyond acquiescence of the resistant is unpardonable injustice (S. 8:61, 5:90). Islam commands the Muslims never to transgress, never to go beyond the termination of injustice, never to give vent to any resentment by increasing the suffering one atom's weight, but to deal to the enemy exactly what he had dealt them, measure for measure (S. 5:45). Islam equally commands its adherents to spare no effort, no matériel, no wealth needed to bring the war to victorious conclusion. It lays no time limit on the declaration or conduct of the war; for a moral religious obligation is *ex hypothesi* timeless. Islam further recommends pardon, mercy and forgiveness (ibid). But these virtues cannot be forced; and they have moral value only if they are practiced from a position of strength and self-sufficiency. Morever, they are strictly personal. They must be the object of a personal decision on the part of a free personal subject for them to have the moral value to which they lay claim.

The injustice perpetrated by Zionism is so complex, so compounded and so grave that there is practically no means of stopping or undoing it without a violent war in which the Zionist army, state and all its public institutions would have to be destroyed. Even if the Western world forsook the Zionist state altogether, its Zionist leadership would still muster enough desperate courage to persist. For it is, by nature, an ideological state, necessarily prepared to save itself at all cost to human life and property. All the more reason, therefore, for the Muslims of the world to take it more seriously, and to prepare realistic plans which they are unquestionably capable of executing.

Once the Zionist state, its army and other public institutions are destroyed, the problem of what to do with its population would have to be faced. That

Islam cannot and will not compromise on Zionism is a lesson which must be taught to every Jew living in the Muslim world. Hence, Islam will not tolerate the establishment of a Zionist alternative to the Zionist State. All Zionists who wish to live within the Muslim world would have to de-Zionize themselves, emigrate, or face prosecution for their Zionist activities. De-Zionization, it must be borne in mind, is the rejection of Zionism, the political program to transform Palestine into a Jewish state on the European or Western model.

ISLAM AND THE JEWISH PROBLEM

The self-same law of Islam which requires of the Muslim to go to the end of the earth to put an end to injustice must equally apply to the goyim as to the Jewish sufferers of injustice. Can there by any doubt in the Muslim's mind that the Jew is a sufferer of injustice at the hands of the Christian West?

The answer is categorical. Certainly, the Jew has been victim of injustice in the West; and certainly, the Muslim is enjoined by God to come to his rescue, to relieve him from suffering and to help him achieve his freedom, security and peace. There can therefore be no doubt, Islamically speaking, that the world of Islam is religiously bound to champion the Jewish cause against Christendom; that it stands indicted as long as it fails to do so. Indeed, championing the cause of the oppressed has been an essential component of the image of Islam in Mecca and Medina, in the Muslim world and in Europe. That is why the Jews of Damascus, of Spain, as well as of Constantinople, the Balkans, and Central Europe, helped the Muslims in their conquest of these lands. The Jews themselves were convinced that Islam's and its adherents' championing of justice was genuine. What can Islam offer to the cessation of Jewish suffering in the modern world?

Islam offers a perfect solution to the Jewish problem which has beset the Jews and the West for two millennia. This solution is for the Jews of the world to be given the right to dwell wherever they wish, as free citizens of the state of their choice. Those who feel themselves reasonably happy where they are and wish to continue to live there ought to be entitled by a world-covenant to do so. As to those Jews who desire to emigrate from the West, they ought to be welcome in the Muslim world. If, for reasons of religious attachment, they wish to live in those areas of the Muslim world associated with their history—Egypt to Mesopotamia—they ought to be entitled to do so by virtue of the respect Islam pays to the Prophets of God and the necessary extension of sympathy and love for those that honor the prophetic tradition and the spaces in which it conveyed its divine messages.

On this question of Jewish immigration Islam gives far more to world Jewry than Zionism. The latter wants only Palestine; Islam forces wide open the gates of the whole Muslim world, and *a fortiori,* of the Arab world; and still more, of the territory of the "Fertile Crescent." "Immigration," however, does not mean seizure of land, displacement or dispossession of others. Neither does it mean seizure of the state, or its transformation into a state for the Jews on the German or French model. *Ex hypothesi,* there must be an Islamic state comprehending these territories; an Islamic state whose constitution is the Quran, whose law is the *shariah,* and whose constituency is only partly non-Muslim. Such an Islamic state, extending from the Atlantic to the Malay Basin, is certainly obliged to open its gates to any Jewish immigrant who travels thither. Such an Islamic state is the haven for world Jewry, as well as the protector and defender of prophecy and its peoples against all outside attack. Such a state is a world state, with infinite geo-political depth, infinite geographic and human resources. Endowed with the life- and world-affirming ideology that Islam is, and with a long history of confrontation with the world, and the richest culture and civilization, such an Islamic state can effectively contend on the world scene and has the capacity requisite therefor.

Contrasted with such an Islamic state, the state of Israel which Zionism presents is a miserable match. It consists of a few thousand square kilometers, a sliver of land, and three million people. True, it is at present armed to the teeth with the most up-to-date and sophisticated weaponry. But it depends for its military muscle as well as the very food it consumes on Western imperialism whose direction may change from moment to moment. Moreover, it is surrounded with a wall of resentment and hatred in the will of a hundred and fifty million Arabs and a billion Muslims, awaiting the shift in international relations which would give them occasion to pounce on it.

If world Jewry, or a substantial number of its members, or, if only the present Jewish citizens of Israel were to exist in an Islamic state, how may they live in accordance with Judaism? How may Jewish genius be given the chance to prosper and flower forth?

The first requisite for any culture, civilization or religion to prosper—which is the same for any community—is peace. The reassurance that one's life and property are safe is absolutely necessary for the mind to operate in any long-term or constructive manner. Without it, no human can develop the taste or the will for truth, goodness or beauty. . . . Such lasting peace cannot be assured to the Jews anywhere except by Islam and under its political dominion. The relation of Islam to Judaism being one of sympathy, even of identity, Islam's religious honoring of the Hebrew prophets as God's prophets and of the Hebrew revelation as God's revelation furnishes the best guarantee. Here is a nation, an *ummah* of a billion souls on the march maintaining this faith as an essential and constitutive element of its own religion, of its own consciousness of God, of itself and of the world. As with Muhammad and his companions, the *ummah* of Islam firmly believes that God is the Guardian of the Jews and other non-Muslims who opt for peace rather than war with the Islamic state. Indeed, in the faith and law of Islam, the guarantee is provided even against corrupt Muslim rulers who might be tempted to exploit or aggress upon the *dhimmis,* or covenanters who covenanted for peace under God's guaranteeship. Finally, there is the guarantee of tested history. Except for the briefest intervals in which Muslims have suffered even more than Jews or Christians at the hands of a corrupt ruler, the history of Islam's tolerance and coexistence with Judaism and Christianity is pure white. Throughout the fourteen centuries of its existence, its record is without blemish. Never has the *ummah* conceived of itself or of its mission, of its past or of its future, as involving a necessary decimation of the non-Muslims living in its midst.

Before leaving the question of Jewish security under Islam, one more problem remains. Is it not necessary for the feeling of peace that the Jews enjoy national sovereignty like the European countries do? No! The feeling for national sovereignty is a very recent development, even in the West. It is an outgrowth of ethnocentrism and political nationalism and the offspring of European romanticism in the last two centuries. The European has existed and prospered for centuries without it. Loyalty to God, to the Church, to the universal community, to king and prince, does not require it. "National sovereignty," as the third constitutive element of the state after "people" and "a piece of earth with defined borders," is itself a part of the disease of romanticism. "Sovereignty" is a vague and woozy concept, supposed to weld "people" and "earth" into mystical unity precisely in order to exclude all other elements. When it was first called for in Europe, it was meant to exclude the jurisdiction of the Church in affairs of the community. Later, as the Church influence withered, it was meant to exclude Christian ethics and values from determining public affairs.

In the domain of concrete personal living, Islam unquestionably yields all authority to the non-Muslims to determine their lives as they alone see fit. It not only permits, but requires them, to live in accordance with their own laws. To this purpose it regards them as an *ummah* community, different and separate from the Muslims and all non-Jews, endowed with traditions and institutions. It requires the Jews to set up their own rabbinic courts, and puts its whole executive power at their disposal. The *shariah,* the law of Islam, demands of all Jews to submit themselves to the precepts of Jewish law as interpreted by the rabbinic courts, and treats any defiance or contempt of the rabbinic court as rebellion against the Islamic state itself, on a par with like action on the part of any Muslim vis-à-vis the Islamic court.

The only area removed from the *dhimmi* community's jurisdiction is that of war and peace. This is the exclusive domain of the Islamic state whose raison d' être is the establishment of peace and the critical presentation of the word of God. This duty is that of defense of Dar al-Islam—that is, the *ummah* of Muslims as well as those of the non-Muslims who have entered the *Pax Islamica*. Since the Islamic state is really a federation of community-states, it is only befitting and right that no community-state be held responsible for the conduct of foreign policy, of peace and war, and that the federal state be so held. Two major differences exist between a federal state such as the Islamic state and one like the United States or Switzerland. The first is that in the latter the constituent is a mini-state based on territory, whereas in the former, it is based on humans in community, thus giving primacy to the humans rather than to real estate. The second is that the law of the Western federal state is positive in the sense that it is what the majority of the constituents (whatever its percentage) decide it to be at any time; whereas the law of the Islamic state is what God has ordained for it for all time.

THE ISLAMIC SOLUTION AND THE STATUS QUO IN THE ARAB WORLD

Finally, it may be asked, How would the application of the Islamic solution affect the actual state of affairs in the Near East?

First, the Arab states of the Near East must undergo a transformation from being caricatures of the Western national states to becoming a single, united Islamic state. The Arab states are literally all creations of Western colonialism. They must all be dismantled and their populations reorganized into the Islamic state. Their laws which again for the most part they inherited from Western colonialism ought to be discarded in favor of the *shariah*. The Islamic state emerging from their union should abolish all frontiers between them, all their individual defense establishments, and assume all responsibility for defense and foreign affairs. Only if this is achieved may the Arab Muslims of the Near East stand ready to implement the Islamic solution of the problem of Israel.

Second, Israel, the Zionist state, would be dismantled; by force, if necessary. The institution of the Zionist state is a positive evil, and so is all its defense establishment. This leaves the *ummah* community of Jews as covenanters with the Islamic state for peace. The Jewish citizens of Israel would not be required to move. On the contrary, they would be invited to dwell in any city or village of the whole Islamic state, not only in some pieces of real estate on the West Bank of the Jordan and in the Gaza strip as Zionism is presently asking. But no Jew may dispossess a Muslim of his land, house or other property as Zionists have so far done. The transaction is personal; and both parties, buyer and seller, have to will the sale and be satisfied with it. As for the Palestinians, they would have to be rehabilitated in their own homes and lands, out of which they were forcibly ejected first by British and then by Zionist arms. Moreover, they would have to be compensated, under Islamic law, for their damages.

This means that the Jews presently living in stolen homes and cultivating stolen lands, will have either to vacate or to compensate their owners. If the owners insist on evacuation, the capital necessary for compensation could be used to buy new land and home elsewhere. If, as Jews claim, the Kingdom of David extended from the River of Egypt to the Euphrates, there is still plenty of land for them to purchase and occupy. According to Islam, as it has been already said, there is no restriction whatever on the number of Jewish immigrants, nor on the area or locality of land they may purchase to dwell in throughout the Muslim world.

Thirdly, once the *bouleversement* this solution brings has settled down, there is no reason why the Jews, as *dhimmi* citizens of the Islamic state, may not keep all the public institutions they have so far developed in Palestine (courts of law, learned societies of art and culture, public corporations, schools, colleges and universities) to continue in their operation, whether in any locality of Palestine or anywhere else where Jews might choose to dwell. Henceforth, their vision and their efforts would be directed toward upholding and promoting Judaism, not the Western ideologies of decadence and aberration. No one will make war against them. No one will persecute or molest them. Their task is to be as Jewish as they care to be.

Then, when the Jews of the emerging Islamic state have organized themselves and begun to breathe as Jews, free from any threat, the chief of the Islamic state might repeat the message which an earlier predecessor of his (Muhammad, "the second," conqueror of Constantinople) sent to the chief of an earlier non-Muslim *ummah* in the Islamic state (Gennadius Scholarius, Patriarch of Constantinople): "Be the Patriarch of your *ummah* in peace. May Allah protect you. To you, our friendship is pledged in all circumstances and under all conditions, wherever it may benefit you. May you enjoy all the privileges hitherto enjoyed by your predecessors!"[1]

Note

1. G. Papadopoulos, *Les privilèges du patriarcat œcuméniques (Communauté grecque-orthodoxe) dans l'empire ottoman,* (Paris, 1924), p. 10.

FIFTEEN

The Islamic Approach to Economic Development

KHALID M. ISHAQUE

WESTERN THEORY AND MODELS

In the West (primarily the First World) human activity in the economic field is primarily directed towards individual gain. It was formerly widely believed that competitiveness generated by each individual's drive for personal gain would somehow bring about an overall harmony of interests and mutual gain. The West is only now discovering that this is not wholly true. Without moral or legal restraints the big fish tend to eat up the small ones. The path recommended and often willingly chosen (i.e., following Western models of development), is not a road to salvation for the Third World, especially in the case of the Muslim part of the Third World which does not share the worldview of the capitalist or the socialist. The problem of under-development has to be tackled within the framework of its Islamic commitment, a commitment not confined merely to some aspects of worship, but to a total life-view in which economic activity has a definite place and purpose. Not enough importance is given by the foreign advisers or by the existing ruling elites to the fact that there is radical difference between the vision of a good and successful life in the worldview of Islam and that of the capitalist or the socialist world. In the former it consists of fulfilling one's covenant with Allah and of living out the worldly life in terms of divine guidance as preparation for a more beautiful life awaiting mankind. The First (capitalist) and the Second (socialist) worlds have an essentially materialistic and earthly worldview. The total picture of good life painted with a mix of hues provided by Freud's vision of a sexual man and Marx's version of an economic man does not coincide with that which Islam portrays.

THE NEW TASK

To be able to utilize all the resources available to the Muslim community, several types of action shall have to be taken simultaneously and on several fronts.

Disabusing Muslim Mind About Imported Economic Models

The first task is to disabuse the Muslim of the necessity of adopting one or the other of the two models projected by the First and the Second Worlds. Both are basically materialistic, have priorities basically different from those of Islam and have had and continue to have aspects which permit wholesale exploitation. In the West it is the big corporations and cartels and in the Socialist countries it is state capitalism and bureaucracy. In the former, some relief is possible because power is diffused in social groups, in the latter the financial and political power is concentrated in one and the same agency. In the former, the capitalist exploits and in the latter the bureaucrat oppresses. In both cases oligarchies run the society and knowing no control or criterion higher than their will, they exploit and oppress without even feeling guilty. There is nothing inevitable about these models as both stand discredited and exposed. The Muslims are and should feel free to devise their own models for solving their problems.

Our second task is to introduce the Muslims to Islam's distinctive approach to the whole range of economic activity. It is the only ideology whose dimensions cover the life in this world as well as hereafter. Islam alone teaches man how to lead a moral and meaningful life in poverty and in wealth; it provides a motivational pattern to an individual for a spiritually meaningful total commitment of his life and all his worldly possessions.

Organizing Development: The third task is to work out models for the Muslim communities to organize their development, by increased self-reliance and where necessary by mutual dependence.

The Way to Will to Develop: The final task is to discover ways and means to kindle a new self-confidence and fervor in the community, to pull itself up by the bootstraps, to participate enthusiastically in fairly creating and justly distributing wealth.

Content of Economic Activity

On the above analysis it is clear that charting of our future will demand consideration of not merely the economic and political factors, but also spiritual and moral factors without which politics becomes a game of oppression and economics a hunt by exploiters. Socio-economic injustices are the first object of attack under an Islamic commitment.

QURANIC PRINCIPLES OF ECONOMIC ACTIVITY

Participation in Economic Activity—According to the Quran, participation in economically creative activity is obligatory for every Muslim (S. 62:10); Muslims are also expected to work hard (S. 73:20). The Jews sought fulfillment of God's blessing in worldly life, and the Christians went to the other extreme by propagating asceticism. Islam in unequivocal terms affirmed the fundamental and absolute precedence of life hereafter over the worldly life (S. 4:77); and expected the Muslims to use the good things of life (S. 24:60; 7:31) and to be grateful to God for his blessings (S. 16:114; 29:17; 2:172) because Allah increases His blessings for those who are grateful (S. 14:7). The blessing in worldly things is abused when a man squanders his wealth (S. 17:26–27), or exalts and makes a wanton public display thereof (S. 28:72); therefore waste and wanton display in contrast to moderate display within the family circle to increase the beauty and charm of life (S. 24:31) is prohibited. The importance of this principle becomes clear when one realizes that contemporary Marxism's strongest criticism against capitalism is in regard to its wastefulness, i.e., both the non-utility of a large number of items produced and also their inequitable distribution and use. One person wallows in ostentatious high living and another barely survives in a condition of extreme poverty and deprivation. The same criticism can be levelled against the socialist system also because therein too once a person has earned his wage he can do with it what he likes. Waste of hard earned wages on alcoholism is a special problem of Russian society.

According to the Quran everyone is entitled to a share in what he earns (S. 4:32); no one is permitted to withhold all that he earns (S. 104:2–2). He is required to use it in the categories prescribed by Allah (S. 28:78) but is prohibited from using it for wanton public display (S. 28:79). Blocking the use of wealth in this fashion carries severe chastisement (S. 28:81), because it causes oppression in land and upsetting of social balance (S. 28:83). The Quran has specifically chosen to mention Korah as an example of a man of means who invited divine punishment on account of abuse of wealth. But throughout the Quran there is repeated mention of the punishment the wealthy ones invite by hoarding their wealth, and not using it in a manner which would save them the hereafter (S. 28:77; 104:2).

Duty to Produce More Than One's Needs—Economic activity is not to be confined to earning or producing enough to meet one's personal needs only. Muslims are expected to produce more because they cannot participate in the process of purification through providing security to others (*zakat* or alms tax) unless they produce more than what they themselves consume. The most recommended use of fairly earned wealth is to apply it to procuring of all means to fulfill a Muslim's covenant with Allah. A Muslim is under a covenant to struggle for establishment of Islamic order with his life and all worldly belongings (S. 9:111). This too would become impossible if individuals only produced enough for personal needs (S. 8:72). This of course does not mean that for those who have no wealth there is no compensation with Allah (S. 9:91–93). They can improve the quality of social life even without surplus economic resources.

The duty to produce carries certain further implications of which due note must be taken. In the production of goods Muslims must give priority to those things which are good and wholesome and help to improve the quality of life. Goods for mere display or for titillating artificially created wants would have very low social priority. The goods whose use is unlawful or prohibited may not be produced at all. Under no circumstances should production be by means which are disapproved because in such circumstances even if there is appearance of an immediate gain as in case of usury, in reality there is a loss which is not immediately apparent (S. 30:30).

The importance of these principles becomes obvious when we realize that one of the major faults of the first economic order of the First World is over production of goods which merely whet the appetite by creating a passing fancy and do little to add to the real quality of life. Every day media of all kinds keep inflicting advertisements for cigarettes, wines, clothes, and innumerable consumer items for which markets are articially created and for projection of these wares, a specious culture is created and inflicted. In the end not all the consumer items reach everyone. A good many go completely to waste. In the process a great many social priorities remain unattended. The individual produced in such a society is morally indifferent and spiritually famished.

The Quran prohibits wagering transactions. In a wagering transaction the winner makes an undeserved gain and the loser suffers an undeserved loss, without both parties being involved in any process of producing more. Such transactions constitute a clear abuse of wealth, be it in the form of goods or the saved power to command goods and services available in form of money. Such transactions cause envy, rancour and enmity (S. 5:90) and destroy dignity and the necessity of productive labor. Through them people acquire power to command more goods and services without participating in any exercise of adding to the sum total of socially available goods.

The Quran explicitly prohibits usury *(riba)* (S. 3:130) because of its evil effects on human society. It constitutes one major cause of social malaise (S. 2:275). Ultimately, usury assures unearned incomes, and converts business into exploitative bargains (S. 2:275) and by and large develops a style of production wherein business transactions do not benefit both the parties to the transaction, but rather become unfair and unjust taking of someone's property (S. 4:16).

The Quran insists that Muslims must not block wealth but must constantly spend it though with wisdom (S. 9:34) and moderation (S. 17:29), and keeping in view the permitted uses of wealth (S. 9:35). The full implications of this command do not become apparent at first glance and stand in need of some explication.

Participation in economically productive activity is the duty of every man and woman. The Prophet (peace be upon him) is reported to have said that hateful in the eyes of Allah is one who does nothing. The individual's savings represent the surplus generated over and above what is consumed in the process of production. Part of this surplus is reserved by the *shariah* for the benefit of those who due to some permanent disability or temporary inacapacity cannot look after their own needs or those of their dependants. This part is contributed and collected by the mandate of Divine Law and is known as the *zakat*. As far as the rest of the savings is concerned, this too needs to be thrown back into the process of production in the form of capital, to further social productivity. Islam seeks maximum use of capital, total utilization of manpower. Severe chastisement is promised to those who withhold socially available capital by storing it up in the form of gold and silver (S. 9:34).

Gold and silver by themselves are at best universally accepted symbols to command services or to buy goods, and by themselves do not carry any intrinsic value to provide direct satisfaction of human needs. So long as the savings in the individual accounts are by and large available as capital for the community, the problem of chronic shortage of capital may not often arise. For example a man "A" works and from his wages he saves a hundred rupees. This amount he puts in a bank. The bank as his agent invests it in a joint venture with someone else, say "B." From the surplus generated the bank and "B" make provision to return the original sum, the bank takes part of the profits made in the joint venture with "B", and "B" deposits say fifty rupees as savings from part of the profit that accrued to him. Now say the bank enters another joint venture with "C" utilizing the amount of rupees deposited by "A" and "B" and makes further profit and generates further savings by "C". In this way the sum total of socially available goods and services increases without destroying the capacity of "A" and "B" to call for certain goods and services to which they are entitled by virtue of their savings. The profits of depositors would of course be calculated annually as *zakat* is also calculated on annual savings. The transaction would then be different from a *riba* transaction or an ordinary banking transaction wherein the lender gets his interest at a predetermined rate irrespective of the benefit which may or may not accure to the borrower. In the former case the money remains that of the investor but in the latter case it becomes that of the borrower.

In joint ventures both parties risk profit or loss but in the latter case the lender does not share the profit or loss but takes the fixed interest. There would be other points of distinction also. In the capitalist banking system only the rich can borrow, because they alone can provide the requisite "safe" securities. Wealth of the borrower is a very important factor for the lender when Islam expressly prohibits "circulation of wealth only amongst the rich" (S. 59:7), and the state guarantees repayment of loans, the utilization of capital will follow a completely different course from that prevalent in the West or in the socialist world.

There are many factors which operate to create profit. The Quranic injunction of equality, and the Prophet's command that in all transactions both parties must profit, and the other principles already referred to above have a direct bearing on the question of the quantum of profit permissible to a Muslim. Until quite recently the First World economists used to say that profit is as much as anyone is willing to pay minus the cost, and often justified it by saying that the competitive market fixes the margin. We know now that there is no absolutely free competitive market like that the academic economists visualize, and that there are too many factors which prevent the market from reaching a fair equilibrium. The Prophet (peace be upon him) is reported to have prohibited making of profit on articles of absolute need like food-grains though he refused to fix prices in spite of requests. On other items he required the believers to make reasonable profits to assure full benefits of each transaction to all contracting parties. The Islamic social framework, insisting as it does on nurturing social confidence, would provide the requisite field for successful operation of these principles.

Quranic principles operate in the numerous patterns of economic arrangements in such a way as to occlude exploitation. They seek to assure that within the limits set by *shariah*, each party shall receive due benefit for its contribution, industry, work, entrepreneurial skill inventiveness. Those who contribute more shall receive more (S. 53:32). There will remain certain inequalities (S. 16:71, 43:32) but they will not hurt the group because strict controls regulate the uses of wealth. Those who have more wealth have more responsibilities, and more to account for.

The Quran recognizes the difference between man and man in terms of intelligence, health, stregnth and morality. It also recognizes the fact that some work harder than others and some work more intelligently and consistently for better objectives. Some work only to get the good things of this life and some use their worldly life as means for betterment of the real life of hereafter. Some save their earnings and others squander them. Recognizing all these differences, the Quran affirms the principle of just requittal by declaring that:

There is naught for man but what he strives for. (S. 53:39)

The Quran also proclaims:

Whosoever desires the present life, We hasten for him therein what we will, for such of them as We please then We have appointed Hell for him he shall burn therein condemned and rejected. And whosoever desires the Hereafter and strives for it as it should be striven for, and he is a believer; these are the ones whose striving shall find favour.

And We do aid these as well as those, out of bounty of thy Lord; and bounty of thy Lord is not held back (from any). See how We have made some of them to excel others. And certainly the Hereafter is greater in degrees and greater in excellence. [S. 17:18–22]

In short, therefore, the Quran makes it clear that principles of just requittal require that the wages of sin and virtue all be reckoned and paid to each according to the labor that he puts in. Any egalitarian philosophy which destroys or even fails to recognize the qualitative differences between a good man and a knave, a hard worker and a waster, is totally unacceptable to Islam. The slogan of the equality of all men is put forward by its proponents as an alternative to the injustices and tyrannies of the few against the many. The answer provided by Islam does not destroy the radical differences between right and wrong, between useful and useless, between good and bad, between the productive and the barren. It does not seek to establish social justice by steam-rolling all into a state of unmerited equality. Nor does it accept the philosophical assumption underlying the theories of those who explain the phenomenon of human culture in purely economic terms. The transfer of legal ownership of means of production to government instead of individuals does not ipso facto establish the equality that is sought. Even in the government-owned farm or factory there is the manager who commands and oppresses like the owner that he replaces. Human dignity and freedom are as effectively choked under the new arrangement as they were under the old; perhaps they are even more effectively and irretrievably lost, because the new master is member of a vast bureaucracy infinitely more powerful and power-drunk than the so-called capitalist that he replaces. Islam protects the individual not on the basis of hatred or class-war, but in a manner infinitely surer, wiser and more human.

At this stage it might be useful to refer briefly to Islam's attitude toward private property. We have already referred to the fact that the first addressee of the Quran is the individual. He is called upon to achieve salvation and ultimate fulfillment by living up to the terms of his covenant with Allah irrespective of the performance of other members of the community; the way to obtain Divine approval is primarily in the social field by performance of his social obligations. Islamic individualism is irreconcilable with the collectivism and moral relativity of socialist thought. The distinctive characteristics that the concept of private property has in an Islamic society must be understood in this context. In Islam no person has an absolute right to his property to use it as he will, except perhaps in the sense that he can use it for some purpose that has been accepted as lawful by the Quran. It is not the property which is in itself the source of trouble but it is the misuse of the property which causes unhappiness and unrest. Korah is cited by the Quran as a classical example of one who misused his wealth. His sin lay in 1) his assertion that because he had earned his wealth he could use it as he wished; and 2) in the wanton display of wealth. The Prophet (peace be upon him) was extremely careful in suppressing ostentatiousness and wanton display of wealth. He constantly warned the community that wealth was one means amongst others whereby to win one's laurels in the life hereafter. All things created were for use of man in his spiritual journey.

That Allah has created the good things of life for the use of mankind is a positive declaration of the Quran.

Allah says:

Say, Who has forbidden (unto you) the good things granted by Allah to His servants, or raised as healthy nourishments? (S. 7:32).

The believers are exhorted to strive for earning their livelihood; the Quran declares:

And when the prayer is finished, then disperse in the land and seek of Allah's grace, and remember Allah much, that you may prosper. (S. 62:10)

But whereas the believers are called upon to lawfully earn what they can, they are simultaneously placed under a duty to spend what they have earned in the path of Allah i.e. for that which is laudable, approved or permitted by the Divine Book and the Holy Prophet. The hoarders of wealth have been promised the most severe punishment. The Quran declares:

Woe to every back-biter, slanderer, who amasses wealth and counts it time after time. He thinks that his wealth makes him immortal, Nay, he shall be cast into crushing punishment. (S. 194:2–6)

It is for this reason that we notice that many of the companions of the Messenger of Allah (peace be upon him) left no wealth worth mention in spite of the vast amount that came to their share as income or as war booty. It is well known that during Umar bin Abdul Aziz's reign there was a shortage not of the bountiful but of the needy.

Islam's way to social justice is the establishment of a brotherhood of believers, thereby destroying tyranny without destroying legitimate differences. In this brotherhood each individual is duty-bound to work for self-support and to help the other, even though each one works for whatever he aspires for. Islam recognizes that ambition for self-development and advancement, for progress and salvation, is the mainspring of an individual's efforts. It puts these urges and ambitions into a constructive channel. It does not prevent a man from acquiring or enjoying the just and lawful produce of his labor, but insists that what is earned be spent in a manner prescribed or approved by Allah. It makes the positive command of morality to provide content for the social framework, which the essentially negative command of law seeks to protect.

It is part of Quranic justice that it does not permit the concentration of capital or of wealth. It refuses to approve hoarding of wealth. It promises a grievous chastisement for hoarders of gold and silver. It directs us to look at the glorious examples of the companions of the Holy Prophet who have left us a brilliant trail to follow. Tabari for instance records of the third Caliph Uthman, declaring to the people who had gathered around him to depose him:

> I have naught but two camels, I have neither a goat nor a she-camel and when I assumed office [of caliph] I had amongst all the Arabs the largest number of the camels and goats; and this day I have no goat nor camel except two camels for performing *hajj* [pilgrimage]. Do you accept this—and they said "By Allah it is so."

It was a singular misfortune of the tradition of Muslim law after the third century, that the right to acquire property came to be emphasized much more than the obligation to spend one's wealth according to the priorities fixed by Allah, even though in the Quran there is far greater emphasis placed on spending. The legal structure of Islam cannot operate effectively independently of the moral framework within which it is found and in so far as law becomes amoralized or secularized it loses one of its mainsprings of effectiveness.

SIXTEEN

The Islamic Resurgence: Prospects and Implications

KEMAL A. FARUKI

THE PLATFORM OF THE ISLAMIC RESURGENCE

Whether the Islamic resurgence expresses itself through the subversive and forceful methods that are often the only recourse under dictatorships, or through speeches, persuasion and elections in semi-democratic states and democracies, its aims are remarkably similar throughout the Muslim world.

In the sphere of personal morality a main object of attention is the communications media. Censorship is advocated for anything thought to be inconsistent with Islamic morality in films, television, books and magazines. In education, courses on "Islamics" and Islamic history (particularly the early period of the Prophet and the Orthodox Caliphate) receive greater stress for teaching time, even at the higher levels of specialized education. Co-education becomes the target of attack and stricter separation of the sexes in mixed institutions at the higher levels is insisted upon. Sizable Muslim communities in Western countries with compulsory education have waged campaigns for "single-sex" schools within the state educational systems besides providing on a private basis "Sunday school" Islamic instruction for their children. In social matters there have been moves to make women's dress conform to a head-covering and a shapeless outer-garment from head to foot. But so far there has been only minimal opposition to women working. In fighting crime, there have been movements to restore the so-called *hudud* punishments and making punishable matters which are dealt with lightly or not at all in Western penal codes. Countries where traditional Islamic criminal law is in force are compared favorably with the rising crime rates in other countries—Muslim and non-Muslim. In terms of economics, the main thrust of the Islamic platform has been to demand the abolition of *riba* (banking interest), the introduction of *zakat* and *ushr* (religious taxes) and the formation of commercial companies along "Islamic" lines.

Where political and constitutional aspects are concerned, as long as an Islamic movement is in the opposition, it states that the future constitution will be based on the Quran and Sunna and that the *shariah* shall prevail. It usually takes as its ideal those states set up by the first three Muslim generations. The paradox here is that while the main theme of Islamic opposition movements has been that a change in the political system is the essential precursor for ushering in an Islamic order (in personal and social morality, economic affairs, etc.), the fact remains that there is considerable vagueness as to what precisely this Islamic political structure should be: does it imply mere toleration or outright rejection of democracy? What is the relationship between its different branches (if they are to be differentiated at all) such as the executive, judicial, and the assemblies? Are its assemblies merely consultative? Are they empowered to "make" laws or merely "interpret" laws? Are they subject to some higher judicial, executive, ecclesiastical, or other authority?

In the cases where avowedly Islamic regimes have obtained power during the current wave of Islamic resurgence, the process was not through a ballot box. Given the nature of things perhaps it could not have been, however widespread the support they enjoyed. Consequently, like the other aspects, the politico-constitutional aspects of new Islamic regimes have been unfolding after the event. The two major cases are Pakistan (1977) and Iran (1979).

ISLAMIC RESURGENCE IN IRAN

The Iranian Revolution which began in 1979 marks the most spectacular example of what is popularly thought of as the Islamic resurgence. Suddenly the pendulum swung from one extreme of a Westernizing Shah to a champion of uncompromising Islamization, the Ayatullah Khomeini. The institutions of the monarchy disintegrated—the ruling class, the imposing armed forces built up over three decades, the secret police, the Westernized educational institutions, and much of the new class of technocrats manning the infrastructure of a rapidly industrializing state.

What gave these events greater importance in international terms was their effect on Iran's substantial oil exports to the rest of the world and the possibility of matters spilling over to the even more vital oil-exporting regions on the other side of the Gulf. Moreover, Iran occupies a position of considerable strategic significance in the global struggle between Russia and the West. Then for a long period the U.S. hostage crisis made Iran a major item in Western news media. But Iran's significance with regard to the Islamic resurgence continues unabated. In the early phase of the revolution, it united together all anti-Shah forces and there was in particular an alliance between the clergy and Islamic modernists; the latter derived a great deal of their ideological inspiration from Dr. Ali Shariati. However, as events unfolded during 1981, power moved almost totally into the hands of the clergy. For this Khomeini has been largely responsible as the initiator, but the pressure of the activist clergy on Khomeini himself should not be discounted.

The importance of revolutionary Iran must be assessed, however, in light of the fact that internal developments remain in a state of flux. Changes of obvious external symbols took place with regard to women's dress and the banning of liquor, night clubs and pornography and, anything in the media which portrayed the permissiveness of the contemporary West. Severe punishments were summarily meted out to those found violating these new rules, but it was by no means clear to what extent these practices of the past had ceased or merely been driven underground. A number of these measures have also been adopted by other Muslim states in deference to the new Islamic mood. What makes their genuine success or failure in Iran peculiarly critical is the fact that its government, parliament and administration are now dominated by the Islamic clergy itself headed by a man with tremendous mass-appeal and support. Failure in Iran cannot be dismissed on grounds that the government was not "really Islamic" or not composed of men of lifelong religious training and conviction.

The Iranian revolution has not attempted to deny the importance of industrialization or the importance of oil exports to its economic well-being. The extent to which certain departures from traditional society are inevitable concomitants of industrialization and technological development remains unanswered. Questions concerning women still await definite clerical responses. The same uncertainty hangs over the question of education. Only medical and engineering faculties remain open in Iranian universities. After the purge of the Humanities teaching staff is completed, the ideologically approved curricula, capable of coexisting with the attitude of mind fostered (and required) by the purely scientific subjects, have to be developed. It is a dilemma very similar to that existing in the Soviet Union.

Another unanswered question is the extent to which the clergy really approve of this activist role which some of them have undertaken. Many of them believed that their function was to supervise, not administer, a temporal government, performing and regulating essential duties prescribed by the *shariah* until the coming of the Twelfth Imam who had gone into occultation in the ninth century. Qum, the theological capital, was to be the conscience of Iran and watchman over the temporal government at Teheran but uncontaminated by its worldly influences and atmosphere.

The other school of clerical thought from the turn of this century maintained, however, that the duty to fight oppression could not be in doubt or held in abeyance pending the Twelfth Imam. Indeed he would surely require it of them. Matters reached a crisis in the Persian Revolution of 1905 and the Constitution of that time. This constitution provided *inter alia* for a committee of five theologians to ensure that legislation did not conflict with Islam. This issue of activist participation versus supervision from a distance is by no means resolved and indeed remains in the shadows only as long as Khomeini himself is there with his overwhelming personality and mass support.

The state of flux in Iran makes even a rough estimate of the possible direction of events extremely hazardous. New institutions have evolved such as the Islamic Revolutionary Guards *(Sepah Pasdaran),* a popular volunteer force which is to number twenty million; a Reconstruction Brigade *(Jihad-i-Sazen-dagi)* for building small welfare projects; *komitehs,* local municipal bodies operating from mosques for local administration and internal security; and a new Bureau of Political-Ideological Affairs within the Army. Each province and organization has a representative of Khomeini reporting directly to him. The imams for Friday Prayers maintain direct control over the people; at these gatherings major policies are announced and issues discussed. In place of disbanded trade unions, industrial workers are now governed by an elected council *(majlis-i-shura)* of each factory's workers and an Islamic society *(anjuman-i-Islami)* for ideological orientation.

All of these are, of course, held together at the moment by the supreme authority of Khomeini. Thereafter, it would appear that much will depend on whether the succession provisions of the new constitution are followed and prove workable. This constitution rests on a substructure of what at first sight appears to be a typical contemporary document—a president, a prime minister, and a *majlis* or parliament—all of them popularly elected or chosen, directly or indirectly.

Superimposed on this, however, is a Council for the Protection of the Constitution (CPC) which in turn is subject to the *faqih,* the final expounder of religious law, who is the Ayatullah Khomeini for the rest of his life. This *vilayat-i-faqih* (leadership by the faqih) will thereafter devolve upon one, three, or five people chosen by an elected Council of Experts to form a council of leadership intended to be composed exclusively of the clergy. It remains to be seen whether these succession provisions for the supreme office of *vilayat-i-faqih* lead to stability at the top. At what is even constitutionally, at best, the second level, namely, the office of President, matters certainly cannot be said to have proceeded smoothly as witnessed by the case of the first President of the new Islamic Republic. Abu-Hasan Bani-Sadr was popularly elected (with Khomeini's approval) at the time when a more plural society, in political terms, was in existence.

The question must arise at this stage as to whether the Iranian version of Islamic resurgence now in full control of the apparatus of the state has sufficiently established itself. Some of the factors which led to the Revolution have been eliminated: the sharp class distinctions with a wealthy privileged ruling class and the blatant aspects of Westernization which offended Muslim moral and social values. The higher ranks in the army and the civil administration of monarchist times have been removed. A new younger generation has taken its place alongside the clergy with its seventy-odd ayatullahs at the top, in part directly involved in the new order and partly wielding influence from behind the scenes. The new institutions described above are still in their early formative stages and their relations *inter se* in the new power structure are far from settled.

Of the possible reasons for the government to falter, the first that comes to mind is the succession provisions for *vilayat-i-faqih* with its overwhelming concentration of power. Even more basic is the unresolved debate within the ulama body as a whole as to whether his clerical activism and direct assumption of temporal power is the proper religious role for the guardians of *shariah*. This may not become an acute problem as long as Iran's internal economic situation does not assume crisis dimensions. However, there is a severe shortfall in industrial production with high unemployment and shortages of even some essentials. It is by no means assured that the problems of the drop in oil production and sales of even the greatly reduced output have been overcome. The full outlines of the new educational system are still unclear as is the degree to which they will establish lasting conviction with the youth, particularly those in the big cities and those who inescapably will be exposed to what is going on in the outside world.

Given these dangers, real and potential, in the post-Khomeini era, the immediate and instinctive reaction of those in power may well be to move to an ever-increasing authoritarian form of rule. The succession struggle may easily burst through the fragile constitutional rules and the new institutions brought into play may find themselves in a struggle based on sheer force. Lurking in the background are the still long unresolved questions of linguistic-ethnic minorities and their demands for regional autonomy.

There is a tendency to minimize these difficulties and dangers, believing that calls for self-denial and even greater austerity can always circumvent pressing economic difficulties. Similarly, the martyr-psyche, deeply imbedded since Karbela in the Shiite outlook, is also brought into the total picture as demonstrating that when people are ready, even anxious, to die for a cause, they will prove irresistible as they did against the powerful army of the Shah. There are limits, however, to the extent to which this can be used. The Japanese *kamikaze* and army willingness to sacrifice all for the semi-divine Emperor of Japan ultimately was overcome by the logic of Allied force in the 1941–45 war.

Thus events in Iran as a pointer to the long-term significance of a resurgent Islamic movement must of necessity remain uncertain to a high degree. If it succeeds, its influence is likely to spill over to an ever-widening circle of Muslim states, Sunni as well as Shiite, giving an enormous accretion of prestige and potential power to traditional clerical and neo-traditional Islamic movements. On the other hand, if the present version of Islamic resurgence in Iran fails or even undergoes a long period of virtual anarchy, the ulama in politics at the very least are likely to suffer a grave setback in the rest of the Muslim world.

ISLAMIC RESURGENCE IN POWER IN PAKISTAN

Islamic motivation or justification was an inherent part of the movement for Pakistan. After the establishment of the state in August 1947 came the complex and controversial task of giving this expression.

With but a few exceptions, until the 1970s implementation of the 1949 Objectives Resolution was held in abeyance pending the solution of the overall constitutional issues in which the alternation of civil and military rule and relations between the Eastern and Western wings of the country became predominant. In the aftermath of the 1971 secession of the Eastern wing (Bangladesh), renewed non-official primacy was given to the fostering of Islamic sentiment to counter provincialism and protect the flickering flame of Pakistan sentiment. The new Pakistan, released from a Southeast Asian role with the severance of its Eastern wing, saw itself more as part of the Muslim Middle East. In the 1973 Constitution (Article 31) the teaching of Arabic was incorporated for the first time and Pakistan played host to the 1974 Islamic Summit at Lahore. Basically, however, the main emphasis of Z. A. Bhutto's People's Party government was concentrated on the socialist rather than the Islamic part of its manifesto under Bhutto's highly personalized form of government. Nevertheless an Islamic resurgence slowly gathered force during the 70s. A coalition of religious and political parties united under Islam in opposition to Bhutto's rule. The government attempted to defuse and deflect from this *Nizam-i-Islam* (Islamic System) movement in 1976–77 by introducing prohibition, banning horse-racing and declaring the Ahmadiyya community a non-Muslim minority. But the alliance of all opposition parties (united in their charges of official rigging of the general elections) eventually brought matters to such a pass that in early 1977 the Army was called in by the government. Inevitably on July 5, 1977 these same Armed Forces themselves took over declaring martial law. The strong personal Muslim sentiment of the new army ruler General Zia ul-Haq was significantly responsible for the widespread Islamization process initiated subsequently but, in any case, irrespective of personalities this new wave of Islamic resurgence would probably have made Islamization politically necessary for any government.

Compared with the pyrotechnics in Iran, with its violent assault on the old order and anything suggestive of Westernism, Islamic resurgence in Pakistan by contrast is regarded, depending on one's point of view, as moderate, evolutionary, anaemic, or superficial and protective of entrenched privilege. It is also much less clerical at the top. However, the prior influence of Pakistan on the Islamic resurgence internationally should not be underestimated. First, the writings of Muhammad Iqbal, particularly his emotional, activist Persian-language poetry played a significant part in the ideological content of revolutionary Iran with respect to Dr. Ali Shariati and his followers. Second, Pakistan has had a more than merely formal two-way religious and cultural relationship with Muslim countries as diverse as Saudi Arabia, Algeria, Turkey, and Iran. Thus it attempts to blend Islamization with the existing long-established infrastructure and momentum of a modern state have made its current efforts the object of close interest by other Muslim governments and movements. Nevertheless, in important respects its current phase of islamization is still at best purely tentative and has still to come to grips with some unavoidable issues.

Moribund Islamic institutions have been activated and new ones have proliferated. For example, in the 1962 Constitution an Advisory Council of Islamic Ideology (ACII) was created of not more than 12 persons knowledgable in Islamic and contemporary matters to advise and give authority to any Islamic recommendations implemented by government. The reactivation of the Council of Islamic Ideology in July 1977 saw changes in its composition until non-traditional and modernist elements were virtually excluded. It has played an essentially traditional, conservative role in the Islamization process, timidly exercising pseudo-*ijtihad* in a peripheral fashion where unavoidable, but voiding basic *ijtihad*.

New institutions were set up such as *shariah* courts composed of judges with common law training and traditions with the traditional ulama as advisers. The relationship of these *shariah* courts with the existing common law judiciary and its courts was subject to evolving change. The full effects of this experiment have still to work themselves out. But the creation of two separate judicial systems could lead to the notion that the Supreme and Provincial High Courts were *"non-shariah"* and therefore "un-Islamic" and that until *madrasa*-trained *qadis* (Islamically educated judges) replaced "British colonial" trained judges, a truly Islamic legal system could not be effective.

As separate Islamic university was set up after a temporary experiment with a *shariah* faculty within the existing University at Islamabad. If Islamization is conceived of as a total process, the question might well arise, sooner or later, of the legitimacy of the existing "secular" university system. Ministries—of religious affairs, education, information, finance, economic affairs, law, etc.—became involved in the process of Islamization and various committees from different disciplines and professions were formed. An elaborate *zakat* administration was created from a central apex down to the village level. The subsequent appointed *majlis-i-shura* or Federal Advisory Council also set up its own Islamization committee.

In the realm of law a series of enactments were announced by Zia ul-Haq and came into force on the Prophet's Birthday, February 10, 1979. They related to the *hadd* offenses of classical Islamic criminal law together with some other enactments designed to eliminate interest *(riba)* from certain state financing and investment corporations, and some amendments to existing criminal law.

Zakat (alms tax) has received the fullest expression. An elaborate mechanism was devised to collect and distribute *zakat*. The collection of *zakat* while trying to keep within the classical framework nevertheless was also applied by a form of peripheral pseudo-*ijtihad* to such latter-day innovations as time deposit bank accounts and state savings certificates of different kinds. This introduced a new precedent into taxation and banking practice of permitting the state to deduct *zakat* directly from accounts held in the nationalized banking system.

On *riba*, Zia ul-Huq pledged to eliminate all forms of "the curse of interest," but there was no attempt to examine any further the meaning of *riba*. Within this predetermined framework the Council of Islamic Ideology with attached *ulama* and multi-discipline committees of bankers, financiers, economists and bureaucrats deliberated. Although writing in his personal capacity as one ardently committed rather than as the head of the largest nationalized bank (Habib Bank Limited), Abdul Jabbar Khan gave an insight into the philosophy behind the official anti-riba measures in an article published in various newspapers in February 1982 in which he asserted at the outset: "Interest-free banking should not be taken to mean that banks-financial institutions would neither pay any return on their deposits nor get any income from their loans, etc." He went on to list four "alternatives to interest," among them: 1.) "mark-up or *mura-baha*" in which on a sale an immediate or deferred, lump sum or installment "margin of profit" would be mutually agreed between the buyer and seller as included in the sale price; and, 2.) "profit and loss sharing or *musharaka*" in which there would be a "temporary partnership" between the bank and a party with the ratio of distribution of net profit agreed upon in advance and with the loss to be "shared strictly in the ratio of funds deployed in the business." To these, others have been later added such as *mudaraba* (profit-sharing) companies.

How far this is in conformity with the classical Islamic understanding of a *riba*-free transaction is an interesting question. The charge has been made that to ban the word "interest" from all discussion and use instead "profit" and "mark-up," particularly when these are agreed to in advance, is more a matter of semantics than a basic change in principles. Nor does the use of the word "partnership" alter what is in effect, in some cases, a "principal and agent" relationship.

In any case, a Profit and Loss Sharing (PLS) Scheme was launched by all the nationalized banks to run parallel with the existing interest-bearing fixed and savings accounts. By the end of 1981, after one year in operation, the equivalent of about $650 million had moved or been moved into PLS, representing nearly 12 percent of the total savings and fixed-term deposits in the country. While interest on savings accounts was 7½ percent p.a. the profits under PLS declared by banks varied between 8½ and 9 percent, remarkably close to each other and curiously enough just that much higher above normal savings accounts to attract confidence in the profit aspect of an avowedly profit- or loss-sharing scheme. A significant proportion of the PLS sums were of government controlled or state corporations who were "persuaded" to move these sums from fixed deposits, etc. A crucial stage will be reached as banks have to really persuade private companies and individuals to move their deposits to the PLS scheme. Here profits can no longer be safely arranged as in bank dealings with monopolistic State corporations, and the risk of loss then becomes as real a possibility to contemplate as the expectation of profit. These risks are illustrated by the fact that there were in early 1982, some 38,000 cases of defaults in bank loans before the courts with a further 11,000 due to be filled if borrowers failed to reach acceptable and secured repayment schedule arrangements with the lending banks.

Many of the problems connected with the PLS scheme were set out by one writer (Sultan Ahmed, "Profit and Loss Sharing Scheme: the Real Perils" published in *Dawn,* Karachi, March 11, 1982) which expressed difficulties about distinguishing between (forbidden) interest-bearing arrangements and (permissible) "guaranteed profits" as in a private Saudi investment in a Pakistani fertilizer factory with a guaranteed profit of 20 percent and a Pakistani company publishing copies of the Holy Quran with a fixed 20 percent "profit" to its lenders. The article concluded by urging "an economic approach which should discourage experts from being seduced by Arabic names" and emphasizing that "what matters are the real contents and market practices in a system and not the labels alone" if the PLS scheme is to become "a genuine third way."

Finally, mention should be made of the *hudud* ordinances which set out in modern statutory fashion laws to give effect to most of the *hadd* (Quranically prescribed penalties) references set out in the Quran and hadith literature as understood in classical times, before the closing of the gate of *ijtihad*. The Ordinances also came into effect on February 10, 1979. The ordinances dealt with theft *(seriqa)*, adultery *(zina)*, false accusation of adultery *(qadhf)* and drinking of intoxicants *(shurb al-khamr)*. By Ordinance No. VI of 1979, theft "liable to *hadd*" is to be punished by amputation of the right hand "from the joint of the wrist" (for the first offense), by amputation of the left foot up to the ankle (for the second such offense) and by imprisonment for life (for the third or more offenses). Amputation is to be carried out "by an authorized medical officer." However although well over three years have elapsed since this came into force, no such punishments have been carried out although convictions have continued.

Similarly with adultery (zina), Ordinance VII prescribes stoning to death at a public place for the married man or married woman guilty of this offense. In this case a difference of opinion has persisted as to the permissibility of stoning which is not mentioned in the Quran but derives its authority from hadith literature references which are imputed by many. This has been the subject of a special examination by expert evidence before the shariah court.

In these and other matters a formidable backlog of cases has built up in the Federal Shariat Court, partly explained by defects in the existing (common-law based) Evidence Act in determining guilt according to classical Islamic criteria. Meanwhile revisions were being drafted to bring the evidence law in line with classical Islamic provisions by the Council of Islamic Ideology. The ultimate outcome is far from clear while the hudud ordinances continue to remain unimplemented. Modernist Islamic shariah understanding would call for a more basic ijtihad on all these matters, but this is beyond the framework of the present Islamization process. Yet another matter on which this process has come up against two diverging views is the position of women, their Islamic rights and their right to work. Here the attempts by traditionalists to change the status quo has generated in reply a movement for the protection of women's rights.

The current Islamization process in Pakistan has been the result of much genuine pushing and prodding by Zia ul-Haq and his associates but it has been within the limitations of reliance on the traditionalist. One extreme conservative reaction to this might be a demand for greater ulama participation even control over the Islamization process. On the other hand, the logic of the unfolding situation might bring the reformist (aligarh) spirit out of its temporary eclipse far sooner than anticipated.

At some point it would seem inevitable that ijtihad (reinterpretation) at a more fundamental level of Islamic exegesis will be required. This is a task unlikely to be undertaken by appointees of a regime lacking a popular mandate. The authentic basis for understanding the shariah, in particular in the Sunni, Hanafi version which predominates in Pakistan, is the consensus of the competent as accepted by the consensus (ijma) of the community. Only after community acceptance is ijma legally complete. Even the acceptance of individuals as competent must relate back to the community's approval directly or indirectly and, indeed, this has been the basis on which the founders and early jurists of the different schools won acceptance and by which their views prevailed over others. Coffee drinking is an early example of how the verdict of the learned prohibiting its use was rejected by the community, thereby upholding the permissibility of coffee drinking. The same process can be observed with regard to the use of many scientific "innovations" during this century such as loudspeakers for reciting the Quran. A mechanism for effective *shariah* understanding is essentially part of the problem of constitution-making. The necessary relationship between the competent and the community in general would seem to imply a constitution inevitably democratic in essentials.

This is part of a larger question of the kind of Islamic political order within which a resurgent Islam has to express itself. It is clearly already an issue of paramount importance in Iran and Pakistan, the two states we have just considered where Islamic resurgence is now in power. The prospects for an Islamic political system may well depend upon the long-range implications of current Islamic resurgence. In light of what has already been considered and in the context of the record of Islamic history itself, the prospects for a viable, enduring Islamic political order within the boundaries of the existing States require examination.

THE PROSPECTS FOR AN ISLAMIC POLITICAL ORDER TODAY

First, the case of Libya. The system existing in Libya today is the work of the Libyan leader, Colonel Muammar Qaddafi, and is highly subjective in quality. Admirable as the insistence on the Quran's supremacy may be, the exclusion of *hadith* and the corpus of Islamic law by his *Green Book* make his conclusions arbitrary, even erratic, and certainly difficult, if not impossible, to relate to the rest of the Muslim world or provide a systematic base for Qaddafi's successor.

Second, in Saudi Arabia, the nature of the Hanbali-Wahhabi doctrines makes it difficult to conceive of them being give wider application or serving as a prototype for other Muslim states. The ulama and the temporal authority of the immediate descendants of King Abd al-Aziz have not fused in a synthesis of outlook but run parallel in harness. From Abd al-Aziz b. Saud through three of his sons including the present king, the succession mechanism has functioned smoothly, but whether in the probings toward an "Islamic consultative democracy" some lessons can be learned by others engaged in the task of finding an Islamic political order for today—this question is still far too nebulous to be considered here. Even such limited popular participation would seem to need the growth of supporting institutions, such as freedom of expression and association, in an evolutionary manner. This may well be indispensable for an ordered curing of any causes for discontent that might exist whether in economic matters or in reconciling strong Islamic convictions with actual practice at different levels. Here it is a question of masterly timing and avoiding the opposing risks of too much too soon or too little too late.

Third, in Iran, the permissibility of continuing *ijtihad* has had a doctrinal base historically without interruption, and for which the need becomes increasingly apparent elsewhere with renewed insistence. By Shii theory this is a task for the *mujtahids* (one who exercises *ijtihad*) of the age alone. The question arises as to whether the succession provisions of the new Constitution will stand up to the great test of the immediate post-Khomeini era for ascertaining the true consensus of the *mujtahids* or higher clergy of the age. Their oligarchic organization has also to be reconciled with the democratic election provisions of the new Constitution and the possible conflict of authority that this may give rise to.

Furthermore an enduring equation between central and regional requirements has yet to be worked out. A unitary solution is not more workable or feasible within Iran today than it has been in past Muslim (including Iranian) history. There is the Farsi or Persian-speaking majority and there are the linguistic-ethnic minorities of Kurds, Turcomans, Baluchis, Khuzistani Arabs, and Azerbaijanis. Some of these groups are Shii while others are Sunni. True regional autonomy (with provision for accommodating sect differences where they cannot be reconciled) is hardly possible in the current ideological one-party state, consisting of the Islamic Republican Party plus the clergy. It is true this exists in theory in the "federal" Soviet Union with its comparable Russian-speaking majority and its constituent separate linguistic-ethnic republics, some with a religious differentiation as well. But the degree of voluntary acceptance of this dispensation is probably minimal not merely in Muslim Central Asia and the Caucasus but also in such European federated "republics" as the Ukraine and the Baltic states and merely waiting for some weakening in the Soviet center. Similarly a Bonapartist outcome to events in Iran is likely to attempt to smother by force this central-regional question besides failing on questions of *shariah*-understanding and on succession provisions. Matters have reached a stage where a negotiated settlement of Iran's internal problems is nearly impossible as between the different options that have been considered. The essential deciding factor between options is likely to continue to be force. In Iran the intrusion of economic imperatives cannot be ignored or derided any more than elsewhere. These are matters on which the IRP and clergy have yet to demonstrate adequate competence. Nor have they dealt effectively with the requirements for creative science and technology and its necessary intellectual milieu.

Fourth, in Pakistan, the sultan-ulama (ruler-clergy) equation of the late classical period has been in a sense resurrected in the relations between the President and a revived traditionalism, with its oligarchic clergy. The need for basic *ijtihad* before the rule of *shariah* can in fact prevail raises the question of the prime role of the community in Pakistan in sanctioning the results of such *ijtihad* and generally in restoring the reformist *(aligarh)* spirit and the Objectives

Resolution of 1949. Recognition of the need for a renewed movement from an oligarchy to a democracy is already there, however weak the degree of official recognition of this need may be at the moment. Such a democratic constitutional structure offers the best hope of finding at long last a legitimate form of succession, something that cannot be said of the manner in which real executive power has moved from one individual to another since the assassination of the first Prime Minister, Liaqat Ali Khan in 1951. A major impediment in devising this constitutional structure has been the failure to reconcile central and regional requirements within a viable federal system.

In Pakistan, the economic issues are still underrated, particularly the question of economic justice. The current traditional type of economic Islamization measures may, in this respect, prove counter-productive. The probable failure of the current *zakat* scheme to alleviate poverty, ignorance and disease in a constructive manner is one illustration. The learned discussions on *riba* and "the curse of interest" may cause anger rather than pleasure as the "experts" draw doubtful distinctions between "interest" and "guaranteed profits," etc. while turning a blind eye to the unmistakable usury perpetrated on the illiterate and the poor by *soodkhuris* (lit. "devourers of usury"). These officially registered moneylenders under the Moneylenders Act are permitted to lend at not more than one per cent below the State Bank rate. In fact they are Mafia-like individuals who charge interest as high as 60 percent per annum collected ruthlessly in monthly installments and refuse to accept repayment of the principal sum indefinitely. Their tactics include intimidation and force. The existence of a partly free press brings these social injustices to general attention but true popular participation in government and a parliament alone seem capable of bringing accountability into action. These matters illustrate another weakness of a non-democratic, oligarchic system.

Beyond this, in assessing the prospects for the Islamic resurgence in the politics of the Muslim world there are the great unknown factors—assassinations, coups d'état, revolutions and counter-revolutions, the emergence or death of a charismatic leader, unrest from unexpected or underestimated quarters, the pressure of external events—which can have profound effects on current Islamic resurgence, either hastening the process or postponing it to another age.

Finally, there are the ever-present possibilities of other Muslim states entering into the mainstream of Islamic resurgence at the level of power, with new approaches or strengthening one or other of the trends we have endeavored to describe. It could be Sudan or in West Africa, North Africa or Southeast Asia. Afghanistan will be a factor to reckon with after it has passed through its present tribulations. Two states in particular require mention: Egypt and Turkey.

The rich religious and intellectual traditions of Egypt have exerted an influence for centuries. It had long been, more than any other Arab country, the fountainhead of the intellectual activity of the Arabic-speaking Muslim states. It is the site of the oldest extant Islamic ulama university, of al-Azhar. Thus its modern and clerical Islamic intellectual activity is prolific and rich. Al-Azhar itself, which produced the great reformer Muhammad Abduh (d. 1905), has been politically quiescent and outwardly under effective governmental supervision. During the last few decades (the extreme phase of Arabism) the dialogue between traditional and modernist Muslim approaches broke off to be replaced by violence and counter-violence. The break in dialogue, however, may not be irreparable and the confrontation methods may diminish and find more constructive outlets. The consequent results for general Islamic thought and practice may be far-reaching, particularly in other Arab states initially.

The other significant country outside the mainstream at present is Turkey. It possesses a persisting tradition of constitutional development, free elections, the rule of law, an independent judiciary, a free press and the right of freedom of association, notwithstanding its bouts of military rule. These have been largely brought on by the extra-legal and terrorist activities of its extremist fringes of right and left, of neo-traditional Islamic groups and groups professing a highly nationalistic form of Turkicism in reaction. The constitutional framework has so far been sternly secular but there are signs that the strongly and majority Kemalist center (with its primary support amongst the armed forces, the administration and the large urban population) consider that the Muslim Middle East and Muslim world generally must play an increasing role in foreign and commercial relations. Disenchantment with the mores of the contemporary West (also provoked by the more uncouth tourists and the experiences of Turkish workers in western Europe) have also had their impact on a changing Turkish outlook. There is recognition of an increasing role for Islamic values in social and public life. Thus Kemalism, seeking sanction from the spirit and not letter of Ataturk's philosophy and from his pragmatic approach, may well recall the basic nature of Turkish laicism—namely, a continuing strong aversion to any clerical entry into politics. This however is not really incompatible with the possibility that a stage may come, through the democratic process, when Turkish legislative activity seeks assistance from the *shariah* and the universal aspects of Islamic principles, understood in contemporary terms. With the clergy *qua* clergy confined to the mosques and to matters of personal devotion, and the new theological group being products of the Kemalist and post-Kemalist *imam-hatip* schools, it would seem that the rigid, traditionally trained ulama establishment of the past is probably well beyond artificial respiration even by some extremist traditionalist group.

Such signs of movement in Turkey may well be influenced by success in devising a modern Islamic political order elsewhere, above all in Pakistan as it recovers the outlook of its founder, M. Ali Jinnah and its Aligarh momentum. Thereafter the interaction between the two states may prove highly instructive. The first Pakistani influence may be in its successful employment of basic *ijtihad*. The corresponding Turkish influence may be with regard to the clergy and the curricula of the *imam-hatip* schools (schools for the training of prayer-leaders and preachers).

Such developments and mutual influences may grow between other Muslim states, transcending perhaps the sectarian obstacles of the past. The possibilities for an overall Muslim world failure or individual state failure in an Islamic resurgence exist and some of the conceivable causes for this have been indicated earlier. On the other hand, the prospects for a successful outcome of the search for an Islamic political order are equally present. It is true that the Islamic resurgence today may prove to be an anachronistic and unfortunate false dawn but, equally, the current Islamic resurgence may prove to be the beginning of an inspiring and beneficial chapter in the history of humanity in this closely interdependent world.

Selective Glossary

adl social justice

ahl al-bayt model family of the Prophet; descendants of the Prophet's cousin, Ali (see also **wisaya**)

ahl al-kitab "People of the Book"; Jews, Christians and others who have received revelation from God

ahl al-shura "house of consultation"; those who resolve public affairs

akhund popular preacher

amanah divine trust

anjuman-i-Islami Islamic society

aqaid belief

asala authenticity

ashab al-ray scholars whose interpretation of law is based on personal opinion

ayatullah al-uzma supreme ayatullah

baya oath of allegiance

bida innovation; deviation from tradition

dar al-harb "abode of war"; non-Islamic country

dar al-salam "abode of peace"; Islamic country

dawah "call"; missionary

dhimmi (also *zimmi*) non-Muslim citizen; convenanter for peace under God

din religion

diwan government bureau; chancery

dua prayer

faqih (pl. **fuqaha**) legal expert; jurisprudent

faraid shares of inheritance prescribed by the Quran

fard ayn personal religious obligation

fard khilafayah corporate religious obligation

fatwa formal legal opinion of a *mufti*

fiqh Islamic jurisprudence

hadd (pl. **hudud**) "limits"; Quranically prescribed penalty

hakimiyya sovereignty

haram prohibited conduct

hijra flight of Muhammad from Mecca to Medina in A.D. 622

hizbullah party of Allah

hukm rule, govern

husayniya center for religious education and propagation (Shiah)

ibadat "worship"; regulations in Islamic law governing religious observance

ijma consensus of opinion

ijtihad independent analysis or reasoning

ikhwan brotherhood

ilm knowledge

inqilab revolution

islah reform

islam submission

istihsan juristic preference; equity as a criterion in development of Islamic law

istihslah "public interest"; general welfare of the community as a criterion in development of Islamic law

jahili ignorant
jahiliyyah period of ignorance
jammah (also **jamaat**) party
jizya poll-tax on *dhimmi*

kharaj land tax
khalifah "successor", caliph
khums "⅕"; tax, ⅕ of annual income paid to religious authorities (Shiah)

madrasa religious school
majlis "session;" assembly; now used for a parliament
majlis-i-shura consultative body; elected council
marja-i-taqlid "source of emulation"; supreme authority on law
millat "community"; nation
muamalat human relationships; Islamic laws (e.g., civil, crimincal, family) governing social relations
mudaraba profit-sharing in economic transactions
mufti specialist on Islamic law competent to deliver a *fatwa*
mujaddid one who brings about *taqlid*
mujahid (pl. **mujahidun**) soldier of God
mujtahid one who exercizes *ijtihad* to ascertain a rule of *shariah;* jurisprudent
mumin believer
murabit murabout; saint (Sufi)
musharaka profit-and loss-sharing in economic transactions
muslihun those who work for *islah*
muwahid believer in *tawhid*

nahda renaissance
nizam system

qadhf false accusation of adultery
qadi judge who administers shariah
qiyas juristic reasoning by analogy

rabb ruler
rabbaniyyah rule of God
riba usury; bank interest

salat daily ritual prayer
seriqa theft
shahadah confession of faith
shahid martyr
shariah "path;" Islamic law
shirk idolatry
shura consultation

tadbir planning
tajdid revival; renewal
taqiyya resort to dissimulation in defense of Islam (Shiah)
taqlid reliance on tradition
tawhid unity of God

ummah Islamic community
ushr religious tax on land
usul al-fiqh principles of Islamic jurisprudence

vilayat-i faqih guardianship or government by the religious authority

waqf endowment of property for religious purposes
wisaya "testament"; designation of Ali as executor of Muhammad's will and testament

zakat alms tax
zina adultery
zimmi see **dhimmi**
zulm oppression; sin